Studies
in
Long Term Memory

Studies in Long Term Memory

Edited by

Alan Kennedy and Alan Wilkes

University of Dundee

JOHN WILEY & SONS

London · New York · Sydney · Toronto

710 000946 -O

Library of Congress Cataloging in Publication Data:

Main entry under title:

Studies in long term memory.

Papers originally presented at a conference sponsored by the Social Science Research Council of Great Britain.

1. Memory—Congresses. I. Kennedy, Alan, 1939– ed. II. Wilkes, Alan, ed. III. Social Science Research Council (Gt. Brit.).
[DNLM: 1. Memory—Congresses. WL300 S846 1973]

BF371.S85   153.1'22   74-13149
ISBN 0 471 46905 X

Printed in Great Britain by J. W. Arrowsmith Ltd., Winterstoke Road, Bristol, England

To
Midge and Judith
Alison, Susanna and Katie

List of Contributors

A. D. BADDELEY	*University of Stirling*
D. E. BROADBENT	*MRC Applied Psychology Unit, Cambridge*
A. CORBETT	*University of Oregon*
N. H. FRIJDA	*University of Amsterdam*
J. M. HOLMES	*University of Oxford*
P. N. JOHNSON-LAIRD	*University of Sussex*
R. A. KENNEDY	*University of Dundee*
G. R. KISS	*University of Edinburgh*
G. KEMPEN	*University of Nijmegen*
W. J. M. LEVELT	*University of Nijmegen*
J. C. MARSHALL	*University of Edinburgh*
D. E. MEYER	*Bell Laboratories, New Jersey*
R. B. MILLWARD	*Brown University*
J. MORTON	*MRC Applied Psychology Unit, Cambridge*
F. NEWCOMBE	*University of Oxford*
A. PAIVIO	*University of Western Ontario*
G. RICE	*Brown University*
B. SCHAEFFER	*University of Oregon*
A. I. SCHULMAN	*University of Virginia*
P. H. K. SEYMOUR	*University of Dundee*
A. L. WILKES	*University of Dundee*
M. WILLIAMS	*Addenbrooke's Hospital, Cambridge*

Preface

In December 1972 the Social Science Research Council of the U.K. agreed to sponsor an interdisciplinary conference on current aspects of research into long-term memory. The conference, which took place in August 1973, in the University of Dundee, drew together researchers with widely differing theoretical orientations ranging from pure linguistics to computer sciences. Papers were solicited in an attempt to cover the topic of long-term memory from the point of view of the clinician, the psycholinguist, and the experimental psychologist. These papers, together with three additional contributions, form the basis of the present book. All the authors took the opportunity to revise their work and in some cases very substantial changes were made. The division of the text into sections on Encoding, Organization, Integration, Retrieval and Pathology was introduced following discussion with the contributors, and changes in some respects the presentation of topics during the conference. As a result, the subject of long-term memory has been interpreted in the broadest sense and no attempt has been made to maintain rigid divisions between memory and problem solving or intellectual processes. The aim has been to set LTM squarely within an overall cognitive system: as a data base and as a repository of rules for operating upon the base. Inevitably, such an approach entails intersections between memory and perception or memory and problem solving and severely taxes the formal descriptive powers of contemporary psychology. Experimental reports form a large proportion of the present book partly because the conference was concerned with current aspects of research into LTM but also reflecting the fact that much empirical work remains to be done. Contributors have, however, tried to orient their work towards a formal synthesis and have discussed problems associated with this goal.

Two of the papers delivered had been accepted for publication elsewhere. The presentation by Glucksberg, Trabasso and Wald is published in *Cognitive Psychology*, (1974), and David Meyer's presentation is covered in a paper by Meyer, Schvaneveldt and Ruddy to appear in *Psychological Review*. His paper on long-term memory retrieval was specially prepared for this book. Our own contributions, and that by Philip Seymour, were also written following the conference and circulated (somewhat late) to the other contributors.

We would like to acknowledge the financial support given by the Social Science Research Council and the administrative advice given by Mrs M. Harris and Miss A. Stevenson. We are grateful to Principal James Drever for acting as host during the meeting and Mrs Drever for generous hospitality. Our

Research Assistants, Barbara Wilkinson, Jenny Brook and Annabel Broadhurst selflessly took on a variety of roles from running the reception desk to counting the silver. Their efforts were largely responsible for the smooth administration of affairs. Mrs Moira Bell who typed her way out of chaos to some semblance of order particularly deserves grateful thanks.

ALAN KENNEDY
ALAN WILKES
Dundee, 1974

Contents

Introduction

'The physiologist Haller performing the first experiments upon the time occupied in psychic processes had estimated that a third of a second was sufficient time for the production of one idea. On this basis Hook and others reckoned that in a hundred years a man must collect 9,467,280,000 traces or impressions of ideas in his brain' (Burnham, 1888, p. 72). We are not inclined to support a literal reading of this estimate except to acknowledge the insight into the formidable dimensions of the problem. It does not need a particularly long life span to acquire an extensive working vocabulary (Oldfield, 1966), a large recognition store of visual images (Standing, 1973) or a complex network of experiences fused together as a sense of personal history and identity. The accumulation of experience in some form of permanent store has been taken for granted by generations of scholars, but the description of this long term store, its organization and operating characteristics, has not until recently been assigned a high priority within experimental psychology.

The current literature on memory postulates a rich array of storage systems; temporary way stations along the route taken by information in the process of assimilation. Memory overlaps with perceptual and decision processes not as a unitary system but as a synthesis of diverse cognitive activity. As an undifferentiated concept it subsumes too much to be useful within a formalized cognitive model, but when partitioned into functional subsystems, descriptive problems become experimentally amenable. The nature of this partitioning has emerged slowly and not without a cumulative record of dissent, but each theoretical step has served to shape expectations concerning the terminal form of storage. The explanatory progression has been away from registration of experience etched upon a suitably receptive surface towards a selective process in which information is encoded, stored and retrieved following the operation of processing strategies which may vary with both task material and requirements. At minimum, three levels of storage are generally accepted: a sensory store with brief trace duration (e.g., Sperling, 1960); a short-term memory with limited capacity (Broadbent, 1958) and a long-term memory of indefinite capacity (Frijda, 1972). These storage systems have been interpreted in relatively concrete terms (Waugh and Norman, 1965; Atkinson and Shiffrin, 1968) or, less specifically, as the consequences of different 'depths of processing level' achieved during perceptual analysis (Craik and Lockhart, 1972). Either interpretation, however, places considerable emphasis on the subject organizing incoming information for storage and retrieval purposes. The experimental techniques that have identified the operating characteristics of sensory and short-term stores can, of course, be adapted to the analysis of LTM. However, the variety of information held in permanent store presents many problems for a formal description of its organization and content. To some extent, this has been handled by concentrating on sub-categories of learned material: verbal lists, sentences, prose, high imagery material etc., but this defers rather than solves the question of how a working synthesis should be formally described. An eventual goal must be a sufficiently powerful language that can handle the diverse features inevitably associated with a permanent store for personal experience. The present book is concerned with both that diversity of content and its organization for structured yet flexible performance.

The contributions have been organized into relatively independent sections dealing with (a) Information Encoding, (b) LTM Organization, (c) LTM Integration, (d) Retrieval from LTM and (e) Pathology. The allocation of papers to such sections is to some extent arbitrary but the concept of the human operator dealing with the flow of information in a sequence of processing stages has been a fruitful one, and provides a useful framework for diverse argument.

Encoding

An account of LTM must ultimately come to terms with the problem of identifying appropriate descriptive units of what is stored. From theoretical principles alone, it is often ambiguous what the processing unit should be, particularly as the category of learned material and the learning task itself may change. The direct observation of acquisition strategies at an encoding stage can, it may be argued, provide a functional definition. Broadbent proposes that the traditional memory span can be reinterpreted as arising from a system working with a module of three items, and discusses implications for storage and retrieval processes. Such a system would constrain both the assimilation and retrieval of information and, possibly, influence the optimal mode of long-term storage. One component of this argument refers to pausing and grouping activity and Wilkes provides further discussion of pausing behaviour as an index for units of encoding. He argues that spontaneous acquisition strategies can be identified from pausing records and at this level an interaction between encoding activity and structural features of long-term memory can be directly investigated. Schulman deals with differences in processing at the time of input and illustrates in another way the influence which the context of encoding may have at the point of retrieval. In all but exceptional conditions it is only when subjects intentionally attend to a particular encoding dimension that it can function as an effective retrieval cue.

Among the most powerful of mnemonic variables is the capacity of certain materials to evoke images, and the distinction between verbal and imaginal coding and between 'concrete' and 'abstract' words has occupied a central position in the research literature. Paivio discusses how it is possible to exchange information between these two representational systems while maintaining the fundamental distinction between the parallel or synchronous processing mode of imagery and the sequential mode of verbal storage.

Organization

The dual-coding proposal covers one aspect of LTM organization but, as Morton argues, permanent memory is not a single system with one operating principle. Several authors deal with the search for a sufficiently powerful descriptive language to encompass the variety of stored 'code' and the repertoire of rules for acting on it. In so doing, discussions of memory organization often take over the formal languages developed for related cognitive areas. Morton illustrates this when considering the manner in which subjects list coded information. The form of output he suggests implies two distinct classes of operation; one to deal with the direct output of a stored list and the other which involves a prior stage of deriving information from a data base. In effect, for retrieval an appropriate model could be that of problem solving.

Analysis of vocabulary storage also presents in a particularly sharp manner the descriptive difficulties already outlined. Kiss presents both a formal network and normative data for word associations in the language. From this basis he goes on to consider not only the relevance of associative models for defining semantic relationships but their utility for retrieval and reasoning. The relation of semantic fields to semantic theory is specifically discussed by Johnson-Laird who considers different formal descriptions that might be applied. Working from both experimental and theoretical considerations he attempts to identify a semantic theory whose primitive terms can be psychologically motivated and concludes that a feature analysis could replace an associative network in describing the verbal lexicon but may need itself to be replaced by 'perceptual and conceptual routines'.

In *Things to Remember*, Frijda lists many of the structural properties which must eventually be incorporated in a model of memory. Such a model must (minimally) encompass the coding of single items; classes; objects; relations between objects; and higher order systems. In addition, any adequate model must deal with methods for transferring data, assimilating new information into the data base and deriving implications which influence future action. In this paper the intersection of LTM organization with related cognitive skills is made explicit through the use of Guilford's structural model of intelligence (Guilford, 1967).

Integration

It has been claimed that memory must contain not only representations of information but also rules for carrying out what Frijda terms 'transformations'. The exercise of any cognitive skill, as in language use or logical reasoning, presents the opportunity to study the integration of information retrieved from permanent store. The papers in this section are all concerned with this interface between memory and structured performance. The problem of the representation of skills in LTM is considered by Schaeffer. Taking a developed skill as a hierarchically ordered representation, he argues that this integration is brought about during the near simultaneous use of subskills in a working memory of limited capacity. On this basis a developmental progression for logical and language skills may be formulated.

In skilled reading it is necessary that controlled associative responses be made to component words of the text. The semantic fields for individual words are constrained by their linguistic context and Kennedy considers the nature of these associative constraints. Using word recognition and reading facilitation procedures, he reports that different associative ranges are elicited by the same words when they occupy logical subject or object positions within sentences. Levelt and Kempen discuss the concept of syntactic plans as LTM operations, arguing that they operate not only in spontaneous speech but also as strategies for subjects in experimental studies showing syntactic effects in retrieval. Subjects memorizing sentences store a semantic representation and, during reproduction, use retrieval plans based upon overlearned syntactic constructions which serve to recreate constituent boundary effects. As Levelt and Kempen point out, the learner's strategy interacts with the experimental task and this provides a cautionary note to the hope that the 'syntax of memory' can be exclusively drawn from formal languages designed for competence models.

Retrieval

It is, of course, an arbitrary separation to consider retrieval processes as distinct from organization and integration, however, a number of papers lay particular emphasis on the output strategies available to subjects. Here a distinction may be drawn between what Millward calls *production* tasks and *verification* tasks. In the latter, subjects must respond simply Yes/No, True/False to report a mismatch present in a stimulus array. The interest in this task lies in the use which can be made of differences in RT to isolate different components of a retrieval search. Production calls for subjects to output material—a task which he uses to examine the concept of semantic memory as well as the properties of the retrieval plan itself.

Seymour presents an extensive review of verbal–pictorial comparison tasks concluding that the data may be subsumed under a model that represents both verbal descriptors and pictures in an abstract (propositional) form. He identifies three possible sources of retrieval priming: priming at access; at output; and a 'generalized threshold adjustment' relating to overall changes in the disposition to produce a particular positive or negative response. Meyer presents evidence, based upon RT's to judge the truth values of various quantified propositions, that sentence negation reduces the rate at which information can be retrieved from LTM. Working from the verification task he presents a two-stage model in which negation increases the time needed for recalling that two categories intersect (Stage 1) and for recognizing that one category is a subset of another category (Stage 2).

Pathology

The fundamental difficulty in attempting to distinguish between the functional subsystems in the structure of memory is perhaps most apparent when one considers the problem of memory loss. Failure to recall may involve impaired retrieval schemes, but may equally well relate to failure at other levels. Clinical observations on the pathology of memory have been available for a long time but major advances have depended on theoretical developments in the main stream of research on normal function. Not until the theoretically critical variables are isolated is it possible to ask appropriate questions of data derived from pathological states. Nonetheless, the breakdown of LTM can provide a unique commentary upon its proposed working characteristics. Assumptions made in the course of model building and factual data derived from controlled experiments often introduce subtle constraints when generalized to human memory and neurological and pathological commentaries can provide a critical perspective for ongoing theory construction.

Marshall, Newcombe and Holmes take up the question of how different parts-of-speech might be organized in LTM. They report that subjects with acquired Dyslexia differ in reading response to Nouns and Verbs, an effect which can be simulated in normals with brief tachistoscopic exposure. It is concluded that the right cerebral hemisphere gives processing priority to high frequency items largely irrespective of part-of-speech whereas the left hemisphere gives priority to noun access largely irrespective of frequency.

In a clinical survey of Retrograde Amnesia, Williams sets out the implications for a theory of LTM posed by memory loss. Baddeley develops this topic by comparing five theories of amnesia and relating them to the clinical evidence. He finds the picture in general to be equivocal but tends not to support the notion of amnesia arising from poor trace consolidation. The remaining alternatives of interference, imagery, construction of cognitive maps and familiarity tagging all at some point bear upon the clinical data. Further progress depends, of course, upon refinements of these theoretical models and sharpening the critical issues between them. It is hoped that the present compilation of studies can help to further this goal.

References

Atkinson, R. C. and Shiffrin, R. M. (1968). Human memory: A proposed system and its central processes. In K. W. Spence and J. T. Spence (Eds) *The Psychology of Learning and Motivation, Vol 2*. New York: Academic Press.

Broadbent, D. E. (1958). *Perception and Communication*. London: Pergamon.

Burnham, W. H. (1888). Memory historically and experimentally considered. I. An historical sketch of the older conception of memory. *American Journal of Psychology*, **2**, 39–90.

Craik, F. I. M. and Lockhart, R. C. (1972). Levels of processing: a framework for memory research. *Journal of Verbal Learning and Verbal Behavior*, **11**, 671–684.
Frijda, N. H. (1972). The simulation of human memory. *Psychological Bulletin*, **77**, 1–31.
Guilford, J. P. (1967). *The Nature of Human Intelligence*. New York: McGraw-Hill.
Oldfield, R. C. (1966). Things, words and the brain. *Quarterly Journal of Experimental Psychology*, **18**, 340–353.
Standing, L. (1973). Learning 10,000 pictures. *Quarterly Journal of Experimental Psychology*, **25**, 207–222.
Waugh, N. C. and Norman, D. A. (1965). Primary memory. *Psychological Review*, **72**, 89–104.

Part I
Encoding

Chapter 1

The Magic Number
Seven After Fifteen Years

Donald E. Broadbent

Introduction

Although the topic of this book is properly long-term memory, this particular paper is more concerned with short-term and almost perceptual processes. The justification for this is that our knowledge of long-term memory must come from material we insert into it and withdraw from it; and it is possible that the features of these input and access systems may colour the performance of long-term memory itself. So at least it will be argued here.

The classic paper of Miller (1956) forms a useful point of departure. As we all recall, he drew attention to two curious and possibly linked phenomena. One of these concerned absolute judgments of sensory quantities, and we shall for reasons of space say nothing about that, simply indicating for completeness that discussion of such judgments does raise many of the same issues.

The second phenomenon mentioned by Miller was the approximate constancy of the memory span in terms of independent units. The span for letters is nearly the same as that for digits, and that for binary digits is little more. Yet if subjects were trained to encode binary symbols into decimal digits they could reproduce after one presentation a long string of binary digits corresponding to about the same number of decimal digits as their ordinary span. These results and other similar ones suggested that there is some limitation on human processing such that only a fixed number, say seven, of independent units can be handled at one time. Each unit could nevertheless be divided into sub-units so that facts and actions of enormous complexity could be handled by calling up a fresh ensemble of sub-units at each stage when it became necessary. In contemporary terms it might almost be better to speak of a 'production system' (Newell and Simon, 1972) in which seven productions can be considered at one time.

The apparent size of the memory span thus depends on the complexity of the encoding processes which the individual has learned; so equally will his utilization of long-term memory. One would expect on this basis that long-term memory will be organized into hierarchical trees or clusters, in which each item at one level can be replaced by a number of alternatives (say, seven) at another level.

This line of thought, with certain variations, has been developed by Tulving and by Mandler. For example, Tulving and Patkau (1962) showed that the words recalled from a long presented list formed a constant number, in the neighbourhood of seven, of 'adopted chunks', if we count as a chunk any words recalled together which had been adjacent in the presentation. If there are in the material a number of words belonging to a certain category, then one will help the recall of those words by giving a cue to the nature of that category especially if there are a large number of categories (Tulving and Pearlstone, 1966). If learners organize the list for themselves, they recall more material as they increase the number of categories they use up to seven (Mandler, 1968). Within each category, the number of words recalled remains about the same if any are recalled at all, i.e. as long as the category itself is recalled. All this suggests a fixed number of items which can be held at any one time, each item being expandable into a fixed number of sub-items. A modification which should be noted parenthetically is that Mandler notes that the constant number of items per category is nearer five than seven, and suggests that the usual memory span is contaminated by the presence of some items in a rather different short-term store. The structure of long-term memory, in this view, would consist of sets of five items, each item perhaps being divisible into five sub-items, and each set perhaps forming one of five making up a super-set. The memory span would then be seven because of the combined reproduction of a set of five from long-term memory and of a couple of spare items from a 'primary memory' or echo-box.

One view in this tradition is that put forward by Broadbent (1971, pp. 376–7). In this particular version, there is a store of buffer type which will hold material only for a very brief time, a longer term store, and a third 'address register' which holds for indefinite time a limited number of addresses. Each address consists of sufficient information to select from all stored information one particular segment, and hence the ordinary memory span requires the successive selection of a series of regions either of long-term or of buffer storage. For this reason the extraction even of items in 'secondary memory' will be limited. The amount recalled in terms of words or other symbols will depend on the amount stored at each address. The structure of long-term memory is thus involved, though this author did not examine the possibility of a hierarchical structure based on a fixed number, nor commit himself about the number of addresses allowed.

In the present paper, various lines of evidence are examined to try and shed light on the elusive question of the number which sets limits to processing. Is it uniformly seven? Or is it five, with an extra two in the case of the memory span? The view towards which we shall be arguing is that the underlying number is more closely *three*; that incoming events, outgoing actions, and transfers of information from one process to another are handled in terms of a module of three. The traditional seven arises (in this view) from the particular opportunity provided in the memory span task for the retrieval of information from different forms of processing.

Memory: Some Doubts About Seven

There are a number of experiments which cast some doubt on the fundamental nature of the usual finding of a seven-item span. These are of a number of different kinds, and can best be considered separately.

The Limit of Perfect Performance

The usual span as reported is the number of items which can be recalled on 50 per cent of occasions. If we rather consider the length of span which can reliably give very high accuracy, we find that it is only three or four items. Further, the span measured by the usual method is somewhat dependent on the nature of the item, being slightly shorter for letters than for digits, slightly longer for binary digits and so on. The length of the perfect span is much more resistant to the nature of the items (e.g., Cardozo and Leopold, 1963). Conceivably, therefore, the extra items beyond three or four are, as Broadbent (1971) suggested, only capable of being stored if they have been learned as units associated with other items.

Running Performance

If there are really seven productions in potential operation at one time, or a single store with space for seven separate items, then when a continuous stream of events occurs one might expect a man to be capable of responding reliably to the stimulus which is at any instant the seventh most distant in the past. This of course is not so: in a continuing string of statistically independent events, human ability to output all the information in the string, but do so with a lag of N items, is much less effective than the ability to output a single stream of length N after its conclusion. The topic was of much interest to psychologists of skill in the Fifties; the ability to follow more than one or two items behind is very limited, and three would be the upper limit (Poulton, 1954).

Modal Rather than Average Category Size

If we ask people to group together common objects such as types of food, and then examine the size of the categories they employ, the mean category size is indeed of the rough magnitude found by Mandler and others. Richard Byrne of Cambridge (1973) has, in such a situation, found average category sizes of six or seven. But it also emerges that the distribution contains modes, at two or three. In one case, there were nearly four times as many clusters of size three as there were of the average size of six. This raises the suspicion that three is the more fundamental category size, and that a larger apparent category has been made to appear by listing two or three fundamental categories under a single more general heading.

Primary Memory

It has already been mentioned that Mandler suggested five as a more fundamental unit for long-term memory than seven, with the extra items carried in a short-term memory. If we follow a long list of words by some brief intervening activity, memory for the words earliest presented is very little affected, but the last few items deteriorate very severely. The number of items affected in this way is about three [see, e.g., Postman and Phillips (1965)].

Effects of Stimulus Duration

If a visual field is exposed for various times, the number of items which can be reported from it increases with increasing duration. There are however two fairly distinct functions which can be determined: for the first fiftieth of a second or so the rate of increase in recall is extremely fast, and after that it becomes slower. Sperling (1967) argues that in the early period partially-parallel processing is going on, because recall of the second and third items on the display starts to improve before the first has reached 100 per cent; certainly the tempting view is that the first period sets up some visual store from which information can only slowly be read into a later (and probably articulatory) store (Coltheart, 1972). If this is the correct interpretation, we can work out the number of items held in the visual store when it is full and extra material can only be held by transfer to the later stage. The answer is three items.

Grouping

It is well known that dividing a string of letters or digits into shorter groups improves its handling by human beings. The best performance is usually obtained with groups of three or four (Wickelgren, 1964; Ryan, 1969). The reason for this is obscure, although Wickelgren has suggested that it may have to do with the unique associations of the beginning, middle, and end of each group of three. There is also the logical point that a retrieval system in which x^n items are stored and retrieved by finding the correct value of each of x features, looking at each of the possible values of each feature in random order until the correct one is located, will work fastest if n is made equal to 3 (Dirlam, 1972).

These explanations would, however, continue to predict an advantage for threes even if the material is made to contain redundancy such that certain sequences of five digits recur unduly often as in telephone exchange numbers; but Broadbent (in Warr, 1971) briefly reports an experiment to confirm that this is not so.

The phenomenon of grouping moreover is more basic than is allowed in most theories; Clive Frankish of Cambridge (1973) has timed the responses to lists presented in various ways, including apparently 'ungrouped' lists, and finds that the pauses in responding reveal that in almost every case the subject imposes on the material a grouping into sections no longer than three or four. Similarly another briefly reported experiment (Broadbent and Broadbent, 1973) in which subjects wrote down alpha-numeric lists on segmented paper showed that the vast majority of responses to eight-item lists divided them into groups of no more than four items. We may strongly suspect therefore that grouping is not an interesting minor phenomenon met with in special experiments on that subject, but rather is imposed by the subject in almost all cases.

Some results suggest another interpretation of grouping. If a list is presented more than once, but with the grouping changed, we do not get the usual Hebb effect of improved recall on the later presentations [see e.g. Winzenz (1972)]. Furthermore if material contains meaningful units of letters such as YMCA, performance is only improved by this meaningfulness when the imposed grouping corresponds to the meaning (Bower, 1972). Thus the grouping appears to separate a small set of items, and to allow a further encoding of this set on their own; meaningfulness and passage to long-term memory occur on the basis of this later encoding. The same interpretation is supported by the brief report by Broadbent and Broadbent (1973) that mixed alpha-numeric sequences are better recalled if they are grouped in a repeated structure such as letter–letter–digit, letter–letter–digit, letter–letter–digit, even if the subject has no advance warning that this will be so. That is, the abstract structure of the group appears to elicit some encoding within the subject, and thus the grouped set of items must have been used as a basis for such encoding.

Another line of evidence leading to the same conclusion follows from the serial-position effect which is found with grouped material. Each group shows the usual recency effect familiar from results over the whole list when presentation is such as to impose no uniform method of grouping (Ryan, 1969). Furthermore, Frankish has found that this recency effect is greater for auditory presentation, in the manner which characterizes the recency effect for the whole list and which is usually interpreted as implying the existence of a pre-categoric acoustic store (PAS) (Crowder and Morton, 1969). This finding, and some of those in the original PAS experiments, mean that Broadbent (1971) was wrong in supposing that PAS operates by holding information precategorically right through the process of response until the last items are required. Rather, the incoming stimuli are held in PAS until a group has arrived, and then the whole group is encoded and ceases to be in pre-categorical storage.

A Preliminary Speculation

The foregoing arguments suggest an alternative to the view that there are seven slots or productions. Baldly, let us suppose that human beings have a register containing three spaces for separate entries, and that this register acts in the fashion familiar from our laboratory computers both as the means of entry to the system in general and also as the means of exit when response is required. Thus when successive events occur in the outside world, up to three such events can be held simultaneously in this register, and then despatched as a single whole to store. The register can then fill up again with fresh inputs. When response is required, the first step must be to call back into the register the grouped information, and the next step to feed it out as three apparently separate items. We can leave till later the question of the way in which this can lead to a seven-item span; for the moment we must deal with the embarrassment that there is little evidence for a packaging by threes in output and especially not in long-term memory. On the contrary, as Miller himself pointed out, many classical ensembles in long-term memory, like the Wonders of the World, and Deadly Sins, or the Sleepers, come in Sevens. An urgent question therefore is whether retrieval from long-term memory shows any sign of packaging.

Experiment I: Grouping In Long-term Recall

Procedure

In this experiment, each subject was asked individually to recall as many items as she could from a familiar category. Her spoken responses were recorded, and subsequently the intervals between the onsets of successive response words were measured from the tape to the nearest half-second. Four categories were used: (1) The Seven Dwarfs (2) The Seven Colours of the Rainbow (3) The countries of Europe, and (4) The names of regular television programmes. All four of these categories, in that order, were obtained from each of 10 members of the APU subject panel, i.e. housewives, in addition data on the first category were obtained from four female members of the Unit secretarial and assistant staff, and on the second and third categories from two each. No particular instructions about the speed of response were given.

Analysis: General

The four categories behaved differently, as we intended, in terms both of amount and speed of recall. The first and second gave fast speech rates, but nobody could produce seven names in the first category and considerable slowing occurred for later names. In the second category only one subject failed to give seven names and the rate of speaking was well maintained. In the third category, all subjects gave at least 11 names and some got over 20; in the fourth, there was a very large range, with enthusiasts reaching double figures and others expiring after as few as four. It was characteristic of the TV programmes that the pauses were normally long even at the beginning of recall.

To bring different people and categories to a comparable scale, the shortest interval for each subject was determined for each category, and all other intervals for that subject and category scaled in units of that shortest one. (It was normally either one or one-half seconds, except for the television programmes.) The data were then examined (1) for changes as recall proceeded, (2) for the number of items in the longest run separated by intervals of one unit, and (3) for the number of items recalled before the first interval longer than the next successive interval.

Analysis: Countries of Europe

It is convenient to consider this category first because it provides the most data, the others are primarily confirmatory. It is known from earlier work such as that of Bousfield, Sedgewick and Cohen (1954), that output in this kind of task slows down as the task proceeds, and the present data confirm this; the average interval for the first set of five intervals is faster than that for the second five in 10 of the 12 subjects. Closer examination reveals however some features which seem to need a complication of the model of Bousfield, Sedgewick and Cohen, which predicts the average rate of response from the number of possible responses still remaining unemitted. Firstly, the shortest response quite frequently occurs in the second rather than the first set of five intervals; in five subjects it is present in both, in three *only* in the second set, and only in four is it present in the first set of intervals without being also in the second set. Secondly, although the mean interval increases as the task proceeds, the short end of the distribution does not; for every one of the first 10 intervals, one or other of the subjects gives her fastest time. Thirdly, the longest run of short intervals is as likely to occur in the second five as the first; in fact, only four subjects have it in the first half and six in the second, the remaining two overlapping both halves.

These results mean that the changes, with increasing time spent on the task, take the form of pauses of increasing duration between runs of responses made with normal speed. The countries of Europe emerge in clusters, and the slowing down occurs as it becomes harder to think of a cluster. Within a cluster however the names came out quickly. The next question is the size of the cluster and this we can get from the longest run of minimal intervals; as will be seen from Table 1.1, nine of the twelve subjects give two or three as their longest burst of fast responding, and no subject gives more than five. For memory, the Seven members of EFTA and the Six of the old EEC are apparently not units.

Table 1.1. Longest Run of Minimum Interval (Number of subjects for each length)

	Length of run				
	2	3	4	5	6
Countries	5	4	1	2	0
Rainbow	5	5	1	0	1
Dwarfs	9	1	1	0	0

(TV programmes are not given, because the shortest interval was usually quite long, and only occurred once.)

Lastly, it is worth looking at the first burst of responses produced, up to th
point where a pause occurs which is longer than the pause between the next tw
responses. This measure is perhaps suspect because it is contaminated by th
gradual slowing up of response, but it has the advantage of being less affecte
by the arbitrary choice of the shortest interval as the only possible interva
between members of a cluster. From Table 1.2, it will be seen that half th

Table 1.2. First Run, Until a Pause Longer than the Next Interval

| | Length of run | | | | |
	1	2	3	4	5
Countries	3	0	3	5	1
Rainbow	0	4	5	2	1
TV Programmes	3	4	3	0	0

(Dwarfs are not given, because once a long interval occurred, there was rarely a subsequent shorte
interval.)

subjects give three or less as the length of their first burst of responses, and a
but one of the remainder give four. The effect of this can be seen in Figure 1.1
which shows the mean value of each successive interval; the mean value i
actually shorter between responses four and five than it is between response
three and four. This drop is not however significant, since of course som
subjects have already paused, started a new group and therefore are faste
between responses three and four than between four and five.

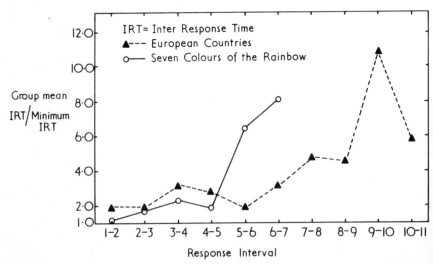

Figure 1.1. The value of the time (sec) between each successive pair of items, when
trying to remember a familiar set. Apart from the familiar general slowing of
response as the set is exhausted, notice the pause after three responses, followed by
an acceleration

Analysis: Other Categories

As the task of retrieving countries has some idiosyncratic features, it is fortunate that the key results are confirmed by the other categories. From Table 1.1 it can be seen that no subject managed to produce either Seven Dwarfs or the Seven Colours of the Rainbow in a single burst of maximum speed, and in each case the longest burst of fast responding was in the great majority of cases three or less. Television programmes create a problem for this score; as responding was slow, even for those who produced many responses, there was rarely more than one occurrence of the minimum interval. Thus there were no 'runs' in the same sense as for the other categories; this may perhaps mean that there are no true clusters in the case of programmes. On the other hand, there do occur cases in which a pause appears which is longer than the next successive interval, and from Table 1.2 it can be seen that this pause is never preceded by more than three previous names of programmes. Fairly satisfactory results by this measure also appear for the Rainbow; the Dwarfs however are useless in this case, because once pausing begins the subject never gives a subsequent burst of responses, and this makes it hard to judge the first pause. Finally, it may be noted that Figure 1.1 shows an insignificant speeding up of response between responses four and five in the Rainbow; the other two categories had too many cases where five responses were not given and so this score was not meaningful.

A Further Step Towards Alternative Theories

The results of Experiment I, rather surprisingly, give some support for the idea that the contents of long-term memory are output in clusters of three or, just possibly, four. We must now think more seriously about the relation between this module, or chunk, of three and the traditional span of seven. Our preliminary speculation was that separate items are collected together in one register until they fill it, and that they are then passed on as a chunk to another stage. Figure 1.2 illustrates the process; it will be plain that by Time Unit 7 there are six items held in the two stages. If both stages can secure an output

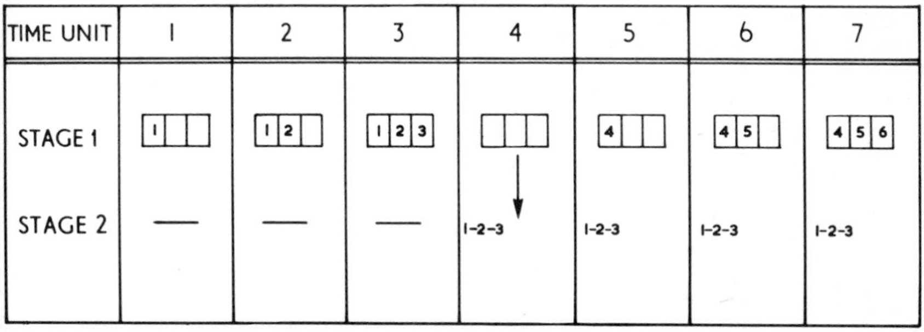

TIME UNIT	I	2	3	4	5	6	7
STAGE 1	I	I 2	I 2 3		4	4 5	4 5 6
STAGE 2	—	—	—	I-2-3	I-2-3	I-2-3	I-2-3

Figure 1.2. A theoretical description of what is happening when items are delivered to a man successively. They accumulate at an early stage until several are present simultaneously, and then an encoded version of the entire combination is prepared at a subsequent stage two

without either interfering with the other, a span of six is possible. If the fundamental module were four rather than three, the spans would be eight. Thus seven might be found as the average of groups of individuals. Alternatively, if the two major stages were preceded by a buffer holding a single item, there would be seven in the total system. Either of these possibilities would however require rather sophisticated extraction of the information from the different stages, and hence would only allow perfect performance on a proportion of occasions.

We suggested earlier a simplistic analogy between our three-slot register and the accumulator through which information travels in and out of a small laboratory computer. It seems parsimonious to think of the same register as both an input and output buffer, but which of the stages in Figure 1.2 corresponds to such a thing? One possibility is Stage 1, since in that the different items are clearly segmented from each other. If that were so, then at Time Unit 7 response to all six items in the correct order can only be arranged by clearing Stage 1 so as to allow the first three items back into Stage 1, as shown in Figure 1.3. This cycle of operations allows further opportunities for error, and on the face of it, if the output of the system is always through Stage 1, then it will be easier to output the last group of items first, immediately after they have arrived, and only then to retrieve the earlier items from Stage 2. Such an apparently paradoxical result is consistent with the findings of Howe (1965, 1966), who asked subjects to recall nine-item lists with the groups of three in various orders including complete reversal. He found better performance when the last group emerged first; so also did Posner (1964). These experiments were not performed in the present theoretical context and further evidence is perhaps necessary. (In particular, the lists were presented ungrouped, and at a fairly slow rate, with some evidence that rate itself was important in producing the effect. The main interest at that date lay in the relative impairment of early and late items in the list as a result of intervening activity between presentation and response.)

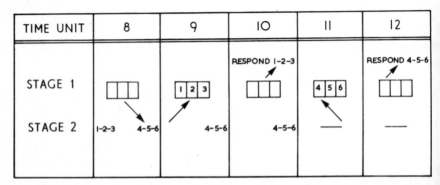

Figure 1.3. A theoretical diagram of the processes which would be necessary for recall in the order of arrival, on the assumption that stage one is an output buffer as well as an input buffer

The alternative possible theory is that Stage 2 is an output register. In that case Stage 1 need not be cleared before response, and recall in the order of presentation will be better than recall of the last group first. We can sub-divide this view into further possibilities, one of which is that Stage 1 is an ikonic or sensory store. In view of all the evidence for such a store, this would be parsimonious, although most theorists would perhaps wish us to add the caveat that transfer to Stage 2 is serial rather than parallel. The key point in this view is however that ikonic store is usually supposed to decay with time. Consequently a slower rate of presentation might in this case be expected to allow more decay in Stage 1 before transfer to Stage 2 becomes possible. This deterioration at slow rates of presentation should apply to any of the groups in the list. Reversed recall should impair performance, since if one were so cruel as to demand recall of the last group first, from a system working on this basis, then output of the whole system would be delayed until the last item had been cleared from Stage 1; one might reasonably suppose that a slow presentation rate would make matters even worse.

The remaining possibility is that Stage 1 is not a time-dependent ikonic store, but equally that it is not an output register. In that event reversing the order of recall would increase the overall error rate, but slowing presentation speed would not. If both conditions increase errors, Stage 1 is a time-dependent store; if neither does, Stage 1 is an output register and Stage 2 a long-term store.

These three possible theories correspond to different views about the point at which the original stimulus has been converted to a 'category state' (Broadbent, 1971). On the first and third views, this recoding of the raw stimulus has occurred before Stage 1; on the second view, it occurs between Stage 1 and Stage 2, and at Stage 1 the item carries its original sensory characteristics. The different views thus give rise to the following experiment.

Experiment II: Reversed and Direct Recall of Slow and Fast Lists

Procedure

Subjects heard 40 sequences each of nine digits, each grouped into threes by a double length interval between the last digit of one group and the first of the next. Repeated digits within a list were allowed but were never adjacent. The lists were divided into four sets of ten, each set being given under one of the four conditions. Group 1 (17 housewives from the APU panel) received two sets with instructions to recall in the order of presentation, followed by two sets with recall of the last group of three, then the first, and then the middle one. The correct answer was read out after the first sequence of each set, as a precaution against misunderstanding. With each instruction, the first set was delivered at a fast speed and the second at a slow speed, 'fast' here meaning two digits per second, with 1 sec between groups, while 'slow' means one digit per second and 2 sec between groups. Group 2 (14 housewives) received the reversed recall

14

instructions for the first two groups and direct recall was required for the later two, with slow presentation preceding fast in each case. Responses were written down. All the following results are for number of complete lists correct in the prescribed order.

Results

In each group alone it is clear that reversed recall order gives fewer correct complete lists whatever the presentation rate: For Group 1, $P < 0.001$ at the fast rate and <0.01 at the slow rate; for Group 2, $P < 0.022$ in both cases. (Tests are by sign test on the numbers of subjects.)

It is also clear that there is no general deterioration at slow presentation rates. When recall is in the order of presentation, each group gives a majority of subjects doing better at the fast rate, and a sign test using subjects from both groups is comfortably significant ($P < 0.2$). However with reversed recall there is a slight majority of subjects who do *better* at the slow presentation rate, though not significantly so. We may test the interaction of instructions and rates by examining the number of subjects who show a larger difference between fast and slow performance in direct recall than in reversed; combining the groups the interaction is significant by sign tests, $P < 0.05$. Figure 1.4 shows furthermore that the beneficial effect of fast rate even in the direct recall order is

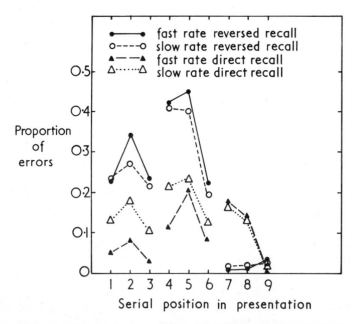

Figure 1.4. The error rate at different serial positions for material presented in three groups of three, either at 2 digits per second, or at 1 digit per second. Notice that this difference of rate has no effect on the last group, but only on earlier groups

emphatically on the first two groups and *not* on the last one; if anything the last group is better performed when presented slowly.

The Implications of Experiment II

On the face of it, these results mean that Stage 1 is *not* an output buffer and that perhaps it is an ikonic form of storage. (The caution expressed in the phrasing of the latter statement arises from the absence of any effect of presentation rate on the last group of the list.)

The conclusions are however at variance with those we would have drawn had the experiment given the same results as those of Howe and of Posner; we ought therefore to consider why this discrepancy of finding has arisen. At the factual level, the key factor is fairly clear: Posner only obtained a beneficial effect from recall of the last group first when he used a very slow presentation rate and not at his faster rate. Howe (1965) noted in his discussion that he also had failed to get his result at a fast rate. It is therefore presumably because of the fast speech rate, almost that of natural speech, and combined with pauses for grouping, that Experiment II gives an impairment when recall order is reversed.

During the last 5 years, most of us would have accepted Howe's explanation of the fact that slow presentation is necessary for reversed recall to be beneficial. Slow presentation, we would have argued, allows more time for encoding and rehearsal of the earlier items, and therefore makes them more resistant to intervening recall of the later items. But Figure 1.4 draws our attention to the fact that slow presentation gives *worse* recall of the earlier items, a curious result of increased encoding and rehearsal. Looking at Posner's results with this in mind, we see that his data also show inferior performance at slow rates when recall is in the order of presentation. We therefore need a new explanation for the fact that slow rates prevent bad effects from reversed recall.

Two possible candidates can be suggested: first, that our previous distinction of only two stages is too simple, and that there is also an earlier ikonic stage which is of no importance at slow presentation rates because each item passes into Stage 1 before the next arrives. At fast rates, however, a back-log builds up in the ikonic store (Stage 0?), and some items are still there when presentation finishes. This makes it difficult to recall those items first. Stage 1 is on this view indeed an output buffer, but at fast presentation rates it still contains early items even when recall instructions arrive. It is not thought that this view will work in detail: if the back-log is so great that the first group is still in Stage 1 at the end of presentation, the ikonic store would still be carrying so many items that a slowing of presentation would surely be beneficial rather than harmful. If on the other hand the back-log is only of two or three items, and after presentation the first group is already into Stage 2, then it is not clear why recall in the original order should be any easier than recall in reversed order. In either case Stage 1 will need to be cleared and a different group moved into it. This possible explanation is therefore unconvincing.

There is a second possible explanation; if we suppose that the slow rate makes combination of each triplet of items into a group difficult, then at such a rate the items might be passed on individually from Stage 1 to Stage 2. This would remove the advantage of grouping and thus make the slow rate harder than the fast one. It would also mean that at the end of each group the memorizer might recall the items of that group into Stage 1 to try and form a group. Then at the end of presentation the last group would be conveniently in Stage 1 whereas in the conditions of fast presentation the last group would differ from the two earlier groups in needing to be emitted rather than passed to Stage 2. This explanation is a little more plausible than the previous one, but apart from its rather complex *post hoc* character, it is not thought that it will survive a detailed comparison with the data. The serial position effects within groups, which show the usual marked recency effect at the end of each group are almost exactly the same at each presentation, which does not look as if grouping was harder at the slow speed. Furthermore, there is the puzzle that none of the items in the last group show any effect of rate; yet that group should surely have as much difficulty in being grouped as any other.

As a final attempt at a satisfactory explanation, let us start with the finding which causes difficulty to our earlier attempts; the resistance of the last group to effects of rate. If we suppose that *Stage 2* rather than Stage 1 decays with time this finding presents no problem. The last group is unaffected by rate because all its items were in Stage 1 until the end of presentation, but at the slow rate the two earlier groups have longer to decay. Furthermore, at the fast rate they will be recalled soon after presentation if recall is in the original order, but if the last group is recalled first they will be held in Stage 2 for longer and thus do worse. At the slow rate the increase in storage time due to reversed recall becomes relatively less large and so makes less difference; except of course to the last group itself, which does improve.

Of the various possibilities then, the author feels that the most plausible is that Stage 1 is not an ikonic store, although it is probably (from all the evidence in the literature) preceded by one. After information has passed through Stage 1, however, it enters a Stage 2 in which it deteriorates with time, rapidly at first and then more slowly. Stage 1 by itself is not an output buffer, but the combination of the two stages may be, in various possible ways of which we shall examine one shortly.

Conclusion: The Meaning of Stage 1

One major point remains undiscussed; what does it mean to say that Stage has three slots? Surely we cannot literally think of a row of three Nixie tubes in the brain, imposing their limits on the groupings of items retrieved even from long-term memory? Of course not, but there is perhaps a functional similarity between the process under discussion and the humble input register of a laboratory computer, despite the obvious differences. When the computer receives a particular 1 or 0, that symbol is marked with the position it occupied within the whole 'word' or string of similar symbols. Similarly in a system like our Stage 1, each item could reasonably be marked with its position in the set of items present simultaneously in the system. Thus as a grouped series of digits arrives at the ear, each of the first three digits is marked as first, second, or third in Stage 1, and passed on to the time-decaying Stage 2 with that mark present. Stage 1 could then be occupied with other information, and yet when retrieval of those items is needed they can be found by the marks assigned to them. Indeed, Shulman and Greenberg (1971) show no impairment when another task is combined with the remembering of lists of less than three items, even though longer lists do produce such an impairment. Similarly Hitch and Baddeley (1973) find no impairment on Baddeley's syntactic reasoning test when two items are being held in memory, although with six items an interference does appear.

Once there are more items than three of the same kind in Stage 2, however, things get more difficult. The three items in a single group can be marked by reference to each other, but to mark a whole group as the first, second, third, or fourth requires comparison with other previous events no longer in Stage 1. It may be possible to mark the first group because Stage 1 was empty when it arrived, and the second because it was not. When both have been passed into Stage 2, therefore, it would be possible to locate each group in turn and the items within each group. They can then be assembled for output; in a sense the marked items in Stage 2, together with Stage 1, thus form an output buffer of the kind we have toyed with earlier.

The 'slots' of Stage 1 could be interpreted then as three possible marks any one of which can be applied to an item for later use as a retrieval cue. But why three? One can answer such a question at two levels. First, to hark back to the introduction, that number recurs in the field of absolute judgments as the number of steps distinguishable on each dimension when a large number of dimensions are being judged; when a single dimension is being considered, five steps can be separated, and this again is the number which could be managed if three standard values were held for comparison (the lowest, the highest, and the middle; the other two steps are the intermediate values).

At a more fundamental level, however, three marks are the minimum which would be needed to conduct certain kinds of processing; for instance, any which require the labelling of two entities and also of the relation between them. Interesting speculations on the relation between the number of properties storable and the possibility of operating at each of Piaget's levels have been put forward by McLaughlin (1963). From the point of view of this book, perhaps the most relevant point is that a three-fold distinction will allow the construction of the fashionable semantic networks with nodes connected by labelled paths. On the other hand, it seems plausible that it would not allow processing of a series of inputs in which two related entities are separated not merely by other terms related to one of themselves, but also by pairs of terms related to each other; and this seems a hopeful approach to the problem of the limits on self-embedding of sentences. That however is a topic for a later occasion.

18

References

Bower, G. H. (1972). Perceptual groups as coding units in immediate memory. *Psychonomic Science*, **27**, 217–219.

Bousfield, W. A., Sedgewick, C. H. and Cohen, B. H. (1954). Certain temporal characteristics of the recall of verbal associates. *American Journal of Psychology*, **67**, 111–118.

Broadbent, D. E. (1971). *Decision and Stress*. London and New York: Academic Press.

Broadbent, D. E. and Broadbent, M. H. P. (1973). Grouping strategies in short-term memory for alpha-numeric lists. *Bulletin of the British Psychological Society*, **26**, 135.

Byrne, R. (1973). Personal communication.

Cardozo, B. L. and Leopold, F. F. (1963). Human code transmission. Letters and digits compared on the basis of immediate memory rates. *Ergonomics*, **6**, 133–141.

Coltheart, M. (1972). In P. C. Dodwell, (Ed.) *New Horizons in Psychology 2*. London: Penguin Books.

Crowder, R. G. and Morton, J. (1969). Precategorical acoustic storage (PAS). *Perception and Psychophysics*, **5**, 365–373.

Dirlam, D. K. (1972). Most efficient chunk sizes. *Cognitive Psychology*, **3**, 355–359.

Frankish, C. (1973). Personal communication.

Hitch, G. J. and Baddeley, A. D. (1973). Working memory. Paper to *Experimental Psychology Society*, April.

Howe, M. J. A. (1965). Intra-list differences in short-term memory. *Quarterly Journal of Experimental Psychology*, **17**, 338–342.

Howe, M. J.A. (1966). A note on order of recall in short-term memory. *British Journal of Psychology*, **57**, 435–436.

McLaughlin, G. H. (1963). Psycho-logic: a possible alternative to Piaget's formulation. *British Journal of Educational Psychology*, **33**, 61–67.

Mandler, G. (1968). In K. W. Spence and J. T. Spence, (Eds) *The Psychology of Learning and Motivation*. Vol. II. New York: Academic Press.

Miller, G. A. (1956). The magical number seven, plus or minus two: some limits on our capacity for processing information. *Psychological Review*, **63**, 81–97.

Newell, A. and Simon, H. A. (1972). *Human Problem Solving*. Englewood Cliffs: Prentice-Hall.

Posner, M. I. (1964). Rate of presentation and order of recall in immediate memory. *British Journal of Psychology*, **55**, 303–306.

Postman, L. and Phillips, L. W. (1965). Short-term temporal changes in free recall. *Quarterly Journal of Experimental Psychology*, **17**, 132–138.

Poulton, E. C. (1954). The eye–hand span in simple serial tasks. *Journal of Experimental Psychology*, **47**, 403–410.

Ryan, J. (1969). Grouping and short-term memory: different means and patterns of grouping. *Quarterly Journal of Experimental Psychology*, **21**, 137–147.

Shulman, H. G. and Greenberg, S. N. (1971). Perceptual deficit due to division of attention between memory and perception. *Journal of Experimental Psychology*, **88**, 171–176.

Sperling, G. (1967). Successive approximations to a model for short-term memory. *Acta Psychologica*, **27**, 285–292.

Tulving, E. and Patkau, J. E. (1962). Concurrent effects of contextual constraint and word frequency on immediate recall and learning of verbal material. *Canadian Journal of Psychology*, **16**, 83–95.

Tulving, E. and Pearlstone, Z. (1966). Availability versus accessibility of information in memory for words. *Journal of Verbal Learning and Verbal Behavior*, **5**, 381–391.

Warr, P. (1971). (Ed.) *Psychology at Work*. London: Penguin Books.

Wickelgren, W. A. (1964). Size of rehearsal group and short-term memory. *Journal of Experimental Psychology*, **68**, 413–419.

Winzenz, D. (1972). Group structure and coding in serial learning. *Journal of Experimental Psychology*, **92**, 8–19.

Chapter 2

Encoding Processes and Pausing Behaviour

A. L. Wilkes

Pausing and Subjective Grouping

In simple serial learning tasks subjects are likely to organize the material into groups. The imposed structure during acquisition readings may follow temporal or spatial cues that are deliberately introduced as part of the experimental treatment or, if none are present, it can be introduced by the learner himself (e.g. Ryan, 1969; Thorpe and Rowland, 1965; McLean and Gregg, 1967; Wilkes, Lloyd and Simpson, 1972).

Grouping tendencies during learning have been familiar to experimental psychologists for many years: Ward (1918), for example, included a section on rhythmizing in his *Psychological Principles* and even then could report that it had been experimentally investigated at great length. A common response, however, was to treat it as an error variable and considerable effort was made to minimize subjective grouping in verbal learning studies. Miller's discussion of chunking (1956) initiated a revival of interest and, more recently, the search for constituent units in sentence perception and learning (Fodor and Bever, 1965; Johnson, 1965) and the growing interest in individual learning strategies (Reitman, 1970) has refocussed attention on the general phenomenon.

The relationship of acquisition structure (the grouping and separation of list items imposed during learning) with later memory search and retrieval is, as yet, unclear but there can be no doubt concerning their interdependence. Bower and Winzenz (1969) reported that a recurrent digit string included within a set of different strings was associated with improved recall if the grouping structure remained the same on each re-occurrence. In contrast, no improvement occurred if the grouping structure was altered. In a subsequent experiment (Wilkes, 1972), it was reported that a single string of letters presented successively for serial learning was associated with a marked impairment in performance if the imposed grouping changed from one trial to the next. (See also Broadbent, this volume.)

The interdependence of acquisition structure and later retrieval need not be restricted to the traditional serial recall procedure. Using a probed recall technique, Wilkes and Kennedy (1970) reported that grouping structure during acquisition was closely related to the response latencies obtained when a subject responded in a later test to a probe-item by giving the item following it in the original list. In the same experiment, however, it was found that latencies to respond to probe words from the original list as present or absent, did not relate to acquisition structure. The 'functional range' of acquisition groupings remains unclear but there is sufficient evidence to warrant their serious consideration in theories dealing with short and long term memory organization.

Any adequate measure of subjective grouping must not only be sensitive to structures that are experimentally imposed (and hence known in advance), but also be sensitive to structures created by the learner and beyond the direct control of the investigator. Following Goldman–Eisler's work on pausing and cognitive processes (Goldman–Eisler, 1972), pausing has been used as such a measure and there are now numerous studies that rely upon identifying imposed structure from the presence of extended pauses. For example, Butterfield, Wambold and Belmont (1973) describe a procedure based upon subjects pacing their own learning of lists of letters. 'By pressing a button, a subject exposes the first letter of a list, then the second letter, and so on. Each letter appears briefly in a unique position. The subject's pauses following each letter and before his next button press are timed, and these times are plotted over serial position to provide a measure of learning processes' (p. 655). The subjective organization of prose material has been investigated using actual or potential pause locations (Suci, 1967; Johnson, 1970) and the preferred constituent groupings within sentences have also been identified from reading pause patterns (Kennedy and Wilkes, 1971a).

Within the serial learning task it has been shown that imposing grouping on an otherwise unstructured string facilitates learning (Ryan, 1969). A common interpretation of this consequence has been that when the learner reaches a group boundary, the content of the group is located in some temporary buffer store and can be maintained in that store by rehearsal or transferred to a long term store, the pause at the group boundary providing the opportunity for the necessary encoding processes. Thus Belmont and Butterfield (1971) write, 'we are certain that pausing involves covert rehearsal of the sort we required to be done aloud in the forced rehearsal condition' (p. 419). Similarly, Bower and Springston (1970) state the pause functions by 'allowing S a moment for rehearsal of the preceding input segment' (p. 421), and Broadbent (this volume) comments, 'Grouping appears to separate a small set of items and to allow a further encoding of this set on their own: meaningfulness and passage to LTM occur on the basis of this later encoding.' Obviously not all investigators share Belmont and Butterfield's certainty that it is covert vocalization that occurs at the boundary pause (Bd.P.) but there is agreement that some encoding operation applied to the group just registered is brought into play at this point. It must be acknowledged that a variety of encoding processes are available to the learner; covert rehearsal is a plausible contender for encoding during the serial learning of unstructured lists but, with structured material, (e.g. sentences and prose), imaging, syntactic and semantic processing are likely to be of greater significance. While a pause measure has not been shown to differentiate between these encoding modes it may provide insight into the types of structure imposed and into the degrees of encoding that may be undertaken.

Consider, for example, serial learning of a letter sequence grouped in three's by double spacing:

ABC   DEF   GHI

If the list is read aloud and then recalled it can be expected that extended pauses will occur at the group boundaries (e.g. Wilkes and Kennedy, 1970). If extended pauses serve as encoding points and separate one functional group from another, then by extension of the argument, when a subject is learning an ungrouped nine-item list and during reading spontaneously introduces extended pauses between say, items (3, 4) and (6, 7), a triplet organization (3:3:3) may well be inferred. The pause measure is seen as providing an analytic key for spontaneously imposed structures and, in principle, the way is open to the investigation of individual differences in acquisition strategies, and the use of learning material far more complex than serial lists, as in the examples given earlier for sentence and prose.

Pausing Times and Imposed Structure

To return to the grouped serial list; the pause measure has been said to index coding at the group boundary. If so, it may be expected that Bd.P. times during reading will change predictably as encoding demands alter. Such alterations may relate to the stage of learning reached, to the number of items comprising the group or again to the articulatory demands of the group items. The use of the Bd.P. for rehearsal of group content would require quite definite changes in pause duration as these factors were allowed to vary. There have been few, if any, systematic studies of such covariation of pause times and rehearsal demands although nearly all studies using pause measures assume this type of relationship. In a series of studies Belmont and Butterfield have provided related evidence (see Butterfield, Wambold and Belmont, 1973 for a recent summary), but the learning materials used have been restricted to letter lists and their self-pacing technique is not obviously related to a faster reading pause measure. It is the aim of the present chapter to report some recent experiments that were directed towards measuring variations in the Bd.P. measure in the context of reading and serial learning and, in the concluding section, to report its utility when no structural grouping had been experimentally imposed.

Pausing and Varying Levels of Encoding: Experiment I

The relation of Bd.P. times and encoding requirements was initially investigated using a variation of the part–whole learning paradigm (Tulving, 1966).

In Tulving's experiment it was found that the learning for free recall of a nine-word list did not facilitate subsequent learning of an 18-word list which contained the first list items randomly interspersed. This was due, it was argued, to organizational units introduced during first-stage learning being carried over, inappropriately, to the second stage. It seemed, therefore, that the learning for serial recall of two separate, spatially-grouped lists would provide different encoding demands if, in a second stage, the task was (a) re-presented for serial learning in the same manner, or (b) presented for serial learning as one combined list although retaining the original items and their order.

Procedure Twelve monosyllabic concrete nouns were used: COAT; NAIL; CAVE; TAP; HOME; CHAIR; BALL; POLE; SHELF; THORN; COAL; DRUM. Two lists of six words were drawn at random and each list was typed on a card with double spacing to provide a 3:3 grouping. An additional list of 12 words was prepared which combined the two lists of six words, again using double spacing to produce a 3:3:3:3 grouping. Thirty students were assigned at random to one of three experimental groups.

Group S.S. (Separate; Separate) $N = 10$. Subjects in this group were first given a 3:3 list (L_1) and asked to read it aloud and then to recall it in serial order. The read–and–recall procedure was repeated until a criterion of three correct consecutive trials was reached. They were then given the second 3:3 list (L_2) to learn to the same criterion. Following this in a second stage both lists were re-learned, separately, to the same criterion. All subjects experienced different random orders of words.

Group S.C. (Separate; Combined) $N = 10$. Subjects in this experimental group experienced the same first stage learning as group S.S. In the second stage they learned a 12-word list derived from combining their first and second lists ($L_1 + L_2$). The same random orders were employed for each subject as had been used for group S.S.

Group C. (Combined only) $N = 10$. These subjects learned only a 12-item list. The spatial grouping was equivalent to that used in the S.C. condition (3:3:3:3) and matching random orders of words were also used.

Pause Measurement. All learning sessions were tape recorded and the readings of each list were measured for pausing between list items. The tapes were used as input to a PDP 12A computer which was programmed to display the input visually. The visual record could be filtered and a moveable cursor aligned with any part of the signal. The visual and auditory signals were used to identify each spoken word and the times between the offset of one word and the onset of another were automatically recorded in milliseconds following appropriate alignments of the cursor. The readings of all lists up to and including criterion trials were processed in this manner.

Table 2.1. Average number of trials to criterion first and second stage, Groups S.S., S.C. and C.: Experiment I

Group	First stage	Second stage
S.S.	(L_1) 5·9, (L_2) 4·6	(L_1) 3·8, (L_2) 3·1
S.C.	(L_1) 4·3, (L_2) 3·5	$L_1 + L_2$ 11·2
C.	— —	$L_1 + L_2$ 15·7

Result and Discussion

The average number of trials to criterion for the experimental sub conditions are given in Table 2.1. List order during first stage learning did not significantly influence trials to criterion for groups S.S. and S.C., nor were the apparent differences between the experimental groups significant. Comparisons from first to second stage learning indicated that group S.S. took significantly fewer trials during the second stage (Wilcoxon T: $(L_1) = 5$, $P < 0.05$; (L_2) $T = 0$, $P < 0.05$).

Comparison of groups S.C. and C. during second stage learning indicated that although group S.C. reached the point of *one* correct recall significantly sooner than group C. (Trials 5·9 *vs* 10·1. Mann Whitney $U = 23$, $P < 0.025$), the trials required to reach the criterion of three correct consecutive recalls were not reliably different for the two groups (11·2 *vs* 15·7; $U = 31$, N.S.).

The reading pauses based upon the three criterion readings, stage one and three initial readings, stage two are given in Figure 2.1.

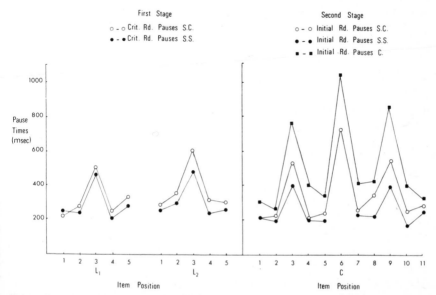

Figure 2.1. Reading pauses between all list items. First stage—criterion trials; second stage—initial trials

Considering only the Bd.P. times for group S.S., there was a significant reduction from first to second stage (F (1, 9) = 10·64, $P < 0·01$). For group S.C. the comparable boundary positions were at list 1, position 3 ($L_1 3$); list 2, position 3 ($L_2 3$) and, in the combined list, positions 3 and 9 (C3 and C9). For these subjects there was no evidence that pause durations at the boundary position dropped ($F(1, 9) = 3·41$, N.S.). In the combined list for group S.C. there is an additional boundary pause, C6, which bridged the two original lists L_1 and L_2. A comparison of boundary position (C3, C6 and C9) over reading trials within stage two (initial and criterion trials) indicated a significant interaction ($F(2, 18) = 8·44$, $P < 0·01$). This was due to the Bd. P. at C6 being reliably longer than the Bd.Ps at C3 and C9 during initial readings of stage two, but not at criterion readings.

A comparison of group S.C. and C. for second stage initial and criterion readings indicated that the Bd.Ps were significantly longer for C. than S.C., (F (1, 18) = 5·84, $P < 0·05$) but the same within-list Bd.P. pattern held for group C. as was found for S.C. The Bd.P. at C6 was greater than that at C3 and C9 for the initial readings but not at criterion readings (F (2, 36) = 14·25, $P < 0·01$).

The pattern of Bd.P. times between groups (S.S. vs S.C. vs C.) and between learning stage (first and second stage) faithfully reflects the presumed encoding load. If the load decreases as from first to second stage (group S.S.) the Bd.P. times drop. If the load is maintained as from first to second stage (group S.C.) the original pause times are maintained and if the load is high as in group C. the Bd.P. times are reliably longer. Taken on its own, the finding that C6 was greater than C3 and C9 for group S.C. seems to imply that the union of the two lists was accomplished at this boundary, particularly since the difference interacts with reading trials during the second stage, having disappeared at criterion. The identical finding for group C. however argues that this cannot simply be due to the novelty of C6 in the S.C. treatment. A more likely explanation is that the Bd.P. at C6 entails not only reference to list items of the immediately preceding group but cross reference to other list groups also. That is a higher order encoding, possibly relating one group to another. Since the absolute duration at this crucial point (C6) was greater in C. than S.C. it is possible that the failure of group S.C. to benefit consistently from prior exposure during the first stage learning resulted in inadequate encoding at this point.

The allocation of encoding operations to boundary pauses suggests a negative correlation between Bd.P. time and trials to criterion. To investigate this, Spearman Rank Order Correlation Coefficients were calculated based upon the total Bd.P. times for each subject learning a given list and his second-stage trials to criterion for that list using the subjects from groups S.C. and C. The coefficients are summarized in Table 2.2.

It can be seen that a significant negative correlation holds between total Bd.P. times during second-stage initial readings and trials to criterion for group C. but not group S.C. However, if *first-stage* Bd.P. totals are substituted for

Table 2.2. Spearman rank order correlation coefficients between total pause boundary times; total encoding times, and trials to criterion, second stage: Experiment I ($\rho = 0\cdot56$, $P = 0\cdot05$, $N = 10$ one tail)

	First-Stage Criterion readings	Second-Stage Initial readings
Total boundary pauses and trials to criterion (second-stage)	Group S.C. $-0\cdot53$	Group S.C. $-0\cdot09$; Group C. $-0\cdot60$
Total encoding times and trials to criterion (second-stage)	Group S.C. $-0\cdot67$	Group S.C. $-0\cdot29$; Group C. $-0\cdot51$

group S.C. a larger negative correlation is obtained. The use of absolute Bd.P. times is not ideal. In particular, it does not differentiate between subjects who read slowly at all positions and subjects who selectively pause at the boundaries. As an alternative measure, therefore, for each subject an encoding time was found by subtracting from each Bd.P., the pause time spent at the immediately preceding position. It can be seen from the second row of Table 2.2 that negative correlations are maintained for group C. second-stage, initial readings, and group S.C. first-stage, criterion readings. This strongly implies the localization of encoding at the imposed group boundaries otherwise the subtraction of the preceding pause times could be expected to reduce the correlation value to zero.

The significant correlation of first-stage encoding times and second-stage trials to criterion argues for S.C. subjects relying heavily upon first-stage learning and not specifically adopting a strategy for the longer combined list. This returns the argument to the reading pause differences already described between S.C. and C. subjects. It would seem therefore on the evidence from Experiment I, that a Bd.P. is associated with encoding of group content, although the interaction of group position within list and Bd.P. duration implies an encoding range greater than the content of an immediately preceding group. This point was investigated further in a second experiment using longer lists and different group sizes.

Pausing and Varying Group Size: Experiment II

Materials. Random lists of 18 words were constructed from the following monosyllabic British place names: CORK; PERTH; DEAL; HULL; CREWE; STAINES; RHYLL; LEEDS; POOLE; KEELE; WELLS; STROUD; WICK; HAYES; FLINT; CRIEFF; HYDE; BATH. Each list was typed as a one-line string on a card with double spacing for the intended grouping.

Procedure. Subjects were drawn from the 5th and 6th year students at Harris Academy, Dundee, and 30 subjects were assigned at random to one of two experimental groups.

E(2) $N = 15$, experienced an 18-item list organized into nine groups of two items and E(3) $N = 15$, experienced an equivalent list organized into six groups of three items. All subjects learned different randomly-ordered lists and were instructed to read and recall in serial order. Learning trials were continued until a criterion of three correct consecutive recalls had been achieved. Up to 20 trials were allowed, subjects needing a longer time were excluded from the analysis. Reading pause measures were taken as described in Experiment I.

Results and Discussion. Three subjects in E(2) and three subjects in E(3) failed to reach criterion after 20 trials and were dropped. For the remainder the mean number of trials to criterion for E(2) and E(3) were 12·7 and 14·5 respectively, and there was no significant difference in learning speed. The initial- and criterion-reading pause times at the group boundaries are given in Table 2.3.

Table 2.3. Boundary pause times (msec) initial and criterion readings: Experiment II

		Position in list of group boundary							
		2	4	6	8	10	12	14	16
E_2	Initial	430	574	635	640	558	598	558	520
	Criterion	501	739	709	755	753	813	601	632

		Position in list of group boundary				
		3	6	9	12	15
E_3	Initial	615	844	801	709	641
	Criterion	759	862	886	840	687

Considering E(2) first, the Bd.Ps differed significantly by group position within list for the initial and the criterion trials ($F(7, 77) = 4·91, P < 0·01$). A similar analysis for E(3) also indicated significant differences in Bd.P. duration with group position ($F(4, 44) = 3·45, P < 0·025$). Generally, following the first group within a list the Bd.P. times tend to increase and to remain high until the boundary separating the last two groups is reached where the pause durations tend to fall. Such a distribution implies that less encoding took place at the beginning and end portions of the list, and is consistent with the rehearsal procedures associated with primacy and recency effects. Thus for E(2) a Newman–Keuls comparison indicated a significant increase from the first- to the second-group boundary in the list and the maintenance of this level until the last two groups were read out. For E(3) the increase from the first- to second-group boundary was not reliably significant although the level of pausing was maintained until the terminal groups were reached where pause durations dropped significantly.

Any direct comparison of E(2) and E(3) Bd.P. times confounds the number of items within an imposed group and the number of groups encoded, except that is, after the first group in each list when group size alone varies. Comparison of the Bd.P. times following the first group in E(2) with those following the first group in E(3) indicated that at both the initial and criterion readings the boundary pause was longer following the larger group ($F(1, 22)=6\cdot97$, $P < 0\cdot025$). At boundary positions 6 and 12 in each list, the total encoding loads are comparable for E(2) and E(3) and there was no consistent evidence at these positions that the boundary pauses differed.

A conditional error probability measure was applied to the recall of the lists by finding the probability of a non-recall of item $n + 1$ given correct recall of item n. In Figure 2.2 is given the error probabilities at each position and the

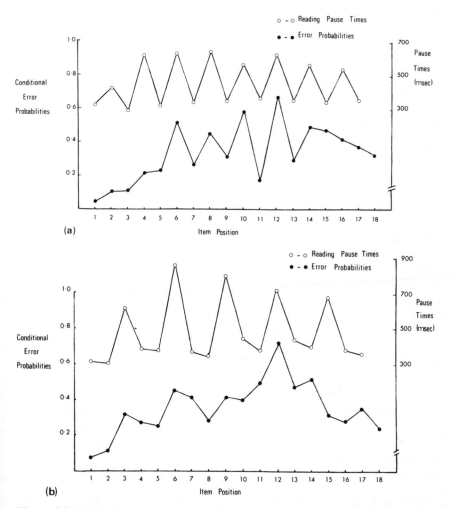

Figure 2.2.(a) Conditional error probabilities at each list position and associated pause times. Initial readings, Group E(2). **(b)** Conditional error probabilities at each list position and associated pause times. Initial readings, Group E(3)

associated pause times during initial readings. Analysis of variance following an arc-sin transformation of the probability scores indicated that the boundary items were associated with higher error probabilities than other within group items but this interacted significantly with the position of the group within the list. In fact the last two groups within each list did not follow this pattern—a result consistent with minimal encoding at the terminal positions. Primacy effects were evident for both E(2) and E(3) treatments. It can be concluded therefore that the reading pauses during acquisition trials specifically related to grouping structure during recall and to some extent to the levels of recall achieved for the imposed groups. The Spearman Rank Order Correlation Coefficient relating total Bd.P. times during initial readings and trials to criterion were E(2), $\rho = 0 \cdot 35$, N.S. and E(3), $\rho = -0 \cdot 57, P < 0 \cdot 05$. The correlations based upon total encoding times, as previously defined, were E(2), $\rho = -0 \cdot 02$, N.S. and E(3), $\rho = -0 \cdot 60$, $P < 0 \cdot 05$. Thus the relationship between learning speed and duration of boundary pauses was confirmed for the triplet grouping but not for the doublet. It is not possible to separate in this experiment the group size of 2 from the number of groups (nine) as the determinant of this result. It seems possible, however, that as the number of groups increases beyond a certain point, the groups coalesce into larger constructions. If this occurred at different list positions for different subjects it would serve to attenuate a correlation based upon all list boundary pauses.

In summary it has been found that the pauses at the group boundaries vary with the position of the group within the list but only relating to known primacy and recency factors. A stepped cumulative sequence for middle portions of a list in which previous groups are encoded along with the immediately preceding group content as suggested by Wilkes (1972) is not supported. The results did establish that group size influenced Bd.P. duration, provided total learning loads were not equivalent. At the level of recall the pause defined reading groupings corresponded closely with recall structures except for terminal groups.

To this point it could be tacitly assumed that pausing at the boundary positions during learning has involved some form of rehearsal through the covert recitation of preceding group content or additionally of preceding groups. This analysis is supported by the finding that pause times following a single group of three are longer than those following a single group of two but is not supported by the finding of equivalent pause times when total load is identical although the group structure remains different. It has been established that reading pauses are critically employed in encoding activity; it remains questionable whether this can be best described as covert recitation. Accordingly, a third experiment was run which attempted to investigate this aspect more directly.

Pausing and Syllabic Structure of Group Content: Experiment III

Materials. Lists of eight words were produced from randomizations of the monosyllabic set: COW; SHEEP; DUCK; PIG; CAT; GOAT; DOG; HEN and the bisyllabic set: LETTUCE; RADISH; CABBAGE; TURNIP; PARS-NIP; CARROT; BEETROOT; SPINACH. Random orders of the monosyllabic and bisyllabic word lists were typed on cards with a double spacing separating groups of two words.

Procedure. The 16 subjects (students) were asked to read one of the lists of words presented in alphabetical order to familiarize them with the list content. They then read and recalled a random order to a criterion of three correct, consecutive recalls. Following this they continued for a further six post-criterion trials and were then tested for their recognition of word order for word pairs drawn from the list. For each word pair they were instructed to respond by pressing a button indicating either 'Yes' for the pair retaining their list order or 'No' for reversals. Latency of the responses was recorded. This procedure was then repeated for the remaining list type. Half of the subjects experienced a monosyllabic list and then a bisyllabic list and the other half the reverse sequence. The reading records for criterion and post-criterion stages for each list were pause analysed as were the criterion and post-criterion recall attempts.

Results and Discussion. The mean number of trials to criterion was 4·9 for monosyllabic lists and 8·6 for bisyllabic lists. It was found that list type (Mono or Bi) was significant ($F(1, 7) = 23·09$, $P < 0·01$) but neither list order (first or second) nor the interaction reached significance. The list of eight bisyllabic items took longer to learn regardless of coming first or second in the learning task.

The criterion reading and recall pause times are given in Figure 2.3 for each position in the two-list types. For the monosyllabic list the reading Bd.P. times are reproduced during recall although they tend to be longer ($F(1, 15) = 4·31$, $P < 0·10$). In both reading and recall the boundary pauses differ by group position ($F(2, 30) = 3·25$, $P < 0·05$) and is due to pausing at Position 4 being greater than that at Position 6. For the bisyllabic list the Bd.P. times during reading are reproduced in recall but are markedly longer ($F(1, 15) = 6·66$, $P < 0·025$). For this list, however, the main factor of group position was not significant.

A comparison of pauses between within group items and boundary pause times for mono and bisyllabic lists indicated that the bisyllabic-criterion readings were consistently slower at all list positions ($F(1, 15) = 7·37$, $P < 0·025$). It has been observed by Klapp, Anderson and Berrian (1973) that the preparatory articulatory time for bisyllabic words is slightly longer than that for monsyllabic words. Thus a direct comparison of monosyllabic and bisyllabic Bd.P. times confounds articulatory preparation and encoding activity. It has been found in Experiments I and II however that the conversion of a boundary pause into an encoding measure by the subtraction of the pause time at the immediately preceding position still retains a functional significance for the acquisition process. Accordingly, the list types were compared using the

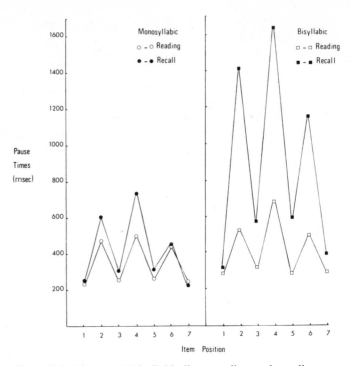

Figure 2.3. Mono and bisyllabic lists; reading and recall pause times. Criterion trials

encoding estimate which removes the articulatory component for utterance of the next word. It was found that on neither the initial nor the criterion readings were the encoding times different for list type: $F(1, 15) < 1$; $F(1, 15) = 1·31$, N.S., respectively. A similar calculation for recall indicated, however, that longer pause times separated the groups in the bisyllabic list, $(F(1, 15) = 5·38,$ $P < 0·05)$.

It appears therefore that the subjects did not spend a longer time encoding during the reading of bisyllabic items and, for this learning task, the use of the reading Bd.P. for covert recitation was not confirmed. The recall differences in Bd.P. times would arise if the bisyllabic list was simply more poorly integrated despite the common learning criterion used. The word pair recognition latencies covered all possible pair combinations from the list and a cluster analysis (Johnson, 1967) revealed that in neither case, monosyllabic nor bisyllabic, had a hierarchically organized structure been achieved. In Figure 2.4 is plotted the mean recognition latencies for correct word order of adjacent word pairs (1–2, 2–3, 3–4, etc.). It can be seen that the latencies for bisyllabic items were much longer although no basic differences in the profiles were present $(F(1, 15) = 12·44, P < 0·01)$. For both list types order judgements of the middle-word pair (4, 5) elicited maximum latencies $(F(6, 90) = 6·09,$ $P < 0·01)$. There are therefore no structural differences that clearly distinguish

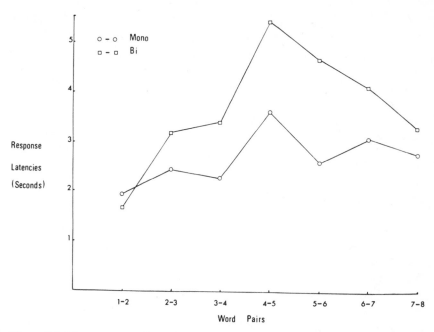

Figure 2.4. Mean response latencies for recognition of adjacent word pairs in correct serial order

the organization of the two list types; only a generally slower processing of the bisyllabic items. It is unlikely that this is solely due to an additional reading load for bisyllabic pairs since a similar difference was obtained in the recall protocols. A parsimonious explanation of these results would be that insufficient encoding occurred for the bisyllabic list and, indeed, it was learned with much greater difficulty. Furthermore, a similar learning difficulty has been reported by Laughery, Lachman and Dansereau (1965). Ironically, therefore, the finding that the boundary pauses during reading did not extend to cover the additional group content in the bisyllabic list may be proof that covert recitation did not occur, but not proof that it is unnecessary.

Pausing and Encoding Operations

The general results for Experiment I–III are taken as clearly substantiating the claim that reading-pause boundaries are employed for encoding activity during acquisition trials. Additionally, they predict the features of recall structures whether immediate or substantially delayed. The negative correlation between total Bd.P. times or total encoding times during initial readings and trials to criterion has reliably emerged for the triplet organization. Similarly Wilkes (1972) reported equivalent negative correlations for subjects learning a 15-item list consistently organized into triplets. On the other hand, there is no evidence of a similar relationship for a doublet organization. It has frequently been observed that adult subjects prefer a triplet grouping (Wickelgren, 1964; Wilkes, Lloyd and Simpson, 1972) and it may well be that composite groupings are more likely to be elicited when groups of two are imposed. If so this cannot be systematically followed by all subjects since the conditional error probabilities in Experiment II did reproduce the imposed pattern.

It is clear that the nature of the encoding activity undertaken has remained elusive. A simple attribution of covert rehearsal gains little support. It is possible that an abstract representation of group content is utilized in covert rehearsal; this would allow for a relationship with group size, yet maintain some independence from item structure, but it is questionable whether an exclusively retrospective focus is in any case sufficient. Neisser (1967) in discussing grouping behaviour suggests that the use of a rhythmic structure creates space in short-term memory at the same time as encoding serial order. On this argument grouping itself constitutes rehearsal since the simple strategy of a repeated rhythm can encode group content and group order. Taking this view, a Bd.P. serves simply as a gap or parenthesis between groups—not as an encoding point. Similarly, Restle (1972) using the task of anticipatory learning for a series of runs and trills in a light display has argued that pauses within the pattern presentation serve as parentheses. 'Good phrasing,' that is long pauses at major subdivisions of the pattern and short pauses at minor subdivisions, was evaluated using *allegro* and *adagio* presentations. In real time the experimental conditions contrasted a 1400 msec pause at the major subdivision with a 600 msec pause. It was reported that there was no gain from the extra time made available in the *adagio* presentation. It is difficult to compare directly Restle's situation with the present serial learning tasks, but it can be noted that subjects left free to set their own Bd.P. times rarely exceeded 900 msec at any point. Ryan (1969) has compared grouping patterns at 'fast' (900 msec Bd.P.) and 'slow' (3400 msec Bd.P.) presentation rates and reported no facilitation at the slow rate for the serial learning of letter strings. From the present pause records, Ryan's choice of fast and slow rates is inappropriate and does not serve as an adequate test of the encoding hypothesis. It seems possible that the same objection could also be levelled at Restle's task. In a second experiment, Restle used *presto* and *allegro* presentation rates with pauses of 200 msec and 600 msec in contrast at the major subdivision and again concluded that there was no important impairment for the faster rate. Nonetheless, comparing good phrasing it is commented that '*allegro* presentation is considerably better than *presto*. This suggests that the perception of the pattern is unaffected by rapid presentation but that some intermediate stage of successful processing analogous to short-term storage, may require more time than was afforded at the *presto* rate' (p. 389). It remains plausible that the Bd.P. time was insufficient for the necessary encoding although this is not Restle's own interpretation. The arguments for a parenthesis function of boundary pauses are equivocal and certainly are not supported by the present findings. However, the anticipatory method of learning used by Restle underlines the possibility that a Bd.P. could be used for initiating the group yet to be read, and many of the factors that associate retrospective encoding with a Bd. P. could equally well operate in a forward direction within the list.

The observations that are basically inconsistent with a parenthesis interpretation appear to be firstly, within Experiment I, the Bd.P. at the juncture of the two combined lists was greater than the pause times at the group boundaries carried over from the first learning stage treatments. This applied for initial reading trials but not criterion trials. Secondly, within Experiment II, the Bd.P. after the first group was greater for the triplet structure than for the doublet, but this did not hold at deeper positions within the list where total encoding loads were equivalent, but the initiation of the two group sizes was still in contrast. Thirdly, in Experiments I and II the correlations of Bd.P. times with trials to criterion held for the initial-reading trials but not for the criterion trials. Of these counter examples, the second and third are not easily assimilated within an anticipatory model. It is noticeable that the retrospective encoding function attributed to boundary pauses is mainly operative for initial reading trials, which suggests both an encoding and parenthesis interpretation may nonetheless be tenable. That is during early reading trials the learner's task is mainly that of assimilating the list material to an appropriate rhythmic structure. Once this has been achieved the boundary pauses can then revert to the role of temporal markers subordinated within an overall rhythmic pattern. Thus the pause measure may well index different functions at different phases of learning, although at all stages it provides a vulnerable point in the acquisition process where diagnostic checks on encoding mode can be most fruitfully located. This argument widens the range of functions that is assigned to boundary pauses during reading but preserves the point that their location in the material learned still provides a direct description of imposed structure.

Pausing and Spontaneous Structure

The monitoring of acquisition strategy allowed to vary free of experimental controls is of considerable theoretical and practical interest. Theoretical predictions of the performance units in sentence and prose learning are often ambiguous and at an applied level the question of the efficiency of learning strategies can be posed with the hope that diagnostic and remedial procedures can be formulated. For the present, however, two studies will be reported that deal with preferences for grouping structure and with contrasting acquisition strategies induced by the features of the learning materials.

Spontaneous Grouping and Serial Learning

Wilkes, Lloyd and Simpson (1972) reported on the groupings imposed by adult subjects during their learning of unstructured serial lists of consonants. In Table 2.4 is reproduced the most frequent examples of recall structures classified by the size of the first imposed group. The structures were identified

Table 2.4. Examples of imposed recall structures. Most frequent grouping for each class with frequency given in parentheses. (From Wilkes, A. L., Lloyd, P. and Simpson, I., *Quarterly Journal of Experimental Psychology*, **24**, 48–54. With permission.)

No. of items	Age (years)	No Structure	Doublet	Triplet	Quartet	Other
	Adult	(9)	2:3(5)	3:2(6)	—	
5	10	(5)	2:3(10)	3:2(5)		
	8	(6)	2:3(9)	3:2(5)	—	—
	Adult	(4)	2:4(4)	3:3(9)	4:2(3)	
6	10	(2)	2:2:2(2)	3:3(12)	4:2(3)	—
	8	(1)	2:4(4)	3:3(10)	4:2(2)	
	Adult	(3)	2:5(2)	3:4(5)	4:3(3)	5:2(3)
7	10	—	2:2:3(1); 2:5(1)	3:2:2(6)	4:3(5)	5:2(3)
	8	—	2:2:3(6)	3:4(7)	4:3(2)	—
	Adult	(1)	2:2:2:2(3)	3:3:2(3)	4:4(4)	6:2(1)
8	10	—	2:3:3(5)	3:3:2(4); 3:2:3(4)	4:4(2)	5:3(1)
	8	—	2:2:4(2) 2:2:2:2(2)	3:3:2(3)	4:2:2(5)	5:3(1)
Per cent incidence	Adult	29·0		46·8	17·7	6·4
of group structure	10 yrs	30·1		49·3	15·0	5·4
All lists and S.'s	8 yrs	41·1		39·7	17·8	1·3

by the presence of pauses in the recall protocols that exceeded the pause at the following position by at least 50 per cent of the mean pause time for the list and which were not lower than the pause time at the preceding list position. In fact this strict definition of boundary pauses simply reproduced grouping patterns that could be identified using pauses that were longer than those at preceding and following positions (inflection pauses). In a further study a partial replication was carried out using random samples of children of 10 and 8 years. Each child started with a consonant list of three items which was read and recalled to the usual criterion. Thereafter list lengths of four, five, six, seven and eight consonants were tackled in ascending order, the lists at all lengths being randomly chosen for each subject. Tape recordings of the criterion reading and recall trials for each list were pause analysed and imposed groupings identified from the presence of inflection pauses. There were 20 subjects at each age level with equal numbers of male and female children. As with the adult subjects the classification of imposed structure is based upon the size of the first-imposed group, and included in Table 2.4 are the most popular groupings observed during the recall at these age levels. The numbers in parentheses refer to the number of subjects choosing a given structure.

Taking adult performance over list length as a reference point a triplet preference is clearly shown. For all list lengths except list 8, the most frequent adult pattern is built around an initial triplet grouping. As Ryan (1969) has observed where symmetrical grouping is possible this tends to be preferred, serving to emphasize a 3: 3 grouping for list 6 and to attenuate a 3: 3: 2 grouping for list 8. If grouping type is expressed as a percentage of all grouping occurrences then strict comparisons are only possible for the doublet and triplet types since list 5 could be divided as 2: 3 or 3: 2 but not as 4: 1 given the dependence on an inflection pause measure for identifying group boundaries. It follows that the incidence of doublet and triplet groupings can be meaningfully compared over list lengths but not groupings in excess of three items. For adults the incidence of doublet structures was 29 per cent and, of triplet, 46·8 per cent.

For the 8-year-old sample no predominance of triplet groupings was found, the per cent incidences being equivalent, 41·1 and 39·7 per cent. In the 10-year-old sample the distribution was close to the adult form, 30·1 and 49·3 per cent. The grouping structures given in Table 2.4 apply to recall during criterion trials and it is possible to compare them with the grouping structures imposed during reading. It should be noted, however, that structural alterations from reading to recall can take different forms which need to be distinguished. Suppose for example that list 8 was read as 2: 2: 4. During recall the grouping pattern could again be 2: 2: 4 (Duplication), 4: 4 (Omission), 2: 2: 2: 2 (Addition) or 3: 3: 2 (Change). Of these possibilities Omission and Addition retain features of the original structure whereas Change need not do so. Of the adults, two subjects introduced a change in their recall of list 5 and four subjects did so for list 8. The 8-year-olds showed a greater tendency to change from reading to recall than the adults but not to the extent found for the 10-year-olds of whom 12 out of 20 changed for the eight-item list. It seems plausible that the age difference is due to a developmental shift in the grouping base—tending to three items for older subjects. The established increase in memory span over this age range would appear to support this interpretation (McLaughlin, 1963).

Wilkes, Lloyd and Simpson (1972) argued that for adult subjects a single repeated rhythm based upon triplet groups was underlying the observed results. Subjects repeatedly imposed groups of three items leaving a terminal group of either two or four items. Assuming Broadbent's estimate of a register capacity to be correct at three items the present results couple the maximum use of that capacity with a single repetitive rhythm. The children's data did not permit a similar conclusion for the repetitive use of a single base but strongly implied a developmental progression in this direction. In general, therefore, the use of inflection pauses to identify spontaneous grouping structures provides an account consistent with other independent descriptions of similar learning tasks.

Variations in Encoding Strategy and Task Requirements: Experiment IV

Given the arguments associating inflection pauses with the encoding of group content, the duration and frequency of such pauses should distinguish acquisition strategies adapted to long-term retention. In an investigation into the influence of acoustic similarity on serial recall, Anderson (1969) replicated a previous finding by Baddeley (1966) that high acoustic similarity within a list led to better long-term retention. Anderson found that lists having consonants of high acoustic similarity were better recalled on a delayed retention task than lists of low acoustic similarity. A deleterious effect for acoustic confusability was obtained during immediate recall but this situation reversed when long-term recall was introduced. In further experiments it was demonstrated that the interaction was eliminated if control procedures were introduced that minimized the role of the short-term memory component during early-learning trials. It was concluded that subjects learning the high and low acoustically confusable lists adopted different acquisition strategies. In particular, the subjects experiencing the low similarity items critically relied upon short-term storage during the learning trials. This difference in acquisition strategies was inferred by Anderson from performance on the delayed retention task but the monitoring of reading pauses would permit a direct comparison of encoding strategies at the time of acquisition. A further experiment was run as a partial replication of Anderson's procedure but with modifications to allow for overt reading.

Materials. Randomizations of the high acoustic similarity set (YBDUCTGP) were printed on cards with equal spacing between all list items. Similar randomizations based upon the low acoustic similarity set (YRLXKMWN) were also prepared. In addition the high and low items were each set out alphabetically on separate cards.

Procedure. The 16 subjects were drawn from a similar housewife population to that employed by Anderson. Subjects were assigned at random to one of two experimental groups and each group read and recalled either the high or low similarity list, three times. Following this subjects participated in a sentence learning task which lasted for 20 min and then produced written recall of the original list they had experienced. As a control for response availability an alphabetical series of the list items was always available for reference. The reading pause patterns were measured as in previous experiments.

Results and Discussion. In Figure 2.5 is given the incidence of correct recall at each trial for the high and low lists.

An arc-sin transformation was applied to the proportional recall scores and a significant interaction effect for list by trials was obtained ($F (3, 42) = 6·49$, $P < 0·01$). In essence the original findings reported by Anderson (1969) were replicated by this experiment.

The reading pause patterns for trials 1 and 3 for each list type are plotted in Figure 2.6. It can be seen that a more deliberative reading strategy has emerged by trial 3 for the high similarity list whereas a faster more evenly paced reading emerges at the third trial for the low similarity list. Inflection pauses were

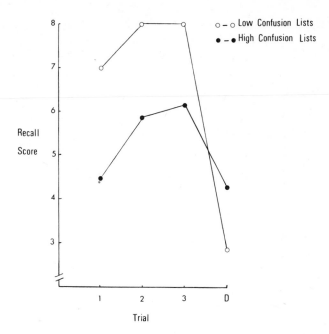

Figure 2.5. Recall scores for low and high acoustically confusable lists. Immediate and delayed recall

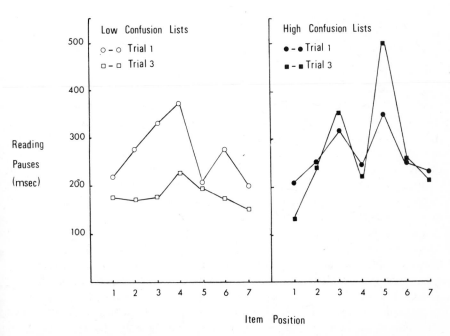

Figure 2.6. Reading pause patterns trials 1 and 3. Low and high confusable lists

38

identified from the pause protocols of each subject and the total encoding times (Inflection pause less preceding pause) assigned by each subject over trials were calculated. (See Figure 2.7.) A comparison of the total encoding times

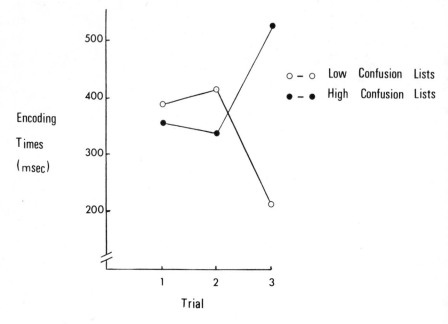

Figure 2.7. Encoding times by trial. Low and high confusable lists

indicated that neither list nor trial was significant as a main factor, and there was no interaction over trials 1 and 2 $(F < 1)$. However, a significant interaction between trials 2 and 3 was found $(F(1, 14) = 4.77, P < 0.05)$. In brief, subjects reading the high similarity list increased their encoding time over the acquisition trials to a significantly greater extent than subjects learning the low similarity list. These changes are consistent with the proposal that subjects learning the low confusable list rely heavily upon short-term memory for immediate recall, whereas subjects learning the high confusable list undertake more deliberate encoding of list content. This pause-defined difference in acquisition strategies is strongly supported by the interaction of list with trial for recall performance, and the smaller retention loss for the subjects experiencing the high confusable list can be attributed to the different acquisition strategy they adopted. It may be noted that at trial 3 the two experimental groups differed in their relative levels of recall and the differential retention loss on delayed recall, it could be argued, is due to 'floor' effects since under one condition there are fewer items to forget. Such an argument would be plausible if the delayed recall scores for both groups were approaching zero but such is not the case. The related argument that the decline be expressed as a proportion of the original learning (see Paivio in this volume) still distinguishes the subjects learning the high similarity list for superior performance following the interpolated task. Finally, it is unlikely that the reading pause patterns associated with the two list types are dependent on their different articulatory demands since the difference in encoding time is not found immediately but emerges over trials, as indeed, Anderson (1969) originally proposed.

Functional Structure and Pausing

The functional utility of knowing the structure imposed on learned material during acquisition not only bears upon learning speed and immediate recall but also extends to long-term memory organization and retrieval. Anderson and Bower (1973) refer to grouped material entered into working memory being checked through a matching process for similarity with information in permanent store. They cite, for example, the finding that immediate recall is better when input groupings correspond with familiar acronyms (e.g., I.B.M., T.V.) than when non-correspondence applies. This variable of cross referencing is minimized in the serial learning of intrinsically unstructured strings but it remains a salient feature for any complete analysis of reading pauses. The choice of appropriate grouping structures and rhythms can be expected to draw upon past performance wherever possible, as for example when sentences rather than word strings are presented. Kennedy and Wilkes (1971b) reported that probed retrieval of sentences produced latency profiles that corresponded with major constituent divisions within the sentence, and a scanning model was proposed which assumed that, when memorizing for verbatim recall, a sentence is stored in a manner that allows separate access to its major constituents. Constituent analysis, as traditionally employed in linguistics, was used as one method of defining the grouping structure of the sentence but, as an independent measure, pausing patterns in the reading of the sentences were also recorded. In fact, a better fit to the retrieval latency profiles was achieved using the reading pause measure than from constituent analysis, mainly because 'extra linguistic' divisions were introduced which could be identified from the overt reading of the sentence but not predicted from its surface structure. In consequence, it was argued that a subject may process sentences at varying levels of complexity, each defined by the task requirements he has been set. Although it may be within the subject's competence to engage in a detailed transformational analysis of a sentence, if the task he faces does not call for any utilization of such knowledge, then less elaborate but more effective constructions of the sentence are possible. The argument denies the *general* applicability of linguistically defined grouping patterns but does not deny that some form of functional groupings of words occurs.

If subjects can adapt their organizational strategy to fit the experimental task, the problem of finding the units of sentence processing is redefined as an empirical issue and not as one that has been conveniently solved by the advent of generative grammars (see also Martin, 1970). Recent work on the relationship between probe retrieval latencies and sentence constituents has led to the suggestion that the effect is not due to the storage of sub-structures determined at the time of acquisition but to syntactic plans brought into operation at the time of retrieval (Levelt and Kempen, this volume). At the outset, it should be noted that the two experimental procedures are not strictly comparable: Kennedy and Wilkes used random probing at all positions within a single sentence, whereas Levelt and Kempen refer to more localized probe procedures ranging over more than one sentence. Even allowing for such distinctions, however, the appeal to syntactic retrieval plans presumes a better correspondence between constituent structure and retrieval latency than is, in fact, found if all positions within the typical sentence are probed—allowing 'extra linguistic' divisions to appear. Explanation of their presence based upon syntactic plans would be at best *post hoc*. On the other hand, the reading pause patterns at acquisition do relate to this effect. Thus while extended reading pauses in sentences may involve cross referencing from syntactic features in long-term store, the operation is itself confounded with *ad hoc* strategies prompted by the experimental task. On a similar point Anderson and Bower (1973) write 'Certain matters such as the representation of active versus passive sentences seemed to be affected by changes in task demands. Furthermore, subjects' introspections indicate that they are engaged in various unscheduled activities in order to improve their recall performance . . . It seems very difficult to use a particular memory phenomenon to obtain firm inferences about a strategy free component of memory' (p. 509). The temptation to treat these strategic variations as an irritating source of error is very strong but when ignored they do not go away. If acknowledged, they raise serious questions of the appropriate descriptive units for syntactic plans, perceptual strategies and for structured material in long-term store. The problem is unlikely to yield to one mode of attack but it is in this context that pausing measures should repay further consideration.

Acknowledgements

The experiments described in this chapter were run as part of a research project financed by the S.S.R.C. The author is also grateful for the valuable help of Mrs J. Brook in the running and analysis of experiments and to Mrs M. Bell for the pause measurements. Professor R. A. Kennedy wrote the program underlying the pause measurement procedures and Mr J. M. Hamilton, Rector Harris Academy, Dundee and Mr J. Gunning, Headmaster Dundee Demonstration School, made testing facilities available. These contributions are gratefully acknowledged.

References

Anderson, J. R. and Bower, G. H. (1973). *Human Associative Memory*. New York: John Wiley and Sons.
Anderson, N. S. (1969). The influence of acoustic similarity on serial recall of letter sequences. *Quarterly Journal of Experimental Psychology*, **21**, 248–255.

Baddeley, A. D. (1966). The influence of acoustic and semantic similarity on long-term memory for word sequences. *Quarterly Journal of Experimental Psychology*, **18**, 302–309.

Belmont, J. M. and Butterfield, E. C. (1971). Learning strategies as determinants of memory deficiencies. *Cognitive Psychology*, **2**, 411–420.

Bower, G. H. and Springston, F. (1970). Pauses as recoding points in letter series. *Journal of Experimental Psychology*, **83**, 421–430.

Bower, G. H. and Winzenz, D. (1969). Group structure, coding and memory for digit series. *Journal of Experimental Psychology Monographs*, **80**, 1–17.

Butterfield, E. C., Wambold, C. and Belmont, J. M. (1973). On the theory and practice of improving short-term memory. *American Journal of Mental Deficiency*, **77**, 654–669.

Foder, J. A. and Bever, T. G. (1965). The psychological reality of linguistic segments. *Journal of Verbal Learning and Verbal Behavior*, **4**, 414–420.

Goldman-Eisler, F. (1968). *Psycholinguistics, Experiments in Spontaneous Speech*. New York: Academic Press.

Johnson, N. F. (1965). The psychological reality of phrase structure rules. *Journal of Verbal Learning and Verbal Behavior*, **4**, 469–475.

Johnson, R. E. (1970). Recall of prose as a function of the structural importance of the linguistic units. *Journal of Verbal Learning and Verbal Behavior*, **9**, 12–20.

Johnson, S. C. (1967). Hierarchical clustering schemes. *Psychometrika*, **32**, 241–254.

Kennedy, R. A. and Wilkes, A. L. (1971a). Functional structure in sentences: a performance analysis. *Quarterly Journal of Experimental Psychology*, **23**, 214–224.

Kennedy, R. A. and Wilkes, A. L. (1971b). Latency studies of human memory with particular reference to language. Final Report S.S.R.C. Project HR/287/1, unpublished.

Klapp, S. T., Anderson, W. G., and Berrian, R. W. (1973). Implicit speech in reading, reconsidered. *Journal of Experimental Psychology*, **100**, 368–374.

Laughery, K. R., Lachman, R., and Dansereau, D. (1965). Short-term memory: effects of item pronunciation time. *Proceedings of the American Psychological Association*, 83–84.

Martin, E. (1970). Towards an analysis of subjective phrase structure. *Psychological Bulletin*, **74**, 153–166.

McLaughlin, G. H. (1963). Psycho-logic: a possible alternative to Piaget's formulation. *British Journal of Educational Psychology*, **33**, 61–67.

McLean, R. S. and Gregg, L. W. (1967). Effects of induced chunking on temporal aspects of serial recitation. *Journal of Experimental Psychology*, **74**, 455–459.

Miller, G. A. (1956). The magical number seven, plus or minus two: some limits on our capacity for processing information. *Psychological Review*, **63**, 81–97.

Neisser, U. (1967). *Cognitive Psychology*. New York: Appleton–Century–Crofts.

Reitman, W. (1970). What does it take to remember? In D. A. Norman, (Ed) *Models of Human Memory*, New York: Academic Press.

Restle, F. (1972). Serial patterns: the role of phrasing. *Journal of Experimental Psychology*, **92**, 385–390.

Ryan, J. (1969). Grouping and short-term memory: different means and patterns of grouping. *Quarterly Journal of Experimental Psychology*, **21**, 137–147.

Suci, G. J. (1967). The validity of pause as an index of units in language. *Journal of Verbal Learning and Verbal Behavior*, **6**, 26–32.

Thorpe, C. E. and Rowland, G. E. (1965). The effect of 'natural' grouping of numerals on short-term memory. *Human Factors*, **7**, 38–44.

Tulving, E. (1966). Subjective organization and effects of repetition in multi-trial free-recall learning. *Journal of Verbal Learning and Verbal Behavior*, **1**, 321–324.

Ward, J. (1918). *Psychological Principles*. Cambridge: Cambridge University Press.

Wickelgren, W. A. (1964). Size of rehearsal group and short-term memory. *Journal of Experimental Psychology*, **68**, 413–419.

Wilkes, A. L. (1972). Reading pauses during serial list learning with fixed or randomly changing groups. *Journal of Experimental Psychology*, **94**, 206–209.

Wilkes, A. L. and Kennedy, R. A. (1970). The relative accessibility of list items within different pause-defined groups. *Journal of Verbal Learning and Verbal Behavior*, **9**, 197–201.

Wilkes, A. L., Lloyd, P. and Simpson, I. (1972). Pause measures during reading and recall in serial list learning. *Quarterly Journal of Experimental Psychology*, **24**, 48–54.

Chapter 3

Encoding Processes and the Memorability of Events

Arthur I. Schulman

Introduction

How should an event be experienced? A mnemonist's question, to be sure, but everyone will concede that the same external event may be experienced in different ways. If an experience is to be of more than immediate value, it should be encoded in a way that will permit its future reconstruction or retrieval.

Knowledge, Experience, and Memorability

The world must be interpreted in the light of previous knowledge. Thus the encoding of events, and hence *episodic memory*, depends on how input is interpreted through *semantic memory* (the italicized terms are Tulving's, 1972). Experience usually involves the rediscovery of already known relations, so that episodic memory, i.e. memory for incidents, should depend, at least in part, on which relations are rediscovered. Now, situational and task demands constrain, and sometimes prescribe, the knowledge called upon to deal with a given input. Whatever the situation, however, we 'operate' upon our input and 'encode' aspects of the encounter. Later we may remember these encodings, but whether or not we do so depends ultimately on the nature of the original experience. In a word, the uses of knowledge have memorial consequences: unrecorded events cannot be remembered, sense is better remembered than nonsense, and content is better remembered than structure.

However, not all meaningful experiences are equally meaningful *or* equally memorable. As Tulving and Thomson (1973) argue, 'what is stored is determined by what is perceived and how it is encoded, and what is stored determines what retrieval cues are effective in providing access to what is stored ... According to the encoding specificity principle, the target item must be encoded in some sort of reference to the cue for the cue to be effective'. In other words, if A is encoded in isolation to B, neither A nor B will serve as a retrieval cue for the other (*cf.* Tulving and Osler, 1968); a 'relational encoding', to use the jargon preferred here, may be a necessary condition for later cued recall. (The absence of a relational encoding may also depress recognition memory and render free recall impossible.) But what 'reference to the cue' should be encoded? While any reference may be better than none, surely not all relational encodings are mnemonically equivalent. Tulving and Thomson's vagueness as to the nature of an effective reference testifies to the need for research on this question. The main purpose of the present paper is to call for such research.

Varieties of Meaningful Experience

The meaning of encoded experience merits analysis, especially for its memorial implications. Events A and B may be separately or relationally encoded, according to situational demands. Suppose they are encoded as a relation, R. Their memorability could easily depend on such factors as: (i) whether R rests upon knowledge of function, state, or structure; (ii) whether R was known prior to encoding or newly established then; (iii) whether R admits many or few possible arguments, of which A and B are only the current representatives; and (iv) whether R links A and B directly or through a third event C (which may relate to A and B in different ways). Research is needed to compare the memorial consequences of tasks which differ demonstrably, or at least theoretically, in the operations they prescribe. Tasks of sufficient complexity should be devised, and both recall and recognition memory tapped, so that the encodings that result from operations on input may be properly assessed.

Contextual Encodings and Memorability

The form and context of an experience usually do not give it its meaning, but their encoding can contribute to its memorability. As for form, we know that mental operations can sometimes be remembered even when what was operated upon cannot. (For a discussion of the memorability of operations, see Kolers, 1973.) As for context—by which here is meant those aspects of an encounter whose encoding is not a logical result of the task requirements—information about the time and place of an experience may be encoded. There is a need for studies of how memory for form and context relates to memory for focal experience. Underwood's (1969) distinction between merely discriminative attributes and attributes useful for retrieval may prove to be of value in guiding such research.

Constraints on Encoding and 'Depth of Processing'

The orienting attitudes reflected in this paper resemble those of Craik and Lockhart (1972), who urge experimenters to exert more 'control over the encoding operations that subjects perform.' We agree that what is encoded should depend on 'the processing demands imposed by the experimental paradigm and the material to be remembered'. Finally, Craik and Lockhart argue that meaningful events 'are compatible ... with existing cognitive structures', receive greater 'depth of processing' than less meaningful ones, and are consequently better retained. The depth-of-processing argument (*cf.* Tulving and Madigan's, 1970, 'elaboration encoding') is a forceful one, especially if one feels constrained to choose between it and short- and long-term boxes as determinants of memorability. Craik and Lockhart point out, for example, that there may be memorial advantages of semantic to structural processing even when the latter is more time-consuming. So long as the notion of processing depth can resist reification and circular argument, it could prove useful. The present position is more neutral theoretically than Craik and Lockhart's depth-of-processing approach. It can be argued merely that certain types of encoding are mnemonically superior to others and that it is worth trying to identify the most important ones. This approach leaves open the possibility that demonstrably greater processing depth will not always leave traces particularly useful for the memory of events. To illustrate this point, assume with Collins and Quillian (1969) that certain searches through 'semantic memory' go deeper than others. Deciding that canaries are animals, for example, might require greater processing depth than deciding that canaries are birds. Yet the memorability of the latter decision could surpass that of the former if the relation between canary and bird were somehow more meaningful than that between canary and animal.

The Importance of 'Relational Encoding'

Certain encoding schemes—the use of imagery, the method of loci, and the mnemonic pegword system are only the most familiar examples—have long been employed by mnemonists to assure the memorability of events. Selz (1913) was one of the first psychologists to assert the importance of encoded relations generally, a view which has strongly re-emerged in the last 15 or 20 years. It may be found in the 'plans for remembering' of Miller, Galanter and Pribram (1960); in the claim that information use depends upon meaningful relations and upon relations between meanings (Deese, 1965); and in Bower's (1970) argument that it is the semantic character of encoded relations that makes possible the effectiveness of certain retrieval cues. The fact that previous experience may be 'redintegrated' (Horowitz and Prytulak, 1969; Horowitz and Manelis, 1972) implies, as Begg (1972) rightly reminds us, the prior existence of 'integrated memory structures'. A recent systematic approach to memory (Frijda, 1972) conceives of the memory store as a relational network, in which the meaning of a relation between A and B resides, in part, 'in the probable or possible nature of their arguments'. If Frijda is right, the memorability of A and B should depend on the degree of their mutual implication, a testable proposition.

Research on Memorability

It has been argued that how we operate on input has memorial implications, and that it is important to develop research strategies that can reveal the determinants of memorability. What follows is a selective and necessarily sketchy review of research that bears upon these concerns, and which I hope may shed some light upon the issues involved. These studies should be viewed as prolegomena, for the systematic work lies before us.

Free association norms suggest the sort of relationships that are important to users of a language. This point has been developed nicely by Deese (1965), whose emphasis on meaningful relations anticipates some of the present arguments. In more recent work, Pollio (1966) and Kiss (this volume) have explored the nature and role of associative structures in cognition.

Strength of Undifferentiated Relational Encodings

On a gross level, it is easy to show that the degree of association, irrespective of its nature, has memorial consequences. For example, the uncued recall of words increases with their inter-item associative strength (Deese, 1959). Effects of associative strength are also to be found in studies of cued recall. In one such study, an undergraduate project carried out by Adlard at the University of Sussex, subjects were asked to scale the degree of association between each of 60 pairs of words. The B members of these pairs had been selected so that an equal number of them were strong, moderate, or weak associates of the A members, according to existing norms. (The strong associates were never those most commonly reported, and the weak associates were never normatively idiosyncratic responses.) An unanticipated cued recall test, with the A member provided as the cue, followed the subjective scaling procedure. Both the normative association values and the scaled values yielded the same results: 80–85 per cent of strong associates were recalled, 70–75 per cent of moderate associates, and 20–25 per cent of low associates.

Tversky and Kahneman (1973, Study 9) report similar effects of word relatedness on cued recall. They presented their subjects with a set of 20 word-pairs. Each pair was shown either two or three times, and then a test of cued recall was administered. They had constructed the pairs so that each response word appeared with two stimulus words, one which was highly related to it and one which was not. Strong relations were either natural (*knife–fork*) or phonetic (*gown–clown*); unrelated pairs included *head–fork* and *bread–clown*. For the pairs presented twice, related response words were recalled with probability 0·77, unrelated ones with probability 0·31. For thrice-presented pairs, the corresponding figures were 0·85 and 0·41.

Types of Relational Encoding

The experiments cited above illustrate only that degree of relation affects memorability; they say nothing of the effect of relational type. In one of the few recent investigations to explore the mnemonic value of different sorts of semantic processing, Elias and Perfetti (1973) required subjects to produce either synonyms or associates to each of a sequence of words. Production of associates led to a poorer recognition memory than production of synonyms, suggesting the mnemonic superiority of denotative to connotative encoding.

At the University of Virginia, recent research has explored the memorial consequences of rediscovering and encoding some well-known semantic relations. An early experiment in this program (Schulman, 1971) required one group of subjects to decide whether each of 96 words denoted a living thing (L) while another decided whether each of the same words denoted a geographical location (G). Half the words belonged to each taxonomic category. On the unexpected test of recognition memory that followed, the pattern of results was the same for both groups: words belonging to the questioned category ('targets') were much better recognized than words ('non-targets') that did not. Thus the discovery of a known class-inclusion relation enhances recognition memory, while finding no such relation—an act surely requiring some sort of semantic processing, however minimal—does not. A similar experiment, informally conducted as an undergraduate 'practical' at the University of Sussex, yielded parallel results for free recall: from a list of 33 animals and 33 place names, about 40 per cent of the targets were recalled freely, but only about 10 per cent of the non-targets. At least two subjects recalled not a single word from the non-target category. This is a fascinating result, especially in the light of what is known about the powerful mnemonic effects of organizational factors (Bower, 1970), since it strongly suggests that the task demands prevented the discovery of the common class membership of all non-target words. (It is possible, of course, that the non-target category was in fact encoded at input, but was strangely unavailable as a retrieval cue afterwards.)

In a related experiment, heretofore unreported, subjects serving in three independent groups judged whether each of 96 words belonged to an individually specified category. For one group, an equal number of words was drawn from each of eight categories (animals, place names, occupations, trees and flowers, boats, games and sports, parts of the body, and musical instruments); for the second, from each of four categories (animals, place names, occupations, and trees and flowers); and for the third, from each of two categories (animals and place names). For each group, the questioned category could change from word to word, but was always one of the possible categories from which the words had been chosen. (The 4CAT group, for example, might be confronted with the following sequence of questions requiring yes/no answers: Tree or flower? DAFFODIL; Occupation? MAGPIE; Animal? BERLIN: Occupation? TEACHER). Following the classification phase of the experiment, all groups were given tests of recognition memory. The 8CAT and 4CAT groups showed our usual pattern of results: targets were much better recognized than non-targets. For the 2CAT group, however, the target advantage evaporated, no difference at all being found in the recognition of target and non-target words. Note that, for this group, unlike Groups L and G in Schulman (1971), the questions kept changing, so that any animal-word or place-word might or might not belong to its questioned category. Now, we know that when a subject decides to which of two known classes each word in a list belongs (Is BERLIN an animal *or* a place name?), the result is target-like recognition for all words (Schulman, 1971, Condition LG). Because their task permitted it, the 2CAT group might thus have encoded each non-target as a member of the only other possible experimental category, thereby functionally transforming it into a target: Is BERLIN an animal? No, it's a place. While the subjects of the 4CAT and 8CAT groups also could, in principle, encode the appropriate class for their non-target words, the stress placed on rapid classifications may have made this psychologically impossible. (Despite its plausibility, the foregoing argument may be misdirected. The 2CAT, 4CAT and 8CAT conditions used different groups of subjects and, of course, different sets of words. As a consequence, comparisons of recognition scores across conditions are risky, and leave open the possibility that all words in 2CAT were encoded equally poorly as non-targets rather than equally well as targets.)

In another experiment (Schulman, 1974), subjects were required to answer 100 queries of attribution and superordination (Is a TWINGE sudden? Is SPINACH ecstatic? Is a CORKSCREW an opener? Is a DUNGEON a scholar?) before being tested unexpectedly on their ability to remember either the upper-case 'keywords' or the lower-case 'descriptors'. Queries were designed to be either obviously true ('congruous') or obviously false ('incongruous', and violative of selectional restrictions). The memorability of keywords and descriptors, as a function of the type of queries relation in which they had originally been processed, was assessed by the methods of free recall, cued recall, and recognition memory. Each of six independent groups of subjects was tested with exactly one of these methods, and was asked to remember only keywords *or* descriptors, not both. The principal results are shown in Table 3.1. They were taken to indicate that, under incidental learning conditions, answering unambiguous queries of attribution and superordination (i) provides a poor basis for the free recall of congruity and almost no basis for the free recall of incongruity; (ii) leaves a trace which can often be 'redintegrated' (Horowitz and Prytulak, 1969; Horowitz and Manelis, 1972) by a congruous cue but seldom by an incongruous one; and (iii) provides a strong basis for the recognition of congruous keywords, and a better basis generally for the recognition of keywords than of descriptors. (Besides being better recognized than descriptors, keywords made better cues. This suggests a role-based asymmetry in the encoding of these words. For adjective-noun phrases, Horowitz and Manelis (1972) and Freedman and Loftus (1971) argue for an asymmetry based upon the roles played by the two parts of speech. But nouns are also more concrete, and easier to image, than adjectives, and this difference may contribute to their memorial superiority (Lockhart, 1969; see also Paivio, 1969 and Kintsch, 1972).) The pattern of results shows a large and pervasive memorial advantage of congruity, arguably because a congruous query, unlike an incongruous one, fosters a relational encoding of keyword and descriptor.

Though congruity mattered, the type of relation did not. Decisions about attribution and superordination resulted in equal memorability, a result

Table 3.1 Percentages correct in the free recall, cued recall, and recognition memory of keywords and descriptors[a] (From Schulman, A. I. (1974). *Memory and Cognition,* **2** (1A), 47–52, with permission)

Condition[c]	Queried Relation[b]			
	S	S̄	A	Ā
FR_K	9·8	3·0	11·3	3·0
	(7·5)	(2·9)	(7·4)	(2·9)
FR_D	12·0	1·7	10·5	3·7
	(7·5)	(2·8)	(6·7)	(4·0)
$CR_{K|D}$	50·8	4·0	42·2	5·0
	(12·8)	(4·9)	(14·0)	(3·6)
$CR_{D|K}$	59·4	5·4	58·7	10·3
	(16·2)	(5·8)	(15·2)	(8·5)
RM_K	95·8	86·0	94·2	88·0
	(4·5)	(6·0)	(5·9)	(7·1)
RM_D	84·7	75·0	81·4	79·7
	(6·8)	(11·5)	(11·5)	(7·2)

[a] Standard deviations are parenthetically noted
[b] An example of an S-query is: Is a CORKSCREW an opener? Of an S̄-query, Is a DUNGEON a scholar? Of an A-query, Is a TWINGE sudden? And of an Ā-query, Is SPINACH ecstatic? To illustrate the use of the table, the entry '59·4' for Condition $CR_{D|K}$ indicates that, following queries like Is a CORKSCREW an opener?, the keyword effectively cued the descriptor with probability 0·594.
[c] Recognition memory was assessed by the two-alternative forced-choice method, so that 50 per cent correct in RM_K or RM_D would denote chance discrimination.

consistent with Kempen's evidence (cited by Frijda, 1972) that these relations have common representations in long-term memory. [The only statistically reliable exception to this rule was that a (noun) superordinate was a better cue for the recall of its keyword than an (adjective) attribute (Table 3.1, 50·8 per cent > 42·2 per cent, $P < 0.05$).] According to Frijda, however, Kempen's (1970) work also suggests that the representations of relations like rose–flower and rose–red differ from those of relations like rose–tulip and rose–nursery. If this is so, future work would show that the encoding of superordinate and coordinate relations have different memorial consequences.

The experiment just described also yielded comparative data on the recall and recognition of individual words. These data, previously unreported, may be of interest here. A word's cue value, much more than its recallability when cued, was positively related to the ease with which it could be freely recalled. Words recalled by more than one subject in free recall were better cues than those which nobody could recall: the comparative figures were 65·6 and 53·6 per cent for keywords and 55·0 and 43·0 per cent for descriptors. When a word's free and cued recall are compared, however, a similar pattern emerges only for keywords from attributive queries: those non-idiosyncratically recalled in FR_K showed better cued recall (54·1 vs. 39·8 per cent) than those that did not. Descriptors best recalled in FR_D were not only more effective as cues in

CR_{KD} but were also better recognized: those freely recalled by more than one subject were recognized 90·3 per cent of the time, compared to 80·6 per cent for those never freely recalled. No such correlation obtained for congruous keywords, probably because of their near-perfect recognition.

There was no persuasive evidence that words effective as cues in cued recall played a similar, but hidden, role in free recall. Though a relational encoding may be a necessary condition for free recall, what triggered recall here was apparently not one of the words involved in the relation, but rather some independent pointer to it. At the same time, the relation as a whole seems to be what is retrieved (see Horowitz and Manelis, 1972, for supporting evidence); the subject retrieves the relation and reports whatever aspect of it the experimenter requires. Consider the support for this allegation deriving from an analysis of queries of attribution. (A similar argument, and comparable data, hold for superordinate queries.) The 17 adjectives and 14 nouns non-idiosyncratically recalled, by independent groups of subjects, included eight pairs of query-mates; the retrieval of integrated memories is thus strongly indicated.

Structural versus Semantic Processing

In the psychological laboratory, paired-associate experiments often deliberately use stimulus pairs which are semantically unrelated; initially, even the individual items may be minimally interpretable. Subjects in such experiments impose 'subjective organization' upon their input and may learn, through instructions or their own discovery, some 'mediator' between the members of an A–B pair. From the present point of view, these subjects are engaged in finding ways relationally to encode their input when few relations are immediately apparent. It is not surprising that large individual differences in encoding practices and, consequently, in learning, are found.

To the experimental subject, a list of paired associates whose 'stimuli' and 'responses' are relatively meaningless may more readily suggest structural than semantic relations; the recall of such lists is not easily mastered. Mnemonically, it is ordinarily better to find meaning in an experience than merely to note its surface features. Only if such were not the case would it be news, and yet the literature pointing out the advantages of semantic to structural processing continues to grow.

Perhaps the greatest variety of tasks involving 'non-semantic' processing (counting a word's syllables, or scanning it for the presence of specified letters, for example) have been used by Jenkins and his co-workers (Hyde and Jenkins, 1969, 1973; Walsh and Jenkins, 1973; Johnston and Jenkins, 1971), who consistently find their semantic tasks to result in superior recall. The following results illustrate the same general point. Words whose sound is to be remembered are more poorly recognized than the same words processed for meaning (Cermak, Schnorr, Buschke and Atkinson, 1970). A small change in the meaning of a sentence is easier to recognize than a small change in its syntax

(Sachs, 1967). Deciding that a word contains the letter A, or that it has a repeated letter, provides a poorer basis for its later recognition than deciding that it belongs to a taxonomic category (Schulman, 1971). Uncued word recall, like word recognition, benefits less from alphabetic than from taxonomic processing, while cued recall of the same words benefits only from a taxonomic, but not an alphabetic, cue (Mondani, Pelegrino, and Battig, 1973).

There is no doubt that tasks that call for semantic processing typically result in better memory than tasks that do not. One might suppose, then, that 'semantic tasks facilitate recall . . . while nonsemantic tasks do not' (Walsh and Jenkins, 1973) and that 'subjects who have performed semantic tasks of any sort will be in a favorable position' (Hyde and Jenkins, 1973). Yet such claims for the general superiority of semantic processing (see also Hyde and Jenkins, 1969; Johnston and Jenkins, 1971; Till and Jenkins, 1973) are in need of qualification, for semantic *processing* does not guarantee—and cannot be identified with—a mnemonically valuable semantic *encoding*. To decide that spinach is not ecstatic is surely to utilize semantic processes, and yet the free recall of words so incongruously linked is virtually zero (Schulman, 1974). And to decide that tiger has no repeated letter makes it as memorable as to decide that it is not a place name, despite the fact that the latter decision presumably calls more semantic processes into play (Schulman, 1971).

Verbal and Nonverbal Relations

Our present emphasis on verbal relations, or at least upon relations that have verbal realizations, in no way suggests that other relations are not of comparable mnemonic importance. A picture of an axe striking a football is more memorable than a picture of those objects side by side (Epstein, Rock and Zuckerman, 1960; Bobrow and Easton, 1972). There is growing evidence, moreover, for independent systems of memory for images and for words (Paivio, 1972; Paivio and Csapo, 1973; see also Baddeley and Warrington, 1973). An item's presentation as a picture is more memorable than its presentation as a word, a result attributed by Paivio and Csapo (1973) to a combination of image superiority and dual encoding. From the present standpoint, at least part of the image's superiority lies in the relations it embodies. Words relate less directly to knowledge of the world than do pictures. One may identify a word without encoding enough of its semantic features (*cf.* Fillenbaum, 1969) to make it memorable. A picture, on the other hand, probably cannot be identified or classified without encoding meaningful relations that enhance its memorability. (One might also argue that relations encoded for pictures tend to result from recognition processes, while those encoded for words tend to result from recall processes). It is instructive to note that when experimental tasks foster distinctive relational encodings of words—encodings which may or may not be image-based—recognition memory begins to approach levels usually found only with pictures (for picture-recognition studies, see Shepard, 1967, and Standing, 1973). Thus the subjective organization imposed by sorting behaviour (Mandler, Pearlstone, and Koopmans, 1969), as well as encodings resulting from classificatory judgements (Schulman, 1974), leads to extremely high levels of recognition memory for words.

Memory for 'Context'

The ability to remember contextual information relates, in poorly understood ways, to the ability to remember 'focal' information. Yet we know from experience that the recall of spatio-temporal context, for example, can lead to memory for events occurring within that context. Restoration of such context can provide access to events and relations stored in memory. (What initiates the recall of such context is completely unknown.) In a recent study, Schulman (1973) presented words in spatial arrays before testing simultaneously for lexical memory and location recall. A word's recognition depended on the ability to recall its spatial location, recall of this attribute increasing with recognition confidence. When words were presented in colour as well as in space, recognition was best when both attributes could be recalled; was better when location alone than when colour alone could be recalled; and was poorest when neither attribute could be recalled. Thus it seems that when such contextual information is encoded, the focal event experienced in that context is more likely to be recognized. Further study is needed, for it is by no means clear that the mnemonic roles of such contextual attributes as colour and location are the same as other aspects—especially, those more meaningful aspects—of encoded events.

A distinction should probably be drawn between contextual attributes, such as time and place, and contextual events. The latter may bias the interpretation of a to-be-remembered event, while the former are unlikely to do so. When 'semantic context' is different at input and at test, recognition memory may fail and cued recall may suffer (Tulving and Osler, 1968; Tulving and Thomson, 1971, 1973; Thomson, 1972; Light and Carter-Sobell, 1970). One may reasonably suppose that a different test context fosters relational encodings different from those produced at input. Viewed in this light, retrieval failure in such circumstances is like the failure of redintegration that typically occurs when a non-syllabic part of a word (e.g., _HO_) is used as a cue for whole word recall (SCHOOL; see Horowitz and Prytulak, 1969).

The questions of availability and accessibility apply as much to contextual attributes and contextual events as they do to focal experience. What can be remembered of context might shed light on focal memory. The failure of cued recall, for instance, might signify only the inaccessibility of encoded context, and not its unavailability; a test of contextual recognition should show which is the case. As part of her undergraduate honours work at the University of Virginia, Good (1972) undertook such an investigation. Her concern was with 'feelings of knowing'—subjective estimates of one's ability to remember something which, for the moment at least, is irretrievable. Good presented subjects with triads of unrelated words, the third of which was underscored and to be remembered. After a single learning trial, and with one or both of the first two words of a triad as cues, the subject tried to recall the word that had been underscored. At the same time he indicated, on a five-point scale, his confidence that he would correctly recognize this word if it were presented in its original context. The 'contextual recognition' test that followed required a choice between two words, both of which had been underscored in the original triads. Thus the subject was being tested on his ability to remember the context of underscored words. The results showed that the accuracy of such discriminative judgements increased with feeling-of-knowing—subjects knew what they knew—ranging from about 60 per cent correct for weak feelings to about 85 per cent for strong ones (chance recognition equals 50 per cent; contextual recognition of words that had been correctly recalled was 98 per cent). Very strong feelings of knowing, it would seem, are tantamount to tip-of-the-tongue experiences (Brown and McNeill, 1966). The fact that such contextual recognition can take place in the wake of cued recall failure raises questions about the nature of the encoding of the input triad. Good's procedure would seem to hold promise for the further study of these questions.

Some Remarks on Incidental and Intentional Learning

While memorability may owe something to mere 'intentionality' (*cf.* Mondani *et al.*, 1973), the usual superiority of intentional to incidental learning is more likely traceable to richer encodings. When memorability is at stake, events may be processed differently than would otherwise be the case. (Differently, but not necessarily with the desired mnemonic advantages; routine processing may sometimes be more effective than *ad hoc* processing.) So long as they induce the same mental operations, however, the memorial consequences of incidental and intentional learning conditions should be the same. For example, the benefits of imagery for free recall do not depend upon instructions to learn (Paivio and Csapo, 1973). On the negative side, instructions 'to learn' should be valueless if the subject, for reasons of ignorance or disinclination, fails to utilize mnemonically effective input operations. Eagle and Leiter (1964), Craik and Lockhart (1972), and others have argued along lines similar to these, and evidence to bolster such arguments has come from Elias and Perfetti (1973) and from Jenkins and his co-workers (Hyde and Jenkins, 1969, 1973; Johnston and Jenkins, 1971; Till and Jenkins, 1973; Walsh and Jenkins, 1973). From the present point of view, the important thing is to curtail idiosyncratic processing so that the memorial consequences of specifiable mental operations can more easily be determined. Incidental tasks that differ, at least theoretically, in the operations they prescribe seem appropriate to this end.

Acknowledgements

This paper was prepared at the University of Sussex during my tenure as Sesquicentennial Associate of the Center for Advanced Studies of the University of Virginia. I am grateful to both Universities.

54

References

Adlard, A. J. (1973). Unpublished thesis, University of Sussex.

Baddeley, A. D. and Warrington, E. K. (1973). Memory coding and amnesia. *Neuropsychologia*, **11**, 159–165.

Begg, I. (1972). Recall of meaningful phrases. *Journal of Verbal Learning and Verbal Behavior*, **11**, 431–439.

Bobrow, S. A. and Easton, R. D. (1972). A confirmation that relational organization facilitates memory. *Psychonomic Science*, **29**(4B), 256–257.

Bower, G. H. (1970). Organizational factors in memory. *Cognitive Psychology*, **1**, 18–26.

Brown, R. and McNeill, D. (1966). The 'tip of the tongue' phenomenon. *Journal of Verbal Learning and Verbal Behavior*, **5**, 325–337.

Cermak, G., Schnorr, J., Buschke, H. and Atkinson, R. C. (1970). Recognition memory as influenced by differential attention to semantic and acoustic properties of words. *Psychonomic Science*, **19**(2), 79–81.

Collins, A. M. and Quillian, M. R. (1969). Retrieval time from semantic memory. *Journal of Verbal Learning and Verbal Behavior*, **8**, 240–243.

Craik, F. I. M. and Lockhart, R. S. (1972). Levels of processing: A framework for memory research. *Journal of Verbal Learning and Verbal Behavior*, **11**, 671–684.

Deese, J. (1959). Influence of inter-item associative strength upon immediate free recall. *Psychological Reports*, **5**, 305–312.

Deese, J. (1965). *The Structure of Associations in Language and Thought*. Baltimore: Johns Hopkins Press.

Eagle, M. and Leiter, E. (1964). Recall and recognition in intentional and incidental learning. *Journal of Experimental Psychology*, **68**, 58–63.

Elias, C. S. and Perfetti, C. A. (1973). Encoding task and recognition memory: The importance of semantic coding. *Journal of Experimental Psychology*, **99**, 151–156.

Epstein, W., Rock, I. and Zuckerman, C. B. (1960). Meaning and familiarity in associative learning. *Psychological Monographs*, **74**, (Whole No. 491).

Fillenbaum, S. (1969). Words as feature complexes: False recognition of antonyms and synonyms. *Journal of Experimental Psychology*, **82**, 400–402.

Freedman, J. L. and Loftus, E. F. (1971). Retrieval of words from long-term memory. *Journal of Verbal Learning and Verbal Behavior*, **10**, 107–115.

Frijda, N. H. (1972). Simulation of human long-term memory. *Psychological Bulletin*, **77**, 1–31.

Good, S. J. (1972). Feeling-of-knowing as a predictor of the ability to recall and recognize words. Unpublished Honors thesis, University of Virginia.

Horowitz, L. M. and Manelis, L. (1972). Towards a theory of redintegrative memory: Adjective-noun phrases. In G. H. Bower and J. T. Spence (Eds) *The Psychology of Learning and Motivation: Advances in Research and Theory*, Vol. 5. New York: Academic Press.

Horowitz, L. M. and Prytulak, L. S. (1969). Redintegrative memory. *Psychological Review*, **76**, 519–531.

Hyde, T. S. and Jenkins, J. J. (1969). Differential effects of incidental tasks on the organization of recall of a list of highly associated words. *Journal of Experimental Psychology*, **82**, 472–481.

Hyde, T. S. and Jenkins, J. J. (1973). Recall for words as a function of semantic, graphic, and syntactic orienting tasks. *Journal of Verbal Learning and Verbal Behavior*, **12**, 471–480.

Johnston, C. D. and Jenkins, J. J. (1971). Two more incidental tasks that differentially affect clustering in recall. *Journal of Experimental Psychology*, **89**, 92–95.

Kempen, G. (1970). *Memory for Word and Sentence Meanings: A Set-Feature Model*. Nijmegen: Schippers.

Kintsch, W. (1972). Abstract nouns: Imagery value versus lexical complexity. *Journal of Verbal Learning and Verbal Behavior*, **11**, 59–65.

Kolers, P. A. (1973). Remembering operations. *Memory and Cognition*, **1**, 347–355.

Light, L. L. and Carter-Sobell, L. (1970). Effects of changed semantic context on recognition memory. *Journal of Verbal Learning and Verbal Behavior*, **9**, 1–11.

Lockhart, R. S. (1969). Retrieval asymmetry in the recall of adjectives and nouns. *Journal of Experimental Psychology*, **79**, 12–17.

Mandler, G., Pearlstone, Z. and Koopmans, H. S. (1969). Effects of organization and semantic similarity on recall and recognition. *Journal of Verbal Learning and Verbal Behavior*, **8**, 410–423.

Miller, G. A., Galanter, E. and Pribram, K. H. (1960). *Plans and the Structure of Behavior*. New York: Holt, Rinehart and Winston.

Mondani, M. S., Pellegrino, J. W. and Battig, W. F. (1973). Free and cued recall as a function of different levels of word processing. *Journal of Experimental Psychology*, **101**, 324–329.

Paivio, A. (1969). Mental imagery in associative learning. *Psychological Review*, **76**, 241–263.

Paivio, A. (1972). Symbolic and sensory modalities of memory. In M. E. Meyer, (Ed.) *Cognitive Learning:* The Third Western Symposium on Learning. Western Washington State College.

Paivio, A. and Csapo, K. (1973). Picture superiority in free recall: Imagery or dual coding? *Cognitive Psychology*, **5**, 176–206.

Pollio, H. R. (1966). *The Structural Basis of Word Association Behavior*. The Hague: Mouton.

Sachs, J. S. (1967). Recognition memory for syntactic and semantic aspects of connected discourse. *Perception and Psychophysics*, **2**, 437–442.

Schulman, A. I. (1971). Recognition memory for targets from a scanned word list. *British Journal of Psychology*, **62**, 335–346.

Schulman, A. I. (1973). Recognition memory and the recall of spatial location. *Memory and Cognition*, **1**, 256–260.

Schulman, A. I. (1974). Memory for words recently classified. *Memory and Cognition*, **2** (1A), 47–52.

Selz, O. (1913). *Die Gesetze des geordneten Denkverlaufs*. I. Stuttgart: Speman.

Shepard, R. N. (1967). Recognition memory for words, sentences, and pictures. *Journal of Verbal Learning and Verbal Behavior*, **6**, 156–163.

Standing, L. (1973). Learning 10,000 pictures. *Quarterly Journal of Experimental Psychology*, **25**, 207–222.

Thomson, D. M. (1972). Context effects in recognition memory. *Journal of Verbal Learning and Verbal Behavior*, **11**, 497–511.

Till, R. E. and Jenkins, J. J. (1973). The effects of cued orienting tasks on the free recall of words. *Journal of Verbal Learning and Verbal Behavior*, **12**, 489–498.

Tulving, E. (1972). Episodic and semantic memory. In E. Tulving and W. Donaldson (Eds) *Organization of Memory*. New York: Academic Press.

Tulving, E. and Madigan, S. (1970). Memory and verbal learning. *Annual Review of Psychology*, **21**, 437–484.

Tulving, E. and Osler, S. (1968). Effectiveness of retrieval cues in memory for words. *Journal of Experimental Psychology*, **77**, 593–601.

Tulving, E. and Thomson, D. M. (1971). Retrieval processes in recognition memory. *Journal of Experimental Psychology*, **87**, 116–124.

Tulving, E. and Thomson, D. M. (1973). Encoding specificity and retrieval processes in episodic memory. *Psychological Review*, **80**, 352–373.

Tversky, A. and Kahneman, D. (1973). Availability: A heuristic for judging frequency and probability. *Cognitive Psychology*, **5**, 207–232.

Underwood, B. J. (1969). Attributes of memory. *Psychological Review*, **76**, 559–573.

Walsh, D. A. and Jenkins, J. J. (1973). Effects of orientating tasks on free recall in incidental learning: 'Difficulty', 'effort', and 'process' explanations. *Journal of Verbal Learning and Verbal Behavior*, **12**, 481–488.

Chapter 4

Imagery and Long-term Memory

Allan Paivio

Recent studies of imagery have firmly established the fact that imagery variables are highly effective in a variety of memory tasks. Indeed, they are among the most potent mnemonic variables ever discovered. Theoretical explanations have also been proposed for the effects and many of these have been supported empirically. Much of the research and theory has been concerned with long-term memory in the sense that the tasks have involved so-called secondary memory, or they have required the subject to generate information from long-term memory, as when he is asked to use imagery mnemonics to learn a list of words. Such research has usually been concerned with the role of imagery as a mediator of memory performance. Recently, however, there has been an increasing interest in providing answers to questions concerning the unique characteristics of images as cognitive representations: What is the nature of the representational unit or image? How are such units organized into high-order structure? What kinds of information processing can go on in the form of imagery? This paper reviews some recent work on each of these questions.

The discussion is organized into sections concerned with (a) theoretical and empirical approaches to imagery and verbal processes in LTM, (b) evidence on the structure and functional characteristics of imaginal representations in LTM, (c) imagery research involving primary and secondary memory tasks, and (d) imagery and long-term retention.

Theoretical Views on Imagery and Long-term Memory

A number of theorists have discussed imagery in relation to long-term memory processes of the kind generally encompassed by the term semantic memory. At least two important general questions can be asked about these theories. First, what degree of abstractness is attributed to the structures and processes presumed to underlie imagery phenomena? Are imaginal representations and processes relatively concrete in the sense that information concerning external objects and events bears a rather direct, isomorphic relation to the perceptual information given by those objects and events, or are they relatively abstract in the sense that perceptual information is transformed into some entirely different format in long-term memory? A number of psychologists have discussed imaginal storage in terms that imply a direct isomorphism with sensory or perceptual processes (e.g., Bower, 1972; Bugelski, 1971; Cooper and Shepard, 1973; Hebb, 1968; Mowrer, 1960; Skinner, 1953; Staats, 1968). The author's own views can be so characterized as well (Paivio, 1971, 1972). Others prefer to conceptualize the underlying representational processes in terms of logical propositions or some other kind of abstract entity (e.g., Anderson and Bower, 1973; Pylyshyn, 1973; Rumelhart, Lindsay and Norman, 1972).

The second question is perhaps more important because more deductive consequences result from the alternative answers to it. The question is whether both verbal and nonverbal information are represented in a common long-term memory system (however abstract) or whether separate systems are postulated. Although the concept of imagery was not in vogue at the time, Osgood (1957) was perhaps the first to propose a common representational system for verbal and nonverbal information in his hierarchical behaviour theory. Linguistic and nonlinguistic (perceptual) signs are distinguished at the projection and perceptual integration levels of his model, but semantic information common to both classes of stimulus input is stored in a single representational meaning system at a third level. The form of representation, as most psychologists know, is the simultaneous bundle of implicit reactions and stimuli that define Osgood's $r_m - s_m$ construct. More recently, Pylyshyn (1973) has argued strongly for a common representational format for both linguistic and nonlinguistic (imaginal) information, his conceptual preference taking the highly abstract form of logical propositions. Rumelhart, Lindsay, and Norman (1972) do not explicitly discuss images but their model involves a common (propositional) memory format for concepts, events, and episodes of all kinds. Collins and Quillian (1972) apparently distinguish images from propositions and assume that the former are generated from the latter. Jorgensen and Kintsch (1973) also distinguished between images and propositions and suggested, on the basis of their data on comprehension, that the two classes of representation are independent.

A Dual-coding Theory

The author's own position on the issue is clear: he believes that it is necessary to postulate separate representational systems for nonverbal and verbal information. Whether these are regarded as distinct symbolic systems or as two kinds of sub-processes within a single system is probably irrelevant in a formal sense, although they are preferably viewed as separate systems. The main point is that the conceptually distinct processes are assumed to be functionally independent at one processing stage at least. First will be given a brief overview of the theory and the empirical procedures related to it, then some of the data that have persuaded the author that distinct systems are conceptually necessary will be reviewed.

The concept of imagery is defined partly by contrast with verbal processes. The two processing systems are viewed as functionally independent but partly interconnected cognitive systems for encoding, storing, organizing, transforming, and retrieving stimulus information. They are assumed to differ functionally in regard to the nature of the information they are specialized to handle, the way that information is organized into higher-order functional structures, and the ease with which the cognitive information can be reorganized or transformed. Thus the imagery system is assumed to be specialized for relatively direct processing of information concerning concrete objects and events: it organizes elementary units of information (images) into higher-order structures that have a synchronous or spatial character, and it is functionally dynamic and flexible in that the organized cognitive information can be quickly reorganized, manipulated, or transformed. The verbal system, on the other hand, is specialized for dealing with abstract information involving linguistic units and organizing such information into higher-order sequential structures. At one time the author tentatively assumed (Paivio, 1971; see also Berlyne, 1965) that verbal processes may also be less transformable, more static, than imagery, but he now believes that the difference may be more a qualitative than a quantitative one, related to the kinds of transformations that are possible given the structural characteristics of each system. Thus dynamic visual imagery involves transformation of spatial information whereas verbal transformations involve rearrangements of the sequential ordering of linguistic units. This issue will be returned to later. The important general point at the moment is that the model attributes different functional characteristics to the two postulated systems—characteristics that have testable empirical implications not suggested, so far as can be told, by the models that propose to handle verbal and nonverbal information in a common format.

A second feature of the theory can be deduced as a corollary of the foregoing, but it will be convenient to make it explicit because it is relevant to later discussions of long-term memory research. The notion of independent but interconnected systems implies distinct levels of information processing, which we have discussed elsewhere in terms of levels of meaning (Paivio, 1971, Ch. 3; Paivio and O'Neill, 1970). These were referred to as representational, referential, and associative levels. The *representational* level refers to the integrated units of cognitive information in long-term memory, corresponding to linguistic and nonlinguistic stimuli. The linguistic or verbal representation can be regarded as analogous to Morton's (1969) logogen, or Bousfield's (1961) concept of the representational response, that is, the immediate perceptual response activated by a verbal stimulus such as a word. Nonverbal representational units, or images, correspond to concrete perceptual entities. This conceptualization raises important issues regarding the size of the representational unit, its relation to sensory modalities, and so on, but it is unnecessary to consider such problems in detail here (see Paivio, 1971, Ch. 3).

The *referential* level refers to the activation of an established interconnection between images and verbal representations, so that a word arouses some corresponding perceptual image, an object can be named, or an exchange occurs between the cognitive representation entirely at an implicit level without being expressed in overt responses. The term 'referential' captures the idea that the interconnection corresponds to the semantic relation between words and things. It is important to note, however, that a one-to-one relation between a verbal representation and a particular image is not assumed (Paivio, 1971, pp. 62–63; 74–75). Instead something analogous to a verbal associative hierarchy is assumed: a word or phrase can activate or generate different images, or an object or event different verbal descriptions, depending on the past experiences of the subject and the context in which the referential reactions occur. The point is that some images are more probable than others given a verbal stimulus, just as verbal responses can vary systematically in their associative probability. This assumption takes account of the variability and contextual determination of referential relations (e.g., Olson, 1970).

The third level is *associative* meaning, which is a rather misleading label because representational and referential level also involve associative relations of a kind. In this case, however, the reference is to associations involving representational units *within* each of the two symbolic systems. Verbal stimuli can arouse verbal responses in an associative chain, and this presumably can occur through the activation of paths connecting verbal representations to each other. Thus the word *boy* elicits the response *girl* directly through their corresponding verbal representations without any involvement of the image system. Conversely, a perceptual object might remind one of some other object directly, through their interconnections within the imagery system.

The foregoing constitutes the main features of the working theory. A more complete model would need to include some kind of statement concerning such matters as operators or control processes within the system. For example, the system must include a component that activates the interconnections between systems when subjects are instructed to image to words or verbalize to pictures, and activates pathways within each system when subjects are instructed or otherwise primed to associate verbally to words or to image associatively to pictures. In other words, it needs a control process that can bias information flow within and between systems. It would also be required to control the transformations and reorganizations of information within each system according to their functional characteristics.

The author has no firm views at present as to how such processes should be conceptualized, and to the extent that the issue has been previously discussed, it has been assumed that the control processes are an intrinsic part of the representational system itself. For example, the author has assumed with various others (e.g., Berlyne, 1965; Hebb, 1968; Piaget and Inhelder, 1966; Skinner, 1953) that imagery includes a motor component, derived from perceptual exploration and manipulation of objects, which permits information to be transformed and reorganized within the system. Similarly, one might propose that linguistic transformation rules are themselves part of the verbal system operating on other informational units within the system in some kind of associative fashion. Instructions to generate verbal mediators or images as mnemonic aids for verbal material also could be viewed as stimulus conditions which prime further processing at verbal associative or referential levels. Thus the control processes might be generalized habits derived from experiences in which one has first learned overtly to make up sentences or phrases incorporating specified words, or to draw or point out pictures corresponding to words or descriptive phrases. These perceptual and motor reactions become internalized so that if I am now told to image to a word it is in effect an instruction to select or generate an internal picture; or, if told to mediate verbally, I generate an inner sentence. Precisely how such processes operate is of course unknown, but they are no more mysterious in this proposal than they are in other contemporary models that incorporate control processes of one kind or another. In any case, it is sufficient for present purposes to assume the control mechanism without taking any firm stand on their derivation or how they should be represented in the model which is proposed.

Operational definitions of imagery. The research relevant to the theory cannot be discussed without reference to the empirical procedures that define imagery as a measurable concept. All imagery researchers have relied on one or other of the following classes of independent variables to define or manipulate imagery: (a) *stimulus materials,* such as pictures, concrete words, and abstract words, which differ in their image-evoking capacity according to various response measures; (b) *experimental procedures* designed to increase or decrease the likelihood that imagery will be used in a task; mnemonic instructions is the most familiar example, but other variables, such as rate of presentation and presentation of material to different cerebral hemispheres, have also been used toward this end; (c) *individual differences in imagery,* as measured by spatial manipulation tests (e.g., Ernest and Paivio, 1969) or self-ratings of experienced vividness of imagery (e.g., Sheehan, 1966). Other behavioural indicators, including physiological responses (see, e.g., Paivio, 1973), have also been used, but always in conjunction with one or other of the three general classes of independent variables just described. The relevant variables have one characteristic in common: they are designed to influence the probability that imagery will be involved in a given task.

Research Evidence on the Functional Distinctions

This section summarizes some of the psychological implications of the theoretical distinctions between imaginal and verbal LTM structures and processes, and presents evidence bearing on those implications.

Functional Independence of the Systems

This assumption refers to independent storage and independent processing within the two systems. More specifically, it implies that information can be stored and processed in either the imaginal or the verbal system, or in both simultaneously. For example, pictures that are not easily labelled might be stored only in a nonverbal form and abstract words only verbally. Pictures that are easily named and concrete words that can be easily imaged might arouse both codes. Independence in the latter case could be reflected in independent retention or forgetting, or additivity of effects, depending on the design of the study. The notion is supported by various kinds of research evidence.

Neuropsychological evidence. Some of the best evidence for functionally distinct verbal and nonverbal memory processes comes from studies of patients with surgically separated cerebral hemispheres (Gazzaniga, 1970; Sperry, 1973) or with localized lesions in one or other hemisphere (e.g., Milner and Teuber, 1968). The evidence generally suggests that linguistic memory information and the processing of that information is in some fundamental sense localized in the dominant (usually the left) hemisphere, whereas certain kinds of nonverbal memory processes are specific to the non-dominant hemisphere. Moreover, functional independence is specifically indicated by the fact that damage to the right (or non-dominant) hemisphere can impair memory for nonverbal material without affecting verbal memory, whereas damage to the dominant hemisphere selectively impairs verbal memory. The same conclusion emerges from studies in which verbal or nonverbal material is selectively presented to the right or left hemisphere of normal subjects (Kimura, 1973). There is even some evidence to suggest that imagery, as defined by mnemonic instructions (Seamon and Gazzaniga, 1973) or individual difference measures (Paivio and Ernest, 1971), may be more a right than a left hemisphere function for most people, as though the long-term memory information required for imaginal processing is stored in the right hemisphere.

Selective interference between perceptual and memory processes. Numerous studies have demonstrated that processing of memory information can interfere with perceptual processing and *vice versa*, and that the interference is greater when both kinds of processes presumably involve a common channel than when they involve different channels (Paivio, 1971, Ch. 5). The best known work is that of Brooks (1968), who showed that reading interfered more with visual memory aroused by the messages themselves than did listening, whereas listening interfered more with verbal memory. Atwood (1971) has recently presented suggestive evidence that the efficiency of visual mnemonics may be disrupted more by a visual than by an auditory interfering task. Klee and Eysenck (1973) similarly showed that the advantage of concrete (high imagery) sentences over abstract sentences in a comprehension task was less under a visual than a verbal interference condition. Such studies indicate that the different perceptual-mnemonic channels are functionally independent insofar as memory activity can go on in one channel (e.g., imagery) while the other is concurrently engaged in perceptual activity (e.g., listening to speech), but the same channel cannot efficiently carry on both perception and mnemonic processing. The evidence for such conflict is not all positive (*cf.*

Baddeley, Grant, Wright and Thomson, 1973; Paivio, 1971, p. 374) and it now appears that it is only obtained when the visual and imagery tasks have a common spatial component rather than a visual-sensory component alone (Brooks, 1972). Nonetheless, the evidence is relevant to the functional definition of imagery, particularly in that it implicates the motor component of imagery in the interference effects.

Additivity of imaginal and verbal memory codes. Csapo and the present author (Paivio and Csapo, 1973) conducted a series of experiments on the free recall of pictures and words in which dual coding was either induced or controlled by orienting tasks, and recall was sometimes tested incidentally. The results provided strong evidence that imaginal and verbal memory codes are independent in the sense that they have additive effects on recall. For example under incidental recall conditions, pictures were consistently recalled better than words except when subjects imaged to words. Successive repetition of pictures, words, and pictures repeated as their verbal labels, or *vice versa*, also increased recall probability relative to once-presented items, but the effect was completely additive only in the case of picture–word repetitions, as though the underlying pictorial and verbal codes are truly independent in storage. Picture–picture and word–word repetitions, however, were less than additive in their effect.

The author has since repeated the item repetition experiment using words only, together with imaginal or verbal encoding reactions to the items. Thus words were sometimes repeated immediately and sometimes not. In either case, subjects were cued either to generate an image to a word or to pronounce the word to themselves. An equal number of repeated words were therefore imaged twice, pronounced twice, or imaged on one presentation and pronounced on the other. Similarly, equal numbers of once-presented words were imaged or verbalized. A surprise recall test following the encoding task revealed a recall pattern that was almost identical to the pattern resulting from repetition of pictures and words in the earlier experiments. Thus recall was equal for items that were imaged twice and those that were imaged on one occasion and pronounced on the other, and both were clearly superior to items that were pronounced twice. Once-presented items also were recalled much better when subjects had imaged than when they had merely verbalized to them. Finally, imaging and pronouncing to a repeated item resulted in recall performance that conformed closely to what would be expected if the individual encodings were independent and additive in their effects, whereas repeated imaging resulted in an increment that was less than additive. Repeated pronouncing also tended to be less than additive although the statistical test of this effect fell short of significance. Except for the last imperfection, the data are consistent with the view that evoked verbal representations and mental images of the corresponding referents are independent memory events, whereas repeated events within either symbolic system are less likely to behave as though the events are independent.

The conclusion that imaginal and verbal storage processes are functionally independent also receives support from a series of experiments by Rowe (1972) which demonstrated that imagery and verbal frequency variables have independent effects in verbal discrimination learning. Nelson and Brooks (1973a, 1973b) also demonstrated independence of imaginal and verbal components of stimulus items in PA learning, as did Bahrick and Bahrick (1971) for pictorial and verbal codes in free recall. These examples suffice to establish a firm empirical basis for the very important assumption that imaginal and verbal processes are functionally independent in storage.

Interconnectedness of Systems

This assumption implies that information exchange can occur between systems during encoding and retrieval of information, as when one images to a word, labels a picture, or when similar exchanges occur implicitly. In this respect the systems are interdependent, rather than independent. While information is stored and can be processed independently in one system or the other, or both in parallel, the *exchange* of information can occur only where interconnections have been established. These connecting pathways presumably are relatively direct in the case of concrete nouns and their corresponding imaginal representations, but generally indirect in the case of abstract nouns and word classes other than nouns. An abstract would like *religion*, for example, presumably arouses imagery by first activating some concrete verbal associate like *church* (the interpretation applies also to general terms such as *animal*; *cf.* Anderson and McGaw, 1973). This assumption is supported by the fact that concrete nouns are consistently rated as easier to image than abstract nouns, verbs, or adjectives, even when the words do not differ in such verbal attributes as familiarity (Paivio, 1971, Ch. 3). More compelling evidence comes from reaction time studies in which subjects have been required to generate either images or verbal associations to concrete and abstract words (e.g., Ernest and Paivio, 1971) or word pairs (e.g., Colman and Paivio, 1970; Paivio and Foth, 1970; Yuille and Paivio, 1967). The studies consistently show that it takes much longer to generate images to abstract than to concrete words, but verbal associative latencies differ very little, it at all, for the two classes of material. Moreover, imaginal and verbal associative latencies are comparable in the case of concrete words but not abstract words. The precise pattern of results changes somewhat when three or four words must be combined in sentences or images (Segal and Paivio, 1973), presumably because sequential constraints increasingly hinder sentence formation in particular as the number of words in the to-be-coded set increases. Regardless of set size, however, coding instruction and item concreteness always interact in a manner which suggests that imaging to abstract words involves an extra step as compared to imaging to concrete words or verbalizing to wither abstract or concrete words.

The important general point regarding the twin assumptions of independence and partial interconnectedness of imaginal and verbal LTM systems is that they imply different patterns of effects at different information processing stages when the task involves both systems. Independence applies to storage effects whereas interdependence applies to the encoding of information from one system to the other, or retrieval of information in one system through the other. Independence is reflected in statistical independence whereas interdependence is reflected in statistical interactions, both of which have been demonstrated in the studies I have reviewed. Which would be expected in other situations depends on what information processing stages are involved in the behavioural task. For example, Paivio and Foth (1970) obtained an interaction in paired-associate recall such that recall was poorer with imagery mnemonics than with verbal mediators when the pairs were abstract, but image mediated recall was superior to verbal when the pairs were concrete. We interpreted the effect in terms of processes operating at different stages: image inferiority with abstract pairs was due to the difficulty of generating images during the encoding stage. This was supported by reaction time data and failures of mediator discovery obtained during encoding. The superiority of images with concrete pairs was attributed to differential properties of imaginal or verbal processes during storage. Alternatively, imagery mnemonics might enhance the probability of dual coding in LTM.

Organization and Transformation of Information in LTM

The distinction between *synchronous* (and spatially parallel) and *sequential* organization of information in imaginal and verbal systems implies that imagery should be advantageous in memory tasks that involve spatial organization of informational units or retrieval of spatial information from LTM, whereas verbal processes should be superior in tasks that require the sequential order of items to be remembered. A corollary of this is that there is greater freedom from sequential constraints in information processing by imagery than by the verbal system. The author now believes that it might be profitable also to relate differences in the transformational capacities of the two systems to this organizational distinction. That is, the imagery system is specialized for the transformation or reorganization of spatial information in memory but the verbal system is not. Conversely, verbal processes involve a specialized capacity for re-arranging the sequential order of linguistic units, as in grammatical transformations, reorganization of free recall lists, and so on. Of course, the precise form that such spatial and sequential transformations can take is likely to be constrained by the cognitive structures already in long-term memory along with the processing habits or rules associated with them. Thus imaginal transformations are likely to result in conventional spatial arrangements of the imagined elements, although novel or bizarre arrangements can be induced by instructional sets. Similarly, temporal rearrangements of verbal information could be gibberish but they are more likely to follow the associative and grammatical patterns of the language. Many of these suggestions are quite speculative at this time, but hard evidence is available on at least some of them.

Sequential versus nonsequential memory. While pictures are generally remembered better than words, we have also found clear evidence that pictures are inferior to words in sequential memory tasks such as immediate memory span and serial reconstruction unless the subject has enough time to name each picture implicitly during input (Paivio and Csapo, 1969, 1971). Even without such labelling, however, pictures are remembered at least as well as words in free recall or recognition memory tasks, which require memory for the items but not for their order. We take this as evidence that the verbal representational system is specialized for sequential processing whereas the nonverbal image system is not. Precisely analogous experiments comparing imaginal and verbal systems in memory for spatial arrangements of items are not yet available as far as I know, but various studies at least suggest that spatial organization enhances the effectiveness of imagery mnemonics. Thus presentation of pictures or requiring subjects to generate images of items in some kind of integrated spatial relationship results in much better paired associate recall than when the items are pictured as separate entities (e.g., Bower, 1970; Epstein, Rock and Zuckerman, 1960; Wollen and Lowry, 1971). Moreover, such relational images sometimes produce better recall than do analogous sentence mediators (Paivio and Foth, 1970; Segal and Paivio, 1973). Some of the mnemonic effects of imagery seem to be attributable, therefore, to the spatial or synchronous organization of information in imaginal representations. This point will be discussed again later in connection with some recent studies of long-term retention.

Images as analogical structures. The perceptual or pictorial metaphor associated with the concept of imagery, and the idea of synchronic or spatial organization of information suggests that imagery involves an analog process rather than the discrete digital process that seems characteristic of the linguistic system. Such a view has been proposed by various people (e.g., Attneave, 1972; Posner, 1973; Pribram, 1971), and some recent experiments provide rather strong support for the proposal. One is a study by Moyer (1973) in which subjects compared the sizes of named animals from memory. The animal names had been previously ranked according to the relative sizes of the animals themselves. The experimental subjects were visually presented the names of two animals and were required to throw a switch under the name of the larger animal. They made a series of such choices with few errors. The interesting result was that the reaction time for the choice increased systematically as animal size difference decreased. Specifically, RT was largely an inverse linear function of the logarithm of the estimated difference in animal size. Since RT is similarly related to size differences when subjects make direct perceptual comparisons (of lengths of lines, for example), Moyer argued that subjects compare animal names by making an 'internal psychophysical judgment' after first converting the names to analog representations that preserve animal size. Smaller size differences between animals presumably are represented as smaller differences between the internal analogs, and the resulting decreased discriminability is reflected in increased reaction times (p. 183). This interpretation is quite compatible with the general conceptualization of the concrete nature of imaginal representations. It seems to me that such results cannot be handled as easily by any model which assumes that the size attribute of animal names is represented in the form of discrete semantic features of propositions.

The same general conclusion emerges from Roger Shepard's recent experiments on mental rotations and other transformations (e.g., Cooper and Shepard, 1973; Shepard and Feng, 1972; Shepard and Metzler, 1971). One of the experiments reported by Cooper and Shepard (1973) makes the point in a way that is particularly relevant in the present context because it demonstrates a direct correspondence between imagined and actual rotations of alphanumeric figures. This was done by requiring subjects to make a timed comparison between a familiar test stimulus presented in an unpredictable orientation and an imagined stimulus of the same kind, sometimes in a corresponding orientation and sometimes not. The figures used were the upper-case 'R' and the number '2'. Each of these characters could appear as a normal or a backward (mirror-image) test stimulus, in any one of six orientations spaced in equal 60° steps around the circle. Thus, on one trial the letter R might be shown in its normal form, but rotated 60° clockwise; on another trial, it might be shown backward and upside down (i.e., rotated 180°), and so on. Prior to presentation of the actual stimulus, the experimenter orally announced which of the two characters was to be presented. The subject understood that he was to imagine the normal version of the character in its upright orientation. The experimenter then presented the tape recorded commands 'up', 'tip', 'tip', 'down', 'tip', 'tip', at one command per half second. The subject understood that at each 'tip' command he was to rotate clockwise through 60° in synchrony with the command. Immediately following a randomly preselected one of these commands, the probe stimulus appeared in one of the six equally-spaced orientations within the circular field. The subject then was to throw one of two switches as quickly as possible to indicate whether this was the normal or backward version of the character. On half the trials, the probe appeared in the orientation designated by the current auditory command (presumably corresponding to the imagined orientation of the figure), and on the other half it was presented in one of the other five orientations. For each position, one half of the probes were presented in their normal and half in their backward versions.

Two results are especially significant. First, when the probe appeared in the expected orientation, the reaction times were short and relatively independent of absolute orientation. Second, when the probe departed from the expected orientation, reaction time increased markedly with the difference between the expected and presented orientations. The latter function was in fact linear for both normal and backward probes (the reaction times for backward probes were uniformly longer than normal probes—a typical result in these tasks). The overall increase from no departure to a 180° departure was about 400 msec.

These results are consistent with Cooper and Shepard's assumption that, when the probe fails to agree with the imagined orientation, the subject must undertake an additional, post-stimulus rotation in order to achieve a match between the probe and the internal representation of the corresponding normal character. The subjects' introspective reports also agreed with this interpretation: they claimed that they were able to imagine the normal version of the designated character rotating clockwise in time with the auditory commands. They also claimed that they used the mental image as a sort of template against which to compare the test stimulus when it appeared. If a match was achieved, they immediately threw the appropriate switch. If not, they had to determine whether the mismatch resulted from the stimulus being backward or in an unexpected orientation, perhaps by performing an additional operation of reflection.

Cooper and Shepard interpreted such mental rotation as an analog process. They did not claim that it is analogous to physical rotation to the extent of being continuous. Perhaps the rotation was carried out as a sequence of discrete steps which individually may not bear a one-to-one relation to external orientations. However, the entire rotation would qualify as an analog process in the important sense that the mental rotations went through intermediate states that had a one-to-one relation to intermediate orientations in the external world. Whatever its precise nature, the internal representation was in a form that was particularly suitable for comparison with the visual stimulus, and Cooper and Shepard find it tempting to refer to this rotating representation as a visual image. This characterization also accords with the author's own conceptualization of imagery as a process specialized for relatively direct representation and transformation of information concerning external objects and events. The representations in the case of visual imagery correspond substantially with the spatial structures of external objects. Moreover, Cooper and Shepard provide strong evidence that the system is dynamic in the sense that it is capable of rapid transformations of such spatial images. While the representations are undoubtedly abstract and schematic in the sense that they contain less detail than a perceptual image, they nonetheless embody the essential structure of the external stimulus in a way that permits quick and definite comparisons. Again, it is difficult to understand how such functional information could be represented as a list of abstract features or propositions, which according to some theorists, differ in no way from the internal representations corresponding to linguistic information. It seems compelling instead to postulate separate symbolic systems, one of which apparently represents external objects and events in an analog fashion.

This completes the discussion of the dual coding model of long-term memory processes and the evidence that supports one or other aspect of it. Manifestations of long-term memory as reflected in performance on so-called secondary (as compared to primary) memory tasks will be dealt with next.

Imagery and Primary versus Secondary Memory

Distinctions between primary and secondary memory are typically based on inferences from performance on particular tasks or task components. Relevant to this issue, we found that pictures are recalled better than words and concrete words better than abstract, in the Brown–Peterson STM task (Paivio, 1971, p. 228; Paivio and Begg, 1971(b); Paivio and Smythe, 1971). This suggests that imagery might be effective in short-term or primary memory, although it could be argued instead that the Brown–Peterson task involves secondary memory to a high degree (Baddeley and Patterson, 1971). Another of our early experiments (Paivio, Rogers, and Smythe, 1968) showed better recall for pictures than words in both recency and primacy positions in free recall, again suggesting that nonverbal images directly aroused by pictures are mnemonically superior to verbal traces in primary as well as secondary memory. Recently, Madigan, McCabe, and Itatani (1972) found that, in the immediate free recall of each of a series of lists, presentation of pictures along with auditory words increased only the secondary memory component of recall relative to a words-only condition. In delayed recall of all lists, however, the negative recency effect (the depressed second recall that has been observed for the last few items of a list, which are ordinarily well-recalled after the first presentations; e.g., Craik, 1970) was observed only with words, but not with lists of pictures or pictures plus words. The recency effects in several experiments were either non-negative or positive when pictures were involved. Madigan *et al.* suggested that pictures might make direct contact with long-term memory at presentation, rather than through a short-term memory buffer, if one prefers that kind of memory model. Alternatively, they suggest that pictures somehow ensure a deeper level of processing (*cf.* Craik and Lockhart, 1972). This can be taken to mean that dual encoding was more likely with pictures than with words alone as items.

Smith, Barresi, and Gross (1971) investigated imagery mnemonic instructions in relation to the primary-secondary memory distinction. Subjects were presented 19 lists, each consisting of 13 paired-associates with concrete nouns as stimulus members and numbers as responses. After each list, one stimulus item was presented as a probe for the response. All probe positions were sampled over all lists. One half of the subjects were given imagery instructions and half were given repetition instructions prior to the paired-associate task. The results showed that imagery benefited recall from secondary memory (i.e., for pairs from early input positions) but not primary memory (especially the last two pairs). In fact, their analysis suggested that imagery hindered primary memory performance. The interpretation proposed by these investigators was that primary and secondary memory both contain acoustic and semantic information, that this information is copied or transferred from primary to secondary memory, and that the retrieval processes in primary memory are mainly sensitive to acoustic information whereas secondary memory retrieval is primarily sensitive to semantic information. Imagery presumably contributed to semantic information and repetition to acoustic information in this case.

Rowe and Smith (1973) investigated the same problem using a continuous paired-associate task in which subjects were instructed to learn concrete noun pairs using imagery mnemonics, rote repetition, or without any reference to mnemonic techniques. Different pairs were tested after 0, 1, 4, 8, 16, or 64 intervening items. Performance dropped sharply up to lag 4 and then more slowly for all groups. The imagery group showed consistently higher recall at longer lags than did the other two groups, but the three groups did not differ at shorter lags even when recall was analysed in terms of primary and secondary memory components. Unlike Smith *et al.* (1971), however, Rowe and Smith found no evidence that imagery instructions actually inhibited recall from primary memory. They suggested that the discrepancy might be due to the difference in the PA task used in the two experiments. The probe task used by Smith *et al.* permitted subjects to anticipate the end of each 13-item list. As a result, the imagery subjects may have relaxed their image encoding strategy as the end of the list approached because the terminal pairs could be remembered well without mnemonics. The continuous PA paradigm would be less likely to encourage such strategy shifts. Be that as it may, the two experiments agree completely in showing that imagery mnemonics enhance secondary but not primary memory in paired-associate learning.

Further recent evidence on the general problem comes from unpublished research by Fraser Bleasdale and Albert Katz at the University of Western Ontario. In one experiment, six lists of high imagery or abstract words were presented for immediate recall of each list, followed by final free recall of all lists. The lists were presented visually at rates of 0·34, 2·0, or 6·0 sec per word. The results are shown in Figure 4.1. Analyses of these data yielded the following results. First, in agreement with Glanzer and Cunitz (1969), rate affected only the long-term memory part of the serial position curves. Second, high imagery words did not differ from low imagery words at the fastest rate, but the former became increasingly superior at slower rates of presentation. This is to be expected, of course, assuming that the image code takes some minimal amount of time to be aroused. Note also that the superiority of high imagery words at the 2-sec rate occurred primarily in final free recall of all lists, and for the early input positions in immediate free recall, which is consistent with a secondary memory interpretation. At the 6-sec rate, however, high imagery words were far superior to the low at all positions in both immediate and final free recall. This result, too, could be interpreted as secondary memory effects, or as a dual-coding effect in the sense that the slow rate provided ample time for the arousal of images to concrete words in all positions while at the same time being too slow to permit formation of an effective verbal-sequential trace for items at the end of the list. Thus the subjects profited from dual coding but not from the special capacity of the verbal system for storing order information.

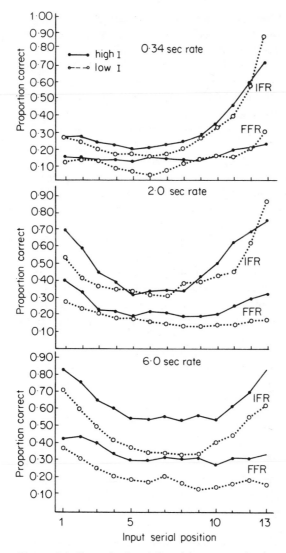

Figure 4.1. Smoothed serial position curves for immediate (IFR) and final free recall (FFR) of high I and low I nouns presented at rates of 0·34, 2·0, and 6·0 sec/item

Further analyses of the data from the above experiment and from two others involved a partitioning of recall scores for items into primary and secondary memory components, where primary memory was defined as a word with no more than six words intervening as an input or output item between its presentation and recall (*cf.* Tulving and Colotla, 1970). The results of two experiments showed an interaction so that recall was better for high imagery than low-imagery words only in the case of secondary memory items. The third experiment yielded a similar interaction when imagery was defined by instructions to image (as compared to pronouncing) concrete words. These results are quite consistent with those obtained by Smith *et al.* and Rowe and Smith.

In summary, the available research on imagery in relation to the distinction between primary and secondary memory shows consistently that imagery conditions facilitate secondary memory performance, perhaps through dual-coding effect on item recall. Imagery is usually not effective in primary memory, perhaps because the defining task sometimes involves a strong component of memory for sequential order as well as for discrete items (e.g. immediate memory span) and imagery does not so effectively represent order information (Paivio and Csapo, 1969). Alternatively or additionally, immediate recall of recent items may be more direct and efficient from a verbal acoustic or phonemic trace than from a nonverbal image, which must be translated into a verbal code before verbal recall is possible. This interpretation is consistent with the assumptions of independence and interconnectedness of coding systems. Imagery conditions facilitate recall from secondary memory because they ensure the arousal of independent memory codes and because retrieval is ordinarily possible from either code through their interconnecting pathways. Image coding would not facilitate verbal retrieval if the verbal trace is available because crossover of information takes more time than direct retrieval from the verbal memory code. This is ordinarily the case in so-called primary memory tasks. In the few studies where imagery apparently facilitated recall from primary memory, it must be assumed that the conditions permitted effective retrieval from the image code.

Long-term Retention

This section deals with the effects of imagery variables on retention over intervals of 24 hours or more. The control of initial acquisition levels is a major problem in this area because imagery conditions usually favour learning. Such control has been achieved in varying degree using different methods. Perhaps for this reason as well as other variations in procedure, the results have also been variable, with imagery sometimes facilitating, sometimes hindering, and sometimes showing no effect on long-term retention relative to a comparison condition of one kind or another. The main findings in the literature will be summarized first and then some recent work will be reviewed in more detail.

Positive effects of imagery have been reported by a number of investigators. Smith and Noble's (1965) subjects learned a list of CVC syllables in serial order, either using an imagery mnemonic technique or under a no-mnemonic control condition. No significant differences in initial learning were found but the imagery subjects were superior to the controls in recall and relearning tests 24 hours later, at least with material of a medium level of meaningfulness.

Schnorr and Atkinson (1969) used a within-subjects design in which half the items in a 32-pair list of concrete nouns were studied by rote repetition and the other half by imagery. Three lists were presented for one study and test trial, and retention was tested again 1 week later. The immediate recall test showed much higher recall for the pairs studied by imagery, the percentage correct for the three lists ranging from 80 to 90, as compared to 30 to 40 per cent for the pairs that were learned by repetition. Imagery also resulted in significantly better long-term retention when the measure of retention was the proportion of items correctly recalled on the initial test that were also recalled correctly 1 week later. Groninger (1971) had subjects learn a list of 25 concrete nouns either by rote or by an imagery mnemonic technique (the classical method of loci). The acquisition criterion was one perfect recitation of the list, which was reached in 14 minutes of study by the imagery group and 17 minutes by the rote repetition group. In recall tests, the imagery group recalled 14 per cent more words after 1 week, and 19 per cent more after 5 weeks than did the rate group.

Other studies have shown quite the reverse when imagery was defined by the concreteness or image-arousing value of the items. In 1970, Butter compared cued recall of noun-digit pairs after 2 minutes, 20 minutes, or 2 days. The nouns varied in concreteness. She found that digits paired with concrete nouns were recalled better than those paired with abstract nouns after 2 minutes, but the effect disappeared after 20 minutes and was completely reversed after 2 days! In a replication of Butter's experiment, Yuille (1971) failed to obtain a reversal of the positive concreteness effect over two days. Nonetheless, he did find that the effect was reduced to nonsignificance after that interval, suggesting that greater forgetting occurred with high imagery than with low imagery stimuli.

Still others show no differential forgetting, higher retention, or somewhat reduced retention as a function of imagery, depending upon how the retention score is calculated relative to some initial value. In considering this issue, Begg and Robertson (1973) recently pointed out that, because memory decay is typically geometrical or exponential (Wickelgren, 1970), conditions starting at relatively higher levels would decline over time relatively faster than conditions starting at lower levels if the decline is expressed in absolute terms. This may not be the case, however, if decline is expressed proportionately. The consequence of such computational differences are clearly seen for free recall data that Csapo and the present author obtained for pictures, their concrete noun labels and abstract nouns (reported in Paivio, 1971, pp. 201–203). The study included incidental as well as intentional recall conditions, and recall tests 5 minutes and 1 week after list presentation for different groups of subjects. Each list contained 72 items of one of the three types. The recall data are shown in Figure 4.2.

The analysis of the mean recall scores showed the usual strong effect of item type, with pictures exceeding concrete nouns, which in turn were remembered better than abstract nouns. This was generally true at both retention intervals and under both incidental and intentional conditions. In fact, retention interval did not interact with item type or conditions. Thus one might conclude that

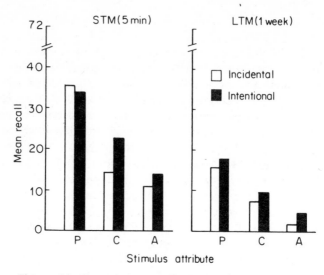

Figure 4.2. Free verbal recall of pictures (P), concrete nouns (C) and abstract nouns (A) after 5 min and 1 week delays under incidental and intentional instructions. From Paivio, 1971 (p. 203)

forgetting was equal for pictures, concrete words, and abstract words, suggest ing that imagery value has no differential effect on retention. The conclusion i quite different, however, when retention at 1 week is expressed as proportio of the recall score obtained for each item type at 5 minutes. Thus, fo intentional conditions, the proportionate retention scores are 0·58 for pictures 0·42 for concrete words, and 0·34 for abstract words. Forgetting was propor tionately less as the material increased in imagery value. The results wer similar for the incidental conditions. Begg and Robertson (1973) similarl compared absolute and proportionate retention effects as a function of imager variables in several experiments reported in the literature and arrived at th same conclusion: the positive effect of imagery appeared to be reduced a longer as compared to shorter intervals when calculated in terms of absolut scores, but it was reduced less or not at all if expressed as a percentage of th short-term imagery effect. Thus the interpretation of the retention effect depends on how the retention score is calculated.

The ideal solution is to equate initial learning for the different conditions although even this presents problems when there are large differences in eas of acquisition. Postman and Burns (1973) recently compared PA learning an retention of four types of stimulus–response pairs which the author ha originally investigated in 1965 and which have been subsequently studied b other investigators. In terms of the imagery or concreteness value of stimulu and response members, the pairs were high–high, high–low, low–high, an low–low. Postman and Burns equated initial learning by taking groups give the different pair types to a common criterion of 12 predicted correct response ut of 16, according to a probability analysis. The trials required to reach this riterion were 4, 6, 9 and 13 for high–high, high–low, low–high, and low–low airs, respectively, reflecting the usual order of learning difficulty as a function f stimulus and response imagery. The startling finding was that this order was ompletely changed on recall tests one week later: retention was poorest for ae high–high pairs, which had been easiest to learn, and best for low–high airs. Low–low and high–low were intermediate in ease of recall. Postman and 3urns interpreted these results in terms of errors of readout from imaginal aediators, basing this on an analysis of intrusion errors. This interpretation will e considered in more detail after reviewing one more series of studies.

Begg and Robertson (1973) reasoned that any one method of equating for aitial learning is open to criticism, so they adopted the strategy of exploring ifferent methods. In addition, they used both item concreteness and anemonic instructions to manipulate imagery in different tasks. Their first xperiment was on free recall of separate lists of concrete and abstract nouns. ach list contained 25 words. Subjects learned one list of each type, with the oncrete–abstract list order counterbalanced for different groups. Learning vas by the incremental method introduced by Mandler and Dean (1969). On he first trial, the subject was presented one word, which he recalled. A second ord was added on the next trial, and the subject then recalled both words. A ew word was similarly added on each succeeding trial, with a recall test after ach, until the subject had been presented all 25 words and attempted recall of he entire list. The procedure produced very effective learning, which did not iffer for concrete and abstract lists. The overall proportions of correct recall ver the 25 trials averaged 0·95 for concrete and 0·94 for abstract lists. In etention tests 48 or 72 hours later, however, concrete words far exceeded bstract words, their respective recall proportions averaging 0·72 and 0·54.

A second experiment compared paired-associate learning of oncrete–concrete and abstract–abstract pairs. Remember that Postman and 3urns had equated pair types in terms of proportion of items correctly recalled, nd that this procedure resulted in large differences in trials to criterion (4 for oncrete–concrete and 13 for abstract–abstract). Begg and Robertson easoned that such a discrepancy inevitably results in a greater total number of orrect recalls for abstract pairs during the learning phase, so they controlled or the number of correct recalls for the two pair types by dropping a pair from he list as soon as it had been correctly recalled once. To determine the effect of acquisition level, different groups were taken to criteria of 50, 75, or 100 per ent correct using the anticipation method. Acquisition stopped at the response hat met the criterion. List length was also varied, different subgroups receiving 6 or 50 pairs that were either concrete or abstract. Long-term retention was ested 72 hours later by one recall trial.

The results for both short and long lists showed that retention was signifi- antly higher for concrete than for abstract pairs in the 100 and 75 per cent riterion groups, but not in the 50 per cent group. The effect was particularly trong with the longer list, where the recall proportions were 0·696 and 0·312 for the concrete and abstract lists, respectively. Thus concreteness strongly facilitated retention over 72 hours when recall was equated at acquisition unless initial learning was at a relatively low level.

Begg and Robertson's third experiment involved both cued and noncued recall of concrete and abstract pairs after five acquisition trials and again after an interval of 1 week. Different groups were given imagery or verbal mnemonic instructions, but this factor did not enter into any significant effects in this experiment—a common finding unless special care is taken to control the subjects' learning strategies (Paivio and Foth, 1971). The results for concreteness were generally the same as in their other experiments: concreteness strongly facilitated both cued and noncued recall at short term and at long term. Moreover, the long-term retention effects held even when recall was conditionalized on short-term recall. In cued recall, for example, 76 per cent of the concrete pairs as compared to 40 per cent of abstract pairs that were correct at short term were also recalled at long term. For noncued recall, the respective conditionals were 60 and 45 per cent. These figures indicate that the long-term retention advantage of concrete over abstract items is greater in cued recall than in noncued recall. This interaction (significant also in other analyses) has important implications for the interpretation of imagery effects in long-term memory, which will be discussed following a summary of the overall picture up to this point.

The Begg and Robertson experiments provide the clearest evidence to date that imagery variables can have strong positive effects on long-term retention even when learning or short-term recall is equated by various procedures. Considering these results together with others in the literature, we can conclude that the majority of studies to date show that imagery facilitates long-term retention at least as much as it facilitates acquisition. A few studies, however, show a diminished memory advantage for imagery over time. Of these, the most dramatic is the virtual reversal of the acquisition effect in long-term retention for high imagery pairs in the Postman and Burns experiment. The contrasting patterns may be a consequence of the different ways in which acquisition has been equated for high and low imagery conditions in the different studies. Although imagery generally has the advantage, however, the Postman and Burns data reveal a possible negative factor related to imagery mediation in associative memory. This factor has appeared in other studies as well and it must be considered in any explanation of long-term memory effects attributed to imagery.

Interpretation of Imagery Effects in Long-term Retention

The kinds of theoretical views reviewed earlier provide a reasonably satisfactory account of why imagery conditions facilitate acquisition and why image superiority might be maintained at a relatively constant level over long retention intervals, but those views do not provide a straightforward explanation of differential forgetting when acquisition level is equated. At least it is not bvious why imagery conditions should result in less forgetting than nonimag-ry (or low imagery) conditions; indeed, greater forgetting as a function of nagery mediation would be more understandable than less forgetting.

The main factors associated with memory effects of imagery variables appear ɔ be dual coding, organization of information, and decoding or retrieval ɔnfusions (i.e., interference). A further real possibility at this time is that trace trength is simply stronger for visual images than for verbal codes in memory, lthough I do not find that statement very satisfying in the absence of any good 1eoretical basis for such a difference. Let us consider each of these factors in ɹrn.

Dual coding. Recall that this hypothesis states that high imagery conditions re superior to low imagery because the former are more likely to arouse nagery as well as verbal coding in memory. Such dual coding simply increases he probability of correct recall because the same nominal response can be ɘtrieved from either of the independent codes provided that they are also 1terconnected. It is important to note, however, that this hypothesis does not 1 itself imply a differential rate of forgetting for dually and singly coded items. f the theory is to encompass differential forgetting it needs elaboration that akes into account qualitative differences in the two postulated codes, related ·erhaps to such factors as organization of information or resistance to 1terference.

Organization of information. Recall that this important theoretical distinc-ion between the postulated memory system states that their information ontent is organized in very different ways. The information in images appears ɔ be structured and integrated in a figural, spatial, or synchronous manner so hat the components of the image are simultaneously available for retrieval, lthough the output or readout from the system is necessarily serial. The verbal ystem, however, organizes information sequentially, that is, it concatenates liscrete linguistic units into higher-order sequential structures. Begg (1972, 973) has recently spelled out and tested an important implication of such a iew. Specifically, he proposed that compound images can be integrated in the ense that multiple components of information are truly unitized in memory. 'hus the compound may take up no more memory space than each of its eparate components, and each component can effectively redintegrate the ntire compound given an appropriate retrieval cue. In support of the memory pace notion, Begg found that subjects could free recall the same proportion of ʋords from a list of adjective–noun phrases as from a list of individual words vhen the phrases were high in imagery value (e.g., *white horse*), but propor-ionately only half as many words from phrase lists as from word lists when the ·hrases were abstract (e.g., *basic theory*). Thus, concrete phrases functioned ssentially like unitary words in memory, whereas abstract phrases functioned ɩke separate word units. A second finding was that the presentation of one 1ember of the pair as a retrieval cue increased proportionate recall relative to noncued conditions only in the case of the concrete phrases. This suggests that the components were truly integrated in high imagery phrases so that redinteg ration was possible, but this did not occur in the case of abstract phrases presumably because each phrase was stored as a string of words rather than as a unitized image. The image interpretation was directly supported in a subse quent experiment (Begg, 1973) which showed that cued recall substantially exceeded noncued recall when word pairs were stored as integrated images but not when each member of a pair was imaged separately.

Begg and Robertson (1973) also tested the implications of the integration hypothesis in the long-term retention experiments described earlier. Re member that their first experiment showed much better long-term retention of concrete than of abstract nouns. They also found that concreteness was highly related to a measure of output organization both during acquisition and long-term retention. They interpreted this as correlational evidence for the imagery-organization hypothesis: the images aroused by concrete words could be organized into complex images in memory and retrieval of part of the compound would provide subjective cues for retrieving or redintegrating the rest of the imagery, thereby enhancing recall.

Further evidence was obtained in their third experiment, which included both cued and noncued recall of pairs of concrete or abstract nouns. They found that cued recall generally exceeded noncued recall but, in support of the redintegration hypothesis, the facilitative effect of cueing was greater with concrete than with abstract pairs. Moreover, this interaction was more pronounced in long-term than in short-term recall, suggesting that imagery particularly enhanced the retention of associative information over time. Finally, as a measure of the degree to which pairs of words became associated even in noncued recall, Begg and Robertson calculated the ratios of word recalled in pairs as compared to recall of individual words. The analysis showed that concrete words were significantly more likely to be recalled in pairs than were abstract words, and the concrete conditional probability of pair recall diminished less over the seven day retention interval than did the abstract. This is consistent with the view that concrete pairs were likely to be stored as unitized images and such image integration often resulted in joint recall of the word pairs even under free recall conditions.

The evidence for the imagery-organization hypothesis seems quite solid, but the theory does not as yet provide a complete account of long-term retention. One problem is that superior recall has been obtained for high imagery nouns even when inter-item organisation scores did not differ for concrete and abstract words (e.g., Frincke, 1968; Paivio, Yuille and Rogers, 1969). This means that higher inter-item organization (at least as measured by current indices of organization) is not a necessary condition for obtaining imagery effects in recall. Secondly, as in the case of the dual coding hypothesis, the imagery organization hypothesis does not suggest why such organization should be increasingly effective in preserving memories over time. More information may be effectively stored in imaginal than in verbal form, but there is no reason to suppose that the rate of forgetting should be less for the images than for the words. Nevertheless, that is what is suggested by the data obtained by Begg and Robertson and others.

Differential interference. Perhaps interference theory can throw some light on the problem despite the difficulties it has recently encountered as a theory of forgetting. The form it takes in this case differs somewhat from classical interference theory, however, and more rather than less forgetting could be predicted from the theory under high imagery conditions. Since image-mediated verbal recall requires that the image or some component of it be transformed or decoded back into the appropriate verbal response, decoding errors should be a strong possibility (Paivio, 1971, pp. 385–386). This can be appreciated most readily in the case of paired-associate recall of concrete noun responses that have synonyms which could be mediated by the same response-term image. The image of an adult female, for example, could generate 'lady' or 'woman' as a response. The same process might operate in a more subtle way in other instances. Just as a visual scene can be described verbally in various ways, so might an internal image generate different descriptions. This hypothetical process is analogous to interference from natural language habits. Rather than being based on purely verbal associative habits, as classical interference theory implies, this version is based on descriptive habits related originally to concrete objects and events but capable also of being activated by internal memory representations of such events through the interconnections between the two systems.

Such a theory could predict relatively more intrusion errors under imagery-mediated than under rote learning conditions because the latter does not require a transformation of the verbal item into a nonverbal memory represen-tation. Forgetting could occur for other reasons as well, but this should not be reflected in extralist intrusion errors to the same extent as image-mediated recall. This prediction would not necessarily apply to verbal mediation, however. Suppose that a subject uses a phrase or sentence to associate a pair of nouns, and one of the nouns is presented as a retrieval cue on the recall trial. That may redintegrate the sentence or part of it, but the response term may be missing. If so, the problem becomes one of response selection, just as in the case of image-mediated verbal recall, and there is no straightforward way of predicting which kind of mediator, verbal or imaginal, would present the greater problem in this regard without more information than we presently have on descriptive habits on the one hand, and verbal-associative or grammat-ical habits on the other.

In any case, we do have some empirical data on aspects of the problem. Reference has already been made to the Postman and Burns study, in which they found quite a different pattern of long-term retention as compared to acquisition of pairs in which stimulus and response nouns varied in imagery-concreteness. Specifically, they found that high–high pairs were remembered most poorly, low–high pairs were best, and high–low and low–low imagery pairs were intermediate in the long-term retention test. They also found that the number of intrusions from outside the list paralleled the recall scores, that is, most intrusions occurred with high–high pairs, and fewest with low–high pairs. Postman and Burns' analysis is along the lines already described. Mediated association of high–high pairs is likely to be predominantly imaginal rather than verbal. Two things are likely to happen as a function of time: (a) the image may change progressively, becoming more blurred or conventional (Reese, 1970, has related such a possibility to the Gestalt concept of 'leveling'); or (b), its translation into the appropriate verbal equivalent is subject to decoding errors. Retention may be best for low–high pairs, they suggest, because the juxtaposition of an abstract and a concrete word represents a unit sequence of low probability in the language, and because the imagery value of the responses may enhance their long-term availability. The combination appears to create a high degree of resistance to interference. The author agrees generally with this analysis, although he also believes that the observed effects of such factors may be exaggerated in the Postman and Burns study because of the great differences in the number of trials that the different pairs required to reach a common acquisition criterion. Their study nonetheless highlights processes that may occur in a less exaggerated form in other studies.

A recent study by Yuille (1973) provided direct evidence on the retention of mediators as well as their mediational effect for the different pair types. Subjects received one study trial with a list containing concrete–concrete, concrete–abstract, abstract–concrete, and abstract–abstract pairs. They were required to form imaginal mediators for half the pairs of each type and verbal mediators for the other half. They drew representations of their images and wrote the sentence mediators. A cued recall test followed immediately for half the subjects, and all subjects returned for a recall test one week later. In the recall test, they were required to recall both the response and the mediator for each pair. Mediator recall was scored as correct or incorrect with high agreement by two independent judges.

Recall as a function of pair type generally showed facilitating effects of both stimulus and response imagery, as in previous research. Recall did not differ for image-mediated and sentence-mediated pairs except for subjects tested only after the one-week delay. These subjects recalled more with images than with sentences as mediators, at least in the case of concrete–concrete and abstract–abstract pairs. The most relevant results for present purposes, however, pertain to mediator recall and decoding errors. Recall of both types of mediators was generally best for pairs with concrete stimuli and poorest for pairs with abstract stimuli. Imaginal mediators were generally recalled better than sentence mediators for all pair types, although in the case of subjects who only received the delayed recall test, the image superiority was especially marked for pairs with concrete stimuli. Thus, Yuille's results do not support the view that images are more likely than verbal mediators to become degraded over a long retention interval. We **must** accordingly look to other factors to explain the finding that response **recall** was not consistently better under imagery than sentence mediation conditions. Decoding errors are the most likely candidate. Yuille defined a decoding error as an intrusion error or response omission that occurred despite correct recall of the mediator. These errors were higher for image-mediated than for sentence-mediated pairs only when the response term was abstract (C–A and A–A pairs), as would be expected from the assumption that the interconnection or referential relation is indirect in the case of abstract nouns and images. In general, then, Yuille's results seem to involve some kind of trade-off between positive effects of imagery conditions, attributable to dual coding or superior memorability of images, or both, and negative effects of imagery associated with their greater susceptibility to decoding errors under some conditions.

These conclusions are consistent with those arising from some earlier studies. For example, Anderson and Hidde (1970) found incidental associative recall to be much better under imagery than under a verbal coding condition, but more intrusion errors (particularly synonym intrusions) also occurred with imagery. Begg and Paivio (1969), in a study that required subjects to detect semantic and lexical changes in remembered sentences, found much better detection of semantic than of lexical changes when the sentences were concrete and high in image-arousing value, but lexical changes were noticed better than semantic when the sentences were abstract. The results suggest that semantic memory was effectively mediated by imagery, but at the expense of memory for the exact lexical items.

In summary, the studies to date have revealed more often than not, that imagery conditions can result in superior recall, perhaps because they enhance the probability of dual coding or because integrated images are mnemonically superior to verbal mediators, or both. Paradoxically, images are also particularly subject to decoding errors under some circumstances, which would explain why more errors might sometimes occur after a retention interval for image-mediated than for verbally-retained linguistic material. But none of the available information satisfactorily explains why image-mediated memories often seem to be more resistant to forgetting than 'pure' verbal memories, despite the greater susceptibility of the former to decoding errors under certain circumstances.

Acknowledgements

This paper was written while the author was on a study leave at the Laboratory of Experimental Psychology, University of Sussex, England, supported in part by a Canada Council Leave Fellowship. The author's research reported in this paper was supported by grants from the National Research Council of Canada (A0087) and the University of Western Ontario Research Fund.

References

Anderson, J. R. and Bower, G. H. (1973). *Human Associative Memory*. Washington, D.C.: Winston.

Anderson, R. C. and Hidde, J. L. (1971). Imagery and sentence learning. *Journal of Educational Psychology*, **62**, 526–530.

Anderson, R. C. and McGaw, B. (1973). On the representation of meanings of general terms. *Journal of Experimental Psychology*, **101**, 301–306.

Attneave, F. (1972). Representation of physical space. In A. W. Melton and E. Martin (Eds) *Coding Processes in Human Memory*. New York: Winston–Wiley.

Atwood, G. E. (1971). An experimental study of visual imagination and memory. *Cognitive Psychology*, **2**, 290–299.

Baddeley, D. A., Grant, S., Wight, E., and Thomson, N. (1973). Imagery and visual working memory. Paper presented at the Fifth International Symposium on Attention and Performance, Stockholm.

Baddeley, A. D. and Patterson, K. (1971). Relation between long-term and short-term memory. *British Medical Bulletin*, **27**, 237–242.

Bahrick, H. P. and Bahrick, P. (1971). Independence of verbal and visual codes of the same stimuli. *Journal of Experimental Psychology*, **91**, 344–346.

Begg, I. (1972). Recall of meaningful phrases. *Journal of Verbal Learning and Verbal Behavior*, **11**, 431–439.

Begg, I. (1973). Imagery and integration in the recall of words. *Canadian Journal of Psychology*, **27**, 159–167.

Begg, I. and Paivio, A. (1969). Concreteness and imagery in sentence meaning. *Journal of Verbal Learning and Verbal Behaviour*, **8**, 821–827.

Begg, I. and Robertson, R. (1973). Imagery and long-term retention. *Journal of Verbal Learning and Verbal Behavior*, **12**, 689–700.

Berlyne, D. E. (1965). *Structure and Direction in Thinking*. New York: Wiley.

Bousfield, W. A. (1961). The problem of meaning in verbal behavior. In C. N. Cofer (Ed.) *Verbal Learning and Verbal Behavior*. New York: McGraw-Hill.

Bower, G. H. (1970). Imagery as a relational organizer in associative learning. *Journal of Verbal Learning and Verbal Behavior*, **9**, 529–533.

Bower, G. H. (1972). Mental imagery and associative learning. In L. Gregg (Ed.) *Cognition in Learning and Memory*. New York: Wiley.

Brooks, L. R. (1968). Spatial and verbal components of the act of recall. *Canadian Journal of Psychology*, **22**, 349–368.

Brooks, L. R. (1972). Visual and verbal processes in internal representation. In E. Galanter (Ed.) *Cognitive Processes*. New York: Academic Press.

Butter, M. J. (1970). Differential recall of paired associates as a function of arousal and concreteness-imagery levels. *Journal of Experimental Psychology*, **84**, 252–256.

Bugelski, B. R. (1971). The definition of the image. In S. J. Segal (Ed.) *Imagery: Current Cognitive Approaches*. New York: Academic Press.

Collins, A. M. and Quillian, M. R. (1972). How to make a language user. In E. Tulving and W. Donaldson (Eds) *Organization of Memory*. New York: Academic Press.

Colman, F. and Paivio, A. (1970). Pupillary dilation and mediation processing during paired-associate learning. *Canadian Journal of Psychology*, **24**, 261–270.

Cooper, L. A. and Shepard, R. N. (1973). Chronometric studies of the rotation of mental images. In W. G. Chase (Ed.) *Visual Information Processing*. New York: Academic Press.

Craik, F. I. M. (1970). The fate of primary memory items in free recall. *Journal of Verbal Learning and Verbal Behavior*, **9**, 143–148.

Craik, F. I. M. and Lockhart, R. S. (1972). Levels of processing: a framework for memory research. *Journal of Verbal Learning and Verbal Behavior*, **11**, 671–684.

Epstein, W., Rock, I. and Zuckerman, C. B. (1960). Meaning and familiarity in associative learning. *Psychological Monographs*, **74**, (4, Whole No. 491).

Ernest, C. H. and Paivio, A. (1969). Imagery ability in paired-associate and incidental learning. *Psychonomic Science*, **15**, 181–182.

Ernest, C. H. and Paivio, A. (1971). Imagery and verbal associative latencies as a function of imagery ability. *Canadian Journal of Psychology*, **25**, 83–90.

Frincke, G. (1968). Word characteristics, associative-relatedness, and the free-recall of nouns. *Journal of Verbal Learning and Verbal Behavior*, **7**, 366–372.

Gazzaniga, M. S. (1970). *The Bisected Brain.* New York: Appleton.

Glanzer, M. and Cunitz, A. R. (1966). Two storage mechanisms in free recall. *Journal of Verbal Learning and Verbal Behavior*, **5**, 351–360.

Groninger, L. D. (1971). Mnemonic imagery and forgetting. *Psychonomic Science*, **23**, 161–163.

Hebb, D. O. (1968). Concerning imagery. *Psychological Review*, **75**, 466–477.

Jorgensen, C. C. and Kintsch, W. (1973). The role of imagery in the evaluation of sentences. *Cognitive Psychology*, **4**, 110–116.

Kimura, D. (1973). The asymmetry of the human brain. *Scientific American*, **228**, 70–78.

Klee, H. and Eysenck, M. W. (1973). Comprehension of abstract and concrete sentences. *Journal of Verbal Learning and Verbal Behavior*, **12**, 522–529.

Madigan, S., McCabe, L. and Itatani, E. (1972). Immediate and delayed recall of words and pictures. *Canadian Journal of Psychology*, **26**, 407–414.

Mandler, G. and Dean, P. J. (1969). Seriation: development of serial order in free recall. *Journal of Experimental Psychology*, **81**, 207–215.

Milner, B. and Teuber, H. L. (1968). Alteration of perception and memory in man: reflections on methods. In L. Weiskrantz (Ed.) *Analysis of Behavioral Change*, New York: Harper and Row.

Mowrer, O. R. (1960). *Learning Theory and the Symbolic Processes.* New York: Wiley.

Moyer, R. S. (1973). Comparing objects in memory: evidence suggesting an internal psychophysics. *Perception and Psychophysics*, **13**, 180–184.

Nelson, D. L. and Brooks, D. H. (1973a). Independence of phonetic and imaginal features. *Journal of Experimental Psychology*, **97**, 1–7.

Nelson, D. L. and Brooks, D. H. (1973b). Functional independence of pictures and their verbal memory codes. *Journal of Experimental Psychology*, **98**, 44–48.

Olson, D. R. (1970). Language and thought: Aspects of a cognitive theory of semantics. *Psychological Review*, **77**, 257–273.

Osgood, C. E. (1957). Motivational dynamics of language behavior. In M. R. Jones (Ed.) *Nebraska Symposium on Motivation.* Lincoln: University of Nebraska Press.

Paivio, A. (1971). *Imagery and Verbal Processes.* New York: Holt, Rinehart and Winston.

Paivio, A. (1972). Symbolic and sensory modalities of memory. In M. E. Meyer, (Ed.) *The Third Western Symposium on Learning: Cognitive Learning.* Bellingham: Western Washington State College.

Paivio, A. (1973). Psychophysiological correlates of imagery. In F. J. McGuigan and R. Schoonover (Eds) *The Psychophysiology of Thinking.* New York: Academic Press.

Paivio, A. and Begg I. (1971a). Imagery and associative overlap in short-term memory. *Journal of Experimental Psychology*, **89**, 40–45.

Paivio, A. and Begg, I. (1971b). Imagery and comprehension latencies as a function of sentence concreteness and structure. *Perception and Psychophysics*, **10**, 408–412.

Paivio, A. and Csapo, K. (1969). Concrete-image and verbal memory codes. *Journal of Experimental Psychology*, **80**, 279–285.

Paivio, A. and Csapo, K. (1971). Short-term sequential memory for pictures and words. *Psychonomic Science*, **24**, 50–51.

Paivio, A. and Csapo, K. (1973). Picture superiority in free recall: Imagery or dual coding? *Cognitive Psychology*, **5**, 176–206.

Paivio, A. and Ernest, C. (1971). Imagery ability and visual perception of verbal and nonverbal stimuli. *Perception and Psychophysics*, **10**, 429–432.

Paivio, A. and Foth, D. (1970). Imaginal and verbal mediators and noun concreteness in paired associate learning: The elusive interaction. *Journal of Verbal Learning and Verbal Behavior*, **9**, 384–390.

Paivio, A. and O'Neill, B. J. (1970). Visual recognition thresholds and dimensions of word meaning. *Perception and Psychophysics*, **8**, 273–275.

Paivio, A., Rogers, T. B. and Smythe, P. C. (1968). Why are pictures easier to recall than words? *Psychonomic Science*, **11**, 137–138.

Paivio, A. and Smythe, P. C. (1971). Word imagery, frequency, and meaningfulness in short-term memory. *Psychonomic Science*, **22**, 333–335.

Paivio, A., Yuille, J. C. and Rogers, T. B. (1969). Noun imagery and meaningfulness in free and serial recall. *Journal of Experimental Psychology*, **79**, 509–514.

Piaget, J. and Inhelder, B. (1966). *L'Image Mentale chez l'Enfant*. Paris: Presses Universitaires de France.

Posner, M. I. (1973). Coordination of internal codes. In W. G. Chase (Ed.) *Visual Information Processing*. New York: Academic Press.

Postman, L. and Burns, S. (1973). Experimental analysis of coding processes. *Memory and Cognition*, **1**, 503–507.

Pribram, K. (1971). *Language of the Brain: Experimental Paradoxes and Principles of Neuropsychology*. Englewood Cliffs: Prentice-Hall.

Pylyshyn, Z. W. (1973). What the mind's eye tells the mind's brain: a critique of mental imagery. *Psychological Bulletin*, **80**, 1–24.

Reese, H. W. (1970). Imagery and contextual meaning. In H. W. Reese (Chm.) Imagery in children's learning: A symposium. *Psychological Bulletin*, **73**, 404–414.

Rowe, E. J. (1972). Imagery and frequency processes in verbal discrimination learning. *Journal of Experimental Psychology*, **95**, 140–146.

Rowe, E. J. and Smith, S. K. (1973). Imagery effects in continuous paired-associate learning. *Journal of Experimental Psychology*, **99**, 290–292.

Rumelhart, D. E., Lindsay, P. H. and Norman, D. A. (1972). A process model for long-term memory. In E. Tulving and W. Donaldson (Eds) *Organization and Memory*. New York: Academic Press.

Schnorr, J. A. and Atkinson, R. C. (1969). Repetition versus imagery instructions in the short- and long-term retention of paired-associates. *Psynchonomic Science*, **15** 183–184.

Seamon, J. G. and Gazzaniga, M. S. (1973). Coding strategies and cerebral laterality effects. *Cognitive Psychology*, **5**, 249–256.

Segal, A. U. and Paivio, A. (1973). Imaginal and verbal cognitive structures: encoding and retrieval differences. Unpublished manuscript, University of Western Ontario.

Sheehan, P. W. (1966). Accuracy and vividness of visual images. *Perceptual and Motor Skills*, **23**, 391–398.

Shepard, R. N. and Feng, C. (1972). A chronometric study of mental paper folding. *Cognitive Psychology*, **3**, 228–243.

Shepard, R. N. and Metzler, J. (1971). Mental rotation of three-dimensional objects. *Science*, **171**, 701–703.

Skinner, B. F. (1953). *Science and Human Behavior*. New York: Macmillan.

Smith, E. E., Barresi, J. and Gross, A. E. (1971). Imaginal versus verbal coding and the primary-secondary memory distinction. *Journal of Verbal Learning and Verbal Behavior*, **10**, 597–603.

Smith, R. K. and Noble, C. E. (1965). Effects of a mnemonic technique applied to verbal learning and memory. *Perceptual and Motor Skills*, **21**, 123–134.

Sperry, R. W. (1973). Lateralization of function in the surgically separated hemispheres. In F. J. McGuigan and R. Schoonover (Eds) *The Psychophysiology of Thinking*. New York: Academic Press.

Staats, A. W. (1968). *Learning, Language and Cognition*. New York: Holt, Rinehart and Winston.

Tulving, E. and Colotla, V. A. (1970). Free recall of trilingual lists. *Cognitive Psychology*, **1**, 86–98.

Wickelgren, W. A. (1970). Multitrace strength theory. In D. A. Norman (Ed.) *Models of Human Memory*. New York: Academic Press.

Wollen, K. A. and Lowry, D. H. (1971). Effects of imagery on paired-associate learning. *Journal of Verbal Learning and Verbal Behavior*, **10**, 276–284.

Yuille, J. C. (1971). Does the concreteness effect reverse with delay? *Journal of Experimental Psychology*, **88**, 147–148.

Yuille, J. C. (1973). A detailed examination of mediation in PA learning. *Memory and Cognition*, **1**, 333–342.

Yuille, J. C. and Paivio, A. (1967). Latency of imaginal and verbal mediators as a function of stimulus and response concreteness-imagery. *Journal of Experimental Psychology*, **75**, 540–544.

Part II

Organization

Chapter 5

Structuring Experience—Some Discussion Points

John Morton

General Background

It is clear that it is no longer profitable to talk about 'Long -Term Memory' as though it were a single system operating on a single principle with a common code. From the kinds of errors (or, more impressively, the lack of errors) I make when reciting well learned speeches or singing a song, I am forced to conclude that they are coded in my memory in some literal (e.g. phonological) form. When I recall the contents of a scientific paper, whatever I do there is little or no literal recall, and the errors reflect the amount of reconstruction and assimilation involved at some stage between the reading and the recall. When I describe the route from Cambridge to Steeple Morden (once travelled, recently) I draw the information largely from visual images and cannot repress the image of the car I was travelling with breaking down on the way. The more familiar route to Oxford, on the other hand, has as its first expression the simple verbal form 'Bedford, Buckingham, Bicester'.

Some groups of items are held in ordered lists which usually reflect a natural or conventional ordering such as the names of the months or the four gospels; other groups, such as Shakespeare's plays or the seven dwarfs, although small, are very labile in order and ease of recall. If we do have lists of such items their organization must be very different from the ordered lists. This reflects the way they are learned and is reflected in the more complex way in which they are retrieved.

Currently there are attempts to formalize a division of long-term memory into two parts. Tulving (1972) proposes a distinction between Semantic Memory and Episodic Memory. Bruner (1969) makes a related distinction between 'memory with record' where specific events are recoverable and 'memory without record'. In the latter case experience is incorporated into some larger structure changing, for example, the rules by which the organism operates, 'but which are virtually inaccessible in memory as specific encounters.' There is, of course, also the possibility of a clear record of an event together with an abstraction based on the event with or without any indication of the relationship between the event and the abstraction. Certain authors have also noted the case where the record of the event is singularly inaccessible but the abstraction plays a considerable role in influencing behaviour. Another example of a division is Mandler's (1967) separation of a buffer memory from long-term storage. Related to this is the division into Lexicon and Topicon suggested by Smith and Claxton (1972). Such divisions incorporate a number of factors including:

Formal (or shared) knowledge *vs* idiosyncratic experience.
Permanent (relatively) storage with limited access *vs* limited storage for currently relevant material with much more free access.
Time independent knowledge *vs* time coded knowledge.
Linguistic information *vs* knowledge of the world.

While suggesting the Semantic–Episodic division, Tulving also stresses the interdependence of the two systems and other workers are confirming what a number of linguists had previously discovered—that a reasonable semantics for a language system has to include knowledge of the world. Thus, Collins and Quillian, who started off with a fairly simple, hierarchial model of semantics with fairly limited methods of operation have had to complicate their descriptions of how people operate in verifying simple propositions (1972). Winograd (1971), Rumelhart, Lindsey and Norman (1972) and Norman (1972) give other evidence favouring the breakdown of sharp divisions.

Local Background

My own interest in this area, apart from the general problem of the language user (Morton, 1968), springs from some problems in applied psychology. The specific issue was the design of computer systems for patients' records using a visual display and a keyboard. As the nurses would be expected to operate the system in addition to their other duties it is not feasible to design a command system involving special syntax and mnemonics. Such systems are suitable for full-time operators, (such as airline booking clerks), but the likelihood of forgetting the correct forms or making a keying error is too high for them to be acceptable to nonprofessionals. Instead, then, the system has to be organized in terms of successive multiple choices. Thus at one stage in the interaction the user might see on the screen the sequence of instructions shown in Figure 5.1.

Suppose the user wishes to enter the information that a patient has recovered sufficiently to have solid foods. She would then press key number 4 and proceed to the next level. If the information to be entered was that the patient had recovered sufficiently to bath himself however the choice is no longer obvious. If the same patient can now also go to the lavatory by himself, can get up for visitors or go into the TV room then the current focus in the users' mind would be Mobility. If, on the other hand, she is in the process of revising the *bathing*

Nursing Procedures

1. Bathing
2. Mobility
3. Care of Pressure Areas
4. Feeding

5. Oral Hygiene
6. Lavatory
7. Dressings
8. Special Treatments

9. Investigations

Figure 5.1. A display which might occur in the middle of an interaction between human and computer where the latter is the repository of patients' records

status of all the patients on the ward then the natural choice would be key 1. A strict single hierarchy would be very inconvenient in this situation.

In one operating system, at Kings College Hospital in London from which the above example is taken, problems of this kind were reduced by involving the nursing staff in the design of the system. The system nevertheless took some time to evolve. The end product can be described by a directed graph whose organization reflects the organization of the information in the user. What we would like to do is find experimental procedures which will readily reveal at least the major part of these structures.

Another problem is that the internal organization is likely to be different for different groups of people. Thus, in a hospital, nurses will be likely to classify patients with tonsilitis and appendicitis together in contrast to throat cancer and prostate operations since the former need little nursing and the latter pair more intensive nursing. For medical staff, on the other hand, it would be more natural to classify the tonsilectomy and the throat cancer patients together and the prostate and appendix patients together on the basis of the parts of the body concerned.

A more dramatic example of the same principle can be seen in the context of a large store. Given that there are too many departments to display on the screen at the same time then some superordinate headings have to be devised. For inter-departmental communication it seems likely that the most appropriate headings would reflect the physical layout of the store since this is the classification with which people in the store are used to working. For customers however, ordering goods via their computer link, such a structure would not be very useful and headings such as 'food, clothing, hardware, garden, kitchen . . . ' would be appropriate as a first-level classification.

Our practical problem, then, is that of devising methods for discovering the principles of organization in memory. There follows preliminary reports on the results of three enquiries.

Colours

Informants, mainly members of staff of the APU, were asked to 'give as quickly as possible as many names of colours you can think of'. This they did with their eyes closed. The spoken lists were taken down in shorthand, and the informants were stopped when they paused for 20 seconds or more, when they made some comment like 'do you want details/sub-divisions?' or 'I don't know any more' or when they started to produce compound names such as 'Royal Blue' or 'Shocking Pink'. When they had finished they were asked if they knew the 'colours of the rainbow'. Of 33 people asked, 18 were able to recite the seven in the proper order. Of these only five had produced the seven in order in the main task. The other 13 either omitted one item or had some colours in a different order from the spectral one. Of the 15 who could not recite the spectrum colours, only one mentioned them all in the main task. Some of these people knew mnemonics for the spectrum, such as 'Richard of York Gains Battles In Vain', 'Read Only Your Garden Book In Verse' or 'Very Idle Blondes Get You On Retreat'. However, it was clear that they only had access to the colours sequence through the mnemonic and not as an independent list.

The performance of the people who could recite the spectrum must be interpreted with care. Some claimed they were not using the spectrum list in the main task but were using some other strategy, or no strategy at all. A list such as RGBOYVI could be produced by a combination of retrieving individual colour names plus inter-colour associations without reference to the spectral list. In the other cases we could suppose that the list was retrieved from store correctly but output incorrectly owing to the pressure for speed. Still, it is unlikely that the alphabet, the months or the four gospels would be subject to such influences. This was checked by an enquiry in which 16 people were asked to 'recall as quickly as possible, not necessarily in the correct order the books of the New Testament'. Twelve produced 'Matthew, Mark, Luke, John' immediately. The other four blocked (i.e. could think of no New Testament books for about 30 seconds) but continued in the usual way when cued with 'Matthew'. There are a number of reasons why this might be so—e.g. amount of experience, length of list and extent of inter-item associations and classifications between items which are non-adjacent and on the list. All we can say is that the spectral list, when it is known, exerts strong influence on recall of colour names but that it does not dominate.

Turning now to colours outside the spectral list we can find other differences between the groups, which seem to illuminate the recall strategies. The two groups produced about the same average number of non-spectral names, 5·2 for the spectral, (S) group and 5·4 for the Non-spectral (N) group. They differed, however, in respect of the triple Black–White–Grey, and in the three most frequent (by Thorndike–Lorge) non-spectral colours, Brown, Pink and Purple. The N group named an average of 4·0 of these six, the S group only 2·2. This difference was tested by calculating for each subject the difference between the number of this set which was mentioned and the number of other non-spectral colours mentioned. The distributions of these differences for the two groups were compared using a Mann–Whitney which gave $z = 3·032$ ($P = 0·0012$). Some of the S group explicitly rejected Black–White–Grey as not being colours (though if one was mentioned it was recorded). However, as performance on Brown, Pink and Purple was equivalent to that on the other names the author is inclined to minimize the influence of such internalized theories. Instead I wish to suggest that a word-frequency effect operated for the *N* group, but the *S* group, being committed to a general strategy of retrieval from LTM, effectively dampened the word-frequency effect. Such a suggestion implies a multi-component model of word retrieval, with colour names being retrieved explicitly from LTM as a result of some strategy or being produced by some more peripheral mechanism, such as the Logogen System (Morton, 1969) as a result of a semantic context 'colour'. The latter method would be expected to show the word frequency effect.

Store Departments

Having claimed blithely that people who work in a store have a model of the store in their heads it was thought useful to present some data backing up the claim. Pennie Ottley persuaded one of the stores in Cambridge to cooperate, and interviewed 29 people who worked there. These interviews took place in the departments where they worked. The informants were presented with a piece of paper and asked:

'Please write down as quickly as possible the departments you would expect to find in a large store. Be fairly specific—for example you might divide "sports equipment" into "Indoor Sports" and "Outdoor Sports".'

These instructions were worded to minimize the likelihood of us being accused of having fixed the data by deliberately biassing the informants, and any questions about the detail of the task were answered guardedly. The 'Sports' example was chosen to make sure we got the right level of detail—the store we used had no Sports department. Subsequently 33 female members of the APU subject panel were asked the same questions with the name of the store we had used thrown in as an example.

We expected to find two clear influences in the lists from the store workers. One of them would be the physical layout of the store; the other would be a classificatory influence, with departments related to clothing all grouped together, for example. These two classifications were related, as in most stores, but we expected the physical layout to reveal itself unambiguously.

In fact we were wrong. The only clear influence of the working situation was that 11 of the 29 people named their own departments first. From then on most people looked as though they were going on a random walk. If we analysed the data in complete detail we would probably be able to show that the store workers produce significantly more pairs of names of physically adjacent departments than do the control subjects, but that was not the point. We thought we were demonstrating something obvious. Several people have been at pains to point out that for a task like the one we gave there are many possible retrieval strategies and influences. All we established was that the other factors, whatever they were, were stronger than that of the layout of the store. Semantic groups were apparent, but what is one to make of a sequence like . . . TOYS, FASHIONS, TOOLS, PERFUMES, CAMPING . . . ? The answer is probably 'nothing'.

Although we have not yet run any further tests on our informants, we have no reason to believe that the subjects had no knowledge of the layout. It was just that we asked the wrong question to reveal that knowledge. Yet there were some appreciable differences between the two groups of subjects. One of them was in the number of departments mentioned which were not present in our store. We checked this by pairing each store worker at random with a control subject who had produced the same number of departments in her list plus or minus one. We were able to match 19 pairs in this way. A Wilcoxon test on the number of extra-store departments gave a $T = 21$ ($P < 0.005$). The reason was clear—the control subjects used other stores as models: the store-workers in general only use their own, in whatever way.

The most common of the extra-store departments were the 'sports' departments which had been given as an illustration in the instructions to the subjects. It might seem that this is a simple case of priming. However, 11/29 of the store workers and 5/33 of the controls did not mention sports, and none of the subjects mentioned it first. For the control subjects the sports departments were evenly distributed through the list; for the store workers there was a strong tendency for them to be at the end of the list, (13/18 put it in the second half of the list, $P = 0.048$; Binomial test). There are many possible reasons for this but we can be sure that models of the process which predict simple priming effects would have problems.

Food

Lists are sometimes more directly revealing of multiple strategies. Thus if you ask people to produce a shopping list for a week's holiday in a country cottage, sequences appear which unambiguously reflect a variety of influences such as:

Dairy goods— . . . eggs, cheese, lard, butter . . .
Desserts— . . . tinned fruit, fresh fruit, jellies, tinned milk, rice pudding . . .
Breakfast— . . . bacon, porridge, cornflakes, milk . . .
Grain products— . . . flour, rice, barley, sago, spaghetti . . .
Cake making— . . . lard, margarine, plain flour, self-raising flour, currants, sultanas . . .
Physical form— . . . tinned soups, tinned meats, tinned fish, tinned fruit . . .

Existence of multiple classifications equally clearly leads to chaining and interleaving of strings. Some examples are given in Table 5.1.

It is not clear what might be made out of these data. Examples can be found to illustrate the influence of virtually any classification one can think of. One exception to this is the contents of the refrigerator, which none of the 22 protocols we have looked at illustrate. No doubt people do know what is in the refrigerator so we must assume that, as with the department store, some kinds

Table 5.1. Multiple classification of food items Examples

A	cream		
	milk		
	butter	dairy	
	lard		
	margarine		
	plain and S.R. flour	cake making	
	currants		
	sultanas		

B	butter	Dairy		Fats
	margarine	Dairy		Fats
	cooking oil			Fats
	eggs	Dairy	B'fast	
	bacon		B'fast	
	cheese	Dairy		
	tea		B'fast	
	coffee		B'fast	
	Marmalade		B'fast	
	jam		B'fast	

of retrieval strategy are less efficient than others in producing responses. It is worth pointing out, however, that when my wife gives me a shopping list it contains logical sequences such as 'cream, orange juice, beef, eggs, spaghetti, apples'. The key to the sequence is the layout of the supermarket round the corner, and the items are generated in the order in which they will be picked off the shelves. This, of course, is a deliberately adopted strategy with a rigorous exclusion from *response* sequence of any out-of-order items. Any model of the list generation process would have to take such factors into account.

It seems likely, then, that a study of shopping lists will tell us more about the nature of the retrieval mechanism than about the organization of the data-base. However Dick Byrne and the author have found another kind of food list that displays different properties: a list of ingredients of a dish. Such lists can readily be generated by people who know how to make the dishes. The problem is discovering how such lists are stored. One likely method is to have a copy of the ingredients as they are listed in a recipe book. One wouldn't expect such a list to be more strictly ordered than the spectrum colours and one would expect priming to be effective. So, if you ask someone what are the ingredients of lemon meringue pie or sherry trifle you might expect the first responses to be 'lemons' and 'sherry' respectively. And you would be wrong. Of 10 subjects asked the ingredients of lemon meringue pie only one said 'lemons' first. The others all began with 'flour', or 'fat'. The reason is quite plain—there is no list of ingredients as such. What happens is that the housewives used as informants retrieve the program for making the dish. They run through this program and extract for verbalizing the ingredients required by the experimenter. They all agree that this is indeed what they do, and this introspective conclusion is supported by two kinds of evidence. First there is a very high correlation (usually unity) between the order of the ingredients and the order in which the ingredients appear when the same people are asked to produce a recipe (at a second interview). Secondly, pauses occur as the lists of ingredients are produced, at the natural gaps in the recipe—corresponding to the pastry, the lemon filling and the meringue. It seems likely that the program for the pastry and meringue sections at least are not stored with the lemon meringue pie recipe but rather have to be retrieved from elsewhere. Listing the ingredients is thus a process which is at least three levels deep.

The list thus turns out to be fairly strictly ordered, but only as a consequence of the ordering of the operations involved in the manufacture. This being so it is not surprising that there was no priming from the name of the dish. The one informant who did give 'lemons' first in her list mentioned them half way through the recipe. When she had finished the recipe she was asked: 'At what point would you actually *grate* the lemons and squeeze them?'. 'Well, I think I'd do it before I began, because I don't like doing things like that in the middle.'

Discussion

The results of the enquiries outlined above lead us to fairly simple conclusions. Basically they show that the kind of organization revealed by an experimental situation is heavily determined by the precise nature of the task. Information concerning a particular topic can emerge in a number of ways and the strategy adopted to start with affects the whole performance. Thus, by the present account, one can start to retrieve colour names either by using 'scientific' knowledge or by relying on a semantic probe into a word store. If the former operates, as it nearly always does when such knowledge is directly available, then the latter method seems to be ruled out. When store workers are asked to list departments they seem not to use what would probably be the most efficient method—that of using special information. Instead they use a mixture of strategies including (we presume) personal experience as well as semantic links. This then prevents any subsequent attempt at a systematic search from becoming effective.

Such accounts make it clear that the form of the organization and the nature of the retrieval mechanism cannot be studied in isolation. In addition, the degrees of freedom open to us in designing a retrieval mechanism are currently greater than those available in describing alternative forms of organization. The likelihood that the retrieval mechanism operates in different ways in different situations means further that unless we adopt the right level of model we will find ourselves with apparently contradictory results. The author's current view is that we will have to conceptualize retrieval in terms of a problem solver.

The appropriate level of description will be to specify the classes of operation that are possible. Restrictions in the operation of the problem solver may take the form of a limited capacity available for current information. Such a limitation may manifest itself in certain kinds of grouping during output (see

Broadbent, this volume) but also, it is to be expected, in other ways. For example we might expect a limitation in the depth to which a search can proceed down some tree-like organization without the speaker losing his place. Alternatively one or more of the current goals of the task might be forgotten. A good example of this occurs when subjects are asked to introspect about an ongoing task—such as generating a menu according to certain restrictions. At certain stages in the proceedings subjects often cease introspecting. We would expect such an event to coincide with some activity which occupies a large number of slots.

Another factor we will eventually have to contend with is the difference between what might be called *directed* and *autonomous* search. The phenomenon of autonomous search will be familiar to most people. If, for ecample, you try to list the contents of your house by adopting a deliberate strategy, such as going from room to room, items will keep on intruding from other rooms. Calling such intrusions 'simple' associations, as is tempting, doesn't really add anything to our understanding of the situation. More dramatic examples will doubtless occur to most people. My most recent example followed a conversation in which parts of the body (separated) were being discussed. Van Gogh's ear was mentioned which led me to remember, from many years ago, that a war with Spain had once been precipitated by the removal of an ear from the head of an English sea captain. His name, however, eluded me and the rest of the company. Three days later, in some of the same company, 'Jenkins', the name we had been searching for, came to my lips apropos of nothing in the conversation. While it would be unreasonable to expect a coherent account of such events at the moment our models should allow for them at least in principle (cf. Shallice, 1972).

Introspection Level

If we are going to understand complex processes we need to have complex data. Mere listings of output items are insufficient. Not only do we need timing information but we also need to have introspections from our subjects. Only by asking them can we discover the way in which they see a test or the particular idiosyncratic strategies used. Collins and Quillian (1972) have recently shown how introspections can cast light on the way in which subjects tackle a seemingly simple task. Two important questions which need to be tackled are the extent to which introspections accurately reflect the underlying processes and the extent to which introspecting interferes with ongoing processing. If the idea of a limited capacity working memory is correct then we might expect the goal INTROSPECT to reduce measurably our information handling capability. Newell and Simon (1969), however, claim that producing protocols makes no difference to performance in cryptarithmetic tasks. Perhaps the nature of the task makes a difference. We need not expect that a difficult task which uses a small data-base, such as cryptarithmetic, would be subject to the same influences as an easy task (in terms of the underlying logic) which uses a large data-base, such as designing a menu.

The question of the accuracy of introspections is more complicated. A group of us at the APU are currently trying to tackle this problem. In the course of developing a program to simulate a housewife producing a menu it became apparent that we had a number of options open to us with regard to what the program output. Suppose we take a very simple program. The data-base consists of lists of dishes under the headings COURSE 1, COURSE 2 and COURSE 3. Under COURSE 1 will be found the list SOUP, OYSTERS, MOULE, SALAD, ROLLMOP, PATE. The COURSE 2 list is STEW, SPAG, OMLET, COQ, SOLE, CURRY and COURSE 3 is ZAB, YOG, ICE, BRIE, CHEDDAR. Each dish is also the name of a list of features. Thus the OYSTERS List includes WHITE, POSH, FISH and MOULE is CHEAP, POSH, FISH, WET.

Goals are entered into the program which then simple-mindedly proceeds to find a meal to satisfy the goals. It does this by taking the first item in COURSE 1 and testing it successively against all the current goals. When a test fails the next item in COURSE 1 is tested and so on until an item is found to satisfy all the goals. Then the same procedure is followed for COURSE 2 and COURSE 3.

The program is written in a local list processing language based on TRAC macros. As the language is unprincipled it is called Simulation Language Under Trac or SLUT. A flow diagram of the program is shown in Figure 5.2. Its mode

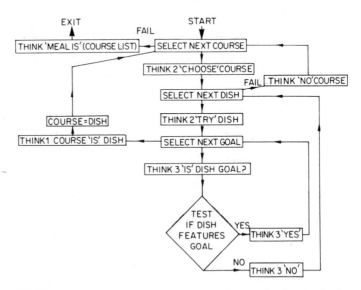

Figure 5.2. Flow diagram of program for selecting a three course meal with given constraints. An 'introspection level' is set before the program is run such that any THINK instruction results in the message attached being printed only if the suffixed digit is lower than the introspection level. Thus the external evidence for the nature of the program's operation differs as a function of the introspection level

of operation is fairly clear from the description. The one unexplained feature is the THINK function. This is an optional PRINT instruction controlled by a numerical suffix on the instruction in the program and an I-LEVEL (introspection level) figure entered by the operator before execution or dynamically. If the THINK suffix is equal to or less than the value of I-LEVEL then there is an output from the program. Output for I-LEVELS of 0 to 3 are given below for GOALS of CHEAP and POSH.

I-level = 0
   MEAL is MOULE COQ YOG.

I-level = 1
   COURSE 1 is MOULE
   COURSE 2 is COQ
   COURSE 3 is YOG
   MEAL is MOULE COQ YOG.

I-level = 2
   CHOOSE COURSE 1
   TRY SOUP
   TRY OYSTERS
   TRY MOULE
   COURSE 1 is MOULE
   CHOOSE COURSE 2
   TRY STEW
   TRY SPAG
   TRY OMLET
   TRY COQ
   COURSE 2 is COQ
   . . . .

I-level = 3
   CHOOSE COURSE 1
   TRY SOUP
   IS SOUP CHEAP? YES
   IS SOUP POSH? NO
   TRY OYSTERS
   IS OYSTERS CHEAP? NO
   TRY MOULE
   IS MOULE CHEAP? YES
   IS MOULE POSH? YES
   COURSE 1 IS MOULE
   CHOOSE COURSE 2
   TRY STEW
   . . . .
   . . . .
   . . . .

The particularly instructive aspect of these outputs follows from playing the game of supposing they are separate introspections from four informants and trying to formulate a model for their production. We might deduce from I-level 0 that the whole meal was accessed directly with a CHEAP–POSH search feature (some of the subjects tested by Dick Byrne do in fact claim they do this, substantiating the claim with details of the guests last time the meal was served). Something like Tulving's (1972) Episodic Memory might be brought to bear as an explanatory construct. From I-level 1 we might conclude a direct access to POSH–CHEAP dishes with the courses treated in series. I-level 2 suggests parallel testing of the features for individual dishes in contrast with I-level 3 where the features are clearly tested in series.

When we then learn that all the outputs were produced by the same program we might be surprised. The lesson seems to be that on the basis of a protocol we can eliminate certain kinds of model. Positive conclusions, particularly concerning possible parallel search, can be dangerous.

A useful distinction can be drawn between real-time introspections and *post-hoc* introspections. The examples given above are of the former type. Suppose we ask our subjects what they did in solving the task. Sometimes it is clear that they have no more information available than the experimenter. On other occasions one can get quite complex, but unsubstantiated descriptions of the underlying operations. In an attempt to understand how such descriptions may be arrived at we can imagine that we are clever enough to have as part of the SLUT system a resident program to which the problem-solving section communicated. The former program would contain a number of inferential processes enabling it to draw conclusions about the operation of the latter. These conclusions could then be part of the output. Their validity, however, is simply a function of the appropriateness of the inferential procedures.

Individual humans differ widely in the extent to which they spontaneously introspect (when not explicitly asked to) and in the extent to which they can introspect when asked. We are only beginning to understand the problems of using such data but feel sure that with continued analysis they can be overcome.

Practical Conclusions

The problem of man-computer systems has become lost from view. We have been on a search for techniques which would enable us to understand the principles or organization of our knowledge. This led to considerations of the nature of the data we can collect. Perhaps more important than trying to find *the* best principle of organization is the task of discovering the adaptability of the human operator. Faced with a particular system, what kinds of discrepencies are likely to create serious problems? What kinds of interference are likely between a prior structure and one imposed by a system? How are new structures incorporated into memory and how should they best be presented for learning? And the trouble is that we need the answers now. Systems are being implemented and if we don't know the right way to do it, nobody does.

Acknowledgements

I am grateful to a number of people for contributions of time and thought to the material in the paper. Notably Pennie Ottley, John Fox, Dick Byrne and members of the THLUTS group.

References

Bruner, J. (1969). Modalities of memory. In G. A, Talland and N. C. Waugh (Eds) *The Pathology of Memory*. New York: Academic Press.

Collins, A. and Quillian, M. R. (1972). How to make a language user. In E. Tulving and W. Donaldson, (Eds) *Organization and Memory*. New York: Academic.

Mandler, G. A. (1967). Organization and memory. In K. W. Spence and J. A. Spence (Eds) *The psychology of learning and motivation*, Vol. 1. New York: Academic Press.

Morton, J. (1968). Grammar and computation in language behavior. In J. C. Catford (Ed.) *Studies in Language Behavior* C.R.L.L.B. Progress Report No. VI. University of Michigan.

Morton, J. (1969). Interaction of information in word recognition. *Psychological Review*, **76**, 165–178.

Newell, A. and Simon, H. A. (1972). *Human Problem Solving*. Prentice-Hall: Englewood Cliffs.

Norman, D. A. (1972). Memory, knowledge and the answering of questions. CHIP 25, N. C. San Diego.

Rumelhart, D. E., Lindsey, P. H. and Norman, D. A. (1972). A process model for long-term memory. In E. Tulving, and W. Donaldson, (Eds) *Organization and Memory*. New York: Academic Press.

Shallice, T. (1972). Dual function of consciousness. *Psychological Review*, **99**, 383–393.

Tulving, E. (1972). Episodic and semantic memory. In E. Tulving and W. Donaldson, (Eds) *Organization and Memory*. New York: Academic Press.

Winograd, T. (1971). Procedures as a representation for data in a computer program for understanding natural language. Project MAC report TR-84. M.I.T.

Chapter 6

An Associative Thesaurus of English: Structural Analysis of a Large Relevance Network

G. R. Kiss

Introduction

Over the last 5 years my colleagues and I in the MRC Speech and Communication Unit have been engaged on a project aimed at the mapping of associative connections over a large proportion of the English vocabulary. At the outset of the project I was convinced that large-scale information of this kind would be interesting and useful for a number of disciplines, and now that the project is reaching the stage of structural analysis of the accumulated data, this feeling is being confirmed. The structure of the Associative Thesaurus promises to be a fascinating source of information on the structure of our minds. The author reaffirms this view, in spite of the ups and downs in the fortunes of research based on an associative orientation. Although the associative approach has come under strong criticism from the Chomskian school in linguistics, now that the dust is beginning to settle it becomes possible to separate associationism from S–R psychology, and to re-examine the role of associative structures in cognition. There is no fundamental reason why associationism should be closely linked to S–R psychology, except a historical one, and the author maintains that associative mechanisms are quite fundamental to cognition.

The main purpose of this paper will be to give a progress report on the structural analysis. The background to the Associative Thesaurus project has been described in a number of papers and reports and only a brief summary of it will be given here (Kiss, Armstrong and Milroy, 1972; Kiss, Armstrong, Milroy and Piper, 1973; Kiss, 1973c; Armstrong and Piper, 1973). Towards the end of the paper I shall give some indication of the kind of memory model which is behind this research, and how the Thesaurus could be used for practical purposes.

Association Networks

There are many tabulations of word association data in existence, but most of them are for relatively small samples of the English vocabulary. Over the last decade it has been increasingly realized by investigators that it is better to regard associations between words as forming a network, rather than to concentrate on the list of responses given to any given stimulus. Deese (1965) introduced the idea of using factor analysis on a matrix of correlations between response distributions to a set of stimuli. Pollio (1966) and Kiss (1968) developed the application of graph theory to word association networks. From these approaches came the idea of 'growing' a large association network systematically, and then applying various methods of structural analysis to the resulting data.

A word association network is a directed linear graph with labelled arcs (links). The nodes of the graph are words (or larger verbal units) and the arcs represent estimates of stimulus–response associative probabilities. In such a graph a path is a sequence of arcs. The length of a path is the number of arcs in it. The number of arcs going into a node is the indegree of the node, while the sum of the values of these arcs is the indegree value of the node. The concepts of outdegree and outdegree values are defined similarly.

It is often useful to regard such a network as a so-called signal flow graph (Kiss, 1968). It is possible to define the transmittance between two nodes A and B as the total signal strength reaching B if a unit signal is injected at A, via all possible paths in the network. If the path length is limited to n, then we obtain the n-step transmittance. The basic rules for calculating transmittances are that the resultant value for two series-connected arcs is the product of their values, while for two parallel-connected arcs the resultant is the sum of their values.

The Associative Thesaurus Data

The procedure for growing the network was to use a smallish nucleus set of stimulus words, obtain responses to them, and then use these responses as the stimuli in the next phase. This cycle was repeated approximately three times. A total of 8400 stimuli were used. The number of nodes is over 55,000 in the network, including misspellings and other oddities. The data cover a wide range of grammatical form classes and inflexional forms (Farvis, 1972; Milroy, 1972).

Each stimulus was presented to 100 different subjects. Each subject gave responses to 100 different stimuli, one response to each. The 100 words were presented in printed form, randomised for each subject. The responses were also written. Most of the data was collected in a classroom setting.

The subjects were mostly undergraduate university students. A stratified sampling procedure was used, with the aim of making the sample representative of the British student population as to geographical origin and faculty of study. The age range was 17 to 22 years. The sex distribution was 64 per cent male, 36 per cent female.

All of the processing of the resulting data was carried out by computer methods. The main result of this work is also a computer data base, together with a set of programs which facilitate its examination from various points of view. It has also been possible to produce a microfilm version directly from the computer magnetic tapes.

The general form of the data is a very densely connected central area, with a progressive thinning out towards the periphery. An interesting kind of information, which is revealed for the first time in this data, relates to the incoming arcs of a word node. It is now possible to ask, for any given word, which stimuli elicit it as a response in word association. Since this is the inverse of the question answered by conventional word association data, it may be called *inverse association.* The corresponding formal concepts are of course the indegree and indegree values. The indegree of a word is the number of different stimuli which elicit it (in our data the maximum indegree is 8400 since we only used that many stimuli). The indegree value of a word is its total number of occurrences as a response token, i.e. its total frequency in the data. The distributions of these are shown in Figure 6.1 on lognormal coordinates.

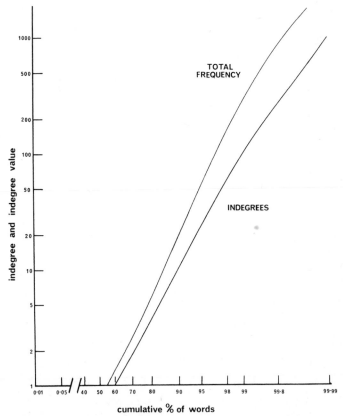

Figure 6.1. Distributions of indegrees and indegree values (i.e. total frequencies) of words in the Associative Thesaurus on lognormal coordinates

Clearly, at the lower end these distributions are close to the lognormal, which is interesting in view of the ubiquitous nature of such distributions in word statistics. There is a deviation from the straight line towards the high-frequency end, particularly for the indegree distribution. The largest indegree in the data is that of *man*, and is 1071. In contrast, consider that over 60 per cent of the words have an indegree of only one.

Impressive regularities are found also when the cumulative contributions to the indegrees and indegree values of individual nodes are plotted as lognormal distributions (Figure 6.2 and Figure 6.3). Notice that the slopes of the lower parts of these distributions are rather similar, indicating similar dispersions, and that the main differences are in the horizontal shift of the curve, i.e. in the mean values. However, the deviation from the lognormal is severe at the upper ends.

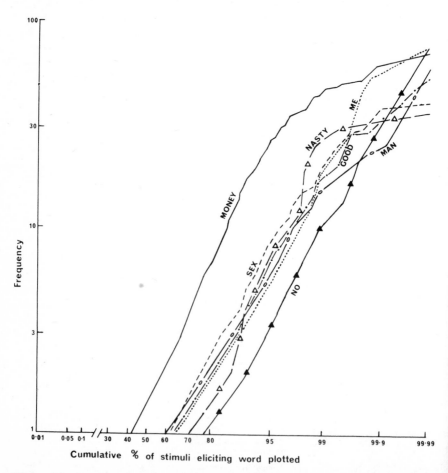

Figure 6.2. Type distributions of stimuli for a set of representative responses in the Associative Thesaurus on lognormal coordinates

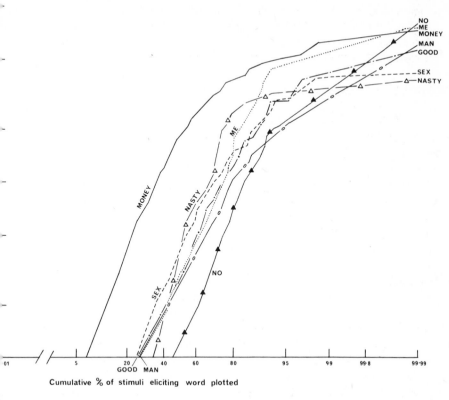

Figure 6.3. Token distributions of stimuli for a representative set of responses in the Associative Thesaurus on lognormal coordinates

One interesting fact which emerges from the availability of inverse association data is that, once the constraint of the response frequencies having to sum to the number of subjects is removed and replaced by the number of stimuli used in the data collection, opposites are not always the strongest associative links. Such changes in the relative strengths may lead to a re-examination of some long established facts about word association.

The Ideas of Relevance and Similarity

Many attempts have been made in the past in linguistics, psychology and in information retrieval to impose a structuring on the lexicon by defining a relationship of similarity. This is usually done by defining a set of attributes for each word, based on things like its distributional information in a corpus, or the contexts in which it occurs in dictionary definitions, or perhaps on what associations it has with other words. Once a procedure is available for identifying the attributes of a word, similarity can be measured in terms of comparisons between sets of attributes. In spite of the widespread use of this framework, the idea of similarity between words (or concepts) remains unclear. Part of the difficulty is due to the lack of any clear cut criteria for delimiting the set of attributes on which the comparison is to be based. Invariably the selection of attributes introduces a point of view into the comparison. It is thus always necessary to state in relation to what body of knowledge or experience similarity is to be defined, and of course this context of comparison is highly variable.

A somewhat clearer notion is that of *relevance*. Relevance simply tells us 'what goes with what'. This aspect of belongingness is to be found both in the world itself, in the sense of causal, spatial and temporal connections and structure, and also in the representation of the world in our minds, commonly referred to as our 'knowledge of the world'. The author maintains the view that one very important aspect of this knowledge of the world is simply knowing these 'what goes with what' connections. This kind of knowledge is clearly not all that we need. In addition to knowing that chair goes with table, we also need to know a great deal of information about the relational (logical) nature of the connection. Considering, however, the extremely large amount of relational information that we all carry around with us in our memory, efficient retrieval of parts of this information demands that we should have the means for quick, global evaluation of what alternative possibilities need to be considered in a situation. In another paper (Kiss, 1973a) the author has argued for a clear distinction between the functions of *generating* alternative possibilities, on the one hand, and deliberating and reasoning about them on the other. The reasoning processes require full knowledge of the relational structure concerning the elements we need to consider. But the decision about the elements to consider and bring in readiness for relational examination into our 'working memory' is based on a different kind of knowledge, which is relevance. I shall not try to give a formal definition of this special kind of relation. As far as our cognitive processes are concerned, two things are relevant to each other when given one of them, the other may also need to be considered or taken into account in some way. A knife is relevant to bread, because it could be used for cutting it. Scales are also relevant because they could be used for weighing it. Clearly, relevance is a matter of degree. It is easy to decide that knife is more relevant to bread than scales are. Why we feel this to be so probably has a number of reasons, including frequency of association, essentiality, etc.

Notice that if we accept the notion of relevance as our primitive basis, then we can also treat similarity by saying that two words are similar to each other to the extent that they have similar distributions of relevance connections to other words. This notion of similarity has been proposed many times in the past, but as we shall see later, it may need critical re-examination.

My interpretation of word associations is that they are direct indicators of degrees of relevance between the concepts for which the words are labels through their word senses. Word association norms, and particularly the Associative Thesaurus network, are thus fairly direct mappings of this aspect of our knowledge. As such they are extremely important indicators of the ructure of the organization in our minds. Not only do they tell us what the ements are which we need to think about in contiguity with each other, but ey also indicate the degree of cohesion existing between them. The detailed udy of this kind of organization is what the Associative Thesaurus makes ossible for the first time on a large scale.

ocal and Global Analysis of Organization

There are two different kinds of structural analysis which can be done on the rge relevance network of the Associative Thesaurus. The first of these is belled *local*, because it is applied to the local environment of a word in the etwork. An environment in the network is defined as the set of words which an be reached from a starting node if we follow all possible arcs up to some xed limit. If the limit on the path length is *n*, then we can talk about an *n*-step nvironment.

The other type of analysis is labelled *global*, because it is applied to the whole f the network rather than to an environment. It is concerned with the overall rganization of the whole network. This distinction will become clearer as ese two approaches are described in more detail.

My colleagues, Jim Piper, Christine Armstrong, and I have now done a onsiderable amount of work on the local analysis, and we are presently xperimenting with global methods.

Within both the global and local approach we can still distinguish methods ming at the derivation of relevance or similarity structure. The analysis of elevance structure is based directly on the connectivity (Transmittance) elations in the network. The analysis of similarity, on the other hand, is based n computing suitable similarity or dissimilarity coefficients (DC) from over-pping sets of relevance connections. Two words are then regarded as iaximally similar if they are connected to the same set of other words and the rengths of the links are also the same.

It turns out that the techniques of similarity analysis are usually a great deal ore laborious than those of the relevance analysis. From what we have been le to do so far, it also seems that similarity analyses on the global scale will be rohibitively expensive, unless some very approximate methods are to be used. he examples to be given in this paper will also show that the local similarity nalysis is strongly dependent on the 'point of view', as discussed in the revious section. Lastly, the major structures revealed by the similarity analysis re not very different in a local environment from those found in the relevance nalysis. For these reasons relevance analysis will be concentrated on in this aper and will merely illustrate the main differences which arise in similarity nalyses.

ocal Relevance Structures

The purpose of this type of analysis is to discover the organization based on e relevance relation within the local environment of a word in the Associative

Thesaurus. The first step towards this is to extract the local environment, which will be described first.

Extracting local environments. As implied previously, the local environment of a word in the Associative Thesaurus is the set of words which can be reached by following all possible pathways, of lengths up to n, starting from the word in question.

Christine Armstrong has written a program in COBAL which does just this, using the computer-based form of the data. The program has various input parameters, determining the value of n, and also the values of thresholds which can be applied in selecting links to follow. It is thus possible to exclude from the environment all links which fall below the threshold, and moreover, the value of the threshold can vary according to the current length of the path being followed. This program can operate either in the forward (stimulus–response) or the inverse (response–stimulus) direction. The output consists of listings of the words in the environment, sorted both according to descending values of transmittances, and also alphabetically. The program calculates the transmittance values as it goes along the various paths originating from the starting word.

Environments extracted in this way can be extremely large. It is not unusual for a 2-step environment to exceed a thousand words. For this reason thresholding at some low frequency is usually applied to reduce the environment to a few hundred words. These limits are set by the capacities of the cluster analysis programs which we are using at present.

Finding the Connection Matrix. Once a suitable size of environment has been found, a connection matrix is determined for its members. This is a square matrix whose columns and rows are the words in the environment, and the entries are measures of the connectivity (transmittance) between them. These matrices are n-step transmittance matrices. The larger the value of n, the better the results, since more of the connection structure is taken into account. However, the computation of transmittances for $n > 1$ gets very expensive, so that this is only done in critical cases. Normally, $n = 1$ is used, which means that only direct word to word connections are considered.

Numerical Taxonomy. The transmittance matrix of the environment forms the input to the procedures which determine the underlying organization. My colleague, Jim Piper, has written a number of programs for well-known cluster analysis algorithms, and we have also extensively used a package of programs written by Wishart (1969), which implements practically all known methods of analysis, with a wide variety of DC's.

The amount of exploration which we have done over the past year or so is too extensive to report here in detail. Similarly, I do not wish to go into a lengthy discussion of the merits and disadvantages of the various methods of numerical taxonomy. Some amount of discussion is given in Kiss (1973b) and in Kiss

Armstrong, Milroy and Piper (1973), where further useful references to the taxonomy literature are also given.

The outcome of our explorations can be summarized by saying that in spite of the mathematical weaknesses in its foundations, the method of average linkage yields the most satisfactory results with our data. In this method, two items (where an item can be either a word or a cluster of words) are joined together on the basis of the average DC between them. Items are successively merged into larger and larger clusters until all of them are in a single large cluster. The result of the procedure is a dendrogram (a tree) which shows the merging sequence.

In local relevance clustering the DC which we use is the sum of the transmittances between a word pair in both directions. For this reason we also refer to this method as *connectivity clustering*. This is a compromise solution, and we also intend to experiment with taking the larger or the smaller transmittance between the pair as the DC between them.

The result of the cluster analysis is printed on the computer line printer as a dendrogram, so that the structural analysis is now completely automatic from designating a starting node for an environment (together with the parameters regulating the size of the environment), up to the printed dendrogram as a result (see Figure 6.4 for example).

Examples of Clustering Results. We have now run a large number of such local analyses, both for our own purposes and also as an aid to other research workers. As examples, the results of analyzing the environment of the word *food* in the inverse direction using 2-step transmittances are reproduced in Figure 6.4. This dendrogram is reproduced here in order to show the general nature of the clustering results obtained. The computation of the 2-step transmittances is rather expensive, so that normally only 1-step connections are used and all other examples in this paper are of this kind.

Tables 6.1 and 6.2 show a simplified representation of clustering the forward and inverse environments of food. The bracketing and semicolons indicate the major divisions about half way up on the dendrogram.

It can be seen that the forward and inverse environments are different, although some elements occur in both. Recall that the inverse environment contains words which elicit the word *food*, while the forward environment is elicited by it. The sizes of these environments are usually quite different, and so are the distributions of linkage strengths, since in the forward direction the links from a node must sum to 100, while in the inverse direction there is no such limit.

In some cases our analysis is done on a combined inverse and forward environment, but usually more insight can be gained by doing the analyses separately and then combining the results.

Detailed inspection of such analyses usually reveals a quite exhaustive set of clusters, each of them representing a more-or-less separate but cohesive group of words sharing some conceptual component which makes them relevant

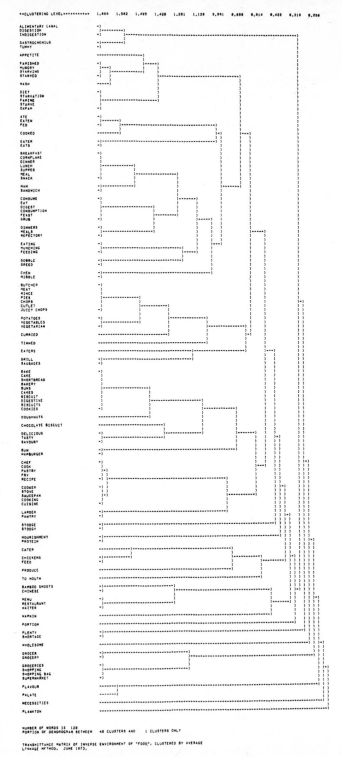

Figure 6.4. An example of local cluster analysis output. This is the inverse environment of *food* analysed by the average link method

Table 6.1. Relevance clustering of the forward environment of 'Food'

(bad good nice)
(bacon eggs; eggs rotten)
(greed fat; pig)
(chips fish steak; meat sausage; chop lamb sheep)
(apple pie fruit orange; bite; green lettuce salad)
(drink beer booze glass wine drunk; bottle milk; drinking eating)
(cold hot water wet; soup)
(hunger thirst; strike; pain stomach; hungry starving thirsty)
(cook; book case)
(bread butter cheese; kitchen knife; table)
(breakfast dinner lunch time supper; coffee tea; consumption digest eat food
    meal; meals)
(cake mix; up; chocolate)
(shop store house; loot money; space storage)
(baby boy; face mouth)
(now again; yes please; dance quickly; me you of)
(thought think mind brain; firm; hard work)
(poison death; deep sleep)

Table 6.2. Relevance clustering of the inverse environment of 'Food'

(digestion indigestion alimentary-canal; tummy gastrocnemius)
(appetite; famished hungry starving starved; fed ate eaten)
(eat digest consume consumption nibble chew; gobble greed)
(feed chickens; to-mouth)
(eating munching feeding)
(restaurant menu waiter; meal feast snack; chinese bamboo-shoots)
(breakfast dinner lunch supper cornflake; napkin; dinners meals refectory)
(meat mince pies butcher vegetarian; cooked; ham sandwich; cutlet juicy-
    chops; tinned; curried; chops eaters; hash)
(diet starve starvation famine oxfam; shortage plenty; protein nourishment)
(bakery buns cakes doughnuts; cake bake shortbread biscuit biscuits digestive
    cookies; bun hamburgers; portion)
(delicious tasty savoury; flavour; chocolate-biscuit eats)
(stodgy; wholesome)
(cooking cook chef cuisine recipe pastry; cooker stove saucepan; fry grill
    sausages)
(larder pantry)
(grocery grocer vegetables potatoes; groceries shopping supermarket
    shopping-bag)
(stodge) (produce) (plankton) (necessities)

(syntagmatically or paradigmatically) to the starting word. One could summarize the picture presented by the analysis of the *food* environments by saying that it shows what kinds of things we need to know in order to have an adequate conceptual understanding of the word *food*. Taken together, these words indicate what is generally known in relation to, or about food. It is an index to this area of our knowledge. The fact that we obtain intuitively satisfactory and interpretable clusters also indicates that this is not a haphazard collection of items, but has its own systematic organization. The question of how this organization can be useful in cognitive processes will be returned to later in the paper.

The various clusters in the inverse environment could be labelled and listed as the following outline. The main headings are italicized, the subheadings are enclosed in brackets:

Digestion.
Eating: (appetite; hunger; manner of eating; feeding; meals; eating places).
Kinds of food: (meat; vegetable; cooked; sandwich).
Nourishment: (starvation; plentifulness).
Bakery: (cakes; buns; delicacies).
Catering and cooking: (cooking; utensils; methods).
Storage of food.
Shopping for food.

The forward environment reveals similar clusters, but is somewhat more impoverished. The clusters relating to digestion, nourishment, catering and storage are not present.

A certain amount of improvement takes place in the assignment of items and in the hierarchial arrangement of clusters if the analysis is based on a 2-step transmittance matrix instead of the 1-step one, as can be seen in Figure 6.4.

One wonders at this point how adequate the coverage and the classification of words into clusters is in this analysis. A comparison with Roget's Thesaurus (1953) could throw some light on this question. if one takes the paragraph indentation of this edition as a guide to the clusters identified by Roget, we find the following outline describes the structure:

Eating:
  Organs of Eating.
  Drink.
  Nourishment.
  Kinds of food: (soup; meat; bakery; sweets; vegetable; fruit).
  Meals.
  Eating places.
  Manner of eating.
  Feeding.
  Catering.
  Adjectives relating to food.

It can be seen that all of Roget's subclassifications are present in the clusters of the associative thesaurus. Roget indicates two of his sub-classes by cross referencing: eating house, and cater. This edition of Roget lists approximately 300 words in his section on food. It is not easy to make a direct comparison with the coverage of the associative thesaurus, since the size of the environment which can be extracted around food can vary up to several thousands, depending on the path lengths and frequency cutoff values. It may give some indication to the reader to consider that the indegree of food (i.e. the number of different stimuli eliciting it) is 676, and these words are only one step away.

Local Similarity Structures

Comment has already been made on the fact that the similarity type of analysis, which is based on the degree of agreement between the relevance connections of a pair of words, is much more laborious to compute and is subject to distortions due to the limited sizes of the local environments. In this section this will be illustrated by giving an example of this type of analysis for the inverse environment of food. The clustering results are shown in Table 6.3, which is to be compared with the corresponding relevance clustering in Table 5.2. It is easily seen that the major subdivisions are, by and large, the same. An example of an odd combination of words is the close clustering of chicken and ham, which is due to both having a strong connection to egg. The similarity analysis of the forward environment (not shown here) also contains the corresponding oddity of joining together egg, eggs, and pig, occurring for the same reason.

Table 6.3. Similarity clustering of the inverse environment of 'Food'

(digestion indigestion tummy alimentary-canal gastrocnemius; digestive)
(appetite famished starve starving starvation starved famine oxfam greed)
(eat; eats; diet; hungry; feed ate eaten; eater eaters)
(stodge stodgy; eating)
(bakery bake bun buns cookies doughnuts biscuit biscuits chocolate-biscuits
 shortbread cake cakes; portion)
(delicious tasty savoury; wholesome)
(digestive consume consumption feed nibble chew gobble restaurant;
 to-mouth)
(breakfast dinner dinners lunch supper meal refectory; feast menu snack;
 meals)
(feeding napkin; munching) (nourishment) (flavour palate)
(butcher mince chops juicy-chops sausage pies cooked cutlet protein; hamburger sandwich) (vegetables vegetarian tinned)
(meat; curried fry potatoes) (chickens ham) (produce)
(chef pastry; cater; cuisine recipe saucepan stove; grill)
(cook cooking cooker; hash) (larder pantry)
(chinese waiter) (grub)
(grocery grocer groceries supermarket; shopping shopping-bag)
(necessities) (plenty shortage)
(plankton) (cornflake)

Global Clustering Structures

Global similarity clustering is unfortunately prohibitively expensive, so that in this section only relevance clustering will be discussed. We are currently experimenting with methods of forming an average-link cluster around an arbitrary starting word according to an algorithm which always joins the next word having the strongest average symmetrized transmittance to the already existing cluster.

This method assumes the availability of both the forward and inverse forms of the data as direct-access data sets on computer disk storage. The process can be pictured as a kind of crystal growth process, in which the already existing cluster seed attracts successive additions on the basis of the adhesion strengths of potential candidate members.

Let us consider the example of growing such a global cluster around food. In the first step of the process food attracts nourishment as the next member, since the strongest symmetric transmittance (the sum of forward and inverse links) leads to nourishment. Among all of the words linked to either food or nourishment, the word with the strongest *average* connection to both is eat. This then becomes the next word to join. At this stage the candidates for joining the cluster, in order of decreasing total transmittance, are: consume, larder, meal, appetite, menu, grub, restaurant, etc. Consume is therefore the next word to join, and so we continue until some arbitrary limiting value is reached for the average transmittance. In this example, the first few members of the global cluster are: food, nourishment, eat, consume, larder, pantry, meal menu, restaurant, feast, appetite, grub, refectory, meals, eating, digest, eats hungry, famished, starving, hunger, etc.

This method thus generates a very strongly connected set of words reflecting the most important elements among the various facets of the starting word One would expect these words to cluster in any local environment of some other word as a self-contained component, and this is the reason for calling such clusters global.

More recently different methods of global clustering have been explored on a much larger scale. In particular, a 3000-word subset of the Thesaurus has been analyzed, using a method which does not require the complete DC matrix to be computed and makes it possible to treat very large sets of words. The results of this work will be described in a separate report.

Let us finish this section by giving another example of such a global cluster in the neighbourhood of the word friend: friend, acquaintance, companion colleague, enemy, foe, comrade, pal, buddy, mate, ally, neighbour, compan ionship, etc.

Retrieval Processes

In this last part of the paper will be discussed the relation of the Associative Thesaurus to a general model of memory, and certain types of retrieval processes which may operate on it. The author's general views on the nature and organization of verbal memory have been outlined in an earlier paper (Kiss, 1972a) in which a state-space approach is proposed. The picture drawn there was a functional system (an automaton with inputs and outputs) composed of subsystems dealing with aspects of verbal representation like auditory features, motor features, relational conceptual structure, etc. The total system can be in many different states, and these states represent the 'contents' of the memory system. The behaviour of the system is determined by the transition and output functions. The retrieval mechanism is the transition function of the system, which enables the system to reach a particular state through a set of state-to-state transitions.

One of the sub-automata into which the system can be decomposed (doing part of the computation of the total system) has been labelled 'verbal units system'. This system is postulated to contain units of the kind we find in the Associative Thesaurus. The state variables of this sub-automaton are continuous variables attached to these units. These variables one might call 'activation' (Kiss, 1969). Activation can be carried from one unit to another by transmission links. The state of this system is accessible to consciousness through readings of the activation levels of units in the system.

The connection structure found in the Associative Thesaurus is assumed to be a reflection of, *among other things*, the structure of the transmission links in the verbal units sub-automaton. This reflection is, however, indirect because of the existence of the several other subsystems and of the output functions. Associative responses are a composite result of the operation of the total system.

Searching for Words

One particular use of the Associative Thesaurus with which the author has started to experiment is to make it into an on-line thesaurus of the Roget type. This might eventually find practical applications in information retrieval, literary and technical writing, and elsewhere. I would like to describe briefly some of the possible mechanisms for search processes in such a data base, since not only is this of interest for such practical applications, but this kind of experimentation also leads to hypotheses about human memory.

The typical way of searching in Roget's Thesaurus is to start from some word, look it up in the index, and examine the corresponding entry for the required target word. In comparing Roget's Thesaurus with the Associative Thesaurus, one could say that the entries under the so-called head in Roget are associative environments, while the index is an indication of some of the network connection structure. Additional connection information is contained in the cross-references in the entries. The explicitly indicated connection structure of the Associative Thesaurus is of course much richer, and accordingly searching is more convenient. In addition, the connection structure of the Associative Thesaurus has been determined empirically and can be expected to be more in tune with most people's ideas about relatedness between words.

Single-entry search. This corresponds closely to what one can already do in Roget, i.e. to follow connection pathways and to examine the list of branches in the network at each node traversed in the search. In the on-line form of search one can simply type in the name of the node and get back the list of directly associated words, or more generally, a whole environment in the network. Having looked at the output listing, one may decide to follow up any of the words, or else to start from another word.

Multiple-entry search. In contrast to what one can do in the printed thesaurus, the on-line form makes it possible to give more direction to the search by specifying several words, together with positive and negative weights for each. The interrogation of the network in this fashion corresponds to injecting excitation and inhibition at several nodes of the net, and using the superimposition of these to determine the response of the system. This enables one to make use of all the information available at any stage of the search in order to narrow it down to more relevant items. The output can be a rank ordered set of words which have received the maximum amount of excitation and the minimum amount of inhibition. This kind of interrogation can be used to 'prime' and bring to the surface items which are only weakly linked to the query words when they are taken in isolation.

Combined method. In practice, a combination of both methods turns out to be a useful way of browsing in the network. One can 'walk' about, following paths and accumulating 'good' cue items, and then use these items simultaneously to ensure that a good relevant environment is retrieved.

Uses of Associative Retrieval in Human Memory

What use are word associations? As suggested earlier in this paper, they are an index of our knowledge of the world. They are the keys to the retrieval processes of our memory. They determine the transition function of the memory automaton. One might say that, after all, these associations are between words only and that we are dealing with a purely linguistic phenomenon. I think this is not the case, particularly if we accept that the main uses of words are as labels and 'handles' for concepts, which are, in turn, our main cognitive structures for knowledge.

Many current accounts of problem solving and reasoning (both in psychology and also in artificial intelligence) ignore the problems created by the enormous size of our everyday knowledge. For example, a typical problem often treated in artificial intelligence as a task for so-called 'advice taker' systems (McCarthy, 1968) is the 'monkey and bananas' problem. Several systems have now been described in the literature which could go through the necessary reasoning procedures showing how a monkey can formulate a plan of climbing on a box, which first has to be pushed to the right position, in order to reach a bunch of bananas hanging from the ceiling. By formalizing the notions of 'can', 'cause' and 'can ultimately', and by specifying the situation in a set of predicate calculus statements, like move (person, location, object) implies cause (at (location, object)), a theorem proving procedure can derive what needs to be done.

If all our knowledge is encoded into such a form, and the deductive reasoning procedures are needed in order to derive even the simplest plans, there seems to be such a vast overhead of searching and theorem-proving, that one wonders whether some short-cuts might not exist, especially for our simpler everyday activities. I suggest that a judicious combination of associative mechanisms with deductive, relational reasoning may provide a more economical alternative. Simply stated, the associative retrieval mechanism may provide relevant alternatives to try, which are then evaluated in the relational sense, using information stored in what many workers now call a 'relational network' representation of knowledge.

The idea of a relational evaluation of associatively produced candidates also gives an answer to the puzzle of how we know in our associative search processes when we have found what we are looking for. The associative production of items of knowledge (especially those which are often needed) may eliminate elaborate deductive procedures. In the case of the monkey and bananas problem the key ideas in the description of the situation are the *bananas*, the *box*, the need to *reach* them, because they are too *high*. Presumably, the problem can be solved by realizing that one has to climb on something. Let us see how soon the associative Thesaurus would lead us to this idea. From box we would get to *top* and *hill*. From reach we get to *up, grasp, get, hold*, etc. From banana we get *monkey, tree*. Tree leads to *climb* and so does monkey too. But there are other routes to the target word as well: up leads to *hill, mountain*, both of which lead to *climb*. Stool leads to *high*, which in turn goes to *hill, mountain, jump*, etc., so that in the next step we again reach *climb*. The idea of climbing would thus certainly be near the top of *our* minds, if not of the monkey's, when thinking about this problem. A relational evaluation of the description of the concept of climbing would presumably show that it is appropriate to the circumstances and to the goal in hand.

Examples of what the relational description of the concept of climbing might look like can be found in Kiss (1972b, 1973a). In contrast to most workers in this field, the author does not think that it is essential or even very useful to regard these descriptions as networks. The essential aspect is that these relational descriptions can be expressed in a suitable language as structured entities. The work of Winograd (1972) and of Charniak (1972) provide examples of how this can be done.

A different, but related, example of retrieving concepts according to some given specification, or clues, can be found in a particularly clear form in the well-known children's game of riddles. Recently the author has been experimenting with a program which implements some of the facilities for searching in the associative network, described in this section. The programs operate on a 3000-word subset of the Associative Thesaurus, which was extracted for certain clinical applications (Kiss, Walton, Farvis and Piper, 1973; Walton, Kiss, Farvis, McIver and Basson, 1973). In addition to the reduced size of the vocabulary, the connection structure is also severely truncated, and the nodes are restricted to stimulus items in the Thesaurus. For these reasons the performance of the associative retrieval programs is not expected to be as good as it could be with the full data. Nevertheless, it may be instructive to look at some examples.

Consider the following riddles from the charming collection compiled by Leeming (1953):

I am forever, and yet was never. What am I?

If we pick on the words forever and never as the key items and use them in a multiple-entry search, the program comes back with a list of 46 items, the beginning of which is: *always* 30, *ever* 27, *never* 12, *again* 9, *love* 7, *eternity* 6, *now* 6, *eternal* 4, . . . etc. The 'official' solution of this riddle is in fact *eternity*, which is the sixth item on the list, with a weight of 6.

Now consider

You can hang me on the wall, but if you take me down, you can't hang me up again. What am I?

Unfortunately the word *hang* is not in the data-base, but iterrogation with *wall* yields: *brick* 16, *stone* 9, *paper* 7, *game* 5, . . . etc. (a list of 27 items). The official solution is *wallpaper*.

As a last example, consider:

I am something that has never been felt, seen, nor heard; never existed; and yet I have a name. What am I?

In this case, *hear* and *heard* are not in the data-base. Starting with *never* (with a weight of 2), *feel* (weight of −1), and *Exist* (weight of 2), we get back a list of 51 items which does not contain the official solution, *nothing*. However, the list contains items which feel relevant, and upon selecting the words *die, no, not, reality, being, impossible, forever* (all with a weight of 1), we get back an additional 45 items. In this new list the 12th item is in fact *nothing*, our target word. The search in this case required two iterations and the examination of 63 items. However, if the first interrogation includes the word *something*, then the word *nothing* would have been the second item on the response list. This is due to the strong link between something and nothing, which are opposites, always having a strong link in word association.

These examples illustrate, if in a somewhat facetious way, that the 'what goes with what' kind of knowledge can serve as an effective aid in retrieving possibilities to aid our reasoning.

References

Armstrong, C. and Piper, J. (1973). The structure of an associative empirical thesaurus of English. Paper presented at the International Conference on Computers in the Humanities, University of Minnesota. *MRC Speech and Communication Unit Report TH-7.*

Charniak, E. (1972). Toward a model of children's story comprehension. *Memorandum AI TR-266*, MIT Artificial Intelligence Laboratory.

Deese, J. (1965). *The Structure of Associations in Language and Thought.* Baltimore: The John Hopkins Press.

Farvis, K. (1972). Index of stimulus words used in the Associative Thesaurus. *MRC Speech and Communication Unit Report TH-1.*

Kiss, G. R. (1968). Words associations and networks. *Journal of Verbal Learning and Verbal Behavior,* **7**, 707–713.

Kiss, G. R. (1969). Steps towards a model of word selection. In B. Meltzer and D. Michie (Eds), *Machine Intelligence* 4. Edinburgh: The University Press.

Kiss, G. R. (1972a). Long-term memory: A state-space approach. *British Journal of Psychology,* **63**, 327–341.

Kiss, G. R. (1972b). Recursive concept analysis. *MRC Speech and Communication Unit Report R-9.*

Kiss, G. R. (1973a). Geometrical and relational approaches to the analysis of concepts. Paper presented at the Annual Conference of the BPS. *MRC Speech and Communication Report R-10.*

Kiss, G. R. (1973b). The acquisition of word classes: A theory and its computer simulation. In G. Bower (Ed.), *The Psychology of Learning and Motivation,* Vol. 7. New York: Academic Press.

Kiss, G. R. (1973c). An associative thesaurus of English and its structure. Paper presented at the 4th Structural Learning Conference, University of Pennsylvania. *MRC Speech and Communication Unit Report TH-5.*

Kiss, G. R., Armstrong, C. and Milroy, R. (1972). *An Associative thesaurus of English (microfilm version).* Wakefield: EP Microforms Ltd.

Kiss, G. R., Armstrong, C., Milroy, R. and Piper, J. (1973). An associative thesaurus of English and its computer analysis. In A. Aitken, R. Beiley and N. Hamilton-Smith (Eds), *The Computer and Literary Studies.* Edinburgh: The University Press.

Kiss, G. R., Walton, H. J., Farvis, K. and Piper, J. (1974). A computer program for the on-line exploration of attitude structures of psychiatric patients. *International Journal of Bio-Medical Computing,* **4**, 37–48.

McCarthy, J. (1968). Programs with common sense. In M. Minsky (Ed.), *Semantic Information Processing.* Cambridge: MIT Press.

Milroy, R. (1972). Index of stimulus words with inflexional and derivational variations. *MRC Speech and Communication Unit Report TH-4.*

Pollio, H. R. (1966). *The Structural Basis of Word Association Behavior.* The Hague: Mouton.

Roget, P. M. (1953). *Thesaurus of English Words and Phrases.* Harmondsworth: Penquin.

Walton, H. J., Kiss, G. R. and Farvis, K. (1973). Clinical evaluation of a computer program for the exploration of attitude structures in psychiatric patients. *MRC Speech and Communication Unit Report CP-8.*

Winograd, T. (1972). *Understanding Natural Language.* Edinburgh: The University Press.

Wishart, D. (1969). *CLUSTAN 1A.* St. Andrews: The Computing Laboratory.

Chapter 7

Meaning and the Mental Lexicon

P. N. Johnson-Laird

The subject of this paper is meaning and, in particular, the meaning of words. Such a large topic can be approached from a number of vantage points by specialists in a variety of disciplines. Logicians, linguistics, psychologists and many others, have all contributed to the problem of meaning and (sometimes) to its solution. Yet the problem is almost certainly too complicated to yield to any one line of attack. Perhaps the best hope of success lies in an enquiry into the psychological representation of meaning because here we can pursue both brute empiricism in the field and genteel indoor reflection. What we can discover experimentally will place certain constraints upon the mechanism of the lexicon; and what we know intuitively about language, or can formulate by sheer hard thinking, will impose further constraints upon its function. The distinction between these two approaches, of course, is not simply one between experiment and theory. There are theories about the phenomena culled from experiments and there are theories about the function of the lexicon. But there is little connection between them. Hence the main purposes of the present paper are to offer a preliminary survey of these two bodies of work, to report a few new empirical results, and to refrain from drawing too many premature inferences about the art of bridge-building.

Experimental Studies of Semantic Categorization

The bulk of the empirical studies of semantic memory have sought to discover whether there are any general principles governing the retrieval of information about a word. What is currently under debate is the relative ascendancy of some alternative theories of the retrieval of hierarchical information. Collins and Quillian (1969, 1972) have argued that words are organized in semantic memory by a network of different sorts of association. This network reflects the way in which knowledge is acquired. For example, a child is unlikely ever to learn that a canary is an animal. Rather he learns that birds are animals and that a canary is a bird. Hence, there will be no direct link between 'canary' and 'animal' in the semantic network; and it should take longer to retrieve the relation between them than to retrieve the relation between 'canary' and 'bird' or between 'bird' and 'animal' which are, of course, directly linked. The results of several experiments are consistent with this notion of the hierarchical retrieval of facts (e.g., Collins and Quillian, 1969, 1970). However, the closeness of items within a hierarchy appears to impede negative judgements about them, e.g., it is harder to evaluate 'a canary is an ostrich' than to evaluate 'a canary is a fish'. This unexpected phenomenon may, indeed, occur because the directness of the associations between neighbouring words creates a misleading bias towards a positive evaluation of assertions involving them (Collins and Quillian, 1972). An alternative explanation of many of these results, however, is simply that in performing a categorization task an individual has to scan a list of items stored with the category label. It may take longer to decide that a canary is an animal than to decide that it is a bird simply because there are more animals than birds to be examined. Such effects have been reported by Landauer and Freedman (1968), Meyer (1970), and others. This theory is certainly more parsimonious than the semantic network theory, but this advantage is paid for by a more restricted range of application.

A major difficulty with both the semantic network theory and the category-size theory is that they fail to predict difference *within* categories. (They also fail to accommodate certain anomalous results, e.g. Rips, Shoben, and Smith (1973) found that it takes longer to decide that something is a mammal than to decide that it is an animal.) It has been evident from the very earliest investigations that there are usually considerable differences in the times taken to classify items within a given category. These differences within categories have been shown to relate to the frequency with which an instance is given as an exemplar of a category (Wilkins, 1971), to the rated semantic distance between an instance and its category (Rips, Shoben, and Smith, 1973), and to the degree to which an instance is rated as an exemplar of the category (Heider, in press). Such measures are likely to predict differences between categories too: for example, 'canary' is probably more likely to elicit the response 'bird' than the response 'animal'. In short, what has been shown is that Marbe's law of associations holds good for categorization. The law states that there is a correlation between the frequency of a verbal associate and its latency: the more frequent an associate to a given verbal stimulus, the faster it will be produced. In the absence of contrary evidence, we might very well assume that the law gives rise to the ratings of semantic distance etc., rather than *vice versa*.

One disadvantage of Marbe's law is that it cannot explain subjects' sensitivity to the logic of class-inclusion: it merely predicts that common associates will be produced faster than rare associates, regardless of the semantic relation between the stimulus and the response. But, of course, this problem is shared by a theory that takes rated semantic distance as primitive, and its solution is presupposed by a theory that takes degree of category membership as primitive. Another more practical difficulty is that when associative frequency is controlled, some hierarchical effects can still be detected (*cf.* Conrad, 1972; Smith, Haviland, Buckley, and Sack, 1972). But the most decisive objection to Marbe's law is simply that the buck should *not* stop here.

On what basis, in fact, do we assign things to categories? It certainly seems that we have different sorts of criteria for, as the linguist Lakoff (1972) has pointed out, they are evident whenever we hedge our remarks in such conventional ways as 'A robin is a typical bird', 'Strictly speaking, an ostrich is a bird', 'Superman is a regular bird'. Heider (in press) has shown that there are apparently different 'degrees' of category membership. Robins and eagles, for instance, are considered to be better representatives of birds than are chickens and ducks. That robins are, indeed, birds is so seldom a topic of discourse that it seems rather absurd to use Marbe's law as the basis for these differences. The ideal bird presumably has feathers, wings, and a beak, and it flies, sings, and lays eggs. Judging from some unpublished results of Hampton, it is the number of such features possessed by an exemplar that determine both its rated membership of a category and the latency of simple 'yes' or 'no' decision about its category membership. It is difficult to resist the view that this variable also gives rise to differences in the associative norms for a category, and in rated semantic distances within it.

The notion that sets of semantic features are involved in categorization tasks was originally proposed by Schaeffer and Wallace (1969, 1970). They suggested that when an individual decides whether an item is a member of a category, he retrieves their respective sets of features and compares them. This comparison involves sampling a certain amount of information from both sets of features in order to satisfy a criterion. Because similar words presumably have more features in common than dissimilar words, the sample for a positive judgement will be relatively small for similar words, but the sample for a negative judgement will be relatively small for dissimilar words. While the details of this sampling and comparison process have yet to be specified, the virtue of this theory is that it offers a unified account of differences within a category and differences between hierarchies of categories. This flexibility is paid for, however, by the uncertain status of semantic features. One possible solution here is to replace them by the actual words that are conventionally used to denote them. Such a step amounts to taking words rather than features as the primitive elements of semantic theory, and would probably lead to a semantic network similar in conception to the sort proposed by Collins and Quillian. Indeed, the empirical data are often compatible with either sort of explanation. It is unfortunate, from this point of view, that the empirical studies have concentrated on nouns. The organization of verbs soon reveals the need for such semantic features as ACTION, CAUSE, and INTENTION, (*cf.* Miller, 1972). The inability of the network theory to free meaning from the explicit verbiage in which it is expressed now becomes embarrassing. It leads to the somewhat grotesque view that children learn the meanings of verbs from statements explicitly involving the words 'action', 'cause', intention', etc.

The retrieval of Non-hierarchical Information

The retrieval of information from hierarchies has been examined at length, but what happens if the information to be retrieved is not hierarchically organized? Linguists such as Chomsky (1965) have regularly pointed out that many classificatory dimensions do not yield hierarchies unless we are prepared to impose an arbitrary ordering upon them. This argument applies to a variety of semantic distinctions, for example, there is no natural *a priori* ordering of the contrast between solid and liquid and the contrast between natural and manmade. A few years ago the author suggested that one determinant of the ease of retrieving this sort of information might be its utility. If it was more useful to know whether something was solid or liquid than to know whether it was natural or manmade, then the former information would be retrieved faster than the latter information. The problem was, however, to obtain independent evidence about the utility of information. The stage at which a concept was acquired by children might have predicted its utility but, unfortunately, there were no relevant data in the literature. One method that was eventually developed in collaboration with Graham Gibbs was to quiz subjects about their knowledge of rare words. We argued that if subjects agreed that, for example, turpentine was a liquid, but disagreed among themselves about whether it was natural or manmade, then it was more useful to know about its liquidity than to know how it was made. If there was a trend of the same sort over a whole sample of words, then we could draw the same moral about the general utility of these two sorts of information. In fact, we also introduced the semantic distinction between consumable (i.e., edible or drinkable) and non-consumable substances into an experiment in which subjects were simply asked to categorize relatively rare words in terms of such contrasts as consumable/non-consumable, solid/liquid, and natural/manmade. The results we obtained with one set of 48 words are given in Table 7.1. Both these trends

Table 7.1. The mean total errors per subject in categorizing 48 words on three semantic contrasts

	Sample 1: University students (N = 24)	Sample 2: Technical College students (N = 12)
Consumable/Nonconsumable	4·7	5·0
Solid/Liquid	6·7	7·3
Natural/Manmade	9·1	10·0

are reliable, but they are to some extent misleading. Many of the words were completely familiar to our subjects, while others of them were sufficiently unfamiliar for subjects only to be able to guess at their meaning. Indeed, in an independent replication, Coope (unpublished) at the City University, London, found that the trend emerged only for those words which were partially, but not completely, known to her subjects. The emergence of a reliable trend may be taken, perhaps, as an index of general utility even though by no means all words conform to it. Does this index predict the speed with which information is retrieved about common words? The results of a preliminary study carried out by Shapiro and the author (unpublished) were promising. When subjects were asked to sort 16 words on each of the relevant contrasts, their latencies showed a reliable trend in the required direction. Table 7.2 gives the mean latencies for the three semantic distinctions in this study and in a more recent study carried out by Coope.

Table 7.2. Geometric mean times (sec) for sorting on three semantic contrasts

	Experiment 1 (Shapiro and Johnson-Laird)	Experiment 2 (Coope)
Consumable/Nonconsumable	13·5	16·3
Solid/Liquid	14·1	15·8
Natural/Manmade	17·3	19·6

In this second study, which involved different material, the natural/manmade distinction took reliably longer than the other two distinctions, but between them there was no reliable difference. It was obviously necessary to examine response times to individual words, and Morton kindly offered to collaborate with us and to test some Cambridge housewives at the Applied Psychology Unit. There was not a trace of the required trend; we comforted ourselves with the thought that certain aspects of the task had seemed unsuited to the subjects. However, Morton did obtain one noteworthy result in a subsequent study.

The judgements typically investigated in studies of semantic memory are of the following form:

(1)

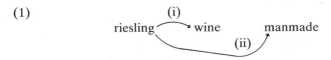

and, as we have seen, the major theories agree that judgement (i) should be faster than judgement (ii). In the original study with Shapiro, there had been no differences in the times to categorize superordinate terms such as *wine, meat, wood*, etc. and the times to categorize subordinate terms such as *riesling, veal, fir*, etc. This comparison is of the following form:

(2)

In this case, the network theory predicts that judgement (iii) should be faster than judgement (ii), the category size theory predicts no difference between the judgements, and it is unclear what is predicted by the semantic feature theory. Morton re-examined the phenomenon in more detail: he recorded subjects' individual response times to decide whether a word denoted something that was natural or manmade. The mean response time for superordinate terms was 1·03 sec, the mean response time for subordinate terms was 1·06 sec, and the difference was not reliable. There was a reliable difference between the two sorts of words only in the case of a third group of low frequency subordinates (mean response time 1·11 sec).

Here for the moment the work inspired by the notion of utility rests. Its great bugbear, of course, is that what is useful to know about one word may not be useful to know about another word, and hence any general prediction is almost certainly false. Unfortunately, the technique of examining knowledge of rare words can yield only general predictions, and, as every literary-minded person knows, words are unique. What is needed is a way of assessing utility for individual words, and such a technique has so far eluded us.

Context and the Facilitation of Lexical Judgements

If an individual is asked whether a given string of letters is an English word, the time he takes to make his decision depends upon a number of factors. One such factor, demonstrated by Meyer and his colleagues, is that there are residual effects from one judgement to the next: a positive response is faster when it has been preceded by a positive response to an associated word rather than to an unassociated word (Meyer and Schvaneveldt, 1971). The facilitation diminishes as the time between the two decisions is increased, with some additional loss when this interval is occupied by a judgement about a non-word: but it is enhanced when the second word is presented in a visually degraded form (Meyer, Schvaneveldt, and Ruddy, 1972). Similar residual effects have been demonstrated in tasks requiring an explicitly semantic judgement (e.g., Collins and Quillian, 1970; Meyer, 1973); but it is interesting that they should occur in a task which does not necessarily require the meanings of words to be retrieved. Since there is likely to be more than one sort of organization for lexical memory, it is natural to wonder whether such effects would occur in tasks where judgements have to be made about some syntactic or phonological property of words.

Meyer and his colleagues have been primarily concerned with delineating the mechanism underlying the residual effects, but an equally important question is what role, if any, these effects play in normal linguistic processing. Is it really advantageous to have a slightly more rapid access to the associates of a recently encountered word?

Before we can answer this question it is necessary to deal with an important peculiarity of the studies of *semantic* categorization. A listener can hardly comprehend a sentence such as 'a canary is a bird', without at the same time verifying it. But, for the vast majority of sentences in discourse, comprehension is virtually involuntary and usually effortless, whereas verification requires a deliberate decision and may involve considerable effort (*cf.* Davies and Isard, 1972). This difference forces us to consider what information a listener is likely to retrieve from lexical memory merely to *understand* an ordinary contingent sentence. What information, for instance, would be retrieved from the lexical entry for 'canary' in order to understand a sentence such as 'The canary won the prize'? One conjecture, which has a superficial appeal, is that a listener retrieves no direct information from the lexical entry but merely accesses it and checks that it contains some semantic information. A subsequent retrieval of this information may take place in, say, trying to verify the sentence, but mere access is sufficient for comprehension, provided that there is at least some semantic information stored in the lexical entry. This sort of access-and-check may very well occur on occasion. But there are strong grounds for supposing that it is not the only mode of using lexical memory in comprehension. A study carried out by Green (1973) provides neat evidence for access-with-retrieval. He devised a task in which listeners had to respond as quickly as possible to a tone presented somewhere in a sentence. He argued that the latency of a response would depend, in part, upon the amount of semantic processing that was going on during the perception of the tone. This hypothesis was borne out by the fact that subjects who had to make up suitable continuations to the sentences, and who were accordingly concentrating on comprehension, were much slower to respond to the tone than subjects who had merely to give a verbatim recall of the sentences. Among a number of variables, Green manipulated the frequency of usage of the words that occurred in the initial nounphrases of the sentences. Because subjects are likely to know more about the meanings of high frequency words than low frequency words, Green predicted that the presence of high frequency words should lead to more semantic processing, and consequently, to slower responses to the tone. The effect should be most noticeable when a listener is trying to combine an interpretation of the initial nounphrase with an interpretation of the verbphrase. Hence, the latency of responses to tones occurring at the ends of sentences should be slower when their initial nounphrases were made up of high frequency words. However, the effect should occur only when a subject was making a thorough-going attempt to understand the sentences, and not when he was merely committing them to verbatim memory. The interaction is clearly evident in the results which are given in Table 7.3: there is little effect of

Table 7.3. Geometric mean response times (msec) to a signal at the end of a sentence

	Initial nounphrase with:	
	High frequency words	Low frequency words
Memorization condition	558	550
Comprehension condition	1015	936

nounphrase frequency on response times in the verbatim memory condition, but high frequency nouns lead to a reliable retardation of response times in the comprehension condition. Since the effect of frequency lies in the opposite direction to what would be expected if the words had merely to be recognized, it seems very probable that semantic information was being retrieved during the process of comprehension.

Yet it is plausible to suppose that a listener does not necessarily retrieve *all* the information he possesses about each word occurring in a sentence. Proper names provide a clear case to the contrary. In understanding the sentence 'Eden resigned after Suez' we plainly do not have to retrieve all we know about either the man or the canal. Indeed, one of the greatest advantages of proper names, as Searle (1969) has emphasized, is that they allow us to communicate successfully even when we have no knowledge in common about a given referent. Proper nouns are the primary example of words that contain encyclopedic information, rather than linguistic information, in their lexical entries; and there is perhaps a continuum from them through common nouns, which often involve a mixture of both sorts of information, to relational terms like verbs and prepositions, which involve only linguistic information. Of course there is no implication that only linguistic information is retrieved in comprehension. The critical point is that what is retrieved for a given word probably depends upon its context. Different features of a word become salient as its context is varied, e.g.

(3) He peeled a tomato   (tomatoes have skins)
    The tomato rolled across the room   (tomatoes are round)
    The tomato gradually ripened   (tomatoes are fruit)

In these examples the selectional restrictions of the verb presumably determine the information that comes to mind about tomatoes. But a similar effect can be obtained without the agency of selectional restrictions, e.g.

(4) He sat on a tomato   (tomatoes are squashy, messy)
    The sun was an over-ripe tomato   (tomatoes are red)
    He likes tomatoes   (tomatoes are eaten)

Let us return to the question of why there is a slightly more rapid access to the associates of a recently encountered word. Such effects may simply be a consequence of our sensitivity to context. We need to hold context in mind in order to decide what information to retrieve. The underlying mechanism may involve opening up access to semantically related areas of the lexicon for a limited period of time. If this conjecture is correct, then decisions about the meaning of a word should be facilitated in certain contexts; and there is, indeed, some corroboratory evidence on this point. Hodgkin has shown in a series of unpublished experiments that selectional restrictions render more salient the relevant aspects of nouns falling under them. In one of her experiments, the subjects had to decide as quickly as possible whether or not a noun of a certain sort had occurred in a sentence. The target class in one condition was ANIMATE nouns, and such nouns occurred in sentences with both relevant selectional restrictions (e.g., 'The milk pleased the butcher, where 'please' selects an animate object) and irrelevent selectional restrictions (e.g., 'The milk soaked the butcher'). Responses where the restriction was relevant had a mean latency of 1·07 sec, responses where it was irrelevant had a mean latency of 1·26 sec, and the difference was reliable. The effect was evident regardless of whether the target noun occurred before or after the verb; and, perhaps surprisingly, there was no difference between the latencies for nouns in these two positions. It remains to be seen whether such effects of context upon semantic judgements can be mediated other than by selection restrictions.

Linguistic Constraints on Semantic Theory

It should be evident that the debate over the empirical findings of the studies of semantic categorization is myopic. Judgements about the merits of the alternative theories have almost entirely been based upon their power to explain phenomena demonstrated in the laboratory. Doubtless there are many psychologists who regard this debating rule as entirely proper. Yet any psychologist who studies semantic memory is confronted by the following question: are the phenomena revealed by an experiment a genuine reflection of human linguistic performance? If they are genuinely revealing, then, of course, a satisfactory explanation of them must form an integral part of a theory of linguistic performance. On the other hand, an explanation of them that is incompatible with what is known about the workings of language can be justified only on the grounds that the phenomena do not reflect ordinary linguistic processes. Theorists cannot have it both ways: either their work is relevant and their theoretical cogs must mesh with others, or else they are in the business of constructing epicycles out of idle wheels.

There are a number of obvious constraints that linguistic performance places on any psychological theory of meaning. The meanings of words must be compatible with the meanings of sentences, and the theory must accordingly be compatible with a viable account of syntax. The only subtlety about this point is that the distinction between syntax and semantics is psychologically neither clearly nor deeply drawn. Children seem to learn their language without any conscious realization of it, adults are often unaware of it when asked to make judgements about grammaticality, and linguists are always arguing about where it should be drawn. Of course, it is far too soon to determine which of the alternative syntactic theories proferred by linguists is the most appropriate. The existence of alternative religions is always a good argument for agnosticism, but it must be said that none of the current theories provides a very plausible basis for syntactic analysis *in vivo*—a situation that is unlikely to improve until linguists regain an interest in performance (but *cf* Kimball, 1974).

It is similarly obvious that a semantic theory should be able to account both for the myriad of semantic relations, such as synonymy, hyponomy, antonymy, that can hold between linguistic expressions, and for the different sorts of semantic properties, such as ambiguity, anomaly, analyticity, that can apply to single expressions. Since it is unlikely that such 'intensional' aspects of language can be accommodated by any theory that takes words as its primitive elements, the analogy between a mental lexicon and a real dictionary is grossly misleading. Dictionaries contain words in their lexical entries and they are notoriously circular: they provide no way of escaping from words. A theory might give a perfectly feasible account of the meanings of words and sentences, and the intensional relations between them, yet if it goes no further, it is severely deficient. Language may apply, or fail to apply, to the world, and this fundamental fact must not be overlooked by semantic theory lest, like a dictionary, it cuts itself off in an isolated lexical limbo. The need to relate language to the world has become more pressing since the advent among philosophers of what might be called the 'extensionalist backlash'. Such philosophers, inspired by Quine and Davidson, and by the development of semantical models of modal logic, argue that a proper analysis of language need concern itself solely with truth conditions and other 'extensional' aspects of expressions (*cf.* Hintikka, (1969); Lewis, (1972)). This attitude is plainly defensible from a logical point of view, but it is almost certainly incompatible with—not to say inimical to—any serious attempt to formulate a psychological theory of semantics.

Yet, of course, semantic theory must be able to handle extensions. What is needed is a way of relating terms to sets of objects, properties, or events, of relating descriptions to referents, assertions to truth values, commands to states of affairs that satisfy them, and so on. Since this problem has been relatively neglected by psycholinguists let us consider in some detail the question of how a word is to be related to the world. A simple assumption might be that a word such as 'table' is associated in semantic memory with a set of visual images—presumably images of those items that the individual has encountered as instances of tables. While it is probably true that 'table' can evoke a set of images, it seems unlikely that its relation to the world is established in this way. Since we can build up complex images from more basic components, it is more plausible to suppose that, instead of a set of images, there is a set of procedures that can be used both to generate images and to identify perceived objects. This view seems close to that version of 'procedural semantics' in which the meaning of a word is simply the operational procedure for identifying objects as exemplars of it (*cf.* Woods, 1968). Yet even this more sophisticated approach will not quite suffice. Let us suppose that we had such a procedure for identifying tables. It would presumably consist of a number of perceptual tests such as:

(5) TABLE: Is it a physical object?
      Does it have a flat surface?

Does it have a leg or legs at right-angles to this surface?
etc.

(An item such as 'leg', of course, may in turn call upon a further set of tests.) Such a procedure might be framed so as to identify conventional tables. It might even be elaborated to include unconventional tables. But, no purely perceptual procedure would contain an appropriate sense of the ridiculous—a sense that would immediately grasp the absurdity of a table with all its legs in one corner (*cf.* Carelman, 1971). In short, the meaning of a word such as 'table' is more than just a set of procedures for handling its extension. It is necessary to distinguish between the *concept* of a table and the perceptual *routine* for identifying a table. The concept will include a variety of information, often functional in nature, that may not correspond to any direct perceptual test, e.g.

(6) TABLE: (moveable) manmade object used in eating, working or playing games, and that serves to support objects used in the course of such activities.

The perceptual characteristics of tables follow from such information: the identification routine must be guided by the concept.

There is a further point to be made. If the meaning of a word were a set of images or perceptual procedures acquired by ostensive definition, then meanings of different words could be acquired totally independently of one another. This notion violates our very strong intuition that the meanings of words are related to one another, i.e. that there are intensional relations between them, constituting semantic 'fields'. That we learn a taxonomy rather than isolated words is obvious in the case of colour terms, since there are no unlabelable gaps in the visible spectrum. But similar interrelations pervade the lexicon; and they are not so much a way of relating already defined words but rather an inherent part of their definitions (*cf.* Harrison, 1972).

It is a commonplace of Empiricist theories of language that, once certain primary words have been related to the world, other secondary words may take their meaning by association with them [*cf.* for example, Osgood's (1953) distinction between *signs* and *assigns*]. This view should be distinguished from what might be called the Basic English Stratagem. The reader may recall that Ogden, who collaborated with Richards in writing *The Meaning of Meaning*, invented a language called 'Basic English'. It consists of some 900 or so common English words; and with them, Ogden claimed, anything that was worth saying could be said—a fact evidently borne out by the translation of such works as *Gulliver's Travels* into Basic. The pedagogical advantage of Basic for second language learners is presumably considerable, but alas it seems never to have caught the imagination of non-native speakers of English, perhaps because of its extremely sketchy syntax and because a speaker is reduced to such circumlocutions as 'The woman to whom I am married is going to have a baby' instead of 'My wife is pregnant'. Nevertheless, it seems likely that given the meanings of a set of basic words, the meanings of other words can be defined in terms of them; and a theorist might devise a program that would simulate the process given the necessary initial data (the meanings of the basic terms) and routines for interpreting sentential definitions. What Ogden does not seem to have assumed, unlike many Empiricists, is that the Basic terms could all be defined perceptually. Whether one wishes to work with basic words, or fundamental semantic components, the fact remains that many of them are irreducibly non-perceptual, e.g. the notions of ownership, kinship, obligation.

Such considerations lead naturally to the requirement that the primitive terms of a semantic theory should be psychologically motivated. There are clearly a number of relevant criteria such as the naturalness of definitions. For instance, it is plausible to define 'bachelor' as 'not married', but it would be ridiculous to take it as a primitive, together with 'spinster', and to define 'married' as 'not a bachelor or a spinster'. Such a system could doubtless be made to work, but its logic would hardly correspond to reality. The relation of marriage is a primitive concept if ever there was one. And this fact should be reflected in the working definitions of everyday life. It should also be noted that in defining 'bachelor' as 'not married' one is (correctly) presupposing that the relevant individual is an adult male. This supposition suggests that the concepts of maleness and adulthood are more primitive than the concept of marriage. A similar, and perhaps related criterion, would be provided by examining children's semantic development—not merely, of course, their explicit vocabulary but the working concepts that underlie it.

Where psychological considerations are not allowed to determine the set of primitives, then a semantic analysis often seems arbitrary, and one is inclined to wonder whether it is, in Burling's (1964) memorable phrase, 'God's truth or hocus pocus'. The point can be illustrated by considering some alternative analyses of the locative preposition, 'at'. Cooper (1968) in her analysis of locatives offered an analysis along the following lines:

(7) x *at* y: x is near or in y, with the constraint that x is portable relative to y, and y is not a geopolitical area.

whereas Leech (1969) suggested an analysis of the following sort:

(8) x *at* y: x is contiguous or juxtaposed with the place of y, where the dimensionality of y is not significant

Neither of these analyses seems entirely satisfactory: 'at' can clearly contrast with 'near' and 'in', and the notions of contiguity and juxtaposition seem more complicated than 'at'. One is reminded a little of Dr Johnson's definition of a 'network' as 'any thing reticulated or decussated, at equal distances, with interstices between the intersections'. Such criticisms are, of course, unfair. The respective definitions seem perfectly well able to handle the intensional

elations between locative prepositions, and this function is what they were
rincipally designed to fulfil. It is instructive, however, to inquire into the
xtensional aspects of 'at', and to ask under what conditions a statement of the
orm x *is at* y is true. This question sharpens up any consideration of what
hould be treated as primitive; and it also demonstrates how it is often difficult
o distinguish between perceptual and conceptual primitives. Let us consider
nder what circumstances the following three assertions are true:

(9) He is at the desk.
     He is at his office.
     He is at Bognor Regis.

Two points are immediately evident. First, no simple constant relation between
objects is involved: the place where x has to be in order to render true 'x is at y'
depends upon y, and probably upon x, too. Second, although there are many
ituations that render an assertion of this form definitely true, and many
ituations that render it definitely false, there are probably other situations that
are more equivocal. One way to try to accommodate both these points is to
ntroduce, as a primitive notion, the idea of a 'region' of an object. Intuitively,
he region of an object, y, is where x has to be in order to interact with it
ohysically, socially, or in whatever way x's interact with y's. We can assume that
ndividuals are capable of making a perceptual judgement about such matters;
his judgement will usually be secure but occasionally it will be uncertain. It is
aow possible to sketch a simple routine for the extension of 'at'.
     In order to determine whether something labelled 'A' is *at* something
abelled 'B', apply the following tests:

(10) (i)   Find something labelled B. [($\exists$ y) (By)?]
      (ii) Determine that B has a region. [($\exists$ w) (Region(w, y)?]
      (iii) Find something labelled A. [($\exists$ x) (Ax & x $\neq$ y)?]
      (iv) Test whether A is included in the region of B. [Include (x, Region(w, y))?]

If the first three operations fail for any reason, then it is unclear whether the
statement is true or false; but provided these 'presuppositions' are fulfilled, the
truth value of the statement hinges upon the outcome of the fourth and final
test. Of course, our previous arguments suggest that it is a mistake to treat
words in isolation: they should be analysed in related groups in order to capture
their 'field' properties. It is not obvious how best to proceed, but the next
constraint upon semantic theory provides a clue.
     In attempting to verify a sentence it is necessary to recognize words and to
retrieve semantic information about them from lexical memory. In describing
the world, on the other hand, it is necessary to go into lexical memory with the
results of conceptual and perceptual tests and to retrieve appropriate words.
But access to lexical memory is even more flexible as may be illustrated by an

example. Let us suppose that a listener attempts to verify a simple locative assertion such as 'John is at the gate'. There are clearly a number of theoretical strategies open to him. The view implicit in the picture-verification models developed independently by Clark and Chase (1972) and Trabasso (1972) is that an internal representation of the sentence is matched against an internal representation of reality. This strategy is certainly feasible when evaluating the description of a picture. It is less feasible when evaluating a locative description of the real world, because it will be unclear what aspects of the world should be examined until the sentence has been understood. Indeed, one obvious function of a locative description is to inform a listener of the whereabouts of some object by locating it in relation to a known landmark. The listener does not match the sentence against reality, rather he uses one part of it to guide his search and another part of it to test what he finds. When he is told that John is at the gate, he first finds the gate, and then checks whether John is there. This search-and-check strategy involves:

(11) (i) Setting up a semantic representation of the sentence.
 (ii) Determining the referent of 'the gate'.
 (iii) Retrieving a specification of the location of this referent from episodic memory.
 (iv) Finding it in the real world.
 (v) Looking within the region specified by 'at the gate' and testing whether John is within this region.

Looking back at the routine (10) for 'at' we see that it corresponds to the last two steps of the present routine. But evidently it was a mistake to include the presuppositional steps (i), (ii), and (iii), within the routine for 'at', since they are part of the verification routine for many locative expressions.

There is no reason why the particular strategy of first finding the gate and then testing for John's presence should form a fixed sequence in a verification routine. It is also possible to use the sentence 'John is at the gate' to locate a particular gate—the one, perhaps, that needs a new coat of paint. The listener's routine in this case might involve:

(12) (i) Setting up a semantic representation of the sentence.
 (ii) Determining the referent of 'John'.
 (iii) Retrieving a specification of John's appearance from episodic memory.
 (iv) Finding him in the real world.
 (v) Looking to see whether he is within the region of anything and testing whether it is a gate.

Of course, this routine is not the end of the story. The listener may wish to verify that it is, indeed, *the* gate that needs to be painted. Alternatively, he may be in no position to verify the statement: its function may be purely informative. In such a case, he may want to store a mental representation of the particular gate which he is, in effect, being told needs to be painted. (It is interesting to note that such a statement would plainly be falsified if there was no gate in John's vicinity; but it could hardly be verified by the listener since its function is to identify something for him.) However, in order to maintain parity with the previous routine (11) let us suppose that the listener is in a position to verify, and wishes to do so. Clearly, the last step of the above procedure would in this case involve:

(13) (v) Looking to see whether John is within the region of anything, and testing whether it corresponds to the referent of 'the gate'.

These examples establish that the presuppositional aspects of locative prepositions should be excluded from their semantic representations, and that the critical operation for 'at' is simply testing whether x is included in the region of y: Include (x, Region (w, y)?). However, the mode of executing such a test is clearly extremely variable. The routines corresponding to x and y may be executed first and then the inclusive test carried out, or the routine for x may be completed and a search initiated for a value corresponding to y, and so on. Moreover, a listener needs to grasp the *illocutionary function* of a sentence in order to determine an appropriate course of action. If an assertion is intended as an implicit command (e.g., 'John is at the gate', so open it for him), then it would be inappropriate merely to verify it. But even if it is intended as a statement it may be a simple verifiable statement, or it may be purely informative (e.g., 'John is at the gate I like') and not open to immediate verification. Hence, the notion of illocutionary function is perhaps wider in scope than Austin's (1962) celebrated concept of illocutionary force. However, whatever course of action is appropriate, the listener must first understand the sentence before he can act upon it. He must, to adopt a potent metaphor (Davies and Isard, 1972), compile the program before he can execute it. But the metaphor does not go far enough. As we have seen, the meaning of a sentence is no mere program, which when executed determines the truth value of a sentence. It is rather a structured set of subroutines that can be called in a variety of orders by general purpose programs responsible for verifying statements, obeying commands, storing representations in episodic memory, and so forth.

Does the reader understand the meaning of the sentence 'John is at the gate'? Doubtless any native speaker of English does. But does the reader understand the *significance* of this sentence? No, he or she does not; for to grasp its significance it is necessary to know what is referred to by the expressions 'John' and 'the gate', and to appreciate the illocutionary function of the sentence. This distinction between meaning and significance emerges naturally from the conception of semantics presented here; and it is a useful distinction, ignored at the peril of unnecessary confusion. For instance, it is increasingly argued that no merely linguistic analysis of sentences is of much value to studies of memory, since it is demonstrable that individuals usually remember *more* than any such analysis would, or should, reveal. At its heart, this view seems to confuse meaning and significance, and therefore to throw the baby out with the bath water. Wherever possible an individual is likely to remember the significance of a sentence, which goes beyond the frontier of language into the extensional world; and where an individual cannot grasp the significance of a sentence, he is unlikely to remember it correctly (Bransford and Johnson, 1972). But meaning is a prerequisite for significance, and a linguistic analysis could be extremely pertinent to the process of comprehension.

The problem of flexible access to lexical memory appears to be trivial in the case of a single locative preposition, but it does raise considerable difficulties when considered together with the need for words to be related to one another in semantic 'fields'. Indeed, a speaker's task of selecting a suitable term to characterize a perceived relation demonstrates again the necessity for such an organization. He needs flexible access to a whole set of words, since once he has established which perceptual tests are satisfied, his task is to emerge with an appropriate word. One way of envisaging the organization of the lexicon, which appears to provide the necessary flexibility, is in terms of interrelated decision tables. A subset of the locative presuppositions may be organized on the lines illustrated in Table 7.4. This table represents the meaning of a subset of

Table 7.4. A simplified decision table for a set of locative prepositions

	'Far'	'Near'	'With'	'At'	'By'	'Against'
(i) Large (Distance (x, y))	+	−	(−)	(−)	(−)	(−)
(ii) Include $(x, \text{Region} (w, y))$			+	+	+	(+)
(iii) Include $(y, \text{Region} (v, x))$			+	−		
(iv) $(\exists z)$ (Between (x, z, y))					−	
(v) Touch (x, y)						+

prepositions, displayed across the top of the table, in terms of a variety of perceptual tests. The analysis is obvious for *far* and *near*. A less obvious feature is that we tend to say *with* rather than *at* when two comparable objects are involved, i.e. where both x is included in the region of y and y is included in the region of x. Obviously, where either of these two tests is satisfied, there cannot be a large distance between the two objects, and hence this test is redundant. Redundant tests are indicated in the table by placing their values in parentheses.

In verifying an assertion involving a locative preposition, it is necessary to locate the preposition within the decision table and then to execute the routine of tests it calls. It is not necessary to execute tests that are redundant, and therefore the verification routine will automatically jump to non-redundant tests, executing first those that require positive outcomes. The sequencing of the tests can be built into the decision table itself to a considerable extent. But when we turn to the use of the table by a speaker seeking to describe a locative relation, this 'built-in' sequence is largely irrelevant. Let us suppose that the speaker has decided that one of the 'distance' prepositions is called for, i.e. he is not concerned with the deictic or dimensional relations between the two objects. He is therefore likely to enter Table 7.4 at its first test (i). If the distance between the two objects is large, then *far* is an appropriate word; if it is not large, then *near* is an appropriate word. Yet, if the distance is not large, it is likely that further tests would be conducted before leaving the Table. The speaker will probably test whether one item is included in the region of the other. If the result of this test (ii) is negative, he may safely leave the Table armed with the word *near*. However, if it is positive, a slight quandary arises: in what order should the remaining tests be executed. A natural solution would be to assume that their order is arbitrary, or that they are conducted in parallel, and that it is only when the results of all of them are known that an attempt is made to select an appropriate word. For example, the set of values:

(14) (iii) Is y included in the region of x?   −
     (iv) Is anything between x and y?   −
     (v) Is x touching y?   +

clearly satisfies the requirements of Table 7.4 for *at, by* and *against*, whereas the set of values:

(15) (iii) Is y included in the region of x?   +
     (iv) Is anything between x and y?   +
     (v) Is x touching y?   +

satisfies the requirements of *with* and *against*. Which word a speaker actually uses in cases where there is a choice, will depend upon a variety of factors, including the degree of precision he is aiming for, the amount of work he wishes to put the listener to, and so on. It is such factors, of course, that will determine his initial predilection for a particular sort of locative preposition.

The most pertinent problem arising from the use of decision tables is the order of executing the tests. It seems evident, on the one hand, that the order is not always arbitrary. It would be extremely uneconomical to carry out all the tests in Table 7.4 if the result of the first test reveals that the objects are far apart from one another. On the other hand, it seems unlikely that there is some standard order that is strictly adhered to in all uses of the Table. Perhaps the most plausible conjecture is that the routine for finding a word is sensitive to various properties of decision tables, such as the disposition of the values of tests.

Recapitulation and Conclusion

The present paper has offered, in effect, some conditions that must be satisfied by a psychologically oriented theory of semantics, and it may be useful to summarize them here:

1 A semantic theory must incorporate what is established experimentally about the process of comprehension and the retrieval of information from the mental lexicon.
2 The meanings of words must be compatible with the meanings of sentences, and a semantic theory must accordingly be compatible with a set of syntactic rules.
3 A semantic theory should account for the intensional properties of linguistic expressions and for the intensional relations between them.
4 A semantic theory should account for the extensional relations between linguistic expressions and the world.
5 The primitive terms of a semantic theory should be psychologically motivated.
6 The illocutionary function of linguistic expressions must be taken into account in order to distinguish between meaning and significance.
7 A semantic theory must provide for the organization of words into semantic 'fields', and for their flexible accessibility in lexical memory.

It would not be difficult to suggest further more stringent conditions; yet it is clear that no existing theory, whether drawn from logic, linguistics, or psychology, meets even these seven simple requirements. What, then, have we achieved by considering them?

The body of experimental results failed to establish conclusively whether words or some other elements should be taken as primitive, and whether the phenomena of categorization are best accounted for in terms of an associative network, lists of category exemplars, or sets of semantic features. However, a plausible explanation of the data could be given in terms of semantic features; the number of categorical features possessed by a word could account for its degree of category membership, for its rated semantic distance from the category, for its associative frequency as an exemplar of the category, and for the latency of a decision about its category membership. The argument in favour of features as primitive elements of semantic theory was strengthened by considering the intensional aspects of linguistic expressions, especially the meanings of verbs. But the need to explain the extensional aspects of language suggested that the somewhat uncertain notion of a semantic feature might be better replaced by the notion of a routine of perceptual and conceptual tests. The analysis of semantic 'fields', and of the demands placed upon them by speakers and listeners, suggested that such routines may be organized in a form resembling decision tables.

Acknowledgements

I am grateful to a number of my colleagues and students for making available to me the results of their experiments, and also to Professor N. S. Sutherland

r some useful criticisms of an earlier version of this paper. I owe a very
onsiderable debt to Professor George A. Miller: most of the ideas about
sychological theories of meaning were developed in collaboration with him,
hough he is in no way responsible for any errors in their present formulation.

eferences

ustin, J. L. (1962). *How to do Things with Words*. Oxford: Clarendon Press.
ransford, J. D. and Johnson, M. K. (1972). Contextual prerequisites for understand-
    ing: some investigations of comprehension and recall. *Journal of Verbal Learning and
    Verbal Behavior*. **11**, 717–726.
urling, R. (1964). Cognition and componential analysis: God's truth or hocus-pocus?
    American Anthropologist, **66**, 20–28.
arelman, J. (1971). *Catalog of Fantastic Things*. New York: Ballantine.
homsky, N. (1965). *Aspects of the Theory of Syntax*. Cambridge: M.I.T. Press.
lark, H. H. and Chase, W. G. (1972). On the process of comparing sentences against
    pictures. *Cognitive Psychology*, **3**, 472–517.
ollins, A. M. and Quillian, M. R. (1969). Retrieval time from semantic memory.
    Journal of Verbal Learning and Verbal Behavior, **8**, 240–247.
ollins, A. M. and Quillian, M. R. (1970). Facilitating retrieval from semantic memory:
    the effect of repeating part of an inference. *Acta Psychologica*, **33**, 304–314.
ollins, A. M. and Quillian, M. R. (1972). How to make a language user. In E. Tulving
    and W. Donaldson (Eds) *Organization of Memory*, pp. 309–351. New York:
    Academic Press.
onrad, C. (1972). Cognitive economy in semantic memory. *Journal of Experimental
    Psychology*, **92**, 149–154.
ooper, G. S. (1968). A semantic analysis of English locative prepositions. *Report No.
    1587*, Bolt, Beranek and Newman, Inc., Cambridge, Mass.
avies, D. J. M. and Isard S. (1972). Utterances as programs. In D. Michie (Ed.)
    Machine Intelligence 7, pp. 325–339. Edinburgh: Edinburgh University Press.
reen, D. W. (1973). *A Psychological Investigation into the Memory and Comprehen-
    sion of Sentences*. Unpublished Ph.D. thesis, University of London.
arrison, B. (1972). *Meaning and Structure: An Essay in the Philosophy of Language*.
    New York: Harper and Row.
eider, E. R. (In press). On the internal structure of perceptual and semantic
    categories. In T. M. Moore (Ed.) *Cognitive Development and the Acquisition of
    Language*. New York: Academic Press.
intikka, J. (1969). *Models for Modalities: Selected Essays*. Dordrecht–Holland:
    Reidel.
imball, J. (1974). Seven principles of surface structure parsing in natural language.
    Cognition, **2**, 15–47.
akoff, G. (1972). Hedges: a study in meaning criteria and the logic of fuzzy concepts.
    In G. Lakoff and R. Lakoff (Eds) *Studies in Generative Semantics II*. Mimeo,
    University of Michigan.
andauer, T. K. and Freedman, J. L. (1968). Information retrieval from long-term
    memory: category size and recognition time. *Journal of Verbal Learning and Verbal
    Behavior*, **7**, 291–295.
eech, G. N. (1969). *Towards a Semantic Description of English*. London: Longmans.
ewis, D. K. (1972). General semantics. In D. Davidson and G. Harman (Eds)
    Semantics of Natural Language, pp. 169–218. Dordrecht–Holland: Reidel.
eyer, D. E. (1970). On the representation and retrieval of stored semantic informa-
    tion. *Cognitive Psychology*, **1**, 242–300.

Meyer, D. E. (1973). Correlated operations in searching stored semantic categorie *Journal of Experimental Psychology*, **99**, 124–133.

Meyer, D. E. and Schvaneveldt, R. W. (1971). Facilitation in recognizing pairs (words: evidence of a dependence between retrieval operations. *Journal of Experimer tal Psychology*, **90**, 227–234.

Meyer, D. E., Schvaneveldt, R. W. and Ruddy, M. G. (1972). Activation of lexic memory. Paper presented at Psychonomic Society Meeting. St. Louis, Missouri.

Miller, G. A. (1972). English verbs of motion: a case study in semantics and lexic memory. In A. W. Melton and E. Martin (Eds) *Coding Processes in Human Memor* pp. 335–372. Washington: Winston.

Ogden, C. K. and Richards, I. A. (1923). *The Meaning of Meaning.* London: Routledg and Kegan Paul.

Osgood, C. E. (1953). *Method and Theory in Experimental Psychology.* New Yor Oxford University Press.

Rips, L. J., Shoben, E. J. and Smith, E. E. (1973). Semantic distance and the verificatic of semantic relations. *Journal of Verbal Learning and Verbal Behavior*, **12**, 1–20.

Schaeffer, B. and Wallace, R. (1969). Semantic similarity and the comparison of wor meanings. *Journal of Experimental Psychology*, **82**, 343–346.

Schaeffer, B. and Wallace, R. (1970). The comparison of word meanings. *Journal (Experimental Psychology*, **86**, 144–152.

Searle, J. R. (1969). *Speech Acts: An Essay in the Philosophy of Language.* Cambridg Cambridge University Press.

Smith, E. E., Haviland, S. E., Buckley, P. B. and Sack, M. (1972). Retrieval of artifici facts from long-term memory. *Journal of Verbal Learning and Verbal Behavior*, **1** 583–593.

Trabasso, T. (1972). Mental operations in language comprehension. In R. O. Freed and J. B. Carroll (Eds) *Language Comprehension and the Acquisition of Knowledg* pp. 113–137. Washington: Winston.

Wilkins, A. J. (1971). Conjoint frequency, category size, and categorization tim *Journal of Verbal Learning and Verbal Behavior*, **10**, 382–385.

Woods, W. A. (1967). Semantics for a question–answering system. *Report No. NSF-1* Mathematical Linguistics and Automatic Translation. Harvard Computation Laboratory, Cambridge, Mass.

Chapter 8

Things to Remember

Nico H. Frijda

This paper presents some reflections on the kinds of information which human memory may retain. When undertaking the construction of a memory model such reflection becomes a necessity: one should know what different structural properties to incorporate. Different kinds of structure, moreover, may require different processes, in a model as well as in human memory itself.

In investigating internal representation of information, we will take as our guide Guilford's taxonomy of informational products and, in particular, his analysis of memory abilities. We think that factor analytic studies can be useful for experimental psychology. Different cognitive abilities or factors reflect, in our opinion, differences in the cognitive processes involved (to the extent that they do not reflect differential familiarity with kinds of material, as may be the case, for instance, with numerical ability). This, obviously, is an assumption, but one which is well supported by considerations of test constructors as well as by introspections of test takers. Guilford (1967) frequently justifies his hypotheses concerning the factor upon which a test is to load by reference to the strategies they permit or induce the subjects to employ. Analysis of thinking-aloud protocols quite often renders the loading pattern of a test intelligible (Elshout, 1974).

In the area of memory, Guilford has demonstrated the existence of six factors for each of the three domains of figural, symbolic and semantic material (Guilford, 1967; Guilford and Hoepfner, 1971; Bradley, Guilford and Hoepfner, 1969; Brown, Guilford and Hoepfner, 1966; Tenopyr, Guilford and Hoepfner, 1966). Part of this work has been replicated and extended in our laboratory by Kamstra (1971). Kamstra confirmed the existence of the six symbolic and the six semantic factors; this is a comforting demonstration of the occasional stability of psychological results, since all tests were newly constructed Dutch versions of the original tests, and performed by Dutch subjects. In addition, the independence of symbolic and semantic factors was demonstrated. Memory for symbolic classes, relations, systems, transformations and implications proved different from memory for semantic classes, relations, systems, transformations and implications. Remembering paired associates consisting of relatively meaningful words (author names and booktitles; names and professions) appeared to involve different processes from that of paired associates consisting of number–letter pairs, and similar differences hold for most other cognitive products. As a general result, his 16 semantic tests showed only four significant loadings on the six symbolic factors (all of which fell on MSU, memory for symbolic units); the 17 symbolic tests had three significant loadings on the six semantic factors (all three on MMU, indicating the relative lack of success in separating the two unit factors).

Differences in materials and products, then, appear to have psychological consequences. This conclusion is supported by still another result, given here with due recognition of the fact that many variables are uncontrolled. In another part of Kamstra's study, 16 tests covering four symbolic and four semantic factors, were given to two groups of subjects. Study time was sufficient for perfect or near perfect recall on a test immediately afterwards. The groups were retested (with different testing modes) following an interval of 3 or 6 weeks.

The results were surprising. The two tests for the same factor behaved quite similarly. Moreover, the tests for corresponding factors, symbolic and semantic, also behaved quite similarly. On the other hand, forgetting curves for different kinds of material, differed drastically. The data are given in Tables 8.1 and 8.2. Admittedly, these results should be considered with caution since learning times, test length, recall-testing mode and scoring procedures, differed

Table 8.1. Immediate and delayed recall of test content [see Appendix]

Test name	Factor	% Correct Immed. reprod. ($N = 138$)	% Correct 3 weeks ($N = 65$)	% Correct 6 weeks ($N = 73$)
Picture recall	MMU	98	72	55
Proverb recall	MMU	75	85	64
Sequence recall	MMS	67	24	21
System recall (M)	MMS	79	22	16
Unusual uses	MMT	96	91	74
Misunderstood words	MMT	89	63	41
Associations	MMI	97	25	6
Pair formation	MMI	98	22	8
Meaningless sentences	MSU	91	85	77
Codewords	MSU	65	61	45
System recall (S)	MSS	80	18	12
Mnemonic aids	MSS	78	31	26
Sentence coding	MST	62	69	56
Spelling changes	MST	93	63	31
Symbolic implications	MSI	49	08	05
Significant correlations	MSI	90	37	15

Table 8.2. Immediate and delayed recall for semantic and symbolic tests

	Semantic tests			Symbolic tests		
	Immediate	3 weeks	6 weeks	Immediate	3 weeks	6 weeks
Units	86·5	78·5	57·5	78	73	61
Systems	73	23	18·5	79	24·5	19
Transformations	92·5	77	57·5	77·5	66	43·5
Implications	97·5	23·5	7	69·5	22·5	10

(Immediate recall is performance of both groups together)

from test to test; they also did so between tests for the same factors, however, none of these variables seems clearly responsible for the differences in slope of the forgetting curves.

The foregoing is to argue the point that Guilford's categories may serve a useful purpose in the study of memory process and of internal representation of knowledge. We must add that, for this study of internal representation, not only memory abilities are relevant. The memory abilities are concerned with what Tulving called 'episodic memory': subjects study lists of some material, and have to give evidence of retention of what was on that particular list. Other abilities have to do with 'semantic memory', i.e. with general knowledge acquired previously. Cognition and divergent or convergent production abilities often tap this general knowledge.

Cognitive Units

Cognitive units in tests of unit factors are either unitary visual or acoustic forms, (such as pictures of objects, printed letters, morse codes, written or spoken words or numbers), or word meanings and unitary ideas generally. Tests for the cognition of figural units involve recognition of letters under near threshold conditions, or incomplete stimuli such as in the Street–Gestalt test. Tests for symbolic units are word recognition tests, the words being embedded in letter strings or hidden in an anagram or otherwise distorted by noise. Cognition of semantic units is measured by vocabulary tests and crops up in every test with difficult words or, presumably, words the meaning of which has to be precisely understood.

Cognitive units can in principle be represented as bundles of properties; this notion has become a generally shared one in recent psychological literature (Brown and McNeill, 1966; Bower, 1970; Rumelhart, Lindsay and Norman, 1972; Wickens, 1972). Property sets formulate word meanings and concepts as well as figural patterns (Neisser, 1967), symbolic stimuli such as nonsense words (Bower, 1967) and the morphological and syntactical aspects of words (Morton, 1970; Kintsch, 1972).

Cognitive units can be considered as bundles of properties, where each property can be represented as an attribute–value pair. Each of these properties, or attribute values, may itself be a cognitive unit, a concept represented as a bundle of properties. In this way a network is created in which the units or properties are the nodes, and the attributes or relations the links.

|n1|, is–a, nonsense syllable; first letter, D; second letter, A; third letter, X.
|bee|, is–a, manipulandum; is–a, insect; has, [6] wings; has, [2] (antennae, size, long); does, (collect, object, honey); name, BEE; [sometimes] does, sting.

The representational convention used here tries to encode data into, possibly nested, triples in which the middle term is a relation, function, operation or attribute, and where the triples predicate their first element. This first element (which may itself be compound) is identified by vertical bars; triples with identical first element are separated by semi-colons. When an item really concerns the relation or function as such, we use a prefix notation, the relation being identified by an asterisk.

Note that for this mode of representation the central node is a dummy: a unit is defined by its attributes and does not exist apart from these attributes. A bee is a cognitive unit having the properties of being a thing, an insect etcetera. Note, also, that the properties, although indicated by means of natural language words, emphatically are not supposed to be represented by words but by entities in the 'inter-language' of internal representation. That is, they refer either to other compound concepts (such as 'wing' or 'insect'), or to perceptual or actional primitives (such as 'red' and 'colour' respectively). Of course, these entities may have names, just like the unit as a whole may have a name (bee, in this case). The assertion that internal representations are not to be thought of as composed of word-analogues is based upon the difficulties in finding the word, or concept, corresponding to a feature-description. The process calls for a separate ability—NMU, convergent production of semantic units; the existence of such an ability can only be explained by assuming that the description-words have to be matched against non-verbal feature representations.

In the representation suggested here properties are represented by attribute-value pairs. Explicit representation of the attributes—the value-categories—is not everybody's idea (e.g. Kintsch, 1972). It seems a plausible assumption however, in part since not all concepts which function as values indicate what category they belong to (for instance, class-names as values of the is-a attribute may be objects of any relation), and in part since attributes often, or maybe always, indicate specific attentional or discriminatory activities: attending to colour, noticing weight or volume etc. Colour, weight or volume are not evident categories for discrimination as is evident both from discrimination learning studies and from work on the development of dimensional concepts (notably Piaget's conservation studies).

The structure of cognitive units has a number of complexities which need entioning. First, the value of an attribute may be imprecise, or even determinate and function as a variable. Objects in general (as a concept) have lour, weight etc., and that is all that can be said about them. Second, tributes are quantified. Universal quantification remains implicit in the resent representational scheme, but otherwise it has to be indicated explicitly. uantification occurs in a numerical manner as well as in a global, imprecise anner: bees *sometimes* sting, they are *rather* pretty, they are *quite* light. It is nportant to notice that quantification brings a new element into representation. Quantifiers refer to operations to be performed upon other elements of ie structure; for specifying these operations other locations in the data store ave to be consulted. Third, properties may often be modified; that is, they are ecifically characterized instances of more general concepts:

|dog|, is, [domesticated] animal.

he notion of modification is not quite clear, and the relationship may be presented in different ways; in any case there is a structural complexity, since eing a domesticated animal is probably not the same as being both domestited and an animal.

Structural complexity of cognitive units goes further. Attributes often cohere such a fashion as to render the notion of a bundle of attributes nearly useless, at any rate too gross a simplification. We will meet examples further on, hen discussing events (and verb meanings). Simple examples can be found in ther domains. Minsky and Papert (1972) point out that relations among tributes are needed to describe even simple visual forms in such a way as to istinguish, for instance

his kind of structure, of course, is at the root of the picture-grammar rmalizations (e.g. Miller and Shaw, 1968; Rosenfeld, 1969). Another xample, informally given, is a property like 'blindness'. Blindness can only be efined as 'not seeing, and still not seeing when the person tries, because the /es are defective'; the property is so understood when perceived in a person, r when communicated by verbal message.

Still, the conception of cognitive units as bundles of properties is not only presentationally simple but has some psychological support. Most of the vidence is reviewed by Perfetti (1972), pointing to experimental evidence for ie independent functioning of properties in memory. This evidence includes cognition errors, word-association data pointing to the minimal contrast rinciple (McNeill, 1966), naming errors in aphasic disturbances or with other ord-finding difficulties (not mentioned by Perfetti), word-sorting studies, and sults from the release-from-proactive-inhibition technique (Wickens, 1972).

It is important to remember, in this connection, the distinction between words and concepts, as cognitive units. Let the label 'concept' stand for any coherent bundle of properties. A concept may or may not have a name attached to it, and it consequently may or may not be possible to call it by means of a name (if not, it may have to be called by means of a description). The link between a word and its meaning, or meanings, is a precarious one as word-finding difficulties indicate. It may be important to note that multiple meanings may present special difficulties; for some subjects it can be quite difficult to produce more than one meaning of homonyms: a test asking for just that loads on a factor which is distinct from vocabulary *per se* (cognition of semantic transformations).

The present representation of cognitive units and, in particular, of word meaning, is incomplete in some important respects. Words in a vocabulary test differ in difficulty, and so do their response times in, say, multiple choice test items. Evidently, variables such as completeness of the property bundle, availability of the separate attributes (Bower, 1967), definiteness of each attribute, or naming difficulty for attributes are involved, and should be incorporated into the representation. Data are lacking, however, to choose between the various possibilities and presumably all of them play a part.

'Semantic' memory for figural, symbolic, behavioural and semantic material involves different processes, for it is based upon independent familiarization histories: cognition of figural, symbolic, behavioural and semantic units constitute different and quite independent abilities. Episodic memory for both symbolic and semantic material, however, may involve closely related processes (when possibilities for clustering or system building have been minimized) tests for free recall of lists of nonsense syllables and of meaningful words or pictures correlate about as highly within themselves as between themselves. Only retention of numbers, correlating higher with other meaningless material than with meaningful material, managed to separate the factors MMU and MSU (Kamstra, 1971).

Classes

A class consists of a collection of distinctly different objects plus a classification rule which applies to these objects:

[set] $((|\langle element\rangle|,$ property 1, x; property 2, y; ...); property w; ...; (member, P, Q, R ...)).
for instance:
[set] $((|\langle element\rangle|,$ is-a, name; contains, letter R); on, list just presented (member, Irene, Roger, Gerald)).
[set] $((|\langle element\rangle|,$ is-a, physical object; (use, $(\langle X\rangle,$ (place, in bathroom (has to do with, water))))); size, small, (member, comb, toothbrush soap)).

Obviously, a class is, logically, similar to, or identical with, a concept. Nevertheless, memory for classes, either figural, symbolic or semantic, is different from memory for the corresponding units. The characteristic property or what, psychologically, constitutes a class is probably that a class is experienced as a collection of individually different things for which no simple class name is quite appropriate and for which the classification rule itself is complex; it may itself be a rule ('second member of the pair is larger than first member'). The above representation tries to incorporate these features. Tests like the following load on the classes-factor. Subjects are presented with a list of triads of names with a common property (symbolic), or of words denoting objects with a common property (semantic). The retention test consists of a list of new elements, or new triads, some of which correspond to classes on the learning list and some do not; it consists of pairs of triads, one of which is appropriate and the other is not. If these tasks were specific because of the detection of the class properties, they would load upon CSC and CMC, respectively, which they do not. If the process consisted of learning and retaining the class names, they would involve MMU, which they do not either. Retention of individual names was involved, producing significant loadings on MSU. The main part, however, of their common variance the tests share with tests such as retaining the classification rules for a list of sets of numbers (e.g. being divisible by 5) (for MSC) or recognizing, in pictures, which picture classes were presented before, and which were not (for MMC). That the classification rules as such are retained is indicated by thinking-aloud protocols: subjects sometimes do not verbalize the class, or rule, at all, and still 'recognize' the correct items on the test page; or they verbalize a classification rule which is vague (such as 'watery things') and often too wide—wider than what appears to have been retained. The correct member of the test pair, in the 'watery things' example, was 'towel–shampoo–sponge' and the incorrect member 'bathtub–tap–washstand'.

Why is retention of symbolic classes a different thing from retention of semantic classes? It can only be guessed at, but it is clear, even from the representations given above, that the symbolic classification rule is precise and applies literally to the test items; whereas the semantic rules are vague, imprecise, and relatively arbitrary since the subject does not know during learning the level of specification which will be required at testing; many different classification rules are usually possible with meaningful materials (as an example consider an item with the learning triad 'sweater–vest–shirt' and the testing pair: 'trousers–shorts–skirt' and 'jacket–pullover–blouse').

Relations

Relations are the structuring elements in the memory network. Explicit representation of these relations, as labelled network links, is necessary for directed memory search and for storing facts. There is no clear-cut difference between attributes and relations, and what follows applies to a large extent to both. Their representation does not differ, at least in the simpler cases:

> Dundee, north of, Edinburgh
> Laertes, father of, Odysseus
> apple, coordinate of, pear
> [often] (bird, sit upon, treetop)
> [usually] (treetop, higher than, roof).

Owing to the relations, the networks of concepts and their attributes are linked together in a total memory network.

Obviously, there exists a 'semantic memory' for relations, which allows subjects to detect them, as he does in the usual cognition-of-relations test figural analogies, symbolic analogies ('on–no; part–?'), verbal analogies and similarities tests. In these tests, any applicable relation can be used in test-items. The set of relations distinguished in the memory network therefore does not seem to be a limited set. Relations are, in principle, entries in the semantic network just as other entries: they are defined by sets of attributes and these sets can be retrieved if desired:

> |higher than|, aspect, ((A, higher than, B), provided, ((* height (A X), >, * height (B, Y)); (A, is–a, physical object; (B, is–a, physical object))

> |father|, is–a, man; [usually] age, [above] 18; opposite, mother; ((has, son) (had, son), time, past); aspect, ((A, father, B), provided, ((B, son, A), or, (B daughter, A))); [usually] ((A, father, B), provided, ((C, mother, B), (C married, A))).

Relations are important in several ways: they frequently are elements in system of relations and therefore permit inferences to be made; they often specify functions; and they entail restrictions with respect to the kinds of elements which can be related, which gives knowledge concerning relations certain predictive power.

Inference

Inferring implicit information from what is explicitly stored has been stressed as an important aspect of human memory functioning (Frijda, 1972; Minsky 1968; Winograd, 1972). The possibility for inference rests primarily upon the meaning-structure of the relations:

> is–a, aspect, ((A, property, C), provided, ((C, is–a, property), (B, property C), (A, is–a, B))).

Inference is based mainly on transitivity rules like this, which apply to relation systems such as the class-inclusion relation, the part-whole relation, and temporal, spatial and magnitude order relations. Inference potential is enhanced by the possibility of the relations themselves being quantified: (kisses [much] sweeter than, wine). Other inference bases are synonymy, inversion and nesting of relations:

> synonym, aspect, ((A, R, B), provided, ((C, R, B), (C, synonym, A)))
> inverse, aspect, ((A, R, B), provided, ((B, S, A), (S, inverse, R))).

[Examples: (precede, inverse, succeed) and (son of, inverse, father of).]

An example of nesting would be: (A, causes, B), implies, ((A, antecedent, C), provided, (B, causes, C)). Where 'causes' among its further components contains time reference, which itself is transitive.

Inferential activity based upon these inference rules is an important aspect of even such simple cognitive activities as ordinary remembering. Dating of memories, construction of search models for remembering ('did I then, as usual, detest this kind of thing?'), reconstructive recollection, all intuitively use rules of the kind indicated (Lindsay and Norman, 1972). The psychological specificity of relations, as informational contents, is also determined by their being connected to other relations by means of these rules. The 'meaning' which is retained whenever relations are remembered consists in some manner of a group of related relations. For instance, in a test for MMR (memory for semantic relations), subjects are presented with items like 'iron is more useful than rust'; retention is tested, for half of the items, by questions such as 'rust is more ... than iron' (Brown *et al.*, 1966; Kamstra, 1971). It should be stressed that relations are further examples of cognitive operations or procedures being embedded in the data structure. Relations refer to operations which can be performed upon other elements of the data structure and which are performed when they are encountered during activities like those just indicated.

Functions

Many relations specify functions; that is, any one element corresponds to only one, or a few, other elements; or an element can, on the basis of the relation, be computed from two or more other elements:

> * similarity (acre, woman,: fertile)
> * difference (mouse, elephant,: size, (larger than))
> * sum (2, 4,: 6)
> * distance (Amsterdam, Rotterdam,: 70 kilometers)

(the colon is used to indicate a function product).

A test which asks for similarities loads on MMR: subjects are to study a list of word pairs, for instance 'acre, woman'; the retention tests involve a list of relation words such as 'fertile', half of which apply to study pairs, while the other half do not. Loadings are 0·44 in the Brown *et al.* study, and 0·53 in that of Kamstra. I mention this test because it points to the retention of similarities, or relations, *per se*; thinking-aloud protocols suggest that it is indeed a common property as such which is retained, along with some of the original list-words.

Predictive Power

Relations specify aspects of the elements related. The elements of 'harder than' are either physical objects, mental attitudes or human personalities. This aspect of relations is probably responsible for the facilitating affect of mediators in paired-associates learning. This conclusion is based upon a study which demonstrates the meaningfulness of a relation (in the sense of its semantic restrictiveness) to be responsible for such facilitation. In this study (Breuker, 1972) subjects had to learn lists of A,R,B triples; every R occurred with more than one different A and B. After learning, they had to recall B on the basis of A,R as the stimulus. A and B were nonsense syllables. There were three conditions: Associative: R. is a letter; Low Meaningful: R is a very general relation such as 'follows' or 'goes with'; High meaningful: R is a more specific relation, such as 'sits upon', 'eats', 'is more powerful than'. Recall under the High meaningful condition was significantly better than under both other conditions; these latter showed no difference, as can be seen from Table 8.3. Incidentally, both the connections 'A–letter–B' and 'A, goes with, B' would be considered implications, not relations, in the Guilford taxonomy; memory tests with such items would load on MSI or MMI, not MMR.

Table 8.3. Recall of ARB triples

	Experiment I (Free-learning procedure)		Experiment II (Anticipation-learning)	
	Mean correct resp.	N	Mean correct resp.	N
High meaningful	44·6	17	60·2	25
Low meaningful	35·0	17	47·2	25
Associative	36·0	17	46·2	25

Comparisons: high meaningful vs ½(low meaning + assoc.):
Exp. I: $P < 0·01$; Exp. II: $P < 0·01$.

The predictive power of relational concepts is clearest in the case of activities, as referenced by action verbs; these however will be discussed under the heading of 'systems'.

Systems

Systems are information complexes consisting of elements, linked by relations which themselves are related; that is, systems are data complexes in which inferences can be made. The string $(A > B; B < C)$ forms a system in that it contains the conclusion A > C. In fact, a test with linear syllogisms is a good test for the factor Cognition of Semantic Systems (CMS), also called "General Reasoning"; this test has loadings of over 0·60 in several analyses (Elshout, 1974). Systems can be represented as structures of elements and relations, but with additional complexity due to dependencies and cross-connections.

The simpler kind of cognitive system is exemplified by what Schank (1972) calls a 'conceptualization'. A conceptualization is the cognitive structure resulting from understanding a simple sentence or precipitated by a simple event. It embodies what at the level of verb-meaning has been called the system of cases; in fact, one of Schank's theses is that cases belong to the conceptual structure underlying a sentence rather than to the words composing that sentence. In addition to these 'conceptual cases', conceptualizations may contain temporal and locative reference:

(($|$Fred$_i$, agent, hit$|$), object, boy 1; instrument,

(($|$Fred$_i$, agent, $\langle$do$\rangle|$), (stick$_u$, trans, (from Fred$_i$ to, boy 1)))); (time, past), (place, $\langle$x$\rangle$))

could be the conceptual structure underlying the sentence 'Fred hit the boy with a stick' or, more precisely, 'Fred did something with a stick so that the stick hit the boy'. (The example is Schank's; the notation, however, differs considerably, because it tries to maintain a nested A,R,B-format, and to denote every relation with a word rather than some kind of arrow. In the example, 'boy 1' indicates that a definite boy is meant; $\langle$do$\rangle$ means that the specific action is unknown, stick$_u$ that an undefined stick is used.)

It is important to realize that the 'conceptual cases' apply to a conceptualization based upon a verbal message as well as to one stemming from perceptual input. Cases and relations are the coding principles for events generally and the resulting internal structure may be considered the basis for recognition as well as for verbal expression or imaginal reconstruction.

The structure as given represents, of course, much more information than is explicitly stated; this information can be retrieved by interpretation of the elements. The first compound element, for instance, contains at least:

(Fred, is–a, man), [probably [intentionally]] does,
(cause to , [violently] touch)

Obviously, the major part of the structures given resides in the characteristics and requirements of the action concerned. Given the action, the case slots and their requirements appear: 'hit' needs an instrument which, as Schank argues, is not a thing but a conceptualization (it is not the stick by means of which Fred hits the boy; it is his moving the stick towards the boy), and 'hit' needs a human (or possibly primate) agent etc. This means that, as hinted at before, verb meanings (or at least action verb meanings) are to be understood as event schemas rather than as mere action descriptions or bundles of properties. In fact, representation of verb meaning as event schemas seems the natural way if one considers the manner in which unsophisticated subjects define action verbs: 'to throw is if you have a thing, say a stick, and you make it fly away'. Internal representation of the meaning of action verbs, then, consists of a conceptual schema (or a set of conceptual schemas, for different meanings), plus a process description.

hit, applies to, $((|\langle agent\rangle, [probably [intentionally]] does,$
$(cause\ to, [violently]\ touch|), (object, \langle physical\ object_1\rangle));$
$(instrument, (|\langle agent\rangle, agent, \langle do\rangle|), (\langle physical\ object_2\rangle,$
$trans, (from, \langle agent\rangle, to, \langle physical\ object\rangle))))$

The relation 'applies to' is chosen instead of 'means' to avoid the impression that the meaning structure corresponds to the word as such. The process description has been embedded at the place of 'hit' itself, and could be extended at the site of the dummy 'do'—as it would be for an action like 'beat'.

Process descriptions themselves contain, or may contain, a large number of attributes: mode of action (swim = move arms and legs etc.), velocity (run = move by foot in a certain manner, and fast), medium (swim = move through water). Miller (1972) has analysed the attributes of motion verbs, identifying at least ten categories which, however, are distributed over process description, instrumental case, and caused change (see below).

One of the interesting things about these representations is the presence of the various predictive aspects hinted at in a previous section. Application of a verb, or knowledge about an action type, involves knowledge about aspects of reality which have to be present in order to fill the case slots; these aspects may not have been mentioned in the message, or have been hidden behind the verbal formulations, or they may not have been visible during perception of the event. Moreover, entire conceptualizations—facts, activities—may be predicted, such as the activity in the instrumental case slot, or the desired event in a sentence like 'the baby wants his mother' (meaning: 'the baby wants his mother to come to him'; Schank, 1972).

It is evident that events, or even the conceptual structures underlying the use of verbs, are highly organized structures. This is particularly so since many of these structures have hierarchical features; they embody what Schank calls conceptual dependencies: there is on the one hand the object of an action, which depends upon that action and its actor, and on the other the entire conceptualization of an instrumental activity (doing something with a stick) which is the instrument whereby the activity is effected.

Conceptual systems usually are composed of smaller systems which are related or integrated in some fashion. This comes out clearest in the case of true events, exemplified by verbs of change. Verbs of change generally refer to a combination of facts, as is evident from several analyses (Miller, 1972; Schank, 1972; Utrecht, 1973), namely a causal action and a resulting change:

(|⟨actor⟩, agent, ⟨does⟩|), causes,
  (object, property, (change, (antecedent, X),
  (consequent, Y)))

for instance;

(John, agent, stabs), causes,
  (Peter, life-state, (change, (antecedent, alive),
  (consequent, dead)))

for 'John kills Peter with a knife'. Elaboration of the instrumental act for 'stabs' has been omitted, as have been the obligatory time and place slots.

Relations between conceptualizations may be of different types, and transitions between simple and compound events occur; examples of these are Schank's 'CACT'S', communication acts, and 'SACT'S', state acts.

((|Jim, communicator, tells|), ((John, agent, stabs ...))) is an example of the former, and

((|Jim, state, believes|), ((John, agent, stabs ...))) of the latter.

Types of event relations other than causation include temporal order (then ..., while ..., during ...) and motivational causation:

((John, sentiment, hates), object, John), motivates,
  (John, agent, stabs ...) etc.

The upshot of all this, in this connection, is that internal representations of events, or systems generally, are to be considered complex structures, organized according to rules. This means that, psychologically, the translation of verbal messages or real events into these internal representations must be a complicated, and probably often quite difficult process.

There is evidence that such translation activity, in fact, often is difficult. 'General reasoning' or CMS, which is one of the major abilities involved in intelligence tests, can probably best be considered as the ability to construct internal representations of complex data. General reasoning is measured by arithmetic reasoning tests where, as Bobrow (1968) indicates, detection of basic structural components and variables may be the major task; by linear syllogisms (Elshout, 1974), where the formation of internal representations appears to be of cardinal importance (see Clark, 1969; Huttenlocher, 1968), and by the understanding of complex verbal material. As regards this last assertion, tests with complex instructions tend to load on CMS, and understanding of difficult prose passages does too, in particular when intricate syntactical relations have to be disentangled (Kunst, 1973).

Episodic memory for semantic systems is measured by any test asking for the sequential order in previously presented meaningful material (sequence in a word list, or of the tests presented, or of elements in a story; Brown *et al.*, 1966; Christal, 1958; Kamstra, 1971). According to protocol analysis, this order is at least in part retained with the aid of constructing meaningful connections. In a study by Meerum Terwogt (1971), protocols of a test of memory for word order were analysed in terms of presumed operations such as noticing rhyme, mere repetition of the word, making sentence-parts etc. Each operation was intuitively assigned to a Structure-of-Intellect factor, and weighted according to the number of words to which, according to the protocols, the operation had been applied. A correlation of 0·67 was obtained between factor loadings and operation scores, with the operation 'words combined as in a sentence or a story fragment' being assigned to MMS, and obtaining one of the highest scores, (the test's loading on MMS is 0·61).

Transformations

Transformations are rules for changing information. These rules specify operations to be performed upon this information, and they are further examples of the fact that so much of memory content is procedural. Retention of transformation rules is often discussed in connection with learning efficiency (Bower, 1972; Katona, 1940; Prytulak, 1971) and in connection with the storage of sentences (Savin and Perchonock, 1965). It has maybe not been sufficiently emphasized that remembering transformation rules is itself a special kind of process. It involves retention of a special kind of information which is not always easily verbalized. Transformations, like classes or relations, are remembered as such. In tests which define the factor MST, the subject may be asked to remember how the spelling of a given word had been changed in the study list (SPY: PSY or SYP?), or how words were embedded in a sentence (was 'pint' hidden as in 'I step into this mess' or as in 'was this pin turned?'). Episodic memory for semantic transformations has been measured by tests having to do with different meanings of the same word, or with unusual ways of perceiving a sentence (given the sentence 'some people go shopping with their wives' the retention question may be: 'what do some people go shopping with?'; or given the sentence: 'schools of fishes do not have pupils', the test question may be 'what do groups of fishes not have?').

These latter examples point to the fact that, psychologically, a transformation often consists of just detaching oneself from a given or current context. One of the CMI tests asks for multiple meanings of given words—presumably because subjects may get stuck on one meaning. A DMT test asks for as many red objects as one can enumerate; the score loading on DMT is the number of category shifts. It is hard to describe the transformation operation involved more specifically than 'find a not-X'; such a description may be meaningful, however, if 'X' is a property-vector and the 'find not-' rule is meant to extend over as many elements of that vector as possible. ('Turn—make round wooden objects' is less of a transformation from 'turn—change direction', than 'turn—dissociation of elements in food-stuffs').

For the reasons given, representations of transformations are simple in principle, but difficult to do non-trivially. The representation follows that of functions in general;

$$*T (A, \ldots ,: P)$$

where T is the transformation rule; A, ... the attributes or properties to be transformed and P the transformation product or transform. T obviously represents an operation or procedure:

*(inversion (first letter, second letter)) (SPY,:PSY)

where 'inversion' points to something like:

> inversion, means, ((. . . b . . . a . . .), provided, ((. . . a . . . b . . .), (inversion (a,b)))).

*(other (*use)) (mop, use, to remove water),: (mop, use, to make Halloween-dress)

where 'other' is defined as:

> other, means, (*max (|X|, property, non-a; property, non-b; . . .), provided, ((|X|, property a; property b; . . .), (*other (X)))).

*(other (*meaning)) ((BAG, meaning, sack): obtain).

*(add, (*function (shower, sandblasting))) ((|shower|, produces, water; function, cleaning),: (|shower|, function, cleaning, sandblasting; produces, water, sand))

where 'add' must involve procedures for finding 'sand' as the means to sandblast. (The examples all stem from transformation tests. The first comes from a MST-test. The second stems from an item of a MMT-test: remember that a mop can be used for making a halloween dress; or a cigarette-filter for a pincushion. The third example asks for the two meanings of 'bag' and, given the word 'sack', to check the other meaning among four alternatives. The last example represents what one is supposed to have remembered after having produced an improvement for a shower, namely, a shower which on request sandblasts—an answer to an 'Apparatus test' item, contributing to a score which loads on DMT). It is a quite plausible assumption that special processes are involved in retaining structures like those presented (apart from its being plausible that special processes are involved in constructing these structures which, if difficult, would load upon non-memory abilities). All memory-for-transformations tests imply retention of two different, and not quite compatible, values for the same attribute.

Implications

Implications; in Guilford's analysis, are extrinsic links; paired associates are implications, and the less mediation is possible, the purer their nature of implication. The existence of MMI (and MSI) as separate abilities supports the view that, all organizational activities in memory being what they are, some place still needs to be retained for sheer contiguity association (just as MMU and MSU indicate that sheer 'sticking in memory' exists). From the point of view of information representation, the simpler kind of implications have not much new to suggest; the only thing to stress is that the relation between stimulus and response in implications is meaningless; that is, it does not carry inferential components of any sort;

list X, consisted of, ((DAX, followed by, TUL),
(WUS, followed by, NEF) etc.)

One of the empirical problems connected with these representations concerns the completeness with which the stimuli are represented; Feigenbaum and Simon (1963) made a case that representation is not necessarily complete. Other problems (see Bower, 1972, Rumelhart, Lindsay and Norman, 1972) concern the question whether paired-associates learning indeed results in structures like the above, or in much richer, and less orderly structures, such as:

list X, consisted of, ((DAX, followed by, TUL),
(place, first half of list), (earlier than, WUS)),
(WUS, followed by, NE-) etc.).

or again:

list X, consisted of, (((D, next, A, next, X),
followed by, (T, next, U, next, L) etc.).

Implications, in the sense of extrinsic connections, comprise a large portion of human knowledge. This knowledge consists to a very large extent of empirical principles: bright things strike the eyes; heavy things usually make a loud noise when falling; highways are full of people, many of them hungry. There are several reasons to stress the existence of this kind of knowledge. First, generating this information from a given starting point implies specific abilities: cognition of semantic implications, CMI, or evaluation of semantic implications, EMI. A test for the first ability is: find improvements for a given apparatus. Improvements are usually found according to thinking-aloud analysis, by remembering problems encountered when using the apparatus, and applying general principles for overcoming the kind of problem. Improvement for a pocket comb (a thing which always gets lost): give it a big, noticeable handle. A test for the second ability, EMI may have items like: On Buna-Buna in the mid-pacific, people play the game of Ticky-Ticky. Which of the following implications is true: Buna-Buna people like to play games; Ticky-Ticky is a difficult game to play; there is an island called Buna-Buna?. Second, acquisition of the principles involved poses interesting learning questions. General principles such as 'bright lights are noticeable' do not seem to be, or have to be, inductions from any experiences, but rather generalizations which may stem from a single experience, as long as not contradicted. Frequency of occurrence or usage may influence the availability of the principle, but its 'generality'. Third, there is an odd sort of quantification involved. The 'usually' or 'sometimes' or 'may' are not really meant to be allotted more specific percentage ranges. They would seem to mean that the connection is not surprising, or is not worth exploring in an instrumental connection.

Representation does not seem to offer problems:

(($*$size ($\langle$thing$_i\rangle$, small)), [easily] causes, ($\langle$X$\rangle$, loses thing$_i$)

for: small things get easily lost, or

(*intensity, (light$_i$, bright)), usually causes, (X, attend to, light$_i$).

(This notation leaves out the 'actor' or 'object' links for readability).

'Using knowledge' means the utilization of implications as mentioned. That is, thought moves along the memory network, from fact to rule to inference. In the test 'Pertinent Questions' one of the items is: which four things should be considered in setting up a new hamburger stand: a hamburger stand is there for his owner to earn money; to earn money, costs should not be too high; stands and shops involve ground rents: a hamburger stand is a stand; ground rent should not be too high? Many authors have pointed out the reconstructive nature of remembering; these rules form some of the bases.

Conclusion

The present investigation was undertaken to scan the structural and procedural complexities of memory. Only part of memory contents, and thus of complexity, has been discussed. Neither figural (visual, auditory) memory nor memory for behavioural data has been treated. It is known, however, both from experimental work (e.g. Posner, 1969) and from factor-analytic studies (Bradley *et al.*, 1969; O'Sullivan *et al.*, 1965) that memory processes in these areas are distinct from symbolic and semantic memory contents or processes.

The complexity discussed, however, already presents a number of problems for both model construction and learning theory. The number of basic structural elements—elementary concepts, relational categories, quantifiers and modifiers etc.—is fairly large. It is one thing to give a formal representation of this complexity, and quite another thing to envisage learning processes that construct the necessary categories as well as the specific structures. It seems to us that the study of learning processes which can account for knowledge acquisition, has hardly begun.

Acknowledgements

The research reported in this paper has been supported by grants from the Netherlands Organization for the Advancement of Pure Research (Z.W.O.). The project was jointly supervized by J. J. Elshout and the author.

References

Bobrow, D. G. (1968). Natural-language input for a computer problem-solving system. In M. Minsky (Ed.). *Semantic Information Processing.* Cambridge. Mass: MIT. Press.

Bower, G. (1967). A multicomponent theory of the memory trace. In K. W. Spence and J. T. Spence (Eds). *The Psychology of Learning and Motivation I,* New York: Academic Press.

160

Bower, G. (1972). A selective review of organizational factors in memory. In E. Tulving and W. Donaldson (Eds) *Organization of Memory*. New York: Academic Press.

Bradley, P. A., Guilford, J. P. and Hoepfner, R. A. (1969). A factor analysis of figural-memory abilities. *Report No. 43. Aptitude Research Project.*

Breuker, J. (1972). Semantic constraints in storage as retrieval strategies in paired-associates learning. *Report ICO. II-161*, University of Amsterdam.

Brown, R. and McNeill, D. (1966). The 'tip of the tongue' phenomenon. *Journal of Verbal Learning and Verbal Behavior*, 5, 325–337.

Brown, S. W., Guilford, J. P. and Hoepfner, R. A. (1966). A factor analysis of semantic memory abilities. *Report No. 37. Aptitudes Research Project.*

Christal, R. E. (1958). Factor analytic study of visual memory. *Psychological Monographs. 72.*

Clark, H. H. (1969). Linguistic processes in deductive reasoning. *Psychological Review*, 76, 387–404.

Elshout, J. J. (1974). *Operaties en strategieën in het denken.* In press.

Feigenbaum, E. A. and Simon, H. A. (1963). Brief notes on the EPAM theory of verbal learning. In C. N. Cofer and B. S. Musgrave (Eds) *Verbal Behavior and Learning.* New York: McGraw-Hill.

Frijda, N. H. (1972). The simulation of human long-term memory. *Psychological Bulletin*, 77, 1–31.

Guilford, J. P. (1967). *The nature of human intelligence.* New York: McGraw-Hill.

Guilford, J. P. and Hoepfner, R. (1971). *The analysis of intelligence.* New York; McGraw-Hill.

Huttenlocher, J. (1968). Constructing spatial images; a strategy in reasoning. *Psychological Review* 75, 550–560.

Kamstra, O. W. M. (1971). *De dimensionaliteit van het geheugen.* Thesis, Amsterdam.

Katona, G. (1940). *Organising and Memorising.* New York; Columbia.

Kintsch, W. (1972). Notes on the structure of semantic memory. In E. Tulving and W. Donaldson (Eds). *Organization of Memory.* New York: Academic Press.

Kunst, H. and van Daalen, M. (1973). SI-faktoren en het begrijpen van ingewikkeld verbaal materiaal. *Report. ICO. 082*, University of Amsterdam.

Lindsay, P. H. and Norman, D. A. (1972). *Human Information Processing: An Introduction to Psychology.* New York: Academic Press.

Meerum Terwogt, M. (1971). Protocolanalytische benadering van de test 'Volgorde Onthouden'. *Report. ICO II-140.* University of Amsterdam.

McNeill, D. (1966). A Study of word association. *Journal of Verbal Learning and Verbal Behavior*, 5, 548–557.

Miller, G. A. (1972). English verbs of motion: a case study in semantics and lexical memory. In A. W. Melton and E. Martin (Eds) *Coding processes in human memory.* New York: Wiley.

Miller, W. F. and Shaw, A. C. (1968). Linguistic methods in picture processing; a survey. *Proceedings Fall Joint Computer Conference*, 279–290.

Minsky, M. (1968). *Semantic Information Processing.* Cambridge. Mass.: MIT Press.

Minsky, M. and Papert, S. (1972). *Artificial Intelligence Progress Report.* Cambridge, Mass.; MIT Press.

Morton, J. (1970). A functional model for memory. In D. A. Norman (Ed.) *Models of human memory.* New York; Academic Press.

Neisser, U. (1967). *Cognitive Psychology.* New York: Appleton-Century-Crofts.

O'Sullivan, M., Guilford, J. P. and De Mille, R. R. (1965). Measurement of social intelligence. *Rep. Psychol. Lab. University Southern Calif. No. 34.*

Perfetti, C. A. (1972). Psychosemantics; some cognitive aspects of structural meaning. *Psychological Bulletin* 78, 241–259.

Posner, M. I. (1969). Abstraction and the process of recognition. In G. H. Bower and J. T. Spence (Eds) *The psychology of learning and motivation*. Vol. 3. New York; Academic Press, 43–100.

Prytulak, L. S. (1971). Natural language mediation. *Cognitive Psychology*, **2**, 1–56.

Rosenfeld, A. (1969). *Picture processing by computer*. New York: Academic Press.

Rumelhart, D. E., Lindsay, P. E. and Norman, D. A. (1972). A process model for long-term memory. In E. Tulving and W. Donaldson (Eds) *Organization of memory*. New York; Academic Press.

Savin, H. B. and Perchonock, E. (1965). Grammatical structure and the immediate recall of English sentences. *Journal of Verbal Learning and Verbal Behavior*, **4**, 348–353.

Schank, R. (1972). Conceptual dependency: a theory of natural language understanding. *Cognitive Psychology*, **3**, 552–631.

Tenopyr, M. L., Guilford, J. P. and Hoepfner, R. (1966). A factor analysis of symbolic memory abilities. *Report No. 38. Aptitudes Research Project.*

Utrecht, L. (1973). Towards a generative-cognitive model of language processing. Paper presented at the Spring Conference of the British Experimental Psychology Society and the Netherlands Psychonomics Foundation.

Wickens, D. E. (1972). Characteristics of word encoding. In A. W. Melton and E. Martin (Eds) *Coding processes in human memory*. New York: Wiley.

Winograd, T. (1972). A program for understanding natural language. *Cognitive Psychology*, **3**, 1–191.

Appendix

Glossary of Main Symbols (See Guilford, 1967)

	Memory Operation	
	Semantic Content	Symbolic Content
Units	MMU	MSU
Classes	MMC	MSC
Relations	MMR	MSR
Systems	MMS	MSS
Transformations	MMT	MST
Implications	MMI	MSI

[Remaining operations within the Structure of the Intellect model are: Evaluation (E); Convergent Production (N); Divergent Production (D); and Cognition (C). Remaining content categories are: Figural and Behavioural.]

Part III

Integration

Chapter 9

Skill Integration During Cognitive Development

Benson Schaeffer

Recently my colleagues and I (Schaeffer, Eggleston, and Scott, 1974) presented data consistent with the view that number development is a process of hierarchic skill integration. Skills A and B are integrated to form skill C, skills C and D are integrated to form skill E, and so forth. Hierarchic integration during cognitive development is not a novel idea; Bruner (1973) described the development of skilled action in infants as the hierarchic integration of modularized skill components; Goodnow and Levine (1973) described the growth of children's copying as the hierarchic integration of rules; and Brown (1968) described the mastery of *Wh* questions as the hierarchic integration of linguistic transformations.

The present paper will develop the notion that hierarchic skill integration implies the hierarchic organization of skills in memory, and attempt to build an information processing model of cognitive development around this core assumption. First a brief outline of the model is presented, then the heart of the model—the processes of integration, automation, and generalization, using number skill illustrations—will be discussed. Finally the author will show how the model might be applied to language acquisition. The memory base for the model's basic processes is provided by a hierarchically organized substratum of skill representatives. Skill representatives may be seen as memory cells, or locations, potentially capable of storing perceptual, motor, and linguistic codes, and potentially open to integration with other memory cells. Skill representatives serve as the programs which guide skill execution. Crucial to successful operation of the memory hierarchy is the fact that multiple skill representatives, that is, tremendous redundancies, exist at every level.

As mentioned before, the three basic processes posited by the model are integration, automation, and generalization. Integration refers to the formation of new skills via the integration of old ones in working memory. During integration, attention is focused on particular components, or subskills, of the old skills and these components are assigned a new memory location. The components thus regrouped in the new location constitute the new skill. Two or more skills can be integrated only during simultaneous processing in working memory or, more colloquially, only when they are kept in mind and used together. Their joint use comes about because they generalize to a new stimulus situation and because they are well automated, requiring no more than the limited processing capacity of working memory.

The processing capacity limits of working memory are defined jointly by the number of skill representatives that can be simultaneously activated and the amount of external feedback required for skill execution. Automation, the reduction of a skill's processing capacity requirements, takes place during generalization. The reduction comes about because with repeated integration experiences multiple representations of the skill develop, and the greater the number of representatives, the lower the skill's capacity requirements. The skill representatives develop as a function of integration experiences and are organized after errors and as a function of the integration of subskills into the old skill. Because only a limited number of them can be activated simultaneously, the greater the number of skill representatives, the more likely the skill is to be activated and the more likely it is to generalize to new stimulus situations. And the greater the number of skill representatives, that is, the more elaborate the internal skill models, the less the external feedback required for skill execution. Hence the greater the number of skill representatives the more likely the skill is to be integrated with other skills. Those familiar with the information processing literature will see that this model draws heavily on the theories and Konorski (1967), Walley and Widen (1973), Newell and Simon (1972) and Keele (1973).

Integration

Two or more skills can be integrated when they generalize to the same stimulus situation and, because they are well enough automated, are simultaneously processed in working memory. A skill is a set of procedures to be used on particular occasions, a schema which embodies stimuli, responses, and the relationships between them, or, in computer terminology, a subroutine, or program. Skills are not integrated in their entirety. Rather, particular components, or subskills, on which attention is focused, are integrated. To illustrate, suppose a child counts the objects in two arrays, finds out that one array contains seven, the other six, and, because the arrays are lined up in optical correspondence notices that the array with seven contains one more than the array with six. In a sense he is integrating the cardinality rule (the last number counted denotes the number of objects in the array), one-to-one correspondences (the determination of numerical equivalence or non-equivalence by the establishment of one-to-one correspondences between the objects in two arrays), and judgments of relative numerosity by visual extent (the use of the apparent fact one array contains more objects than another if it is of greater visual extent), to learn that seven is greater than six. More precisely, he is integrating only particular components of these skills, i.e. the last numbers named during the counting of the arrays, seven and six, and the tag 'more' appended to one of them. The other sub-skills—the numbers counted before the last, the object–number–name connections established, and the comparison procedures which lead to tagging the array of seven objects as having one more—are not integrated; their use is necessary for the integration, but is only indirectly reflected in it. Because the appropriate skills are well automated, the child can, so to speak, read the result 'seven is greater than six' off the internal representation provided by the simultaneously available components.

The above description may be fitted into a hierarchic framework. It may appear that skill integration is strictly a process of moving upwards from lower to higher levels in the memory hierarchy. However, as integration involves focusing attention on subskills and the assignment of these subskills grouped in a particular way, to a new memory location, integration should be viewed as a movement from higher levels in the hierarchy to lower levels, and back again to higher levels. To illustrate by way of the example of integration just presented, before the child learns that seven is greater than six he activates the cardinality rule, one-to-one correspondences, and judgments of relative numerosity as unitary skills at 'high' levels in the hierarchy. The focusing of attention on the crucial components, 'seven more than six', which follows represents a downward movement to 'lower' levels, and the assignment of the regrouped components to a new memory cell represents an upward movement to even 'higher' levels.

The idea of integration will be developed more completely in the sections Automation and Generalization. Before this, however, two points should be made about integration. Firstly, the integration of different skills can yield the same result. The integration of the cardinality rule has been described, as has one-to-one correspondences, and judgments of relative numerosity by visual extent, in the formation of the knowledge that seven is greater than six. The cardinality rule and acquiring more x's (the ability to give, take, or ask for more x's) can also be integrated to form the knowledge. A child may notice, for example, that an array of six objects becomes an array of seven when it acquires one more object. Another example of how the integration of different skills can yield the same result is provided by the learning of number conservation (Piaget, 1952). A child can integrate the cardinality rule and judgments of visual extent to learn that visual extent may not determine relative numerosity, i.e. he can count arrays that appear to differ in number of objects to find out they do not. However, he can also integrate one-to-one correspondences and judgments of visual extent, i.e. he can set up one-to-one correspondences between the objects in two arrays to find out that two arrays which appear to differ in number of objects really do not. That different integration experiences can yield the same results suggests that initial integration experiences are stored in different memory cells, which cells are themselves integrated at some later time (this point will be considered again when the notion of multiple skill representatives is developed). Secondly, integration may be viewed as a guessing process. The child engages in such guessing because he is active and because he strives for competence. The structure of the guesses, the new skills, are jointly determined by the child's old skills and by the stimulus situations to which they generalize.

Automation

Automation, the reduction of processing capacity requirements, and how it is related to integration will now be discussed. First will be described how automation allows integration in the case of the cardinality rule. Next, the automation of the counting procedure, one of the skills integrated in the formation of the cardinality rule will be dealt with in some detail. Having considered these examples, a theoretical outline of sources of automation and integration will follow.

The author has argued elsewhere (Schaeffer, Eggleston, and Scott, 1974) that the child integrates the counting procedure and the pattern recognition of small numbers to form the cardinality rule: the rule that the last number named during counting denotes the number of objects in an array. Thus, the child would recognize an array as 'three', count the three objects in it, and notice that the label arrived at via pattern recognition was the same as the last number named during counting. In thus forming the cardinality rule the child is not actually integrating counting and pattern recognition, but only one component of each. He is not focusing attention on the first two objects counted, but only on the last one; and he is not focusing attention on the pattern recognition procedures that give rise to the label 'three', but only on the label itself. Nevertheless, he has counted the first two objects and employed the pattern recognition procedures, but because the counting procedure and the pattern recognition of small numbers are well automated, requiring little processing capacity, he is able to focus attention on the crucial components and integrate these to form the cardinality rule.

Again, it must be emphasized that integration appears to represent downward followed by upward movement in the skill hierarchy. The child activates the counting procedure and pattern recognition of small numbers as unitary skills at 'high' levels of the hierarchy, moves downward to focus attention on 'lower' level components, the last number counted and the pattern label, then moves upward again to assign the regrouped components, the cardinality rule, to a 'higher' level memory location.

How were the skills involved in the formation of the cardinality rule automated? Only part of this question will be answered, for the author can only describe the automation of the counting procedure. The summary presented here is worked out in detail elsewhere (Schaeffer, Eggleston and Scott, 1974). Mastery of the counting procedure involves the integration of sequential number naming and sequential pointing for the purpose of creating consistent one-to-one correspondences between number names and objects. During learning, the child's major difficulty is remembering which objects he has and has not counted. Sequential pointing is apparently used as a mnemonic device to overcome this difficulty. The child has previously mastered sequential pointing and the kinesthetic-visual memory capacities it requires, and appears to use the memory capacity allied to sequential pointing to help him remember which objects he has counted. The processing capacity reduction effected by the use of sequential pointing as a mnemonic frees capacity for unitizing complex stimuli and applying spatial plans. The child begins to count complex events that are not visible and touchable, such as the number of people who entered his house yesterday. He also begins to use spatial plans to facilitate systematic counting. He begins to count regular arrays, such as rectangles, with clear-cut 'starting and stopping points', more easily than irregular arrays; he might, for example, count the objects in a rectangle from the object in the top left corner to the one immediately below it. And he begins to count arrays with subgroups of contiguous identical objects more easily than arrays without them: by counting first the objects in one subgroup, then those in another, and so forth, until he has covered all subgroups. The spatial plans he uses function as mnemonics, as did sequential pointing. Their use effects a processing capacity reduction by reducing the necessity for rote object and position memory.

The above describes some of the processing capacity reductions which occur during the automation of the counting procedure. The author does not know of any work which shows that these reductions allow the focusing of attention on the last number named during counting, as my portrayal of the formation of the cardinality rule requires. It is certain, however, that the application of Posner's and Keele's (1970) probe technique could be used to show that automation allows focusing of attention. In other words, if one asked the child to respond to an irrelevant stimulus during counting, over the course of automation the irrelevant stimulus would come to interfere more with the counting of the last object than with the counting of earlier ones (even though the absolute effect of the irrelevant stimulus would decline).

What the author will now present constitutes the speculative heart of the skill integration model: a theoretical description of automation. For skills to be integrated they must be used together in working memory, and for them to be used together in working memory they must be sufficiently automated so as not to exceed the limited capacity of working memory. But how exactly is a skill automated? The major assumption used to solve the problem of automation is multiple representation. It is assumed that with repeated integration experiences multiple representations of newly formed skills, called multiple skill representatives, develop. This assumption derives from Konorski's (1967) theory of gnostic units. Multiple skill representatives are crucial to integration because in the author's view the limited capacity of working memory is defined by the number of skill representatives that can be simultaneously activated, a view similar to that of Walley and Weiden (1973). In the following pages will be summarized the evidence for the development of multiple skill representatives, in working memory and integration from a skill representative viewpoint, showing how multiple representatives allow for skill organization.

Before proceeding, however, the author would like to state his theoretical reasons for positing the existence of multiple skill representatives. Firstly, as mentioned earlier, different integration experiences can yield the same new skill. For example, a child can learn that seven is greater than six as he compares two arrays of toys, as he sees a toy added to an array, as he compares two arrays of candies (or cookies), as he sees a candy (or cookie) added to an array, etc. It seems reasonable to assume that different classes of initial integration experiences produce different skill representatives which are at first stored independently. Secondly, and related to the above, it can be shown that the integration of multiple representatives after errors in skill use provides a means of automatic skill improvement. And thirdly, the existence of multiple representatives allows both the formation of new skills and the improvement of old skills to be viewed as examples of integration. These points will be elaborated on in the discussion.

There is considerable evidence which argues for the development of internal skill models. The evidence does not argue directly for multiple skill representatives but is consistent with the assumption. Sokolov (1963) has shown that with repeated presentation the orienting reaction to a given stimulus habituates, but that a perceptible change in the stimulus immediately reinstates it. From these findings he argues that a 'neuronal model' of the stimulus is formed with its repeated presentation; and Keele (1973) summarizes a good deal of evidence for motor programs, responses executed upon command of the central nervous system independent of external feedback. These findings argue for internal stimulus and response models, respectively. Shepard and Metzler (1971) showed subjects two complex forms which appeared three dimensional and required them to respond 'same' if the two figures could be made congruent by rotation. The time to respond was a linear function of the amount of rotation required. This finding argues that the subjects form internal models of stimulus-response relations.

Of course, one cannot conclude from the above that internal models are constructed of multiple skill representatives, for it is always possible that construction involves only the strengthening of a single representation. However, several types of evidence do argue indirectly for multiple representatives. Konorski (1967) summarized data which suggest that numerous gnostic units represent a given bit of information. Walley and Weiden (1973) argued that sensory systems exhibit both convergent and divergent hierarchical organization, and that because the number of neurons increases at higher levels of the hierarchy, the degree of divergence appears to be greater than the degree of convergence. And finally, Hintzman and Block (1971) concluded from the results of a combined frequency-judgment and list-discrimination experiment that the internal representation of frequency preserves the identity of individual repetitions. Thus, there is indirect evidence consistent with the view that multiple skill representatives exist.

If multiple skill representatives exist, then skill use is likely to require the activation of some minimum number of skill representatives. This assumption pushes one in the direction of defining the limited capacity of working memory (Newell and Simon, 1972; Posner, 1967; and Keele, 1973) in terms of the number of skill representatives that can be simultaneously activated (Walley and Weiden, 1973) and making a skill's capacity requirements an inverse function of the number of its representatives. If the number of skill representatives that can be simultaneously activated is limited then the more representatives there are, the more likely a skill is to be used with other skills, i.e. the lower its processing capacity requirements, and hence, the more likely it is to be integrated with other skills. Integration of skills A and B thus involves unification of components in many representatives of A and in many representatives of B.

The idea that the capacity of working memory is limited by the number of skill representatives that can be simultaneously activated suggests a structural as opposed to an attentional view of processing capacity. Broadbent (1958), Posner (1967), Keele (1973), Kahneman (1973), and others suggest that man's processing capacity is defined by the limited amount of attention he can bring to bear on a task, in part as a function of the number of other tasks he must accomplish at the same time. Konorski (1967), Walley and Weiden (1973), and the author suggest that man's processing capacity is limited by the fact that different tasks share structural components, skill representatives in my terms, and by the fact that the same or similar structural components cannot be used simultaneously to accomplish two different tasks. Walley and Weiden (1973) argue that similar gnostic units, their structural components, cannot be used simultaneously in two different tasks because activation of some produces recurrent lateral inhibition which interferes with activation of the others. I prefer to say that the simultaneous use of skill representatives at a given level in a hierarchy is difficult when they converge on the same representative at some higher level.

Several recent findings support a structural rather than an attentional view of processing capacity. Brooks (1970) reported that the mental transformation of a series of spatial relations, a visual task, was performed more slowly by subjects who read sentences about the relations, also a visual task, than by subjects who listened to sentences about them, an auditory task. Kinsbourne and Cook (1971) reported that concurrent verbalization interfered with the balancing of a dowel on the right index finger, both left hemisphere tasks, but facilitated balancing of the dowel on the left index finger, the latter a right hemisphere task. And Turvey (1973) reported findings which support the notion that the simultaneous use of representatives at a given level in a hierarchy is difficult when they converge on the same representative at some higher level. He found that letters were masked both by random visual noise and by letter-like patterns when the mask was presented to the same eye as the letter, but that only the letter-like patterns masked effectively when either was presented to the eye not shown the letter. Further, the dichoptic effectiveness of letter-like patterns as masks could be eliminated by showing the eye not shown the letter, random visual noise after the letter-like pattern. These results make hierarchic sense if one assumes that letter-like patterns and letters converge on a single representative centrally (at a 'high' level in the hierarchy), but that random visual noise and letters, or random visual noise and letter-like patterns, only converge on a single representative, the stimulated eye, peripherally (at a 'low' level).

The skill representatives under discussion are in effect internal skill models. The more skill representatives, the more elaborate the internal models; and the more elaborate the internal models, the less environmental feedback required for skill use, i.e. the lower capacity requirements. Newell and Simon (1972) argue that external memory in the form of blackboards, pencil and paper, and diagrams and charts serves as a great aid to problem solving, and it may be that external memory aids are crucial to early skill learning. Within the present framework, external memory aids would appear to facilitate problem solving and learning by activating more skill representatives.

Two additional remarks concerning skill representatives as internal models. Firstly, internal models probably act as reverberatory circuits in a neural net, circuits which continue firing after the stimuli, responses, and stimulus-responses relationships they represent are absent. Their reverberation probably occurs automatically, without deliberate rehearsal, and serves to reduce processing capacity requirements, by automatically maintaining for a short while, a memory which is available for reference. Secondly, it should again be emphasized that the view of processing capacity taken here is that as skill use is likely to require the activation of a minimum number of skill representatives, processing capacity requirements are an inverse function of number of skill representatives.

In the above discussion, the focussing of attention on skill components that integration involves has not been considered. The reason is that the author cannot really claim to understand the phenomenon in detail. Nevertheless, I would like to comment very speculatively and tentatively on what might determine which components of a set of skills are attended to during integration and what such attention achieves. It seems plausible to assume, within the framework of a hierarchic memory organization, that activation of skill representatives at lower levels of a hierarchy triggers the non-specific activation of representatives at higher levels. If this is so, it may be that subsequent feedback down the hierarchy is possible, and that such reverse feedback determines which components of lower level representatives are focused on during integration. Further, it may be that focused attention triggers a multiplexing mechanism that makes copies of the focused-upon components and assigns the copies to a new memory location.

Thus far the author has argued strongly for multiple skill representatives at every level of the memory hierarchy without showing in detail how the development of multiple representatives over the course of many integration experiences might promote skill organization. There now follows a discussion of the ways in which multiple representatives are integrated over the course of skill mastery, how subskills are integrated into old skills, and how the existence of multiple representatives allows one to treat improvement in skill use and the formation of new skills in a unified manner.

There is no data known to the author which directly bear on the organization of skill representatives, so what follows must remain highly speculative. Let us assume, as has been argued, that over the course of repeated integration experiences in different situations multiple situation-specific representatives develop and fill up potential memory locations (Konorski, 1967). It seems clear that such multiple skill representatives would facilitate skill use by providing elaborate internal models that might lessen the necessity for environmental feedback. A child who has learned in many different situations that seven is greater than six, when asked 'Is seven more than six?' will probably not need to rely as much on actual array comparisons as a child who learned the same fact in only a few situations. But how might such independent situation-specific representatives be organized over the course of skill mastery?

The hypothesis put forth is that they are organized after errors. That is, multiple representatives provide an excellent internal error detection system. Suppose that when asked to use a skill A the child activates N situation-specific representatives of A, and that $N-1$ of these program a certain response while 1 programs another. It is likely that the aberrant representative has programmed an error. In the context of the other active representatives this error as a discrepancy is likely to activate an orienting response that prompts error correction. The error correction probably serves to integrate the N previously independent representatives into a new higher level, less situation-specific, representative of skill A. An example might help clarify the notions. Suppose a child is asked, 'Is seven more than six?' In deciding on an answer the child might activate several representatives specific to different previous integration experiences. Their activation would probably activate memories of the specific integration experiences. If $N-1$ of the representatives programmed a 'yes' response and 1 programmed a 'no', the 'no' representative's response would probably be treated as an error and corrected. This correction would lead to the integration of all N situation-specific representatives into a higher level, less situation-specific representative.

Such self-improving integration has several useful properties. It obviates the necessity for a mechanism which copies every response and compares it to previous knowledge for feedback purposes, as each response is automatically modelled by already available representatives. It allows for the possibility that a skill may be used correctly and thereby strengthened, without necessarily having its error characteristics changed. In addition, higher level representatives of skill A formed during post-error integration may coordinate the activation of lower level representatives of A, and coordinated activation allows for better error-correction and temporal synchronization. Error-correction is more efficient because when different representatives program the same response at the same time discrepancies between the responses programmed, i.e. errors, are more easily detected than when the representatives program the same response at different times. Temporal synchronization is improved because many representatives program the same response at the same time, rather than many different responses at the same time.

Whereas there is no data on the organization of multiple representatives, after errors, there is data on the integration of subskills into old skills. An example is the integration of pointing and spatial plans into the counting procedure, described earlier in the paper. It should be clear that the integration of subskills into old skills represents the same phenomenon as the integration of old skills to form new ones. The difference is merely one of emphasis. As the proposition is that the automation of a skill involves the development of an increasing number of representatives, it is reasonable to ask how the integration of subskills into old skills affects the number of representatives. The integration of subskills into old skills appears both to increase the number of representatives available as guides for skill execution and to decrease the number of representatives required for skill execution. Let me illustrate this by way of the example of the integration of spatial plans into the counting procedure. The child's use of spatial plans to facilitate counting increases the number of representatives by making available for counting the representatives, the memory capacities, normally used for dealing with regular patterns. The child who uses spatial plans can count objects arranged in a rectangle by representing the objects as a pattern; however his use of spatial plans also decreases the number of representatives the child must employ to remember counted objects by making a higher level representative, such as that of a rectangle, available for the guidance of counting.

The assumptions that multiple representatives develop with repeated integration experiences, that skills are organized after errors, and that subskills are integrated into old skills allows a unified conceptualization of skill improvement and new skill formation. Developmental psychologists have long discussed the question as to whether cognitive development is a continuous or discontinuous process (Flavell and Wohlwill, 1969). Within the present framework the issue tends to disappear. As skills are integrated over and over again in different situations multiple skill representatives develop. As multiple representatives develop it is more likely that errors in skill use will be detected, and hence that the representatives will be integrated to form 'high' level, non-situation-specific representatives. At the same time it is more likely that two or more skills will be activated by the same stimulus situation, and hence that new skills will be formed via integration. It appears, furthermore, that the orienting response (Sokolov, 1963) guides both integration after errors and new skill formation. The orienting response during integration after errors is a response to discrepancy while the orienting reaction during the formation of new skills is a response to novelty.

Generalization

The author would now like to leave automation and briefly discuss generalization. It has been claimed that integration can occur when two or more skill generalize to the same stimulus situation, i.e. when their representatives are activated by the same stimuli. The stimulus situation which activates the cardinality rule consists of one or more object arrays and, very often, the question: 'How many?' The stimulus situation which activates one-to-one correspondences and judgments of relative numerosity by visual extent consists of two or more arrays and, very often, the question: 'Which has more?' When all three skills are activated in the same situation, they can be integrated to form the knowledge that $x+1$ is greater than x. Over the course of repeated use the new skill is organized and strengthened, and itself begins to generalize to new situations. As it generalizes subskills are integrated into it.

The more automated the subskills, the easier is the integration; the more external memory support available, the easier the integration; and the more consolidated the new skill, the easier the integration. Clearly the number of skill representatives underlying the new skill and the subskills to be integrated into it are important here. But an equally important determinant of whether or not generalization of a new skill takes place is the number of competing representatives potentially activated by the situations to which the new skill could generalize.

A more complete discussion of generalization will not be attempted because the processes of pattern recognition which determine the activation of skill representatives are not understood. Notwithstanding, the author would like to suggest that pattern recognition can be speedily accomplished within a hierarchically organized memory. In such a memory a pattern constitutes a net of representatives at some arbitrary level j. Assume that representatives at level $j-1$ are activated by a sensory stimulus, and that these representatives activate in a non-specific fashion representatives at level $j+1$. It is possible that the sensory stimulus as a pattern at level j could be speedily constructed in response to convergent feedback upwards from level $j-1$ and downwards from $j+1$.

Lastly, it should be mentioned, and Piaget (1953) rightly stresses, that generalization is an intrinsic motive for intellectual growth. The tendency to generalize skills to new situations, (generalizing assimilation), creates the conditions which produce changes in the skills, (accommodation).

Language Acquisition

The model presented will now be tried out on the problems of language acquisition. If language acquisition is to be understood in terms of hierarchic integration, skills must be found out of which language can be fashioned. It is proposed that the child's first words emerge as a result of the integration of intentional, goal-directed behaviour and vocal skills. In emphasizing hierarchic integration the author is following Braine (1971) and Schlesinger (1971) and in emphasizing intention he is developing Schlesinger's (1971) ideas on intention-markers.

The infant develops clearly intentional behaviour sometime between eight and twelve months of age according to Piaget (1953), earlier according to Bruner (1973). An example of intentional behaviour would be the infant pulling towards himself a pillow on whose farther side there was a toy he wanted but could not reach. He intentionally pulls the pillow towards himself then intentionally grasps the desired toy. As the infant masters the skill of intentional behaviour he integrates the actions of others into his skill. He lifts his hands to be lifted, points to desired objects, and shakes his head 'no' when someone gives him an object he does not want. That is, he communicates without language.

At the same time that he develops intentional behaviour he develops vocal skills. Between 8 and 12 months of age he learns to imitate both sounds he has and has not produced (Piaget, 1951), becomes sensitive to sounds and patterns of intonation and stress, and babbles a lot (Kaplan and Kaplan, 1971).

Sometime between 12 and 15 months of age the child emits his first word. According to my hypothesis the first word is emitted by the child as he endeavours to attain some goal. Suppose, for instance that he wants his father to give him his toy bear and points to it, but that his father is distracted and pays him no heed. To force his father to give him the bear the child emits the bear's name 'Teddy'. Where did he learn the name? He learned it earlier as he pointed to the bear and as his father said 'Teddy?' and gave him the bear. He was able to focus his attention on the bear and on the sound 'Teddy', and integrate the two because three skills had been previously automated: intentional behaviour which uses others to attain a goal, vocal competence (imitation and sound, intonation, and stress sensitivity), and the ability to isolate objects visually. Of course the integration that produced the first word occurred in an especially propitious context: the child's interest in and preoccupation with the object concept (Piaget, 1954), his parents' awareness of this interest and willingness to support it, and his parents' awareness of the apparent necessity to produce simple, concrete, somewhat impoverished speech in order that their child learn words (Slobin, 1968).

The first words the child learns fall into two classes according to Bloom (1973): function forms, such as 'gone', 'more', 'there', and 'up', and substantive forms, such as 'chair', 'Dada', 'Mama', and 'horse'. Both classes of words relate to the child's interest in the object concept: function forms refer to the existence, non-existence, recurrence, and location of objects, and substantive forms refer to objects themselves (see Clark (1973) for a discussion of how the child defines substantives). The question arises, however, as to whether or not function forms and substantives are two different classes for the child, or only for the observer. A skill integration view of language learning suggests that the two are different classes for the child. It seems reasonable to hypothesize that during the integration experiences that yield function forms the child focuses his attention on a particular action of his, but during those that yield substantives he focuses his attention on a visual object. To illustrate, it may be that the child focuses attention on his own repeated attempts at grasping andies as he learns the word 'more', and on the candies themselves as he learns the word 'candy'. (As integration experiences probably do not involve vocalization on the part of the child it is reasonable to expect, and Meadow (1974) has found, considerable receptive language to appear before the equivalent productive language.)

At about 2 years of age, after the child has learned to use many single word utterances and is beginning to produce them in close temporal proximity, he begins to put words together, integrate them, to form two-word utterances. The two-word utterances fall into a small number of classes according to Schlesinger (1971): agent + action, action + direct object, agent + direct object, modifier + head, negative + object, demonstrative pronoun + object, object + locative, etc. A skill integration view of language acquisition suggests that the single-word utterances the child uses before he produces two-word utterances serve to focus his attention on events, as opposed to objects, and to prompt the generalization of language skills beyond goal-directed behaviour and toward description.

A person looking at the world seems normally to scan events in an agent–action–object direction. A child who scans an event in this way and produces the name of the agent is likely to focus attention on and learn the name for the agent's action or the object of the agent's action, and is then likely to integrate the new and old names to produce agent + action, agent + object, or object + action. An agent or object name produced by the child can also serve to focus attention on the name of a property of the agent or object, on the agent's or object's disappearance, on its existence, or on its location. And such focused-attention, integration experiences are likely to prompt the child to use a function form and a substantive to produce modifier + head, negative + object, demonstrative pronoun + object, or object + locative (assuming that the child focuses attention on names as people talk to him).

A child who produces many single- and two-word utterances is likely to focus attention on the utterances themselves and to begin playing with and generalizing them. As he does this his language will become more descriptive and less a part of attempts to attain specific goals. In other words, the child's focusing of attention on utterances seems to motivate the development of a complex, description-oriented language.

The birth of complex language raises the problems of language improvement and refinement: the acquisition of functors, auxiliary verbs, inflections, etc. A skill integration view suggests that improvement and refinement are guided by imitation. Ervin (1964) has argued that imitation is not a productive force in language development on the basis of data showing that grammars based on the child's imitative speech are no more advanced than those based on his spontaneous speech. Slobin (1968) argues, however, that as the child imitates his mother's expansions of his own utterances he sometimes adds the copular verbs, the inflections, the articles, the pronouns, or the prepositions his mother added to his original utterance. What the author would like to propose is a more general version of the language-stretching imitation Slobin describes.

Sometimes the child imitates his mother, sometimes she imitates him and/or expands his utterance; sometimes his spontaneous utterance contains many of the elements of an utterance she produced in close temporal proximity, either before or after. It is suggested that the young child learns very early that his mother knows more about language than he and is more proficient in its use. It is further suggested that after he learns this any close similarity between an utterance of his and one of his mother's produced nearby in time will prompt him to correct, change, the underlying representatives he used to construct his (now remembered) utterance so as to make them more capable of constructing his mother's (now remembered) utterance. Such internal imitation–correction allows the child to refine his language by slowly adding new functors and inflections, and allows him to improve his language by correcting errors. As a consequence it pulls his language towards that of the adults around him. Internal imitation–correction, however, does not make the grammar of his overt imitations any more complex than the grammar of his spontaneous speech.

Internal imitation–correction should be viewed as only one of the child's language-learning devices. The author has previously described the integration which takes place under conditions of focused attention and which allows the learning of very new language forms. Under conditions of less highly focused attention internal imitation–correction allows for language refinement and improvement. The change and self-correction that might follow self-imitation would demand even less focused attention, and the integration of multiple language representatives after errors would demand almost no focused attention.

From a hierarchic integration viewpoint language grows out of intentional behaviour and vocal skills and, when the child learns enough words to focus his attention on his own utterances, develops into a complex system for describing events. During the time that descriptive language capabilities are developing the child's actions do not seem to be as closely tied to language as they were at the latter's inception. However, after the child learns to ask and answer questions and give and obey commands language and action probably grow closer once again. To illustrate, a child might ask his father, 'Where is my doggie?' His father might say, 'Find it yourself, I'm busy right now.' And the child might go and look for the dog. This type of interchange would allow the child to integrate information and learn that he can both ask himself questions and answer them. Such integration experiences might be the precursors of language-guided problem solving and action (Luria, 1961).

In summary, the author has proposed a model of skill integration which he believes can account for the creation of new skills and the improvement of old skills during cognitive development. The model relies on a hierarchically organized memory with multiple representation at every level and on a basic skill integration process involving the unification of diverse skill components under the influence of focused attention. Integration is assumed to take place in a working memory whose capacity limits are defined by the number of skill epresentatives that can be simultaneously activated. And the skill representatives are assumed to develop and become organized over the course of epeated integration experiences. If the model is somewhat correct it would ppear reasonable to propose more detailed research into the nature of skill epresentatives, focused attention, and integration experiences, the three least pecified aspects of the model. In addition, it would appear reasonable to propose extending the application of the model to topics such as the acquisition of language (a preliminary attempt has been made in the present paper), the ormation of the object concept, and the development of reading skills.

References

Bloom, L. (1973). *One word at a time*. The Hague: Mouton.

Braine, M. D. S. (1971). On two types of models of the internalization of grammars. In D. I. Slobin (Ed.), *The ontogenesis of grammar*. New York: Academic Press.

Broadbent, D. E. (1958). *Perception and communication*. New York: Pergamon Press.

Brooks, L. R. (1970). An extension of the conflict between visualization and reading. *The Quarterly Journal of Experimental Psychology*, **22**, 91–96.

Brown, R. (1968). The development of Wh question in child speech. *Journal of Verbal Learning and Verbal Behavior*, **7**, 277–290.

Bruner, J. S. (1973). Organization of early skilled action. *Child Development*, **44**, 1–11.

Clark, E. V. (1973). What's in a word? On the child's acquisition of semantics in his first language. In T. E. Moore (Ed.), *Cognitive development and the acquisition of language*. New York: Academic Press.

Ervin, S. M. (1964). Imitation and structural change in children's language. In E. H. Lenneberg (Ed.), *New directions in the study of language*. Cambridge, Mass.: M.I.T. Press.

Flavell, J. H. and Wohlwill, J. F. (1969). Formal and functional aspects of cognitive development. In D. Elkind and J. H. Flavell (Eds), *Studies in cognitive development*. New York: Oxford University Press.

Goodnow, J. H. and Levine, R. A. (1973). 'The grammar of action': Sequence and syntax in children's copying. *Cognitive Psychology*, **4**, 82–98.

Hintzman, D. L. and Block, R. A. (1971). Repetition and memory: Evidence for a multiple-trace hypothesis. *Journal of Experimental Psychology*, **88**, 297–306.

Kahneman, D. *Attention and effort*. (1973). Englewood Cliffs: Prentice-Hall.

Kaplan, E. and Kaplan, G. (1971). The prelinguistic child. In J. Eliot (Ed.), *Human development and cognitive processes*. New York: Holt, Rinehart, and Winston.

Keele, S. W. (1973). *Attention and human performance*. Pacific Palisades: Goodyear Publishing.

Kinsbourne, M., and Cook, J. (1971). Generalized and laterilized effects of concurrent verbalization on a unimanual skill. *The Quarterly Journal of Experimental Psychology*, **23**, 341–345.

Konorski, J. (1967). *Integrative activity of the brain*. Chicago: University of Chicago Press.

Luria, A. R. (1961). *The role of speech in the regulation of normal and abnormal behavior*. New York: Liveright.

Meadow, S. G. (1974). Language in the two-year-old: Receptive and productive stages. Unpublished study.

Newell, A. and Simon, H. A. (1972). *Human problem solving*. Englewood Cliffs: Prentice Hall.

Piaget, J. (1951). *Play, dreams, and imitation in childhood*. New York: Norton.

Piaget, J. (1952). *The child's conception of number.* New York: Norton.

Piaget, J. (1953). *The origin of intelligence in children.* London: Routledge and Kegan Paul.

Piaget, J. (1954). *The construction of reality in the child.* New York: Basic Books.

Posner, M. I. (1967). Short-term memory systems in human information processing. Proceedings of the Symposium on Attention and Performance. *Acta Psychologica* **27**, 267–284.

Posner, M. I. and Keele, S. W. (1970). Time and Space as measures of mental operations. Paper presented to the American Psychological Association.

Schaeffer, B., Eggleston, V. H. and Scott, J. L. (1974). Number development in young children. *Cognitive Psychology.* In press.

Schlesinger, I. M. (1971). Production of utterances and language acquisition. In D. I. Slobin (Ed.), *The Ontogenesis of grammar.* New York: Academic Press.

Shepard, R. N. and Metzler, J. (1971). Mental rotation of three-dimensional objects. *Science,* **171**, 701–702.

Slobin, D. I. (1968). Imitation and grammatical development in children. In N. S. Endler, L. R. Boulter, and H. Osser (Eds), *Contemporary issues in developmental psychology.* New York: Holt, Rinehart, and Winston.

Sokolov, Y. N. (1963). *Perception and the conditioned reflex.* London: Pergamon Press.

Turvey, M. T. (1973). On peripheral and central processes in vision: Inferences from an information-processing analysis of masking with patterned stimuli. *Psychological Review,* **80**, 1–52.

Walley, R. E. and Weiden, T. D. (1973). Lateral inhibition and cognitive masking: a neuropsychological theory of attention. *Psychological Review,* **80**, 284–302.

Chapter 10

Contextual Effects in Reading and Recognition

Alan Kennedy

It is a commonplace observation in research on reading that subjects make great use of context to guide their activity. At times this can produce difficulties, as for example in proofreading when errors may go unnoticed. In the main, however, contextual effects seem to produce large though short-lasting alterations in selective attention, without which fluent reading would scarcely be possible. Typically, as reading continues a more and more consistent and well-elaborated set of presuppositions and expectations is formed by the reader. Particular words within the text come to be seen as bearing the major part of the communicative message while other words are given less attention. This chapter is an attempt to identify formally some of the determining features in this complex activity.

A fundamental demonstration of the effect of (minimal) context can be seen in the work of Underwood (1965) and Kimble (1968) on 'implicit associative responses'. These studies showed that subjects make a variety of consistent errors in a recognition task. Following the presentation of a set of words in a list, false positive responses are made to words bearing a variety of associative relationships to items in the original list. Underwood argued initially that these false responses were mediated by the presence of covert associations during the inspection of the original list and that the evocation of these associates in the recognition task led to false recognition. However, Fillenbaum (1969) suggested that such an interpretation was implausible since subjects show an equal rate of false recognition for both synonyms and antonyms of critical items. This argues for an explanation in terms of the large number of shared features present in sets of antonyms and synonyms of stimulus words and the confusability generated by these in a recognition task; since an antonym and synonym pair may differ by one semantic feature only, it is plausible that subjects should produce equal rates of false recognition. Whatever the mediating process it is now well established that subjects are willing to report as 'old' in a recognition task both synonyms and antonyms of previously presented words. This 'associative priming' can be shown in error rates and also marked retardation in the latency of successful identifications of 'new' (Hall, Sekuler and Cushman, 1969).

While it is intuitively reasonable that subjects, having seen or heard a list containing the word 'open', should later falsely identify the word 'shut' it is much less plausible that such an undifferentiated priming would take place when the critical word forms part of a simple proposition (e.g. *open door*). Anisfeld (1970) examined this using judgments of orally presented phrases which were, in his words, 'minimal propositions'—that is, adjective–noun pairs (e.g. *black dress*). For each two-word phrase in the original set, a later recognition test contained synonymous, antonymous and matched control phrases, together with the original items. The results show that false recognition of synonymous phrases was higher than for antonymous and control phrases, which were identical. It appeared that the effect of embedding the original words in short propositions was to produce context which effectively restricted the range of associative priming.

The theory developed by Morton (1968) provides a suitable general heuristic for considering the priming effects of semantic context. The key concept in this theory is the notion of a 'logogen', a hypothetical unit underlying a single word response. The logogen may be considered as a statistical device or counter which sums information from a variety of sources and releases a response after exceeding some critical threshold level. 'Each logogen is defined by its output which can be represented by the set of phonological features [P], and by the sets of acoustic, visual and semantic attributes $[A_i]$, $[V_i]$, and $[S_i]$.' (Morton 1970, p. 206). Whenever there is an input to a logogen from any source which is a member of one of its defining sets of attributes, the counter is incremented.

In a free association task Morton argues that presentation of a stimulus item affects the effective threshold level of other logogens in direct proportion to the extent of the overlap of 'semantic attributes'. For example, significant members of the set of attributes relating to the word *cat* might be (a) mammal, (b) domestic, (c) quadruped, etc. and in addition such relational attributes as [milk: drink] and [mouse: eat] etc. To the extent that these sets have elements in common with the sets of attributes relating to '*mouse*' and '*dog*' these responses will also be made available, (Morton, 1968).

The theory accounts for the false recognition of antonyms and synonyms of stimulus items presented singly in a list by assuming that each stimulus presentation effectively reduces the threshold of logogens underlying the response words sharing semantic attributes (both synonyms and antonyms). This reduced threshold produces occasional false positive responses in a recognition task, and slows down successful identification because of the need to assess more evidence to make a correct response.

The model assumes that the free association task is in fact atypical in that a normally obligatory rule relating to the release of antonymous responses is relaxed. This rule specifically treats polar semantic attributes such that when these appear in the logogen system all logogens containing the polar attribute of opposite sign are normally inhibited. It has been frequently noted that dyslexic patients with severe reading disorders appear to operate this rule even in free association situations: while synonymous reading errors are frequent, antonymous errors almost never occur (see Marshall *et al.* this volume). The results of Anisfeld's study showing the effects of minimal context in reducing antonymous false responses can be seen to follow from the application of this general rule. However, a prediction from logogen theory, not tested by Anisfeld's data, relates to the pattern of errors to synonyms and antonyms of qualifying adjectives when they are used either in their normal role of attribution (e.g., *bitter drink, hungry tiger*, etc.)—what Claxton (1973) called a 'topical' relationship; or are employed in a 'lexical' qualification (e.g., *bitter lemon, striped tiger*, etc.) where the adjective identifies some property of the noun. The model predicts that the frequency of synonym errors should be greater (and the latencies of correct identification longer) when the adjective is employed in a role of 'lexical' qualification, since in this case the number of shared semantic attributes is greater.

Experiments I, II and III set out to test this prediction using as a measure the response latency of correct rejection in a recognition task. This procedure has the advantage of allowing situations to be used in which error rates are very low. Formally, the use of the reaction time procedure rests on a model of the recognition process which assumes that increments in the judged 'familiarity' of words accrue as a result of their presentation in a particular context. In addition, though to a lesser extent, effective increments in the familiarity of associated items not presented will also take place, since changes in the thresholds of other logogens will occur. In a typical experimental situation the subject is assumed to establish a criterion on the perceived familiarity dimension and if, on any given trial, perceived familiarity exceeds this value the item is judged as 'old'; otherwise it is seen as 'new'. In terms of this model the probability density functions for different classes of stimulus items lie at different points along the dimension of perceived familiarity, response latency in the recognition task being a function of the distance between the perceived familiarity and the established criterion (Egan, 1958).

Experiments I, II and III

Materials for these experiments consisted of a set of 14 words (a + b + c below) for inspection (two fillers and 12 critical items) and a test list containing these words together with distractors. The inspection items were as follows:

(a) *paint clean* (fillers)
(b) *torn bell funny chair heavy carpet*
(c) *bitter black tall fast hot pretty*

In Experiment I the materials were presented in random order as a serial list at a 3-sec rate. In Experiments II and III the words were presented embedded in short sentences. The distinction between Experiments II and III related to the role played by the set of adjectives (c). In Experiment II these appeared embedded in short sentences of the form, 'the drink was bitter'—a topical qualification; in Experiment III they appeared in sentences of the form, 'the lemon was bitter'—a lexical qualification. In other respects the materials used in Experiments I and II were identical.

In each Experiment the same recognition test list was employed, consisting of the two fillers which always appeared first; the set of words (b); and a set of synonyms and antonyms of the adjectives (c). Each word, other than the fillers, appeared twice in the list in a random sequence.

Thirty undergraduate volunteer subjects, all women, were used, 10 in each Experiment. The materials were presented to the subjects by means of a computer-generated display linked to a PDP-12A laboratory computer which scheduled random presentations and recorded response latencies. Two complete presentations (Trials) of the presentation list were given in different random orders. Responses consisted of a right-hand button-press for judgments of 'old' in the recognition test and a left-hand response for judgments of 'new'. The inspection list was presented at a 3-sec rate and items in the test list were presented 3 sec after each response.

Table 10.1 Response latency (msec) to reject synonyms and antonyms of critical words

| | Trial 1 | | Trial 2 | |
	Synonyms	Antonyms	Synonyms	Antonyms
Experiment I	818	801	742	729
Experiment II	824	802	722	687
Experiment III	890	831	739	683

A summary of the results is shown in Table 10.1. Analysis of variance of these data showed a significant effect for Trials, $F(1,9) = 23.85$, $P < 0.01$ in Experiment I and a similar effect in Experiment II, $F(1, 9) = 29.20$, $P < 0.01$. There was no consistent difference in response latency to synonyms and antonyms in Experiment I, confirming the earlier findings of Fillenbaum. Experiment II, which is similar to the Anisfeld situation also failed to show a significant difference, although latencies to synonym judgments were slower than to antonyms particularly on Trial 2. This suggests that embedding adjectives in 'propositions' may produce synonym–antonym differences, but not reliably. However, in Experiment III a highly significant difference was found when the adjectives were used to form a lexical relationship. Here correct rejection of synonyms is greatly retarded relative to antonyms, $F(1, 9) = 8.16$, $P < 0.01$. A Trials effect was also found, $F(1, 9) = 43.83$, $P < 0.01$.

Discussion

The results of Experiments I to III suggest that Anisfeld's conclusions need some qualification. Embedding adjectives in propositions may indeed alter the false recognition of synonyms and antonyms, but the nature of the proposition and in particular the presuppositions surrounding it appear to be crucial. Whereas drinks may be either sweet or sour, lemons are in normal usage marked as [sour]. This difference is critical when examining priming effects since the inhibition of antonymous responses is, as predicted by Morton's model, greater in the second case.

Hall and Crown (1970), using a measure of false recognition of synonyms and antonyms of words taken from previously presented sentences, attempted to control the effect of sentence content and presupposition on priming. They argued that in a sentence like, *'the flames were hot'* the antonymous associate *'cold'* would not be falsely recognised in a later test since it is not 'interchangeable' in the sentence frame. That is, no sentence of the form, *'the flames were cold'* can occur in normal usage. On the other hand, in *'the weather was hot'* such a later false recognition would be likely since here the antonym is interchangeable—it is possible to say *'the weather is cold'*. The results of their study broadly supported this contention: the rate of false recognition appeared to be in part a function of the acceptability of the to-be-rejected word in the sentence frame as a whole. Unfortunately, in a later study they argued that the effect could not be replicated and dismissed it as a Type I error (Hall and Crown, 1972). However, on consideration, it is clear that no definite conclusion could have been predicted for this experimental material, either from the specific results of Anisfeld or from more general theoretical considerations such as Morton's. Since false response rate to all antonymous responses is depressed by a short propositional structure, and since a more elaborated sentence frame might be expected to depress the rate further, Hall and Crown appear to have loaded the odds badly against their hypothesis. 'Interchangeability' may be an important concept in considering the effects of context in a later recognition task, but alterations in the meaning of the sentence are surely more important, and antonymous 'insertions', even interchangeable ones, radically alter the meaning of a sentence.

Experiment IV (Kennedy, 1972) set out to examine the effect of a more elaborated sentential context using a procedure similar to that of Hall and Crown, but examining in more detail the changes in meaning produced by interchangeable words. Again a measure of response latency rather than errors was used.

Experiment IV

Four simple active sentences were constructed, each of the form: $Adjective_1$ $Noun_1$ $Verb$ $Adjective_2$ $Noun_2$ using words from published association norms (Palermo and Jenkins, 1964; Postman and Keppel, 1970). For the five 'content' words in each sentence a set of four experimental words was derived.

This consisted of: (a) a synonym or near-synonym; (b) an associate with similar associative value to that of (a) which would make a 'meaningful insertion' into the sentence frame, but produce a change in the meaning of the proposition (an 'interchangeable' word in Hall and Crown's terminology); (c) a control associate not satisfying the conditions in either (a) or (b); (d) an unrelated neutral control word with matched length and frequency-of-occurrence.

A sample of 48 volunteer undergraduate subjects was used. Subjects read a sentence from a card and then recalled it with the card concealed, continuing to a criterion of three successive correct recalls. Subjects then responded to a presentation of 40 test items (the 20 to-be-rejected words, together with four presentations of each content word from the sentence) in random order. The words were presented in a tachistoscope for 2 sec and response latency was recorded from a digital timer, subjects pressing a right-hand button for 'old' judgments and a left-hand button for 'new'. The orders of presentation of the sentences were completely counterbalanced twice in the design and different random orders of presentation of the test list were used for each subject.

The response latencies of correct rejection for the four classes of negative items are shown in Figure 10.1. In the case of sets (a) and (b) the responses have been broken down with regard to the role played in the sentences by the related word (i.e., Adj_2 refers to responses to items related to the second adjective).

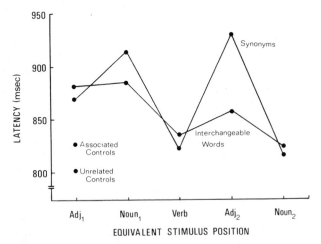

Figure 10.1. Mean response latency of correct rejection of synonymous, interchangeable and control words used in Experiment IV. (Adapted from Figure 2, *British Journal of Psychology* **63**, 387–393, with permission.)

The absolute differences in latency between the four classes of item was highly significant, $F(3, 141) = 27 \cdot 44$, $P < 0 \cdot 001$, but of more interest is the fact that for the sets of words (a) and (b) there was a very significant interaction of Word Type (synonym or meaningful interchangeable associate) and Equivalent Stimulus Position, $F(4, 180) = 4\cdot03$, $P < 0\cdot01$. Response latencies to synonymous associates vary considerably as function of the particular word in the sentence frame to which they relate, whereas no such consistent pattern can be found for 'interchangeable' associates.

Discussion

Clearly, any conclusions drawn from the size of the mean difference in response latency between 'interchangeable' items (855 msec) and associated controls (827 msec) will be misleading since the most powerful effect present in this situation interacts with Equivalent Stimulus Position. In the light of this finding the failure of Hall and Crown to replicate their earlier study becomes more understandable. While subjects are slower overall to respond to synonyms than to associates the absolute difference is quite small, and would be difficult to detect using an error measure, whereas *within* the responses to synonyms a complex pattern of highly significant differences is revealed. Response latencies to synonyms of sentence subjects are significantly slower than to synonyms of objects, a pattern which is reversed for the adjectives qualifying these two nouns.

Before this pattern of differences can be unambiguously related to the effect of the logical relationships asserted by the sentence a number of controls are necessary. Firstly, to demonstrate that the differences related specifically to sentential effects, Kennedy (1972) showed that when the critical words were presented in a serial list, followed by an identical recognition task, no significant differences in recognition latency were shown for 'subject' and 'object' words, $F(4, 36) = 1\cdot22$. Secondly, in a further study Kennedy (1973) showed that when the same materials are used in a passive voice a reversal of the pattern of subject–object differences obtains, $F(4, 44) = 4\cdot79, P < 0\cdot01$: in this case responses related to the *logical* subject remain slower than to the logical object.

The changes in response latency to subjects and objects represent in fact a constellation of inter-related experimental findings. Reading a sentence produces systematic changes in the latency of successful rejection of words relating not only to both the subject and object nouns, but also to the adjectives qualifying these nouns. In different ways, Experiments V and VI attempted to examine some of the boundaries of the effect: firstly for nouns, in particular looking at the stability of the subject–object difference arising from exposure to longer passages of connected discourse; and secondly exploring in more detail the difference for adjectives, looking again at the role of topical and lexical qualification.

Experiment V

The materials consisted of a specially constructed passage of prose containing only active sentences and making use of 30 nouns with a concreteness rating greater than 5 (Paivio, Yuille and Madigan, 1968) as either subjects or objects within a sentence or major clause. The passage was as follows (critical nouns in italic):

'Many *authors* use old *papers* to discover facts about our past. By reading their books we can learn how once foreign *armies* marched across Britain. They burned the peasants' humble *dwellings*, stole their few *belongings* and took captives. They left behind a trail of desolation, bodies littered the countryside, both men and *beasts* suffered as the *flood* of barbarism swept across the country. It was as if a *hurricane* had hit the land.

In later years the threat to life and property came from within; the *serfs* fought their lords for a better deal. Many *robbers* rode the highways and stole *money* and *jewels* from those whose rich *clothing* betrayed their wealth. *Merchants* now formed a large part of the wealthy classes. *Voyages* of discovery had mapped the *world* completely and *ships* flying the British *flag* sailed to remote parts. Britain acquired new *colonies* and sent her *ambassadors* to many countries.

Then came the industrial *revolution*. The *machine* took over. Mass production ousted the *craftsmen*. These ugly *structures* soon marred the countryside and the *stain* remains to this day. The factory workers' *homes* were identical, built close together in rows so that their small *windows* admitted even less light. The *streets* of the developing industrial towns resembled a *maze*, there was so little difference between them. At first children also worked in the factories then an Act of Parliament rescued them and sent them to school. These unwilling *pupils* were the first to enjoy a compulsory education.

The industrial working class had such a dismal *environment* that they escaped whenever possible to the country; here too things gradually changed. The tractor and other inventions replaced the horse and the old farm *implements*. Still the air remained pure and industrial grime seemed far away'.

For each critical noun a synonym was selected using Webster's Dictionary of Synonyms as a primary source. Words chosen were matched as far as possible for letter length and, where data were available, for association value. The stimulus material was presented from a tape recorder and individual probe words together with subjects' responses were also tape-recorded and later written out as traces on a Mingograph jet ink recorder from which response latencies were measured directly.

Two groups of subjects were used, the first (control) group heard the 30 critical nouns read in random order as a *list* at a 2-sec rate. The whole list was presented twice, using distinct random orders for each presentation. Following this, a set of test items was presented, each preceded by a warning tone, and the subject was instructed to say aloud, 'yes' as quickly as possible if the word had featured in the original material, and otherwise to respond, 'no'. At the end of this test phase (Trial 1) the subjects were given a further presentation of the list of critical words in random order followed by a second recognition test (Trial 2). The second (experimental) group of subjects received identical treatment in the recognition memory phase, but heard two presentations of the stimulus nouns embedded in the above passage of prose. Two groups of 12 female undergraduate volunteers acted as subjects.

The result can be seen in Table 10.2 which shows response latency of correct rejections in the various sub-conditions of the design. In the case of the

Table 10.2. Mean response latencies (msec) for correct judgments of 'no' to synonyms of subject and object nouns presented in list form (control) or embedded in prose (experimental)

| | Control | | Experimental | |
	Subject	Object	Subject	Object
Trial 1	1077	1033	1505	1437
Trial 2	990	932	1316	1174

experimental group, significant effects were found for Trials $F(1, 11) = 14\cdot94$, $P < 0\cdot01$; and Grammatical Function of words $F(1, 11) = 19\cdot47$, $P < 0\cdot01$, responses to subjects being significantly slower than to objects. In the control group a Trials effect was shown $F(1, 11) = 9\cdot8$, $P < 0\cdot01$. The apparent tendency for responses to be faster to objects was not significant $F(1, 11) = 4\cdot24$, $P > 0\cdot05$.

Discussion

This pattern of results confirms the earlier findings: response latencies to synonyms of logical subjects are significantly slower than to synonyms of objects, even when the sentences or clauses containing these comprise part of a larger sequence of continuous prose. The control condition however suggests that at least some of this difference is inherent in the particular words chosen. Since there is a tendency, for example, for subjects of sentences to be [+ animate] to a greater extent than objects, some systematic differences may be expected between the two sets of words. The results of the control experiment however show that such differences are small in this situation and statistically non-significant. The question of these systematic biases will be taken up again later, with a discussion of possible controls.

Experiment VI

The materials for this experiment consisted of four sets of 14 active sentences, each set being identical in regard to eight (two fillers and six sentences containing words featuring later as positive items in the recognition tests). The remaining six sentences in the four sets contained the adjectives *hot*, *sour*, *black*, *tall*, *fast* and *pretty*, these being used in four conditions to modify either subject or object nouns in either a topical or lexical relationship,

e.g.	*The HOT weather was nice*	(subject–topical)
	The HOT flame was blue	(subject–lexical)
	They liked the HOT weather	(object–topical)
	They felt the HOT flame	(object–lexical)

190

The recognition phase again consisted of a test list containing as in Experiments I, II and III two fillers which always appeared first; six repeats; and six synonyms and six antonyms of the critical adjectives. Each word, other than fillers, appeared twice in the list, in a random sequence. Materials were presented and response latencies recorded using the computer system described earlier. Separate groups of 10 subjects were tested on the four different sentence types. Each subject saw the 12 sentences in two unique random orders preceded in each case by two filler sentences. They were instructed to read each sentence aloud and think about what it meant. Sentences were displayed for 3 sec with a 3-sec interval between each. The test list was presented at a 3-sec rate in three distinct random orders for all subjects, the blocks being separated by short breaks.

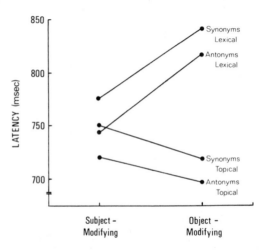

Figure 10.2. Mean response latency of correct rejection of synonymous and antonymous words used in Experiment VI

The results are illustrated in Figure 10.2. Certain general trends apparent in this figure were examined using analyses of variance. The difference between topical and lexical relationships was significant in the case of object-qualifying sentences, $F(1, 18) = 4·79$, $P < 0·05$, but not in the case of subject-qualifying, $F < 1$. Responses to synonyms were slower overall than to antonyms, $F(1, 36) = 8·01$, $P < 0·01$, but the absence of an interaction suggests that subject–object differences are in fact superimposed on any difference in absolute latency.

The exact nature of the subject–object difference was explored using Wilcoxon matched-pair analyses which took advantage of the fact that identical words were tested in all four conditions of the design. Significant (and highly consistent) differences ($P < 0·05$, $N = 6$) were found for both synonyms and antonyms in 'lexical' qualification—latencies to object-qualifying sentences being slower than to subject-qualifying. The effect for 'lexical' relationships was also significant ($P < 0.05$) but in the reverse direction.

Discussion

These results can be seen as an extension of the findings of Experiment II and III, and as further evidence that the pattern of associative priming is different in the case of subject-qualifying and object-qualifying adjectives. Although the drop in latency from subject to object in the case of topical relationships was present for all words the absolute size of the difference is small and should perhaps be viewed with suspicion in the absence of replication. The increase in the case of lexical relationships is, on the other hand, substantial and significant. Quite clearly subjects are slower to identify both synonyms and antonyms of adjectives bearing a lexical relationship to the sentence object than to the same words relating to the sentence subject.

The Subject-object Effect

The results presented so far offer support of a general kind to the model of word recognition and sentence processing proposed by Morton. The specific findings relating to the differential priming resulting from marking a particular noun as subject or object, together with the pattern of results for qualifying adjectives, relate to what Morton termed the 'Ideogen System'. This offers a way of realising in long-term memory the ability of lexical items to enter into a particular grammatical relationship, (e.g., subject–verb; verb-object). In linguistic terms, these represent general selectional restriction rules.

Morton's theory is expressly designed to deal with sentence production but it is not difficult to extend the operation of ideogen-level rules to produce predictions in the recognition situation discussed here. It is suggested that associative priming depends on contextual effects built up as a sentence is perceived. These effects are in a sense a consequence of the pattern of selectional restrictions and presuppositional constraints imposed at the time the sentence was produced. This 'associative residue', it is argued, acts so that the particular verb form limits from the total set of primed associates the set of possible alternative subject–nouns for the sentence; for example, constraining these to other [+ animate] or [+ human] words. In this way thresholds of a range of possible synonymous associates are lowered in the recognition phase as a consequence of perception of the sentence. In addition, however, the net effect exerted by (subject + verb) in a simple active sentence will be to constrain the total set of primed associates relating to the object–noun to a greater degree. It cannot of course be assumed that the pattern of constraints associated with either the subject or the (subject + verb) is easily predictable. On the contrary, it will be at times exceedingly idiosyncratic. As McCawley (1971) has pointed out, selectional restrictions are less a property of syntax and more a question of presuppositions about the denotation of lexical terms.

However, the eventual result will in most cases *for normal sentence forms* be to produce a greater degree of priming to sentence subjects than to sentence objects which will in turn lead to relatively slower correct identification of synonymous subjects in the recognition situation.

Selectional restrictions of course obtain equally between nouns and the adjectives which qualify them, but it is clear that in terms of the associative consequence of sentence perception, a pattern of results directly opposing the subject–object difference for nouns will arise; that is, the greater the set of primed attributes relating to the subject, the smaller will be the set of possible synonymous qualifying adjectives. Hence, rejection times for adjectives qualifying the sentence subject should be faster than for those qualifying the object. Experiment VI suggests, in line with this argument, that the effect is most pronounced when adjectives are present in a lexical relationship, employed to identify a particular attribute of the noun. The possibility that the effect is absent, or even reversed, in the case of topical relationships must wait on further evidence.

The concluding section of this chapter represents attempts to find supporting evidence for the kind of theoretical account given above. Two experiments are reported. In the first, alterations in the degree of associative priming are shown to relate to the particular choice of verb in a sentence frame. In the second a new experimental procedure is introduced to illustrate the generality of the subject–object differences.

Experiment VII

If alterations in associative priming indeed relate in part to the operation of selectional restriction rules within a sentence, then the most direct test of this is to compare sets of sentences which differ only with respect to the verb, containing matched sets of subject and object phrases. Although the status of the distinction is somewhat unclear a reasonable starting point for research of this kind is provided by the comparison of 'stative' and 'non-stative' verbs (see Lyons, 1968, pp. 315–317). Experiment VII made use of two sets of sentences differing only with respect to the 'aspect' of the verb.

'Stative' verbs (e.g. *like, know, own*, etc.) impose fewer specific constraints than those non-statives which refer to some action which integrates the subject and predicate. Sentences containing statives tend to be rather poorly integrated and often arouse only weak images. The long-term retention of these sentences is also probably poorer: having read *the tall vicar knew the old house*, subjects may later remember that a vicar knew something or that the sentence concerned a house, but there is a high probability that over a long retention interval these constituents will not be integrated in memory. Such an effect is less likely in sentences of the form, *the tall vicar burnt the old house*, which contain activity verbs.

From considerations such as these it was predicted that since stative verbs in general impose fewer specific constraints, associative priming for nouns when

nctioning as stative subjects should be greater than when functioning as
ibjects in non-statives, and consequently, the reverse effect should be
ound for the nouns functioning as objects. The design allows for precise
ontrasts since responses to identical stimulus words are compared, only the
lteration in context provided by the choice of verb being changed.

Two sets of four sentences were constructed which differed between sets only
ith respect to the verb which was stative in one set and non-stative in the
ther. Each of a group of 24 volunteer subjects was presented with four
ntences, two stative and two non-stative, with the restriction that no subject
ceived both versions of any particular sentence. The procedure was identical
or each sentence: subjects read it from a card and were asked to think about a
tuation which it might describe. They were then presented with a series of
imulus words in a recognition test and asked to respond with a right-hand
utton press if the word was present in the original sentence, and otherwise to
ress the left-hand button. The test list, consisting of the adjectives, nouns and
erbs from the presented sentence together with synonyms of these words, was
esented in a tachistoscope for 2 sec at a 3-sec rate. In the case of the
ljectives and nouns, the same synonyms were employed for both 'stative' and
on-stative' sentences. Different random orders of presentation of sentences
ere used for each subject.

able 10.3. Mean response latency of correct judgments of 'no' to synonyms of words in
'stative' and 'non-stative' sentences

| | Equivalent stimulus position | | | | |
	Adj_1	$Noun_1$	Verb	Adj_2	$Noun_2$
tative'	814	855	770	822	785
Jon-stative'	801	791	822	867	802

The results are shown in Table 10.3, which gives the mean response latency
or correct identification of a synonymous stimulus item. Analysis of variance
these data showed that the predicted interaction between Sentence Type and
quivalent Stimulus Position was significant, $F(4, 92) = 3·81, P < 0·01$. Sepa-
te analyses of variance of each sentence type showed a significant effect of
osition in both statives, $F(4, 92) = 2·50$, $P < 0·05$; and non-statives,
$(4, 92) = 3·56, P < 0·05$.

It was, of course, not possible to use identical test synonyms for the different
erbs. However, for the four other positions identical words were used and
atched comparisons can be carried out between the two sentence types for
oth adjectives and nouns. Response latencies to $Noun_1$ were significantly
ower ($P < 0·05$) when embedded in stative sentences; similarly latencies to
dj$_2$ were significantly slower ($P < 0·05$) when these were embedded in
on-statives. The differences for Adj_1 and $Noun_2$, although in the predicted
rection, were not significant.

Discussion

Experiment VII satisfactorily demonstrates that times to identify the *same stimulus items* when these are synonyms of critical words within a sentence can be significantly altered by changing the nature of the verb. An embarrassing feature of this Experiment, is that the subject–object difference as such was present only for the nouns in statives, and for the adjectives in non-statives. However, the experiment was not constructed with specific within-sentence comparisons in mind, and a near significant mean effect for Equivalent Stimulus Position was found in the overall analysis of variance $F(4, 92) = 2 \cdot 21$, with a general pattern of latencies similar to that shown for synonym responses in Figure 10.1.

Although Experiment VII provides convincing evidence for the effect of changes in verb structure on later recognition it is evident that the results discussed so far can be generalized only to a very restricted sample of sentence types and a single experimental situation. The results of Experiment V suggested that some effect in this experimental situation may be attributable to inherent differences in the particular words chosen. Obviously in constructing experimenting material the experimenter is liable to fall prey to these systematic biases: not all nouns come equally naturally as sentence subjects and in particular mostly [+ animate] words were used in this role. Similarly, though to a lesser degree, sentence objects tended to be inanimate.

Experiment VIII attempted to control for differences in the sample of words chosen, and simultaneously to examine the possible interaction of animate and inanimate phrases used either as sentence subjects and objects.

Experiment VIII

For this Experiment a new task was employed, involving a measure of reading-time (Jacobson, 1973; Meyer, 1973). In a number of studies these and other workers have demonstrated that the effect of reading a word is to produce a facilitation in the time to read associated words. The models proposed to account for this effect are not in principle different from that discussed in the introduction to this chapter. Meyer considers the facilitation to result from spreading 'lexical excitation' and Jacobson uses a similar theoretical concept. In both cases it is assumed that the identification of the first word produces priming of features common to both words, resulting in a faster recruitment of the pronunciation response to the second. The findings relating to subject–object differences in recognition latency lead to the prediction that in general, and for the sentence types so far considered, words related to sentence subjects should be read faster than words related to the object. That is, the associative priming which leads to retarded recognition responses should in fact produce faster pronunciation.

The Experiment made use of 80 sentences, eight sentence-types with 10 instances of each type. These involved combinations of animate and inanimate phrases containing associates of the same single set of 10 animate and 10

anible words. Examples of the sentence types and their associated words
re shown in Table 10.4. In a further experiment the same materials in the
assive voice were used.

Table 10.4. Examples of active sentence types with animate and inanimate subjects and objects (AS IS AO IO) used in Experiment VIII. Critical words in italic

Example sentence	Structure	Primed associate
Animate associates		
The rich *lady* lost the leather gloves	*AS* IO	Woman
The leather gloves pleased the rich *lady*	IS *AO*	Woman
The rich *lady* dismissed the lazy maid	AS AO	Woman
The lazy maid insulted the rich *lady*	AS *AO*	Woman
Inanimate associates		
The steep *hill* exhausted the weary climber	*IS* AO	Mountain
The weary climber approached the steep *hill*	AS *IO*	Mountain
The wooded *hill* obscured the bright sun	*IS* IO	Mountain
The rising sun brightened the wooded *hill*	IS *IO*	Mountain

Four separate groups of 10 subjects were each randomly allocated to a pair
of active sentence types, one priming animate words and one priming
inanimate, with the restriction that each subject received an equal number of
subject-priming and object-priming sentences. A further group of 40 subjects
was allocated in a similar fashion to the passive versions. The subjects were all
senior pupils (aged 17–18 years) from a local secondary school.

For each subject the test session began with a sequence of 10 practice
sentences each presented for 3 sec in a tachistoscope. Subjects were instructed
to read the sentence aloud, then, after an interval of 4·5 sec, a single word was
presented and the subject read it aloud as quickly as possible. A throat
microphone and voice key were used to measure response latency. Feedback
was given by reading the latency in msec to the subject after each response.
Following the practice series the 20 test sentences were presented in an
identical manner in a completely randomized sequence interspersed with 20
filler sentences of a variety of constructions equalised for animate and
inanimate subject and object frequency.

The results are shown in Figures 10.3 and 10.4 in which each point
represents reading time for the *same* set of 10 animate and 10 inanimate words.
The data for passive sentences are shown as a function of priming by the *logical*
subject and object of the sentences used. The differences in latency were highly
consistent within the sets of words, nearly all comparisons showing either nine
or 10 out of the sample of 10 words moving in the same direction.

The design of necessity confounds the effects of subject- or object-priming
with the content of the rest of the priming sentence which takes the form of

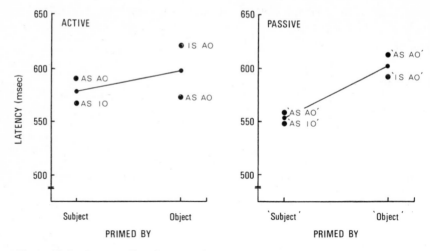

Figure 10.3. Mean reading times for the same set of ten animate words primed by active and passive sentences

either animate or inanimate phrases. For this reason it is not possible to ascrib the difference in reading latency following presentation, for example, of *AS* IC and IS *AO* priming sentences, to the effect of the function of the logical subjec and object as such. It could equally well be determined by the fact that th subject priming sentences had inanimate objects and the object primin sentences had inanimate subjects. The interactions which are obviously larg cannot be disentangled in the present design and for this reason no lines ar drawn connecting points in Figures 10.3 and 10.4. However, a precis comparison of the effects of subject- and object-priming can be found b

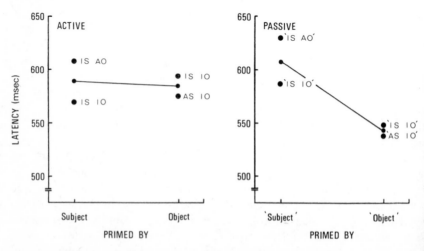

Figure 10.4. Mean reading times for the same set of ten inanimate words primed by active and passive sentences

comparing the mean of the two observations at each subject position with the corresponding object-priming means (the solid lines in Figures 10.3 and 10.4). Examination of these differences with Wilcoxon tests showed that animate words were read faster following a subject-priming sentence in both active ($T = 8 \cdot 0$, $N = 10$, $P < 0 \cdot 05$), and passive ($T = 0 \cdot 0$, $N = 10$, $P < 0 \cdot 01$) versions. In the case of inanimate words, no significant differences were found following subject- and object-priming sentences in the active voice; but they were read faster following *object*-priming in the passive ($T = 0 \cdot 0$, $N = 10$, $P < 0 \cdot 01$).

The most clear-cut observation that can be made on these results is that the experimental situation is extremely sensitive since comparisons can be made between responses to identical sets of stimulus words under different priming conditions. As a result quite small absolute differences in latency achieve statistical significance. The general trend of the results suggests that significant alterations in the speed of pronunciation of single words can be brought about by selective priming from the subject and object of sentences. The exact form of the relationship suggests that for animate words priming from the logical subject position almost invariably leads to faster reading responses. This is true both for active and passive sentences and confirms the hypotheses which led to the experiment. However for inanimate words, differences occur only when priming is produced with passive sentences and these take the form of reading facilitation relating to the logical object.

It is, of course, possible to interpret the results for passive sentences in terms of surface structure and to identify in the case of inanimate words the reading facilitation relating to the grammatical subject. This issue cannot be settled on the basis of the present design, but two arguments suggest that it would be an inappropriate interpretation. Firstly, the results already reported for the recognition latency situation show that subjects are influenced primarily by the *logical* relationships in the passive form. Secondly, since the trends in the passive data are in opposite directions for responses to inanimate and animate words, reversing the interpretation in the case of one would call for similar action in the case of the other. No significant subject-object differences were found with animate words primed by passive sentences and in the case of inanimate words it is clear from Figure 10.4 that most of the variation is contributed by sentences of the '*IS* AO' or 'AS *IO*' form, that is in which the non-priming phrase was animate. It should be noted that sentences with inanimate subjects and animate objects do not go easily into the passive voice (e.g., *the weary climber was exhausted by the hill*) and at least part of the retardation in reading time following '*IS* AO' sentences may relate to the difficulty in interpreting slightly unnatural sentence forms.

Conclusion

This chapter set out to identify some of the changes in associative priming which result from reading sentences. The sequence of experiments taken as a whole tends to support the model proposed by Morton (1968, 1970) which suggests that selective alterations in the 'availability' of words, either as specific reading responses or as possible sources of covert interference, result from the presentation of verbal material. The particular findings relating to subject–object differences place additional emphasis on the role played in sentence perception by the precise nature of the logical relationships asserted. Marking a word as the logical subject produces consequences in terms of associative priming which are radically different from those produced by marking it as an object.

It has been suggested that the mediating mechanisms in this process are general selectional restriction rules operating as part of the interaction between the logogen system and long-term or 'semantic' memory, but whatever the form of the model eventually proposed to account for these effects, it is clear that the combination of recognition latency and reading facilitation studies offers the possibility of a sensible attack on some of the higher-level processes in skilled reading. It could be that in the course of the next few years it will become possible to sketch into process models of reading, which are already well advanced in their treatment of the earlier stages dealing with feature extraction and letter or word identification, some suggestions as to how the attentional mechanisms at higher levels operate to allow the skilled reader to experience not a sequence of words, or even a grammatical structure, but a steady progression of ideas.

Acknowledgements

The research reported in this chapter was carried out as part of a research project supported by the Social Science Research Council of the UK. Grateful acknowledgement is due to Mrs Barbara Wilkinson who tested all the subjects and gave invaluable help with the analysis of results. She also composed the passage of prose used in Experiment V.

References

Anisfeld, M. (1970). False recognition of adjective–noun phrases. *Journal of Experimental Psychology*, **86**, 120–122.

Claxton, G. (1973). The lexicon in action: studies of the semantic memory. Paper read to Psychology Department, University of Dundee.

Egan, J. P. (1958). Recognition memory and the operating characteristic. *Technical Report No. AFCRC TN-58-51*. Indiana University.

Fillenbaum, S. (1969). Words as feature complexes; false recognition of antonyms and synonyms. *Journal of Experimental Psychology*, **82**, 400–402.

Hall, J. W. and Crown, I. (1970). Associative encoding of words in sentences. *Journal of Verbal Learning and Verbal Behavior*, **9**, 303–307.

Hall, J. W. and Crown, I. (1972). Associative encoding of words in sentences by adults and children. *Journal of Verbal Learning and Verbal Behavior*, **11**, 92–95.

Hall, J. W., Sekuler, R. and Cushman, W. (1969). Effects of IAR occurrence during learning on response time during subsequent recognition. *Journal of Experimental Psychology*, **79**, 39–42.

Jacobson, J. Z. (1973). Effects of association upon masking and reading latency. *Canadian Journal of Psychology*, **27**, 58–69.

Kennedy, A. (1972). Semantic constraints on location operations in simple sentences. *British Journal of Psychology*, **63**, 387–393.

Kennedy, A. (1973). Associative encoding of words in passive sentences. *British Journal of Psychology*, **64**, 169–172.

Kimble, G. A. (1968). Mediating associations. *Journal of Experimental Psychology*, **76**, 263–266.

Lyons, J. (1968). *Introduction to Theoretical Linguistics*. London: Cambridge University Press.

McCawley, J. D. (1971). Where do noun phrases come from? In D. D. Steinberg and L. A. Jakobovits (Eds) *Semantics*. London: Cambridge University Press.

Meyer, D. E. (1973). Correlated operations in searching stored semantic categories. *Journal of Experimental Psychology*, **99**, 124–133.

Morton, J. (1968). Grammar and Computation in language behavior. In J. C. Catford (Ed.) *Studies in Language and Language Behavior*. Centre for Research in Language and Language Behavior Progress Report No. VI. University of Michigan.

Morton, J. (1970). A functional model for memory. In D. A. Norman (Ed.) *Models of Human Memory*. New York: Academic Press.

Paivio, A., Yuille, J. C., and Madigan, S. A. (1968). Concreteness, imagery, and meaningfulness values for 925 nouns. *Journal of Experimental Psychology*, **76**, No. 1, Part 2.

Palermo, D. S. and Jenkins, J. J. (1964). *Word Association Norms*. Minneapolis: University of Minnesota Press.

Postman, L., and Keppel, G. (1970). *Norms of Word Association*. New York: Academic Press.

Underwood, B. J. (1965). False recognition produced by implicit verbal responses. *Journal of Experimental Psychology*, **70**, 122–129.

Chapter 11

Semantic and Syntactic Aspects of Remembering Sentences: a Review of Some Recent Continental Research

W. J. M. Levelt and G. Kempen

The study of sentence memory and retrieval, which had become a dominant issue in the psycholinguistic work of the sixties, underwent a major change at the approach of the seventies. It need not be explained here that the original theorizing was more or less directly derived from normal syntactic notions in linguistics (for a review see Levelt, 1973–1974). The change was induced by renewed attention to semantic and extralinguistic aspects of internal representations. It became doubtful whether an implicit assumption of the earlier work could be maintained, namely the presupposition that what is stored in memory is some sort of linguistic object. And one can now rightly question, as Flores d'Arcais (1974) does in the title of a recent paper, whether there is a memory for sentences at all.

The alternative point of view has been expressed most attractively by Bransford and Franks (1972), and by Barclay (1973). Their position is that a person who reads and tries to memorize a sentence or text does this by building an internal representation of the object, action or situation which is described in the text. In case the text contains more than a single sentence, the person integrates the contents of the different sentences into a 'holistic' semantic representation in which there is no trace of the original syntactic boundaries. The linguistic structure of the stimulus material is normally quickly lost. This can only be prevented by giving the subject the explicit additional task of verbatim reproduction (Fillenbaum, 1966; Sachs, 1967; Flores d'Arcais, 1974).

A seemingly obvious consequence of these developments is a devaluation of the paradigm in which verbatim sentence reproduction is required of the subject. In this way, it is said, the subject is forced to store the linguistic object, namely the sentential form, over and above what he normally extracts from it. Since only the latter process is natural and interesting, the paradigm only diverts attention to an artifact. Such would be the case for Johnson's (1965) results which seemingly indicate that surface constituent structure is stored into memory, but from which it cannot at all be concluded that normally such storage takes place, let alone that this would be *the* format in which sentential material is recalled. An additional argument for this interpretation might be derived from Johnson's later (1970) work, in which he can correctly predict transitional errors in the recall of nonsense letter strings from the way letters are grouped, just in the same way as he could predict transitional errors in the recall of sentences from the way words are grouped into constituents. Intuitively, however, the memorization of a meaningful sentence is clearly different from the memorization of a nonsense letter string. Johnson's original study might therefore have concerned an artificial grouping effect which had no relation to sentence memory per se, but only to the additional task of verbatim recall.

A similar critique seems applicable to Blumenthal's (1967) work. Though this author suggests that sentences are coded in terms of their deep structures instead of their surface forms, it might again be due to the verbatim recall task that subjects are forced into creating such codes. They may have little relation to what a subject normally abstracts from a sentence. (It should, by the way, be noted that Blumenthal's results could also be an artifact for other, purely experimental reasons. If one repeats his prompted recall paradigm for ambiguous sentences giving rise to the same case shift as in the *John is eager/easy to please* sentence pair, the original effect disappears, as Levelt and Bonarius (1973) have shown for Dutch and *mutatis mutandis* for Finnish.)

Though these arguments unmistakably have some face value, one has to be careful not to throw out the baby with the bath water. The verbatim recall paradigm is not only attractive from the experimental point of view of easy scoreability, but there is also strong evidence that it does not necessarily create the artificialities. On the one hand one can use the paradigm for the analytic study of the role of semantic factors in the recall of sentential or text material. In the next paragraph we will discuss a few, mostly continental, studies along these lines. Some of these studies have up till now only taken the form of unpublished dissertations or reports. On the other hand, we will show that, just in the context of the verbatim recall task, it is probably not the case that subjects base their reproductions on an internal *sentential* representation (surface or phonetic), this in spite of the fact that they do show clear constituent boundary effects. It will be argued, again on the basis of as yet mostly unpublished continental work, that such effects are at least partly due to syntactic retrieval plans, not to syntactic traces in memory. This is done in the second section of the chapter. In a last, concluding section we will try to relate these findings to some diverse non-continental studies; this may be taken as an exercise in bridge building.

Semantic Effects on Verbatim Reproduction of Sentences

One of the first to demonstrate semantic effects in verbatim reproduction of sentences was Rosenberg (1968). He studied the operation of a factor which he called 'semantic integration' and which is determined by interword associations within the sentence to be remembered. A case of high semantic integration is the sentence *The old king ruled wisely* as opposed to *The poor king dined gravely*, which has little semantic integration. Rosenberg showed that the pattern of transitional errors only reflected constituent boundary effects in the case of weakly integrated sentences, i.e. more transitional errors between than within constituents. For highly integrated sentences, it seemed, subjects were apparently able to construct larger units than (major) constituents.

In a follow up of this finding, Hörmann and Engelkamp started a more analytic approach to this matter. They tried to isolate one factor in semantic integration which they called 'semantic implication' (Hörmann, 1971; Engel-kamp, Merdian and Hörmann, 1972). In the latter paper semantic implication is defined as a property of a subject/predicate/object sentence in the following way: semantic implication of such a sentence is high if it is hard to change one of the three constituents given the other two; it is low in the other case. An example of high semantic implication is the sentence *The river erodes the bank*, since there are only few other things than rivers which erode banks, few other things than banks that are eroded by rivers, and few other things than eroding which rivers can do to banks. Low semantic implication, it is remarked, is the case for the sentence *The pupil finds the book*. It will not surprise that the authors are indeed able to show that learnability increases with degree of semantic implication. However, together with this factor Engelkamp *et al.* varied a second factor that might contribute to semantic integration, namely negation. They theorized that semantic implication would only contribute to semantic integration if the implication is not denied. They did an experiment in which the subject had to give verbatim reproduction of the sentence on the occasion of a prompt word from the sentence. Their general finding was that high-implication sentences were reproduced better than low-implication sentences, but only for affirmative sentences. For negative sentences semantic implication showed no effect. It is necessary, however, to make one qualification. The experimental material contained three types of negation: negation of subject, of predicate, or of object. Instances of these are:

Not the river has eroded the bank (subject negation)
The river has not eroded the bank (predicate negation)
The river has eroded not the bank (object negation).

(The latter construction is quite normal and acceptable in German.) It turned out that the interaction of negation and semantic implication only occurred in the latter two cases. Subject negation did not reduce the effect of semantic implication on sentence reproduction. The authors relate this to the relative independence of the subject constituent, even in sentences with high semantic implication (this independence is given credit in linguistics by the classical subject/predicate phrase dichotomy). In our opinion a more obvious explanation should be explored first. It might well be that the finding is due to a property of the sentential material used in the experiment. It may, further-more, be the case that the subject can ignore the negative element more easily if it precede (or follow) the rest of the sentence. In the experimental sentences this is only the case for subject negation, but in German this could easily be done for predicate (verb) negation as well:

Der Schüler findet das Buch nicht
(The pupil does not find the book)

In his dissertation Engelkamp (1973) extended the notion of semantic implication to relations between constituents other than subject, predicate and object. In fact he analysed sentences in terms of case relations and expressed semantic implication in terms of case structure. In one of his experiments he used sentences such as (a), (b) and (c):

(a) *The tradesman with the merchandise hit the boy*
(b) *The tradesman with the spot hit the boy*
(c) *The tradesman with the stick hit the boy*

According to Engelkamp's analysis the type (a) sentence contains two relation terms, namely *trade* with arguments (cases) *man* and *merchandise* in subject and object position, and *hit* with *man* and *boy* as arguments:

(a) *trade (man, merchandise)*
  hit (man, boy)

Here, the prepositional phrase *with the merchandise* participates in the *trades* relation. In the type (b) sentences the prepositional phrase expresses an independent relation that we will characterize by the verb *possess*:

(b) *trade (man)*
  possess (man, spot)
  hit (man, boy)

In sentences of type (c) it seems that the prepositional phrase relates to the main verb as an instrument:

(c) *trade (man)*
  hit (man, boy, stick)

Engelkamp found in a verbatim recall experiment that transitional errors between *tradesman* and *with*, i.e. within the grammatical subject, were highest for type (b) sentences, in accordance with his analysis. In that sentence type, where the prepositional phrase is neither integrated with *trade*, nor with *hit*, it has low semantic implication.

Studies such as these certainly demonstrate the effect of semantic variables in verbatim sentence recall and give a first theoretical analysis, though a number of new problems arise. Are the semantic effects on reproduction due to the memory code or to some retrieval strategy? Is the degree of semantic implication more than or different from the sum of word association strengths, i.e. is it possible to construct sentences for which the associations between words are controlled and equal and where there is nevertheless a difference in semantic implication? Is semantic implication different from *combinability* of phrases? This latter question needs some explanation which can be done by means of another continental study (Levelt, 1967; Noordman and Levelt, 1970). In this one, Osgood's (1970) 'word intersection' method was used. It consists of having subjects judge the acceptability of word combinations such as verb/adverb (*apologize proudly, kill instantly*, etc.), adjective/noun (*lazy stone, diligent nurse*, etc.) noun/verb (*cars eat, children play*, etc.). The intention is to infer from such judgments something about the feature structure of the words involved. The underlying notion is that acceptability is low in the case of words opposed on some feature. For *lazy stone* the critical feature might be *animateness*. Levelt (1967) studied the combination of interpersonal verbs and adjectives. Noordman and Levelt (1970) analysed verb/noun combinations in the sentence frame 'They *verbed* the *noun*' (e.g., *they received the growth*). The study involved 13 verbs and 480 nouns and all combinations were judged. It turned out that a specification on only four features was sufficient to predict nearly all acceptabilities (errors: 3·5 per cent), though these features were not sufficient to predict all non-acceptibilities; in fact, many of them were predicted as acceptable (errors: 24 per cent). The four features were concrete/abstract, living/non-living, human/non-human, and generic/non-generic. Findings of this sort may lead to further analysis of the notion of semantic implication. Can semantic implication be partly or fully expressed in terms of (non-) opposition of certain general semantic features? Does verbatim recall of sentences increase if certain case or modifier relations go with feature similarity between the arguments?

Another approach can be found in Loosen's (1972) dissertation. Returning to the point of departure according to which memorizing sentences is in fact memorizing representations of subjects, situations, events; it is not a big step to assume that in the process of decoding a sentence the first things to be memorized will be the basic structure of such situations, events, etc. More peripheral details will only be added if time and memory load allow. The notion of 'basic' or 'essential' traits, as opposed to peripheral aspects is not well defined in its generality, but within restricted domains of objects it might be possible to give a more stringent definition. For instance, if the described object is a visual pattern one could define a hierarchy of traits in terms of coding systems such as Leeuwenberg's (1971). A more intuitive version of this 'essentials first'-hypothesis is quite old in psychology. In 1894 Binet and Henri presented data from which it appeared that the most important parts of a text were reproduced better than parts of secondary importance. However, in

206

this and in all later studies no attempt was made to provide an independent
estimate of the importance of various words in a sentence, or of passages in a
text.

Loosen has filled this gap. He developed an elegant method to extract the
'kernel idea' from a sentence. He presented subjects with written (Dutch)
sentences and asked them to underline one to three words that they considered
most essential for the meaning of the sentence. Next, he determined over
subjects for each pair of words the relative frequency that both words had been
underlined together. The resulting symmetric data matrix was then analysed by
Johnson's hierarchical cluster analysis (see Levelt, 1970). (This procedure was
justified because the matrices turned out to be highly ultrametric, i.e. hierarchi
cal.) The result of such an analysis can be pictured as a tree diagram, an
example from Loosen's dissertation is given in Figure 11.1a. It shows the

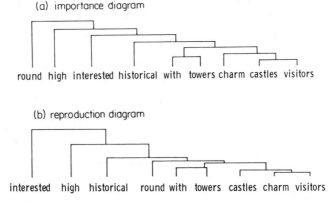

(a) importance diagram

round high interested historical with towers charm castles visitors

(b) reproduction diagram

interested high historical round with towers castles charm visitors

Figure 11.1. Importance and reproduction diagrams for *Historical castles with high round towers charm interested visitors*
(after Loosen, 1972)

importance hierarchy for the sentence *Historical castles with high round towers
charm interested visitors* (Historische kastelen met hoge ronde torens bekoren
belangstellende bezoekers). The lower the node, the higher the relative
frequency that words dominated by that node were jointly underlined as most
important to the meaning of the sentence. It is clear from the diagram that the
kernel idea of the sentence is contained in *castles with towers charm visitors*, or
even more strongly: *castles charm visitors*. Other words such as function words
and modifiers are more peripheral to the idea expressed by the sentence.

These 'kernel idea' data were now compared with the results of a verbatim
recall experiment. In that experiment a different group of subjects performed
what was essentially *a continuous memory* task. A long list of sentences was
acoustically presented; the subject's task was to listen to each sentence, to
judge (by 'yes' or 'no') whether it was plausible (this in order to stimulate real
understanding of the sentence), and finally to reproduce verbatim the test

entence from memory. This was a high-loading task, which resulted in a ubstantial amount of reproduction errors. The data were analysed in different vays, but the main procedure was to determine for each pair of words from a entence the relative frequency (over subjects) with which they were *jointly* eproduced. For each sentence the obtained symmetric data matrix was nalysed in the same way as the importance data previously referred to.

The main finding of the experiment was that there was a striking similarity etween the importance diagrams and the verbatim reproduction diagrams. An example of the latter is given in Figure 11.1b which summarizes the eproduction data for the same sentence as in Figure 11.1a. The correspon- lence between the diagrams is self-evident. Furthermore, it turned out that, at east for the content words, the chance of being underlined was highly orrelated with the chance of being reproduced. For the same sentence this elation is depicted in Figure 11.2. It may be noted in this connection also that Teigeler (1972) found a positive relation between importance and probability of reproduction, but his importance measure is based on purely linguistic considerations. His results are, moreover, rather atypical, as Engelkamp 1973) remarks.

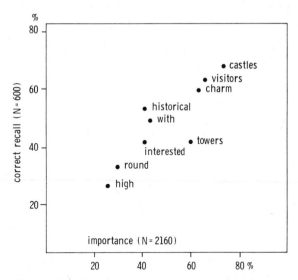

Figure 11.2. Relation between importance and repro- ducibility for the sentence *Historical castles with high round towers charm interested visitors* (after Loosen, 1972)

As a conclusion to this section we can state that the different studies clearly lemonstrate the semantic character of verbatim sentence recall. Even if a ubject learns a sentence by heart he does not treat it as a purely yntactic–linguistic object, but tries to create an efficient code from which the entence may be reconstructed. There is no evidence that the code is isomorphic to the syntactic structure of the sentence, or stronger, that it is to a substantial degree linguistic in character. This conclusion makes it all the more interesting to study the origin of the syntactic effects that are usually found in verbatim recall experiments. This is the subject of the following section.

The Origin of Syntactic Effects in Verbatim Reproduction of Sentences

Two types of experimental paradigm have been used in order to demonstrate that surface constituent structure is reflected in the pattern of transitional difficulties in sentence recall. The first has been mentioned above: it consists of registering transitional errors during sentence memorization. The other type of procedure consists of measuring reaction times from presentation of a word from the learned sentence to subject's reproduction of the next word in the sentence (probe latencies, or probe reaction times). In both ways it is possible to show constituent boundary effects.

A common element in the different explanations which have been put forward for this phenomenon (*cf.* Johnson 1965, 1970; Wilkes and Kennedy, 1969) is that the cohesion of words within the same constituent results from *learning during the experiment.* One may, of course, differ in opinion about the character of this learning. The sentences may have been stored in LTM in the form of chunks that are more or less related to clauses or constituents. Or sentences are stored in a different format, but during the learning an additional retrieval program is constructed which consists of subroutines that are related to different major parts of the sentence (*cf.* Johnson, 1970). In both cases, however, syntax comes in *during* learning. In this section we will present data which strongly suggest that this assumption is wrong, and, more particularly, that syntactic effects in sentence reproduction are caused by retrieval plans which have a pre-experimental existence, i.e. which are not created during the experiment but which are part of our stock of syntactic skills.

A first indication in this direction was obtained by Loosen (1972). He repeated Levelt's (1970a) experiment with one essential change. In the original experiment subjects had been presented with sentences embedded in noise. Their only task was to write down everything they could reconstruct from what they had heard. The pattern of transitional errors showed not only strong constituent boundary effects, but from computing conditional recall probabilities for all word pairs in a sentence it was possible, moreover, to show that the chunking pattern was highly hierarchical in nature. Levelt explained these findings in terms of perceptual partitioning procedures. Loosen argued that the results could as well be explained by syntactic retrieval procedures, and to show that the actual stimulus was of relatively minor importance and that therefore a perceptual explanation might be less attractive, he repeated the experiment in the following way: instead of presenting whole sentences in noise he presented the words of each sentence in haphazard order (and noise), and instructed the subjects to try to reproduce the list of words as a sentence.

The results were about identical to the original results: they showed the same
ᵉrarchical constituent boundary effects in spite of the absence of prosodic
ᶠormation or order information in the stimuli. Also, no particular syntactic
ᵗme was given or suggested during the experiment. Apparently, subjects are
ᵈe to apply syntactic structures of their own making to haphazard word lists,
ᵒugh to show strong syntactic structuring in their reproduction. This is
ᵗnsonant with the idea that syntax comes in during reproduction and is neither
ᵖroperty of the memory code, nor of a retrieval plan that is learned *during* the
ᵖeriment. At the same time, however, the experiment does not prove this. It
ᵗy be the case that the subject listens to the word list, constructs and stores a
ᵗntence and finally reproduces the sentence from memory. Stronger results
ᵗ required apparently.

More definite conclusions can be drawn from a series of experiments by
ᵗmpen (1974). It is good practice in memory research to unravel storage and
ᵗrieval processes by investigating which aspects of the memorized material
ᵗn be retrieved in the reproduction phase of the experiment by means of
ᵗrieval procedures that are distinct and independent from retrieval proce-
ᵗres which have been learned during the acquisition phase. Kempen applied
ᵗs method to a number of variations of the probe latency technique which was
ᵉntioned above.

In each of his experiments subjects learned a set of four Dutch sentences by
ᵃrt. The sentences could be qualified as having weak semantic integration;
ᵗir verbs were 'middle verbs', i.e. they could be used transitively as well as
ᵗransitively. Examples are *Those two Finns wrote texts; Those three Greeks
ᵗrned laboriously*. The critical manipulation was the paradigm by which the
ᵗferent transitions were measured. If the usual probing paradigm was used,
ᵗ presentation of probe words in random order—each probe word followed
ᵗ the subject quickly mentioning the next word in the sentence—significant
ᵗnstituent boundary effects were obtained. These effects were even stronger if
ᵗ subject was instructed to react with the *preceding* word in the sentence
ᵃckward reactions) instead of the following word. Since in these two
ᵗradigms the probe words could be taken from the whole sentence, they are
ᵗled the 'sentencewise' paradigms ('forward' and 'backward', respectively).
ᵗe results for these two sentencewise paradigms are summarized in the upper
ᵗr of dotted lines of Figure 11.3. It is clear that the transition from subject
ᵗun to main verb and inversely (*Finns, wrote*) gives longer probe latencies
ᵗn the transition from main verb to object noun and inversely (*wrote, texts*).
ᵗe first transition corresponds to a major constituent break, the second is a
ᵗhin-constituent transition.

However, the profile of probe latencies changes drastically if a different
ᵗradigm is used, which Kempen called the 'pairwise' paradigm. In this case,
ᵗjects were (after learning) instructed that all probe words would come from
ᵗe of the two positions around a predetermined syntactic transition, for
ᵗance the noun/verb transition, and that if the one word is presented (e.g.,
ᵗ noun) the subject has to reproduce the other (the verb) and conversely.

After this instruction a particular transition was chosen at random and a backward and forward probes were done for all learned sentences. Then the experimenter announced a shift to another transition and again all forward and backward probes were done. This went on systematically until all transition had been measured. This pairwise paradigm led to a complete disappearance of the constituent boundary effect. This can be seen in Figure 11.3, where the continuous horizontal lines summarize the forward and backward latency data for this paradigm. [A control experiment could successfully eliminate a alternative explanation according to which the subjects engaged in silent rehearsal of the word pairs from which the probes were selected during a given series of pairwise latency measurements. For the details see Kempen (1974).

Before interpreting this disappearance it is necessary to describe the result of a third experiment. In that experiment Kempen was able to generate constituent boundary effect by means of the pairwise paradigm. This important because one might 'accuse' the pairwise paradigm of being insensitive, or at least too insensitive to measure subtle constituent break effects. I order to explain this third experiment a quick course in Dutch is required. The experiment differed from the second one only in terms of its syntactic material. In Dutch the order of the main verb and object is different for a main clause and a subordinate clause. For *Those two Finns wrote texts* the word order in Dutch the same as in English: the verb precedes the object. However, in the subordinate clause the order inverts in the following way: *Because those two Finns 'texts wrote', they needed some light.* It should be obvious that for Dutch ears these two orders sound equally natural if used in the correct context. The third experiment differed from the second in that the subjects learned a set of subordinate clauses where subject nouns were always followed by object nouns. So a typical stimulus clause was *Because two Finns texts wrote* (there was no main clause added, so the stimuli were incomplete sentences). Here the constituent break is between *Finns* and *texts*, the subject and the object which are juxtaposed in these constructions.

It turned out that this latter transition led to relatively long probe latencies both forward and backward, whereas the within-constituent transition between *texts* and *wrote* gave short latencies. These results are summarized Figure 11.3 as the bottom pair of dotted lines.

In order to interpret these data, Kempen reasoned as follows. (For a detailed description of the argument, see Kempen, 1974.) First, it seems clear that the constituent boundary effect depends on the retrieval task which the subject have to perform, not on what the subjects learned during acquisition. The latter was namely identical for Experiments I and II; these experiments differed only in retrieval task for which instructions were given after learning had been completed. In the first 'sentencewise' paradigm the subject could not know advance which transition would be probed. At any time he could expect a probe word. In the second 'pairwise' paradigm, however, the subject did know in advance which transition was going to be tested. The second step, then, was to consider what advantage the subject could have from this knowledge. In

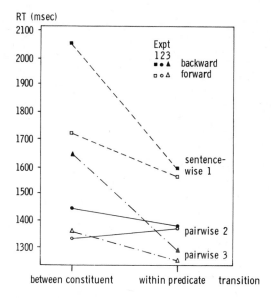

Figure 11.3. Probe reaction times for three experimental conditions (after Kempen, 1974)

rst approximation, Kempen hypothesized that in the pairwise paradigm the ubject could somehow limit his attention to a subpart of the semantic epresentation of the sentences, whereas in the first paradigm the whole nternal representation had to be kept accessible and retrievable. The pairwise aradigm only required the subject to consider a small (meaningful) part of the nternal representation, namely the information that Finns wrote for the first ransition, and that it is texts that were written, for the second transition. This xplains, to start with, why probe latencies are smaller in the second paradigm. ut how to explain the difference in constituent break effect between Experinents II and III? For this Kempen made the additional assumption that the ubject, in retrieving such semantic units, makes use of particular syntactic onstructions. A syntactic construction is a string of syntactic categories, xpressing one or more case or modifier relationships. (In this paper we will fer to specific syntactic constructions by means of labels for the expressed elationships, e.g. S-V, etc., since the intended category sequence is always ear from context.) That is, the subject tries to map a maximally specific yntactic construction on the information to be retrieved. What is the most pecific construction that the subject might use in the first 'sentencewise' aradigm? Since in that case the subject does not know which transition is oing to be tested there is no other recourse for him than using as a retrieval ame the syntactic construction of the sentence as a whole. The subject first xpresses the semantic information in phrases corresponding to the syntactic ame and only then he is able to find the particular transition. The transition, therefore, is 'read' from such parsed information and thus shows the con stituent boundary effect. In the pairwise paradigm, however, the subject know in advance what part of the information is to be retrieved and can use a muc more efficient syntactic construction. In Experiment II the information th Finns wrote can be efficiently captured in the syntactic construction S–V; n other constructions have to be considered. And similarly the information th texts were written is easily caught by using a V–O construction. There is no priori reason to think that one of these is easier to apply than the other so that r differential effect is to be expected, which is in accordance with the data. other words, the subject can perform his task in Experiment II by applying completely overlearned syntactic construction, be it S–V or V–O. The constructions can be different from the syntactic structure of the learne sentences, and still be very effective for retrieval purposes. They are pr experimental in the sense that they are part of the subject's syntactic skills.

Let us now turn to Experiment III and consider why the constituen boundary effect reappears in that case. It should be remembered that the ma difference between this and Experiment II is in the order of subject, verb an object, which is not S–V–O any more, but S–O–V (*Because Finns 'texts wrote* In this case the smallest meaningful unit related to the pair *Finns, texts* is th information that Finns wrote texts. The sequence S–O does not capture th information, it is moreover not a syntactic construction such as S–V and V–(For retrieving *texts*, given *Finns*, it is therefore necessary to first use the larg construction S–O–V for retrieving *Finns texts wrote* and then to read off *Fin texts*. The retrieval of *wrote* given *texts* (or inversely) can again be easily done b applying the overlearned O–V construction to the information that texts wer written. The pattern of latencies is in correspondence with this analysis.

If this analysis is correct, we are able to reconcile the now popular viewpoi that sentences are memorized in semantic or imagery-type format with th always recurrent finding of syntactic effects on verbatim reproduction. Th reconciliation can be made, moreover, without agreeing with the critics wh explain these effects by saying that during a verbatim recall experiment th subject not only stores the content of the sentence, but also sets himself th additional and completely artificial task to memorize the syntactic frame, eith independently, or as a retrieval plan. Kempen's experiments showed that syntactic construction used for retrieval is in principle independent of th syntactic structure of the learned sentences. It depends on the experimen task what sort of syntactic construction is going to be used by the subject order to retrieve (parts of) the stored information. In a verbatim rec experiment the subject may use the construction which he perceived in th learned sentence, but at least for simple sentences such constructions a overlearned already and it should not require much effort to label a particul construction for retrieval purposes; this is quite different from learning a ne syntactic construction which would indeed be an artificial task.

As a summary conclusion it can be stated that the data in this section led us seek the origin of syntactic effects in verbatim sentence recall in the reprodu ion phase instead of the storage. They are caused by the use of retrieval programs that correspond to overlearned syntactic constructions and that are applied to read out and verbalize the semantic information in memory.

Discussion

The experiments discussed in the preceding two paragraphs lead to the following global description of what a subject does during verbatim sentence learning. He creates a semantic representation and in some cases an image of the subject, event, etc. of which the sentence is a description. If under memory or time pressure, he tries to store the syntactically parsed string of words, but depending on his expectations with respect to the recall task, he may label a particular syntactic frame as a retrieval program. Only in the case where relatively complex sentences are learned and the subject is anticipating verbatim recall will the storage of the retrieval program involve some syntactic learning. During the reproduction phase, the subject will, dependent on the instructions, choose from his stock of overlearned syntactic frames one which is most specific to retrieving the information required by the task. Only these syntactic frames can cause syntactic recall effects.

At this point we want to make three qualifications. Firstly, it seems unlikely that any frequent syntactic construction can be used as a retrieval program. As we have remarked earlier, the construction should be appropriate to be mapped on some unit of information in memory. Our knowledge of the structure of such units is still very limited but many theories of semantic memory (for a review see Frijda, 1972) represent sentential information in the form of a predication over arguments or cases. If this is correct we would expect that certain syntactic constructions would be particularly suited for retrieval, such as subject–main verb, main verb–object, main verb–prepositional phrase, as well as different types of modifier relations, e.g. verb–adverb, adjective–noun. There may in fact be a close correspondance between effective retrieval programs and the syntactic constructions that figure in Bever's (1970) perceptual strategies. There also the subject tries out syntactic frames which have a high chance of leading him to the most important semantic relations.

Secondly, by promoting syntactic constructions to retrieval programs we do not intend to deny the existence of other means to retrieve sentential information from memory.

Thirdly, we want to be careful in drawing conclusions with respect to spontaneous sentence production. It should be clear from the above that, contrary to the present trend in text memory work, we do not consider syntactic effects in sentence recall as peripheral, artificial, or unnatural phenomena. On the contrary we want to take them as expressions of LTM-operations which are of much more general use, especially in spontaneous speech. Also there the speaker tries to frame information from memory into syntactic construction of his choice. And similarly, a syntactic construction may guide his search for those aspects of the activated information that have to be verbalized at a particular instant in speech. Care is required, however, because we do not intend to say that in speech the syntactic program precedes the retrieval of information from memory in all cases, nor that it is the only or most important means of retrieval.

To round up this discussion we finally turn to mentioning some non continental studies which in some form or another have also pointed to syntactic constructions as retrieval plans.

Ervin-Tripp (1961) has suggested that in order to carry out a free association task the subject might use syntactic constructions to find a response word. If he does, the result is a syntagmatic association. Paradigmatic associations can be explained similarly: the stimulus word activates a syntactic frame, the response word can replace the stimulus word in that frame. A possible reason for the availability of replacer sets is their useful function in speech perception: the listener can anticipate the speaker by activating one or more words which would be a likely completion given the syntactic frame under construction.

Miller (1969) proposes that certain asymmetries in the occurrence of word associations be explained in a manner which is quite close to our view. One typical asymmetry is the frequent association from exemplar to category (e.g. *collie-dog*), whereas the converse is rare. Another case is the whole-part association (*hand-finger*) which is more frequent than the converse. According to Miller the subject tries to find an association word by making use of *predicates* like ' . . . *is a* . . .', or ' . . . *has a* . . . '.

Polzella and Rohrman (1970) found in an association experiment that transitive verbs as stimuli were more effective in evoking noun reactions than intransitive verbs. They explain this by supposing that in the internal lexicon transitive verbs have a slot for a nominal object constituent. Apparently the subject uses a little V–O construction in order to generate an appropriate response. This construction is not activated in the case of intransitive verbs. Extending this line of thought, Bacharach, Kellas and McFarland (1972) performed a free recall experiment from which it appeared that a pair of intransitive verb and CVC trigram was easier to learn than a pair of transitive verb and CVC trigram, but only in the case where the trigram *precedes* the verb. Apparently, trigrams subsume the role of subject phrase; in the case of transitive verb the 'sentence' remains incomplete and is therefore harder to learn. The difference disappeared completely, however, in conditions where trigrams *followed* the verbs: there trigrams could either be in the role of object phrase for transitive verbs or of adverb for intransitive verbs, leaving the 'sentence' equally incomplete in the two cases.

Wright (1972) determined error rates for subjects answering questions such as *The doctor helped the nurse. By whom was the nurse helped?* The results led her to suggest that in order to retrieve the answer (e.g. *the doctor*) from LTM is necessary for the subject to use a mediating sentence context (e.g., *the nurse was helped by* . . .).

Probably closer to our view is a recent paper by James, Thompson and Baldwin (1973). They related retrieval of a sentence from memory to the constructive process in normal speech production, as we did above. More specifically they select two characteristics of normal free speech for study in a free recall task, namely preference for active constructions over passive, and a tendency to start a sentence with the (semantic) theme. They were able to demonstrate that errors in free recall show the same biases, which is consonant with our view that subjects may use syntactic retrieval plans which are quite different from what they learned during acquisition. It should be added, however, that the authors only mention the reconstructive role of syntax, not its role in memory search.

It is our opinion that both the reported continental studies and the heterogeneous collection of results in this latter section demonstrate the importance of syntactic factors in getting access to non-syntactic information in memory. One would like to see that the presently active study of semantic storage is complemented by an equally active and systematic study of the (partly syntactic) procedures employed in the retrieval and verbal recasting of information from memory.

References

Bacharach, V. R., Kellas, G. and McFarland, C. E. (1972). Structural properties of transitive and intransitive verbs. *Journal of Verbal Learning and Verbal Behavior*, **11**, 486–490.

Barclay, J. R. (1973). The role of comprehension in remembering sentences. *Cognitive Psychology*, **4**, 229–254.

Bever, T. G. (1970). The cognitive basis for linguistic structures. In J. R. Hayes (Ed.) *Cognition and the development of Language*. New York: Wiley.

Binet, A. and Henri, V. (1894). La memoire des phrases (Memoire des idées). *Année psychologique*, **1**, 24–59.

Blumenthal, A. L. (1967). Prompted recall of sentences. *Journal of Verbal Learning and Verbal Behavior*, **6**, 203–206.

Bransford, J. D. and Franks, J. J. (1972). The abstraction of linguistic ideas; a review. *Cognition*, **1**, 211–249.

Engelkamp, J. (1973). *Semantische Struktur und die Verarbeitung von Sätzen*. Bern: Huber.

Engelkamp, J., Merdian, F. and Hörmann, H. (1972). Semantische Faktoren beim Behalten der Verneinung von Sätzen. *Psychologische Forschung*, **35**, 93–116.

Ervin-Tripp, S. M. (1961). Changes with age in the verbal determinants of word-association. *American Journal of Psychology*, **74**, 361–372.

Fillenbaum, S. (1966). Memory for gist: some relevant variables. *Language and Speech*, **9**, 217–227.

Flores d'Arcais, G. B. (1974). Is there a memory for sentences? *Acta Psychologica*, **38**, 33–58.

Frijda, N. H. (1972). Simulation of human long-term memory. *Psychological Bulletin*, **77**, 1–31.

Hörmann, H. (1971). Semantic factors in negation. *Psychologische Forschung*, **35**, 1–16.

James, C. T., Thompson, J. G. and Baldwin, J. M. (1973). The reconstructive process in sentence memory. *Journal of Verbal Learning and Verbal Behavior*, **12**, 51–63.

Johnson, N. F. (1965). The psychological reality of phrase-structure rules. *Journal of Verbal Learning and Verbal Behavior*, **4**, 469–475.

Johnson, N. F. (1970). The role of chunking and organization in the process of recall. In G. H. Bower (Ed.) *The Psychology of Learning and Motivation*, Vol. 4. New York: Academic Press.

Kempen, G. (1974). *Syntactic constructions as retrieval plans*. Report 74FUO2, Department of Psychology, University of Nijmegen, Nijmegen.

Leeuwenberg, E. L. J. (1971). A perceptual coding language for visual and auditory patterns. *American Journal of Psychology*, **84**, 307–350.

Levelt, W. J. M. (1967). *Semantic features: a psychological model and its mathematical analysis*. Report, Center for Comparative Psycholinguistics, University of Illinois, Urbana.

Levelt, W. J. M. (1970). Hierarchical clustering algorithm in the psychology of grammar. In G. B. Flores d'Arcais and W. J. M. Levelt (Eds) *Advances in Psycholinguistics*. Amsterdam: North-Holland.

Levelt, W. J. M. (1970a). Hierarchical chunking in sentence processing. *Perception and Psychophysics*, **8**, 99–102.

Levelt, W. J. M. (1973–1974). *Formal Grammars in Linguistics and Psycho-Linguistics*. Vol. I: Introduction to the theory of grammars and automata, 1973. Vol. II: Applications in linguistic theory, 1974. Vol. III: Applications in psycholinguistics, 1974. The Hague: Mouton.

Levelt, W. J. M. and Bonarius, M. (1973). Suffixes as deep structure clues. *Methodology and Science*, **6**, 7–37.

Loosen, F. (1972). *Cognitieve organisatie van zinnen in het geheugen*. Dissertation, Leuven.

Miller, G. A. (1969). The organization of lexical memory: are word associations sufficient? In G. A. Talland and N. C. Waugh (Eds) *The Pathology of Memory*. New York: Academic Press.

Noordman, L. G. M. and Levelt, W. J. M. (1970). *Noun categorization by noun-verb intersection for the Dutch language*. Heymans Bulletins HB 70–59, Department of Psychology, Groningen University, Groningen.

Osgood, C. E. (1970). Interpersonal verbs and interpersonal behavior. In J. L. Cowan (Ed.) *Studies in Thought and Language*. Tucson: The University of Arizona Press.

Polzella, D. J. and Rohrman, N. L. (1970). Psychological aspects of transitive verbs. *Journal of Verbal Learning and Verbal Behavior*, **9**, 537–540.

Rosenberg, S. (1968). Association and phrase structure in sentence recall. *Journal of Verbal Learning and Verbal Behavior*, **7**, 1077–1081.

Sachs, J. S. (1967). Recognition memory for syntactic and semantic aspects of connected discourse. *Perception and Psychophysics*, **2**, 437–442.

Teigeler, P. (1972). *Satzstruktur und Lernverhalten*. Bern: Huber.

Wilkes, A. L. and Kennedy, R. A. (1969). Relationships between pausing and retrieval latency in sentences of varying grammatical form. *Journal of Experimental Psychology*, **79**, 241–245.

Wright, P. (1972). Some observations on how people answer questions about sentences. *Journal of Verbal Learning and Verbal Behavior*, **11**, 188–195.

Part IV

Retrieval

Chapter 12

Category Production Measures and Verification Times

Richard B. Millward, Glenn Rice and Albert Corbett

Although we seem to be long way from a satisfactory theory of how information is stored in memory, most researchers agree that experiences are coded into numerous and complexly organized concepts. Some of these concepts are labelled linguistically and, insofar as the concepts are related, the labels (words) also become related. When a subject is presented with a word in some context, a concept is evoked. The word and the context determine what this concept is. Because vocabularies and contexts are, from a practical point of view, infinite, experimental and theoretical work on how memory is organized has been rather difficult.

An early attempt to deal with organization of memory was made by Bousfield (1953), who had subjects learn word lists composed of 15 words from each of four natural categories. Despite random input, the free recall of the words (presumably reflecting memory organization) was clustered according to the four categories. Since Bousfield reported this result, the use of conceptual categories has dominated experimental work in studies of organization in verbal learning (see Kintsch, 1970).

Recently, interest has shifted to a more direct investigation of the organization of categories in memory by using reaction time (RT) measures. Studies in semantic-memory retrieval require a subject to produce a member of a category as rapidly as possible (Freedman and Loftus, 1971) or to decide whether an object denoted by one word is a member or a property of a category designated by another word (Collins and Quillian, 1969; Landauer and Freedman, 1968). The RTs of these decisions are assumed to be determined by the structure of the information stored in memory, by the processes involved in retrieving this information, and by comparison processes if they are required. Whereas earlier work in verbal learning concentrated more on the influence of semantic relations over relatively long time spans and using complex learning processes (e.g., free recall), the emphasis in RT tasks has been on the immediate influence of organization on semantic information retrieval.

Theoretical Positions

Three major theoretical positions have been taken on how to describe the semantic retrieval process. Because current research is extensive and theoretical statements have been only qualitatively supported, major theoretical reorientation will surely occur in the near future. Nonetheless, we will review briefly the current theoretical positions since they provide the necessary background for an understanding of the experimental results to be reported.

Collins and Quillian (1969, 1970a, b) introduced a highly structural and complex theoretical model of semantic memory. In their model, concepts are stored at the nodes of a hierarchical tree structure or network. Associated with each concept node are links or paths to other nodes and to properties belonging specifically to the concept; i.e. two types of links are explicitly assumed: links to the superordinates of the concept node and links to the properties of the concepts. For example, BIRD has a link to the superordinate ANIMAL and links to the properties FLYING, HAVING FEATHERS, etc.

'Cognitive economy' is an important auxiliary assumption made by Collins and Quillian. It states that a *property* of a concept is stored at the highest possible or most general level of the tree. Thus, high-level concepts such as ANIMAL contain more universal properties (e.g., SELF-LOCOMOTING), while low-level concepts such as DOG contain more specific properties (e.g., HAVING FOUR LEGS). The fact that a dog, as an example of an animal, is also self-locomoting, is not stored at the DOG node.

In a semantic retrieval task in which a subject must decide whether it is true or false that, for example, 'a canary can sing,' the subject presumably starts at the CANARY node and checks its properties. Its unique singing ability is stored at the CANARY node and so a fast decision is made. On the other hand, when asked to verify whether 'a canary can fly,' the subject enters the CANARY node but does not find the flying attribute. He must move to the superordinate node, BIRD, where the more general property of FLYING is stored because it is associated with all birds. Nonflying birds such as penguins have this special nonflying property stored at the PENGUIN node. The retrieval process takes varying amounts of time, depending on the number of nodes which must be checked in the network.

The assumption of cognitive economy has been refuted experimentally by Conrad (1972). She showed that Collins and Quillian (1969) failed to control for the frequency with which subjects stated that a property belonged to a category. She measured the properties associated with each concept by having subjects generate properties of concepts and found that the cases in which one or more nodes had to be considered were cases where the frequency of associating that property to the concept was low. When the frequency with which a property was elicited by a concept was controlled, there was no cognitive economy effect. For example, FLYING is a property very frequently produced for the concept BIRD and only rarely elicited for CANARY. However, Conrad supported the notion that memory was hierarchically structured with respect to superordinates. Subjects respond faster to 'a canary is a bird' than to 'a canary is an animal.' Thus, the assumption that concepts are related hierarchically through superordinate links received experimental support. This is a critical result for our purposes. Collins and Quillian's model assumes that RT differences are due to the processes of retrieving the information from memory. It makes strong structural assumptions and makes no assumptions about comparison processes.

The set-theoretic or category-search models make fewer assumptions about the structure of memory. Although a wide variety of models has been considered (Meyer, 1970), the simplest one-stage version of the theory assumes that a list of exemplars is stored with each category. When one asks whether 'a canary is a bird,' the BIRD category is searched, in parallel or serially, until the CANARY instance is encountered. When negative examples such as 'A dog is a bird' are presented, the search must be exhaustive and therefore will take longer (Landauer and Meyer, 1972). Landauer and Freedman (1968) suggested this model because of their observation that retrieval took longer for larger categories than for smaller categories. Furthermore, the RT difference between small and large categories was greater for negative instances (items which do not belong to the category) than for positive instances, suggesting that with negative instances categories were searched to completion. The necessary exhaustive search for negative instances would tend to lead to larger differences between small and large categories than would the terminating search for positive items.

The fact that negative-instance decisions show a larger category-size effect is not only supportive of a search model but is also rather difficult to explain with the network model proposed by Collins and Quillian. However, there are two possible problems with the research showing category-size differences for positive and negative instances. The size effect with positive items has not always been observed (Freedman and Loftus, 1971). Furthermore the category-size effect has generally been produced using nested categories so that the smaller category is a subset of the larger one. In cases where the larger category includes the smaller one as a subset, the size of the category is confounded with the level of storage in the network model. Hence, the size effect might simply be caused by the need to check a higher-level node. Within the network models, a category-size effect for negative instances is considered to be caused by semantic relatedness. Collins and Quillian (1970a) argue that the results for negative items arose from the manner in which the items were selected. Negative instances were more likely to belong to a category which could be confused with larger categories than to a category which could be confused with smaller categories. To use their example, when TULIP is tested against either DOG or ANIMAL, because ANIMAL is more likely to be confused with PLANT than DOG is, the time required to decide that a TULIP is not an ANIMAL is increased because of the category confusion. They cite results by Schaeffer and Wallace (1969, 1970) in support of such a semantic–distance effect.

Discussion of semantic distance brings us to the third theoretical position. Central to this position is the notion that categories are not simply nodes in a network of related nodes, nor are they homogeneous sets of instances (or attributes) as in the set–theoretic models. Rather, each concept has an internal structure. In retrieving information about an instance, the internal structure will play a role in the process. The results of Wilkins (1971) and Schaeffer and Wallace (1969, 1970) support this position. Rosch (1973) has discussed the idea that semantic space consists of a set of 'focal' instances and a distance function for instances not in the focal set. This semantic space determines how we use categories generally and not how we formally, or logically, define them. The implication of her ideas is that semantic retrieval will function according to this semantic space and not according to logical definitions.

Schaeffer and Wallace used a 'same–different' *RT* task in which subjects had to decide whether two words presented simultaneously both denoted LIVING THING or both denoted NONLIVING THING (a *same* response), versus deciding whether one word denoted LIVING THING and the other NONLIVING THING (a *different* response). The words from the category LIVING THING were from the two subcategories MAMMAL and FLOWER, and the words from the category NONLIVING THING were from the two subcategories METAL and FABRIC. Two words were defined as similar when they were both from the same subcategory, and they were defined as dissimilar when they were from different subcategories. A strong similarity effect resulted: A *same* judgment to two words from the same subcategory was 176 msec faster than a *same* judgment to two words from different categories. In a second experiment, two category words were presented and followed by an instance of one of them. The subject had to indicate, by pressing a button under the correct category, the category to which the instance belonged. The similarity of the categories in this experiment increased *RT*. Thus, the effect of similarity can be facilitating or inhibiting, depending on whether the categories involved lead to the same response or to a different response. Schaeffer and Wallace's theoretical account of their results is incorporated in the Rips, Shoben, and Smith semantic–distance model (1973) which we describe later.

Wilkins (1971) did not explicitly support a semantic–distance model, but because he showed that not all instances of a category were retrieved with the same *RT*, his results can be interpreted as lending support to such a position. Instances of a category can be scaled according to their *production* frequency or *dominance*. (Wilkins called it *conjoint* frequency, a misnomer because it is really a conditional frequency.) If subjects are asked to generate instances of a category, the dominance of an instance is the proportion of subjects who produce it. This frequency is quite different from word-count frequency as tabulated by Thorndike and Lorge (1944) or Kučera and Francis (1967). Wilkins obtained his dominance ratings from the Connecticut Norms (Cohen, Bousfield, and Whitmarsh, 1957). He also measured category size by counting the number of different words (types) produced for each category. Dominance and category size were varied factorially with word-count frequency held constant, and both dominance and category size significantly affected verification RT.

In Wilkins' second experiment, negative instances belonging to a superset of the test category were presented. For example, for the category ALCOHOLIC BEVERAGE, COKE is a negative example which belongs to the superset BEVERAGE. Landauer and Freedman (1968) had excluded this type of negative instance, using only negative instances which belonged to neither the test category nor its supersets. Wilkins found that, if a negative instance belonged to a superordinate category, the subject took longer to respond than if it did not. Wilkins' first experiment suggests that, within a category, instances differ in their retrievability. It further suggests that category size (when categories are not nested) has an effect on RT. The second experiment shows that the distance between the category to which an instance belongs and the category against which it is being tested determines RT. This result extends the Schaeffer and Wallace result and suggests that the large negative effects observed by some researchers may be due to a failure to control this distance carefully enough.

The most clearly developed version of the semantic–distance position is by Rips, Shoben, and Smith (1973). In their experiment, distance was measured by ratings and was a better predictor of RTs than superset or size relationships. In fact, for the MAMMAL–ANIMAL categories, RTs were opposite from the predictions of the subset model. They found that measures of the distance between an instance and its category were predictive of the verification RT while, at the same time, the subset–superset relationship yields RTs which were reversed from those predicted by network and search models. They argue that the size effect or subset effect, as they call it, is really a semantic–distance effect.

To understand their model, it is necessary to define a lexical item or word. First note that a word is often a category and a member of a category. For example, TREE is a category designating exemplars such as ELM, BIRCH, PINE, etc., but it is also an exemplar of the category PLANT. Thus, any definition of a word must be able to handle the dual role that it can assume. Each word has associated with it a list of functional features, values of attributes which generally characterize the word. Some of these features are criterial for the concept or category designated by the word, while others are only characteristic of it. When two words are compared, the total set of functional features come into play to define the distance between the two words. The semantic distance between two words is inversely proportional to the number of functional features they have in common. When one must be absolutely sure that a word is a member of a category, the criterial subsets may be isolated and used to make the decision, but such an analytical approach is not generally used. Thus, in an experimental situation in which a subject must verify whether one word is a member of a category specified by another word, the RT depends on the distance between the two words.

The verification process consists of two stages (see also Meyer, 1970). In the first stage, the degee of overlap of the functional features of the instance and of the category is determined. If there are few features in common, similarity is low; if there are many features in common, similarity is high. Only the first stage is needed for words which are either extremely high or extremely low in similarity. Decisions based on only the first stage will, of course, be relatively fast ones. That is, if the instance is a member of the category and is a very good example of it (high similarity), fast decisions will be made. If, on the other hand, the instance is not a member of the category and has very little relationship to it, then a fast negative decision is made. Presumably, one has few high-similarity instances which are not members of the category and few low similarity instances which are members of the category.

With the second stage, the criterial features come into play. These allow the true relationship between an instance and a category name to be determined, but at a cost in time. In the Rips *et al.* model then, the semantic–distance effect is carried by the overlap in the features, which allows a fast decision as a function of similarity. Their model closely resembles the Atkinson and Juola (1974) model for list searching in long-term memory.

Purpose of the Present Research

Although the experiment to be reported was designed before some of the above studies were published, the results are pertinent to an evaluation of the different theoretical positions. However, since we were not trying to make a critical test of these positions, no definitive conclusions with respect to these theories will necessarily be forthcoming.

In the experiment to be discussed, category size was deliberately varied by using a measure derived from a production task. This would seem to provide a size measure which does not confound size with set inclusion. There are several procedures for measuring category size. One class of procedures bases the category size on the number of category items recorded in a dictionary, thesaurus, or word-frequency count (see Loftus and Suppes, 1972, for example). Landauer and Meyer (1972) mention some of the difficulties with such measures of category size. A second class of procedures determines the size from category-production tasks in which a subject is presented with a category and asked to generate as many examples of the category as possible (e.g., Battig and Montague, 1969). One advantage of using the production task is that a subject can define his own category examples so that group norms do not have to be relied upon exclusively. Furthermore, a variety of different measures based on the results of the production task can be used to further refine the concept of semantic memory. Since category size may covary with other variables, as Collins and Quillian (1970a) suggest, it is desirable to control as many characteristics of categories as possible.

In order to disentangle the apparent confounding of semantic structure and category size, both must be independently varied. Our aim in this experiment was to find two measures of categories based on the production task, one of which would reflect the category size and the other the category structure.

Consider the results of a typical procedure to obtain items of a category. Subjects are presented with a category name and are asked to list examples of the category. Table 12.1 illustrates a hypothetical set of results for 10 subjects.

Table 12.1. Category production measures

Subject: S_i: i =	Types (ranked by dominance)								No. of Instances for each S_i: I_i^b
	T1	T2	T3	T4	T5	T6	T7	T8[a]	
1	2	4	1	5	3	8	7	6	8
2	1	5	3	4	2	6	8	7	8
3	1	6	2	5	7	3	8	4	8
4	1	2	—	3	6	4	5	—	6
5	3	2	1	4	5	6	—	—	6
6	4	3	1	2	5	—	—	—	5
7	1	3	4	2	—	—	—	—	4
8	2	1	3	—	—	—	—	—	3
9	1	—	—	—	—	—	—	—	1
10	1	—	—	—	—	—	—	—	1
$I_{.j}^c$	10	8	7	7	6	5	4	3	50
Dominance rank	1	2	3·5	3·5	5	6	7	8	

[a] The number of Types, $T = 8$
[b] The average number of instances generated, $I = 50/10 = 5·0$
[c] The Dominance measure, D (not normalized for the number of subjects)

From the 50 items generated by the 10 subjects, eight different items are mentioned. The 50 instances can be called *tokens* and the eight different words *types*. The entry in the ith row and jth column of Table 12.1 is left blank if the jth type was not produced by the ith subject, while if the ith subject did produce the jth type, the cell is filled with a number corresponding to the order in which the subject produced that type. The absolute size of the marginal numbers is not very meaningful since the time allowed to produce examples and the number of subjects involved would change these greatly and probably non-linearly.

For our purposes here, there are four main variables represented in Table 12.1: The number of different types produced over all subjects (T), the number of instances produced by the ith subject (I_i), the number of subjects who generated an instance for the jth type (I_j), and the individual subject's order of production, the value of the ijth cell. The types listed in Table 12.1 have been ranked from highest to lowest according to $I_{.j}$. The value of I_j has been referred to traditionally as the dominance (D) of a type. There is another measure of the category as a whole which is the average $I_{.j}$ (D) measure: $\bar{D} = (1/T) \sum_{j-1}^{T} I_{.j}$. Then, $NI = T\bar{D}$: The average dominance, $\bar{D}$, is related to the ratio, I/T (assuming norms based on a fixed N). However, the $I_{.j}$ of different items varies greatly within a given category. Furthermore, the $I_{.j}$ of an individual word can be quite independent of T and I.

In order to get a measure of the number of instances produced for the category as a whole, we average the individual production measures, I_i, over subjects: $I = (1/N) \sum_{i=1}^{N} I_i$. A scatter plot of I and T for the 56 categories listed by Battig and Montague (1969) shows very little of a systematic nature relating the two measures. A correlation of I and T for 49 of the 56 categories in Battig and Montague yielded a non-significant correlation coefficient of -0.25 (Herrmann, Chaffin and Corbett, 1973). Generally, the I measure in Battig and Montague indicates that in the 30 sec allowed the subject for writing down instances of each category the average subject can list between five and 10 words. The T values range from 66 to 440 but the majority of the categories vary between 100 and 250 different types.

The value of T seems to measure the category size in that, with a large category, there would be a large number of different examples to choose from and different subjects would choose different examples, thus increasing T. On the other hand, I may reflect the degree of structure of the category in that structured categories would tend to lead to rapid production of instances. To the extent that items are semantically related as measured by I, one would expect smaller RTs for larger I values. The D measure probably reflects associative strength or saliency of the example as a member of the category. The average dominance, $\bar{D}$, will be lower for larger categories and higher for organized categories since the organization provides high associate strength to the set of organized words.

Since previous studies had failed to control systematically both variables, the present study investigated T and I by varying them factorially. Freedman and Loftus (1971) used I as an estimate of category size in an experiment in which the category name was followed by a modifier. For example, if the category ANIMAL was followed by the adjective STRIPED, then the subject could respond SKUNK or ZEBRA. Freedman and Loftus found a slight negative correlation between their size estimates (I) and RT and concluded that size (measured by I) was not an important variable in this type of semantic categorization task. Wilkins (1971) estimated category size by using the T measure computed from the Cohen, Bousfield, and Whitmarsh (1957) Connecticut norms. He found a significant category-size effect consistent with the effect observed by Landauer and Freedman (1968). The contradictory results of Freedman and Loftus and of Wilkins suggest that T and I do not measure the same thing, i.e. category size. Since neither experiment controlled for both the variables, one cannot be sure of either result. Our assumption here is that T measures category size but that I measures organization, which would be negatively correlated with RT as Freedman and Loftus found. For example consider the following four categories taken from the Battig and Montague norms (1969), which differ in number of types (T) and number of instances (I (see Table 12.2 for statistics): MALE NAME, OCCUPATION, RELATIVE and PRECIOUS STONE. People know a great many names and there are a great many different names to be known. Thus, each individual gives many names in the 30-sec production period allowed by Battig and Montague (10·7 on the average), but each individual has his own set to select from. In contrast, although there are a great many occupations, people are not able to recite a great number of examples. Perhaps the retrieval strategy for names is to think of relatives and friends, most of whom will bear different names; while the retrieval process for occupations is to think of one's own occupation and a small set of 'standard' occupations such as policeman, fireman, etc. RELATIVES and PRECIOUS STONES are small categories—people do not know many examples of either. But people generate a large number of relative names in 30 sec (9·3 on the average) and a smaller number of precious stones (5·2 on the average), (see Pollio, Richards, and Lucas, 1969). Again the retrieval strategy seems important. This kind of analysis has led us to suggest that T and I measure different aspects of categories and the four categories cited above indicate that T and I can vary independently. One purpose of our study was to vary T and I factorially to see if RT varied differently for the two variables. If T measures category size, and if RT varies with size, then larger T (size) variables should produce slower RTs. In contrast, if I measures category organization and if RT varies with I, then larger values of I should produce faster RTs.

Both T and I are measures characterizing categories as a whole and are necessarily based on average data. The third measure in Table 12.1, dominance (D), measures how likely an example is to be produced relative to the other examples produced for the category. Following Rosch (1973) and Rips, Shoben, and Smith (1973), we assume that categories have an internal structure. By 'internal structure' we mean that each category has a core meaning represented by 'clearest cases' or 'best examples' which is surrounded by other category examples of decreasing similarity to the core meaning. This assumption implies a category centre and a metric by which one can measure the distance from the centre point to each example. Our theoretical hypothesis is that D measures this distance. The relationship between dominance and RT is of interest since Wilkins (1971) and Freedman and Loftus (1971) found that items with high dominance were responded to faster than items with low dominance. However, Wilkins used only two levels of D in each category and did not control for I while Freedman and Loftus controlled neither experimentally and looked at D correlationally.

Finally, Table 12.1 also indicates the order in which each instance is produced by each subject (the rank order of the item, R). Like D, the rank order would seem to measure the structure of the category for the individual subject. The role of R in categorization time is based on the following set of assumptions and arguments. First, although different subjects probably organize the internal structure of a category in similar ways, there is no doubt that some individual differences exist in this organization. Thus, since D is a measure of semantic distance based on an average over subjects, it will not correspond exactly to each subject's ordering of examples. The R measure should do so with more accuracy, in any case. Second, the more central an example is to a category, the faster that example will be recognized as a member of the category. Third, in a production task, subjects tend to generate

Table 12.2. Category names, production measures, and *RT*s for positive items

| Group | | Category name | Production measure | | Dominance rank | | | | | | | | | | Average | |
T	I		T	I	1 D	1 RT	2 D	2 RT	3 D	3 RT	4 D	4 RT	5 D	5 RT	D	RT
		A human body part	170	11·3	326	1229	225	1116	184	1198	127	1196	306	1151	233	1178
		A country	187	8·8	215	1099	154	1160	86	1126	107	1189	269	1103	166	1136
High	High	A building part	257	7·4	184	1284	155	1420	114	1382	67	1331	205	1458	145	1375
		A male name	449	10·7	114	1192	77	1265	59	1296	49	1279	239	1094	108	1225
		A city	430	7·4	156	941	103	1129	48	1180	45	1122	235	972	117	1069
High	High	Average	298	9·1	199	1149	143	1218	98	1237	79	1223	251	1156	154	1197
		An occupation	349	6·2	155	1233	105	1154	49	1126	11	1256	152	1013	94	1156
		An earth formation	243	5·9	248	1125	90	1447	97	1292	15	1408	209	1192	132	1293
High	Low	A type of music	237	5·5	226	1191	94	1363	87	1445	26	1376	232	1154	133	1306
		A toy	285	6·2	103	1137	58	1246	54	1215	37	1459	204	1153	91	1242
		A type of ship	196	5·5	81	1295	60	1282	78	1351	33	1277	162	1221	83	1285
High	Low	Average	260	5·8	163	1196	82	1298	73	1286	24	1355	192	1147	107	1256
High	—	Average	279	7·5	181	1173	112	1258	86	1261	52	1280	221	1151	130	1226

Low		A unit of time	94	8·8	365	1178	396	1155	200	1174	165	1253	213	1316	268	1215
		A relative	61	9·3	361	959	315	988	230	1153	128	1129	225	1008	252	1047
High		A colour	106	9·7	428	958	362	1039	171	1127	109	1072	253	998	265	1039
		An article of clothing	117	9·5	229	1008	247	1115	190	1154	132	1159	280	1137	216	1114
		A musical instrument	86	8·3	238	1137	147	1125	158	1299	100	1190	287	1107	186	1172
Low	High	Average	93	9·1	323	1048	294	1084	190	1181	127	1160	252	1113	237	1117
		A precious stone	68	5·2	425	1095	237	1073	111	1202	76	1244	175	1313	205	1185
		A member of the clergy	93	5·8	280	1117	182	1435	142	1238	84	1400	208	1230	179	1284
Low		A science	125	5·8	278	1005	208	1237	73	1280	45	1176	242	1249	169	1189
		A type of insect	88	6·0	249	1211	166	1174	95	1315	59	1281	233	1274	161	1251
		A flower	110	6·1	269	1009	119	1027	92	1090	87	1086	183	1056	150	1054
Low	Low	Average	97	5·8	300	1087	183	1189	103	1225	70	1238	208	1224	173	1193
Low		Average	95	7·5	311	1118	238	1137	146	1203	99	1199	230	1169	205	1155
—	High	Average	196	9·1	261	1048	218	1151	144	1209	103	1192	251	1134	195	1157
—	Low	Average	179	5·8	231	1142	132	1244	88	1255	47	1296	200	1186	140	1225
—	—	Average	187	7·5	246	1120	175	1198	116	1232	75	1244	226	1160	168	1191

the best examples first, and to follow these with examples more and more distant from the core meaning of the concept. Given these assumptions, if RT is plotted as a function of R, it will have a steeper slope than RT plotted as a function of D. This is because rank order (R) should be a more exact measure of internal category distance than dominance. A predicted difference in slopes would tend to support all the above assumptions and, in particular, provide a more refined substantiation for R and D as measures of internal category distance. Further, if both large and small categories have internal structure as defined here, then the distance of a word from its core meaning would be a variable making RT 'noisy' with respect to the size of the category. The control of the distance an instance is from the core meaning of its superset could make measures of category size much more reliable. The experiment to be reported varies T, I, and $R(D)$ factorially with the use of R measures for the Experimental subjects and D measures derived from the Experimental subjects for yoked Control subjects.

Method

Subjects

The subjects were 22 female and 20 male undergraduates of Brown University who were fulfilling a course requirement.

Procedure

The experiment was run in two parts. In the first part, all subjects were given a pad with a category name printed at the top of each of 20 pages; the names were in a different order for each subject. The subjects were instructed to list, in the order in which they came to mind, 12 examples of each category. They were instructed not to look back at pages they had already completed or ahead to pages they had not yet started and were given as much time as they needed.

The second part of the experiment was run 10 to 14 days after the first part. Each subject was randomly placed in either the Experimental group or the Control group. Each Experimental subject was asked to categorize 200 test words, 10 from each of 20 test categories. Of the 10 words for each category, five were examples of the category (positive items) and five were not examples of the category (negative items). Of the five positive items, four had been produced by the Experimental subject himself in the first part of the experiment and one, *not* produced by the subject, was drawn from the Battig and Montague (1969) norms (see the Stimulus section below for further detail on stimulus selection). Each Control subject was yoked to an Experimental subject in that he responded to the same set of five test words.

After reading written instructions, the subjects were given 40 practice trials followed by 200 experimental trials. The subject initiated the trial by typing the space bar on a teletypewriter keyboard. Following a random delay (varying between 0·15 and 4·0 sec), the stimulus was presented. The test category name and test word were presented simultaneously, with the category name appearing above the test word. The subjects were to indicate as quickly as possible whether or not the test word was an example of the specified category. The stimulus remained in view until the subject responded. One-half of the subjects pressed a left-hand key for a positive response and a right-hand key for a negative response; the other half used the opposite response assignment.

Stimuli

The 20 test categories used in the experiment were selected from the Battig and Montague (1969) norms. They were divided into four sets of five categories each so that I and T varied factorially. Table 12.2 presents the test categories used along with their I and T values. Four words in each test category produced by each Experimental subject in the first part of the experiment were selected as stimuli for that subject in the second part. The words were the first, fourth, eighth, and twelfth words produced by the subject. If he produced fewer than 12 words, the four words selected were evenly spaced throughout the sample he did generate. The four words will be referred to as the words having Dominance Rank 1, Dominance Rank 2, Dominance Rank 3, and Dominance Rank 4. A fifth word was selected from the examples of the relevant category in the Battig and Montague norms. This word was the one with the highest dominance (D) value which had *not* been produced by the subject in the first part of the experiment. It was assigned Dominance Rank 5. Table 12.2 also presents the average Dominance value (D) from the Battig and Montague norms for these words. That is, each word an Experimental subject produced was looked up in the Battig and Montague norms and the dominance values averaged over subjects.

Some editing was performed on the subject-produced words. Spellings were corrected; plurals were eliminated unless the plural was the normal usage (e.g., trousers) or where the use of the singular might be ambiguous in the context of the particular category. Certain words were rejected (and an adjacent word used) for several reasons: the example contained the name of the category (e.g., New York City) and the deletion of the category name made the example ambiguous; the response was incorrect, or the example consisted of an emotionally loaded item (e.g., breast).

The negative examples, presented in Table 12.3, were chosen from 20 different non-test categories (presented in Table 12.4) appearing in the Battig and Montague norms. An attempt was made to select the items ranked first, third, sixth, ninth, and twelfth in dominance from the nontest categories. However, it was necessary to exclude some items for the same reasons that positive items were excluded. The average ranks of the five words selected across the twenty categories were 1·25, 3·9, 6·8, 9·6, and 12·55. These words were distributed throughout the 20 test categories in such a way that each test category had negative examples from five different non-test categories and each of the five negative examples was at a different dominance level. Table

Table 12.3 Information about, and *RT* of negative items

Group		Pos. Cat.	Dominance rank 1					Dominance rank 2					Dominance rank 3				
T	I	No.	word	Cat.	D	Freq.	RT	word	Cat.	D	Freq.	RT	word	Cat.	D	Freq.	RT
High	High	1	knife	3	382	76	1312	sergeant	2	332	28	1176	bluebird	14	138	1	1255
		2	house	7	396	591	1327	eagle	14	161	5	1231	chisel	10	103	4	1249
		3	car	15	407	274	1420	banana	5	283	4	1294	salmon	18	142	3	1223
		4	sparrow	14	237	1	1247	theft	9	171	10	1239	scotch	8	208	5	1414
		5	hammer	10	431	9	1206	wine	8	293	72	1195	peso	13	131	—	1830
		Average			371	190	1302			248	24	1227			144	3	1394
Low	High	1	carrot	16	316	1	1256	cave	7	155	9	1170	arson	9	60	3	1366
		2	apple	5	429	9	1109	newspaper	1	295	65	1221	birch	17	134	2	1188
		3	salt	11	412	46	1092	elm	17	210	3	1731	sword	6	110	7	1138
		4	lieutenant	2	362	29	1109	tennis	12	329	15	1151	lettuce	16	189	—	1018
		5	chair	4	440	66	1270	screwdriver	10	214	—	1211	cherry	5	183	6	1234
		Average			392	30	1167			241	23	1297			135	5	1189
High	Low	1	dollar	13	331	46	1250	sofa	4	232	6	1256	pamphlet	1	200	3	1348
		2	football	12	396	36	1239	bomb	6	122	36	1359	corporal	7	169	4	1447
		3	California	19	297	65	1203	pan	3	242	16	1494	Princeton	20	84	7	1221
		4	Yale	20	133	13	1300	dime	13	261	4	1211	trailer	7	107	11	1578
		5	oak	17	394	16	1283	Florida	19	225	20	1279	couch	4	168	13	1204
		Average			310	35	1255			216	26	1320			146	8	1360
Low	Low	1	gun	6	394	118	1203	train	15	257	82	1171	stove	3	74	15	1315
		2	beer	8	384	34	1088	garlic	11	120	4	1180	Virginia	19	144	75	1291
		3	trout	18	216	4	1148	bean	16	237	5	1267	cloves	11	94	2	1250
		4	magazine	1	375	39	1221	shark	18	176	3	1314	motorcycle	15	174	—	1216
		5	murder	9	387	75	1139	UCLA	20	92	—	1279	golf	12	153	34	1208
		Average			351	54	1160			176	24	1242			128	32	1256

Group		Pos. Cat.			Dominance rank 4					Dominance rank 5					Average			
T	I	No.	word	Cat.	D	Freq.	RT	word	Cat.	D	Freq.	RT	word	Cat.	D	Freq.	RT	
High	High	1	Maine	19	116	9	1308	embezzling	9	40	1	1341			202	23	1278	
		2	admiral	2	146	1	1434	mustard	11	61	20	1167			173	124	1282	
		3	swordfish	18	127	—	1329	wren	14	83	—	1314			208	94	1316	
		4	lemon	5	134	18	1373	shillings	13	46	1	1374			159	7	1330	
		5	Duke	20	57	(11)	1491	spear	6	51	7	1178			193	25	1380	
	Average				116	8	1387			56	6	1275			187	46	1317	
Low	High	1	pliers	10	58	1	1244	dish	11	42	16	1228			126	6	1253	
		2	shack	7	81	1	1293	bowling	12	96	3	1225			207	16	1207	
		3	hawk	14	111	14	1163	commander	2	86	28	1221			185	20	1269	
		4	penny	13	243	25	1203	Indiana	19	98	13	1262			244	21	1148	
		5	rye	8	72	4	1305	Cornell	20	37	5	1312			189	20	1266	
	Average				113	9	1242			72	13	1250			191	16	1229	
High	Low	1	redwood	17	71	2	1318	ship	15	47	83	1176			176	28	1269	
		2	larceny	9	46	2	1506	rug	4	51	13	1154			157	18	1341	
		3	badminton	12	96	1	1525	essay	1	28	19	1289			149	22	1346	
		4	bowl	3	69	23	1541	cottage	7	66	19	1322			127	14	1391	
		5	wagon	15	86	72	1519	cabbage	16	94	4	1293			193	25	1315	
	Average				74	20	1482			57	28	1247			161	21	1333	
Low	Low	1	oregano	11	73	—	1678	walnut	17	64	11	1219			172	57	1317	
		2	spear	6	51	7	1209	apricot	5	102	1	1098			160	24	1173	
		3	broccoli	16	126	1	1183	vermouth	8	55	1	1218			146	3	1213	
		4	journal	1	39	42	1244	screws	10	43	10	1407			161	24	1280	
		5	stool	4	72	8	1258	sunfish	18	80	—	1193			157	39	1215	
	Average				72	15	1315			69	6	1227			159	26	1240	

12.3 presents the dominance value and the word frequency as listed in Kučera and Francis (1967).

The practice categories and test items were also selected from the Battig and Montague norms (see Table 12.4). None of the words used in the practice trials appeared in the experimental trials.

Table 12.4. Names of the negative categories and practice categories

Number	B&M[a]	Negative category name	Number	B&M[a]	Negative category name
1	6	A type of reading material	13	33	A kind of money
			14	37	A kind of bird
2	7	A military title	15	39	A type of vehicle
3	11	A kitchen utensil	16	43	A vegetable
4	14	An article of furniture	17	50	A tree
5	16	A fruit	18	52	A fish
6	17	A weapon	19	55	A state
7	19	A type of human dwelling	20	56	A college or university
8	20	An alcoholic beverage	Practice category name used for the first 20 trials		
9	22	A crime			
10	23	A carpenter's tool	1	5	A metal
11	25	A substance for flavouring food	2	9	A kind of cloth
			3	26	A type of fuel
12	29	A sport	4	30	A weather phenomenon

[a] Number in the Battig and Montague norms

Design

The 200 stimuli, 20 categories × (5 positive examples plus 5 negative examples), were divided into five blocks of 40 stimuli each. Within each block, each of the 20 category names appeared twice, once with a positive item and once with a negative item. In order to avoid confounding the dominance rank and block variables, a Latin Square (category number × dominance rank) was used. The entries within the 5 × 5 square determined in which block of 40 trials the word with a particular dominance rank (rows) and particular category (columns) would appear. For example, if a 4 appeared in the second row and third column of the Latin Square, then a word from the second category and dominance level 3 would appear in the fourth block of 40 trials. Thus, within each block of trials, all five dominance levels appeared, with a different dominance level associated with each of the five categories within a $T–I$ set. The negative items were treated in the same manner. Each of the 21 Control subjects received exactly the same sequence of stimuli as his yoked Experimental subject and differed from him only in that the selected words were not the ones he himself had generated.

Apparatus

The categorization task was controlled by the PDP-8/L computer in the Brown University Human Learning Laboratory, operating under the GASPS control program (Wickens, Howard, Rice, and Millward, 1972). The stimuli were displayed on small television screens (black letters on a white background). Subjects indicated their responses on solenoid-reset teletypewriter keyboards. Reaction times were recorded by the computer and were accurate to within 1 msec. (See Millward, Aikin, and Wickens (1972) for a more detailed description of the experimental apparatus.)

Results

Preliminary Summary

Table 12.2 presents the *RT*s for positive items averaged over the 42 subjects for each of the five categories within each of the four *T–I* groups at each of the five levels of dominance rank. We have collapsed over the Experimental Control variable because, as will be shown below, the difference of 53 msec between E (1164 msec) and C (1217 msec) for the positive items was not large enough to be significant in the face of large individual differences. Table 12.2 also contains the average dominance values (*D*) computed by taking each word that each subject generated (100 words/subject) and looking up its dominance value in the Battig and Montague norms. Words not in the norms were given a value of zero. Of course, averaging within dominance-rank levels is arbitrary, and the fact that the *D* values decrease across dominance-rank levels simply indicates that the word-generation procedure we used is reliably related to the Battig and Montague procedure. These *D* values will be important in later analyses of the results.

Table 12.3 presents the *RT*s for negative items averaged over the 42 subjects for the same conditions as presented in Table 12.2. Again, the Experimental and Control subjects were combined since the groups did not differ significantly. The difference was 55 msec (*E* = 1254 msec and C = 1309 msec). Table 12.3 includes the actual negative words used, the dominance of the negative word as determined from its own category, and its frequency as determined from the Francis and Kučera (1967) norms. Table 12.4 lists the negative category names, i.e. the category from which the negative word was chosen. The dominance values decreased with dominance rank for the negative items because they were chosen to vary in dominance. Since every subject had the same negative words, the *D* values are not averages.

Error rates. Error rates for the Experimental subjects were all below 3 per cent for both positive and negative items. The Control subjects had error rates comparable to those of the Experimental subjects for negative items but larger error rates for the positive items, i.e. between 5 and 9 per cent. The Control subjects were responding to items generated by the Experimental subjects, and it is possible that Control subjects did not consider some of these items as members of the category. Perhaps the reason why the negative items, which were not generated by any of the subjects in this experiment, did not also have higher error rates is that they were based on 442 subjects and are very reliable, while the positive items for the Experimental subjects were generated by only 21 subjects and all generated words were used, not just the more dominant ones. Many of these words may have been unique to an individual subject and his yoked Control was tested with these unique items. This difference between the Experimental and Control subjects was exactly what we intended, of course, but we expected it to produce a difference in RTs as well as in error rates. In order to maintain equal cell frequencies in the statistical analyses, the error responses were replaced with an average RT computed from the other categories in the particular T–I group at the same dominance rank.

Statistical Analyses

The Latin Square balance was different for each pair of subjects, and practice effects, on the basis of preliminary analyses, did not interact with other variables. Since others have also found that practice effects do not interact with main effects (e.g., Meyer, 1970), the data were collapsed over trial blocks.

Analysis of variance design. The analysis followed Clark (1973) in assuming that the category variable was a random-effects variable. Words nested within categories was also a random-effects variable but was not included in the analysis explicitly because, as Clark indicated, when a random-effects variable is randomized and sampled anew for each subject, the treatment effect can be tested against a treatment-by-subjects interaction error term by collapsing over that variable (Clark, 1973, p. 24). Words were nested within categories which, in turn, were nested under the T and I variables, thus meeting the second design condition mentioned by Clark (see also Winer, 1971, p. 364) which justifies collapsing over words. Subjects were also treated as a random effects variable while all other variables were treated as fixed.

In the analysis of variance, Experimental vs. Control subjects was the only between-subjects variable (EC). Subjects were nested under EC and crossed with all other variables (S(EC)). The T and I variables were combined to yield a single variable with four groups instead of being treated as crossed factors. (The combined variable will be abbreviated T–I.) By this procedure, the analysis could be simplified and the interactions could be treated later by orthogonal contrasts. Although the procedure eliminated certain interactions which might be of interest, the results will indicate that the simplifying combination of T and I was adequate for the questions of interest here. Categories were nested under the four groups of the T–I variable and so are designated $C(T$–$I)$ while dominance rank is designated D. The theoretical model is presented in the Appendix along with the expected mean squares and

F ratios. Some of the F ratios are 'quasi' or F' ratios (see Winer, 1971 and Clark, 1973) in which the appropriate error term is computed from a number of directly estimated error terms. The Appendix contains the two analysis of variance tables for the positive and negative items which were treated separately. We will refer to some of the mean-square error terms below because the interpretation of the data depends critically on having used an analysis that treats categories as a random effect.

Results. For both positive- and negative-item analyses, subjects and categories were highly significant, emphasizing the importance of Clark's thesis that categories (subjects, words, etc.) should be treated as random-effects variables. For the positive items, the only other significant result was due to dominance rank (D) and, in particular, the $T–I$ variable had an F' with a probability less than 0·90. Although the graphic presentation of the $T–I$ results below suggests that there was a large interaction between T and I, the lack of a significant effect for $T–I$ eliminates that possibility and justifies our simplifying procedure of combining the two variables. Negative items showed two significant effects of importance: dominance and $T–1$. For both positive and negative items, no interactions approached significance. The Experimental vs. Control Fs for positive and negative items were both less than 1·0, providing the grounds for averaging over these two groups of subjects in Tables 12.2 and 12.3.

Dominance Rank and T–I Results

Interactions. Figure 12.1 presents the average RTs for the four groups that make up the $T–I$ variable as a function of dominance rank for the positive items, and Figure 12.2 presents the same results for the negative items. The dominance rank for the negative items is based on the ordinal position of the word in its own category. According to the statistical analysis just discussed, the four curves in Figure 12.2 for the negative items are significantly different while the curves in Figure 12.1 for the positive items are not. These results as graphed do not appear to agree with the analysis of variance. The reason for the lack of agreement is in the error terms for these two F' ratios. The denominators of the F' ratios depend on terms 4, 11, and 13. The differences for the positive and negative analyses in term 4 (see Appendix), which is the variance of $C(T–I)$, is very large: 1,606,987 vs 508,483, and, even though the numerator of the F' for the positive items is larger than the numerator for the negative items, it is not enough larger to compensate for the larger variance of $C(T–I)$. From Table 12.2, we can see that the variation in the dominance values (D) averaged from the Battig and Montague norms is much larger for the positive items than for the negative items, perhaps accounting for the larger variance. This is an important factor and will be discussed more thoroughly below. Generally, the four curves are parallel in each group and, as expected from the statistical tests, no interaction is evident.

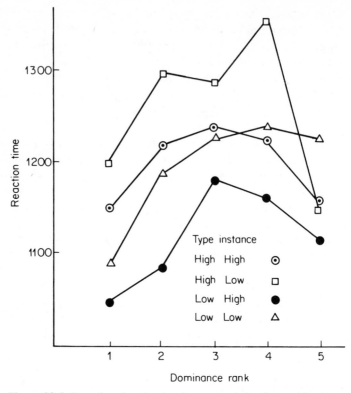

Figure 12.1. Reaction time by dominance rank for the positive items for the four *T–I* groups. Each point represents the average over the experimental and control subjects (42) and the five categories in each of the *T–I* groups

Dominance Rank. In both Figure 12.1 and Figure 12.2, *RT* generally increases with dominance ranks 1–4 and then decreases for dominance rank 5. Dominance rank 5 for the positive items was selected from the Batting and Montague norms so as to have as low a value of dominance as possible and still be a word not generated by the subject himself. As Table 12.2 indicates, the dominance value of the 5th ranking word is much larger than dominance values for ranks 4, 3, and 2 (except in one case), thus explaining the decrease in *RT* for dominance rank 5 (see *Dominance* below).

The dominance rank effect for negative items is unexpected; the dominance rank level is determined by the relative frequency of production of the word as a member of its own category and does not relate to the category involved in the decision in any way. At each dominance rank position, words from every different negative category are involved so it must be a dominance effect and not an artifact of the negative categories involved. The fact that the 5th rank falls for these negative items as it did for the positive items is puzzling and we have no explanation for the fall. In the Discussion Section, we consider a

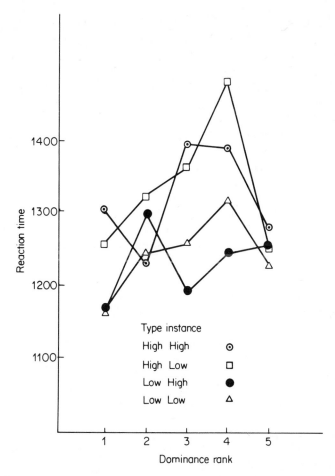

Figure 12.2. Reaction time by dominance rank for the negative items for the four *T–I* groups. Each point represents the average over the experimental and control subjects (42) and the five categories in each of the *T–I* groups

theoretical explanation of these results that might explain the dominance effect but not the drop in the *RT* at the 5th dominance rank.

T–I *Results*. Although the *T–I* variable was not significant for the positive items, the average *RT* values are interesting because they conform exactly to our predictions. We expected high-*T RT*s to be longer than low-*T RT*s and low-*I RT*s to be longer than high-*I RT*s. For the high-*T* and low-*T* groups (averaged over *I*) the *RT*s are 1226 and 1155, respectively, with a difference of 71 msec, while for the high-*I* and low-*I* (averaged over *T*) groups, the average *RT*s are 1157 and 1225, respectively, with a difference of −68 msec. Thus it appears that *RT* increases directly with *T* and inversely with *I*, as expected.

However, as we will show after considering the dominance values more carefully, the implication of these differences is misleading. Of course, they were not statistically significant either.

For negative items, the average RT of the high-T groups was 1324 and for the low-T groups 1234, with a difference of 90 msec. The high-I and low-I group averages were 1273 and 1286, respectively, with only a 13 msec difference. Thus, the T–I effect for the negative items is due to the differences in the type variable and not to the instance variable. Hence, for the negative items, if T measures category size as we have hypothesized, there is evidence for a category-size effect.

Dominance Reconsidered

The consistent and large effect due to dominance rank raises the question whether we have controlled dominance carefully enough simply by controlling the rank-order of the generation of the items. Also, since the average dominance value for each category within the T–I groups (Table 12.2) seems to show a strong relationship to RTs, it is reasonable to reconsider the data using dominance value instead of dominance rank as the controlling variables.

Table 12.2 presents the average dominance value at each rank-order position for each category averaged over the 21 Experimental subjects. For each rank-order position, the dominance value of the particular word generated by the subject was looked up in the Battig and Montague norms, and these values were averaged to yield the average D values presented in Table 12.2. Note that the means of the dominance values of the positive items of the four T–I groups differ significantly, $F(3, 16) = 12\cdot4$, $P < 0\cdot001$. In fact, the mean RTs of the four T–I groups and the mean D values have a nearly perfect linear correlation. This suggests that the T–I RT differences, although not significant, are due to the variation in the dominance values and not to any effect that T and/or I might have on RT.

Figure 12.3 presents the RT-by-dominance value for the positive items for all five dominance ranks of each T–I group. Each point represents the average RT at a given rank plotted against the average dominance for the words generated at that rank. The results are clear: The differences observed in the T–I variable for positive categories are due to the uncontrolled dominance values of the categories used in each of the T–I groups. Furthermore, the T and I 'effects' noted previously are simply a reflection of these dominance values. The straight line in Figure 12.3 is a line drawn by eye through the means of the four T–I groups. It seems to capture the very strong linear relationship between dominance and RT observed in this study. The strong linear relationship also explains the lack of a significant effect for positive items. The categories within each T–I group differed greatly in their dominance values, producing a large variance among categories within each T–I group. The analysis of variance did take into account the fact that dominance rank and T–I varied factorially, but the rank did not take into account the actual value of the dominance variable.

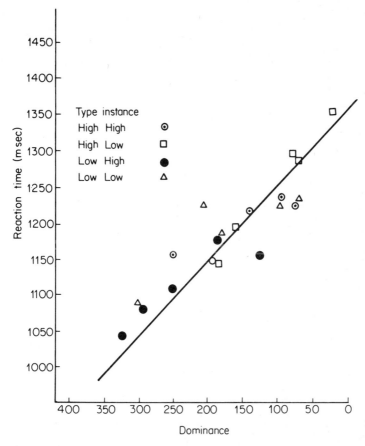

Figure 12.3. Reaction time by dominance value as measured by the Battig and Montague norms (1969) for the positive items. The five points for each *T–I* group represent the words at each of the five ranks. The straight line is simply drawn through the four means for the *T–I* groups by eye. See Table 12.2 for means

Using the rank-order of dominance determined by group data is not an adequate control for dominance because apparently dominance must be measured on more than an ordinal scale of measurement.

The mean dominance values (*D*) (Table 12.3) for the negative items did not differ among categories or among *T–I* groups because the words were assigned to categories randomly. Thus, unlike the positive items, the results involving *T–I* for the negative items are controlled for dominance values. Figure 12.4 presents the *RT*s for each rank-order position plotted against the average dominance value for that position. Here, the differences due to *T* are clearly evident in the vertical shift in the high-*T* groups. The top and bottom straight lines connect the high-*I* and low-*I* mean values for the two high-*T* and two low-*T* groups, respectively. The lines provide a fairly good estimate of a linear

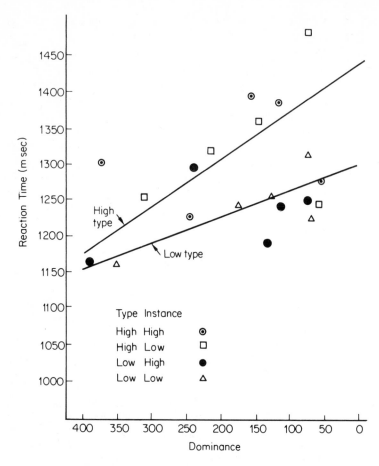

Figure 12.4. Reaction time by dominance for the negative items. The five points for each *T–I* group represent the words at each of the five ranks. The High Type straight line is drawn through the means of the two high type means (High-*I* and Low-*I* groups) and the Low Type straight line is drawn through the means of the two Low Type means (High-*I* and Low-*I*). See Table 12.3 for means

fit to the data. We suggest that the two groups (high-*I* and low-*I*) are a random sample from the same bivariate distribution at each *T* value. The shift in *RT* for the *I* conditions is due to a slight shift in the dominance of the *I* groups.

Discussion

Implications of Results for Original Hypotheses

Control of individual subject organization. The attempt to find an *RT* function that depended on the individual subject's order of production was unsuccessful: there was no difference between the RTs of the Control and Experimental subjects and, in particular, there was no $EC \times D$ interaction. Second, the variable obviously controlling the RTs for both groups was the average dominance values computed from the Battig and Montague norms. In retrospect, these results do not seem unreasonable and suggest that we were expecting too much from the individual production orders. Such productions no doubt have an intrasubject as well as an intersubject variance. Our attempt required the former variance to be much smaller than the latter, despite the fact that the estimate of intrasubject variance is based on a frequency of 1 and the estimate of intersubject variance on a frequency of 442.

In concluding our discussion of individual production measures, we should not like to leave the impression that group norms are necessarily better than individual subject productions. There is, without doubt, a between-subjects variance as well as a within-subjects variance. Furthermore, the slope of the $RT \times D$ function for the experimental subjects was slightly steeper than the same slope for the control subjects, perhaps suggesting that we were tapping some of the idiosyncratic structure of memory. However, more reliable techniques of measuring individual semantic structure are needed if we are to use individual subject measures to predict RTs.

Category size and category organization. By using the number of types (T) and the average number of instances (I) produced in a production task, we separated two variables previously confused in the literature (*cf.* Loftus, 1973 and Wilkins, 1971). Although we observed effects consistent with our original hypotheses (RT increasing with T and decreasing with I), the effects were not significant. But even more enlightening was the clear linear relationship of these effects to the dominance variable. Since the dominance variable and both T and I had never before been varied simultaneously, our results raise questions about previous results which have found a category-size effect. Although some researchers (e.g., Landauer and Meyer, 1972) question the appropriateness of measuring category size by variables such as T, the use of nested categories makes the control of dominance very difficult. Control is particularly difficult if the same word is used for nested categories because the dominance value of the word with respect to the superset category is very likely to be smaller than the dominance value in the subset category. It follows that there will be a change in dominance value because the superset is likely to have a larger T value and the average dominance, D, is equal to I/T. On the basis of our results, we find no evidence for a category-size effect or a category-organization effect for positive items.

Although we made no particular predictions for negative items, the frequently observed effect of category size (T) appeared. In our case, the dominance of the negative items in their own category was controlled; hence the generality of the category-size effect for negative items is increased. No effect of the I variable was observed for negative items.

Dominance rank and value. Previous experiments have demonstrated an effect due to dominance but our results are more extensive. Wilkins (1971) used only two levels of dominance, and others (e.g., Freedman and Loftus, 1971) have controlled dominance only statistically. Our results strongly suggest that dominance is best measured quantitatively and not just by relative rank within a category. Further quantitative work is needed here. We interpreted dominance as a measure of the 'strength,' 'goodness of example,' or 'distance' relationship between a word and its superordinate category. From our results, we must conclude that it is a potent variable.

The dominance effect for the negative items is surprising. Why should the dominance of a word as measured in its own category determine *RT* when that word is a negative instance of another category? Of course, our first thought was that there was some confounding agent at work here. Two variables came immediately to mind: word frequency and word length. Correlations between dominance rank and word frequency and word length were -0.29 and 0.18, respectively. That is, words given most frequently as instances of a category tend to have high absolute frequencies and are shorter words. Since *RT*s to more frequent words are faster in a word–nonword categorization task, these correlations could provide the answer to the above question.

In a recent study by Mervis, Catlin, and Rosch (1973), a correlation between category dominance, word frequency, and goodness-of-example showed only three of nine categories with significant correlations between word frequency and dominance. On the other hand, eight of the nine categories showed that goodness-of-example and dominance correlated significantly. Goodness-of-example was measured by having subjects judge how good an item was as an example of a category (Rosch, 1973). Therefore, the results of Mervis *et al.* suggest that the frequency variable is not strongly related to dominance. Thus, the evidence suggests that there is no relationship between dominance and word frequency.

Perhaps more important here is the evidence for a relationship between word frequency and *RT* in a verification task. In our study there were virtually zero correlations between word frequency and *RT* and between word length and *RT* for negative items. Furthermore, in a study performed by Rice (1973) in which word frequency and dominance were varied factorially, there was no significant interaction between these variables and no word frequency effect at all. In the light of these results, it does not seem appropriate to account for the dominance effect for the negative items by word frequency, despite the fact that there is some tendency for more dominant words to have higher absolute frequencies. Another interesting result was reported by Rice: for the negative items in his experiment, there was no dominance effect at all, even though he used a wider range of dominance values than represented in the negative items here. Certainly the relationship between a word's dominance in its own category and its *RT* as a negative item for another category needs further investigation since it is a puzzling effect which might be critical for theoretical analysis.

Implications for Theoretical Positions

How do these results relate to the three theoretical positions discussed in the introduction? Because the design of the experiment was not intended to differentiate between theories, the results of this experiment cannot, of course, be expected to be definitive with respect to current theoretical approaches.

Network models. The lack of a category-size effect neither supports nor provides evidence against network models since such models predict a subset effect but not necessarily a category-size effect. Of course, insofar as larger categories have more intermediate nodes between the word and the category node, the size effect should also be maintained. At this point, we see no way to estimate the number of such nodes and must leave the issue unresolved. The effect of category size on the *RT*s for negative-item decisions is not predicted by network models. However, Collins and Quillian (1969) explain this result as an artifact of semantic relatedness. Their explanation rests on the consideration of some very specific negative instances which were more related to the superordinate category than to the subset category. In the results reported here, nesting was not used and a very large sample of of negative instances and positive categories were used. Although an explanation based on semantic relatedness appears to be required, our results seem to have a good deal more generality than is suggested by Collins and Quillian's explanation.

We assumed that *I* measured organization, but there is no way to relate organization as measured by *I* to the network model. Thus, the lack of an effect here is also a neutral finding with respect to the network models.

A simple network model cannot easily handle the dominance results. However, if the nodes are assumed to be connected by links of varying strengths, then the dominance effect would presumably be a reflection of the link strengths. The dominance result seems to require some flexibility in the types of links connecting modes within a network model.

Set-theoretic models. In set-theoretic models the category is considered to be a set of elements. Although the elements are left undefined, they presumably represent the category as examplars, names of subsets or supersets, or as attributes (Meyer, 1970). The search process should take longer for larger categories, and therefore our failure to find a category-size effect for positive items is detrimental to this theoretical position. Of course, not every positive item in a larger category takes longer to retrieve than every item in a smaller category, but, on the average, larger sets should show longer retrieval times. We believe that the number of categories and instances within the categories in our experiment was sufficient to detect such a difference, so our results seem conclusive. After all, we observed a category-size effect with the negative items and we controlled for dominance. It is true that *T* may not measure category size, accurately, but, since over 20 categories were used, it seems reasonable to assume that, on the average, the high-T categories are larger.

The I-variable is not part of the predictive machinery of this theoretical position. The dominance effect would be difficult to explain by the rather general notions of the set-theoretic position. However, the T-effect for the negative items is a result predicted by the set-theoretic position.

Semantic-distance models. Many of the difficulties with the set-theoretic models are overcome when the elements in the set are assumed to be related by a distance function. The network models are rigidly structured and the set-theoretic models completely unstructured. In order to account for dominance effects, a strength variable was added to the links between nodes in the network model. In a similar, although opposite, way, an amorphous set must be structured in order to handle the dominance effects.

One advantage to imposing a distance function on semantic space is that the category-size effect is no longer a necessary prediction of the set-theoretic model. Rather, the distance function is all-important and category size is an artifact of changing distance when changing set size. The lack of an I effect is not critical either since the theory has not been developed to predict the influence of semantic distance on production measures.

The T-variable effect for negative items is not easily explained by any of the current theoretical positions. The semantic-distance model must assume that larger categories show more overlap with negative items and thus require the second comparison process more often. However, larger categories have fewer characteristic attributes and thus may not have a larger overlap. So, at this time it is not clear whether a more formalized version of the semantic-distance model can handle the category-size effect for negative items. A similar remark must be made for effect of the dominance values of the negative items on RTs.

In conclusion, we would like to note that, although there are certainly difficulties involved in using production measures as control variables (Landauer and Meyer, 1972) in semantic-retrieval experiments, the typical alternative—using nested sets—may be equally difficult. From the point of view of a set-theoretic model, two categories in a subset–superset relation (i.e., a nested set) differ in size; from the point of view of a network model, they differ in hierarchical level. Further, an instance belonging to both categories probably also has a different dominance or semantic distance within each category. In her experiment involving the retrieval of properties of concepts, Conrad (1972) found that it was also necessary to control for the likelihood that a property belonged to a category. Semantic memory does not change from experimental situation to experimental situation and it seems a necessary part of an adequate theory of semantics to say how words of a category will be generated as well as to say how they will be recognized as members of the category. These procedures of recognizing a word and of generating a word should have something in common.

Acknowledgements

This research was supported by Grants NIMH-11255-07 from the National Institutes of Mental Health and GB-34122 from the National Science Foundation to Richard Millward. Albert Corbett conducted this research for his Honors Thesis in Psychology at Brown University under Richard Millward's direction.

References

Atkinson, R. C. and Juola, J. F. (1974). Search and decision processes in recognition memory. In D. H. Krantz, R. C. Atkinson, R. D. Luce, and P. Suppes (Eds), *Contemporary Developments in Mathematical Psychology*. San Francisco: W. H. Freeman.

Battig, W. F. and Montague, W. E. (1969). Category norms for verbal items in 56 categories: A replication and extension of the Connecticut Category Norms. *Journal of Experimental Psychology Monograph*, **80** (3, pt. 2).

Bousfield, W. A. (1953). The occurrence of clustering in the recall of randomly arranged associates. *Journal of General Psychology*, **49**, 229–240.

Clark, H. H. (1973). The language-as-fixed-effect fallacy: A critique of language statistics in psychological research. *Journal of Verbal Learning and Verbal Behavior*, **12**, 335–359.

Cohen, B. H., Bousfield, W. A. and Whitmarsh, G. A. (1957). Cultural norms for verbal items in 43 categories. *Technical Report No. 22*, University of Connecticut.

Collins, A. M. and Quillian, M. F. (1969). Retrieval time from semantic memory. *Journal of Verbal Learning and Verbal Behavior*, **8**, 240–247.

Collins, A. M. and Quillian, M. R. (1970a). Does category size effect categorization time? *Journal of Verbal Learning and Verbal Behavior*, **9**, 432–438.

Collins, A. M. and Quillian, R. M. (1970b). Facilitating retrieval from semantic memory: The effect of repeating part of an inference. In A. F. Sanders (Ed.), *Attention and Performance III*, Amsterdam: North Holland Publishing Company, pp. 304–314.

Conrad, C. (1972). Cognitive economy in semantic memory. *Journal of Experimental Psychology*, **92**, 149–154.

Freedman, J. I. and Loftus, E. F. (1971). Retrieval of words from long-term memory. *Journal of Verbal Learning and Verbal Behavior*, **10**, 107–115.

Herrmann, D. J., Chaffin, R. J. S. and Corbett, A. T. (1973). A factor analysis of six measures extracted from the Battig and Montague (1969) category norms: Evidence for three properties of categories in semantic memory. *Journal of Verbal Learning and Verbal Behavior*, **12**, 666–674.

Kintsch, W. (1970). *Learning, Memory and Conceptual Processes*. New York: Wiley.

Kučera, H. and Francis, W. N. (1967). *Computational Analysis of Present-Day American English*. Providence, R.I.: Brown University Press.

Landauer, T. K. and Freedman, J. L. (1968). Information-retrieval from long-term memory: category size and recognition time. *Journal of Verbal Learning and Verbal Behavior*, **7**, 291–295.

Landauer, T. K. and Meyer, D. E. (1972). Category size and semantic-memory retrieval. *Journal of Verbal Learning and Verbal Behavior*, **11**, 539–549.

Loftus, E. F. (1973). Category dominance, instance dominance and categorization time. *Journal of Experimental Psychology*, **97**, 70–74.

Loftus, E. F. and Suppes, P. (1972). Structural variables that determine the speed of retrieving words from long-term memory. *Journal of Verbal Learning and Verbal Behavior*, **11**, 770–777.

248

Loftus, E. F. and Scheff, R. W. (1971). Categorization norms for 50 representative instances. *Journal of Experimental Psychology*, **91**, 355–364.

Mervis, C. B., Catlin, J. and Rosch, E. Relationships among category norms, word frequency, and goodness-of-example. Unpublished manuscript.

Meyer, D. E. (1970). On the representation and retrieval of stored semantic information. *Cognitive Psychology*, **1**, 242–300.

Meyer, D. E. and Ellis, G. B. (1970). Parallel processes in word-recognition. Paper presented at the meeting of the Psychonomic Society, San Antonio, Texas, November, 1970.

Millward, R. B., Aikin, J., and Wickens, T. (1972). The Human Learning Laboratory at Brown University. In *Computers in the Psychological Laboratory*, Vol. II Maynard, Mass.: Digital Equipment Corporation, 35–48.

Pollio, H. R., Richards, S. and Lucas, R. (1969). Temporal properties of category recall. *Journal of Verbal Learning and Verbal Behavior*, **8**, 95–102.

Rice, G. A. (1973). Dominance and word frequency effects in the retrieval of semantic information. Technical Report No. 11, Studies in Human Learning. Psychology Department, Brown University, Providence, R.I.

Rips, L. J., Shoben, E. J. and Smith, E. E. (1973). Semantic distance and the verification of semantic relations. *Journal of Verbal Learning and Verbal Behavior*, **12**, 1–20.

Rosch, E. (1973). On the internal structure of perceptual and semantic categories. In T. E. Moore (Ed.), *Cognitive Development and Acquisition of Language*. New York: Academic Press.

Schaeffer, B. and Wallace, R. (1969). Semantic similarity and the comparison of word meaning. *Journal of Experimental Psychology*, **82**, 343–346.

Schaeffer, B. and Wallace, R. (1970). The comparison of word meanings. *Journal of Experimental Psychology*, **86**, 144–152.

Thorndike, E. L. and Lorge, I. (1944). *The Teacher's Word Book of 30,000 Words*. New York: Columbia University Press.

Wickens, T., Howard, J., Rice, G. and Millward, R. (1971). General asynchronous processing system: GASPS-71. *Technical Report No. 8*. Studies in Human Learning. Psychology Department, Brown University, Providence, R.I.

Wilkins, A. (1971). Conjoint frequency, category size, and categorization time. *Journal of Verbal Learning and Verbal Behavior*, **10**, 382–385.

Winer, B. J. (1971). *Statistical Principles in Experimental Design*. New York: McGraw-Hill.

Appendix

Analysis of Variance Design

The variables and their abbreviations included in the design are:

(1) The high and low values of Types (T) and Instances (I) yield four values ($t = 4$) of a single treatment variable T–I. Since the interaction of T and I can be checked with orthogonal contrasts and since other higher-order interactions were not of great importance, this simplifying combination was performed. This was considered a fixed-effects variable.

(2) The five values ($d = 5$) of the Dominance Rank (D) were considered as fixed effects.

(3) The only between-subjects variable was the Experimental and Control subjects difference (EC) which was also considered a fixed-effects variable ($e = 2$).

(4) The Category variable (C) was nested under T–I and so is designated $C(T$–$I)$. It is a random-effects variable with five levels ($c = 5$) at each level of T–I.

(5) Subjects (S) were nested under EC and crossed with all other variables. It is designated $S(EC)$ and is a random-effects variable. There were 21 subjects at each level of EC ($n = 21$).

The theoretical model of the design will be described using the following abbreviations:

μ . . .	grand mean
T–I_i	ith value of the T–I variable
D_j	jth value of the D variable
EC_k	kth value of the EC variable
$C(T$–$I)_{l(i)}$	lth value of the Category variable in the ith T–I condition
$S(EC)_{n(k)}$	nth subject in the kth EC condition
$X_{ijkl(i)n(k)}$	an individual score.

The model is:

$$X_{ijkl(i)n(k)} = \mu \ldots + T\text{–}I_i + D_j + EC_k + C(T\text{–}I)_{l(i)} + S(EC)_{n(k)} + T\text{–}I \cdot D_{ij}$$
$$+ T\text{–}I \cdot EC_{ik} + T\text{–}I \cdot S(EC)_{in(k)} + EC \cdot C(T\text{–}I)_{kl(i)} + D \cdot EC_{jk}$$
$$+ D \cdot C(T\text{–}I)_{jl(i)} + D \cdot S(EC)_{jn(k)} + C(T\text{–}I) \cdot S(EC)_{l(i)n(k)}$$
$$+ T\text{–}I \cdot D \cdot EC_{ijk} + T\text{–}I \cdot D \cdot S(E)_{ijn(k)} + D \cdot EC \cdot C(T\text{–}I)_{jkl(i)}$$
$$+ D \cdot C(T\text{–}I) \cdot S(E)_{kl(i)n(k)}.$$

The analysis of variance model is presented in Table 12.5. The table contains the sources of variance, the degrees of freedom of each source, the expectation of the mean square term for each source, and the appropriate F ratio to test the significance of the source. The definition and justification of the quasi-F ratios can be found in Winer (1971, p. 375). The degrees of freedom for the denominators of the quasi-F ratios require special computation. The formulas for these degrees of freedom can also be found in Winer.

Table 12.6 presents the results of the analyses for the positive and negative items. The F' ratios used to test D (term 2), T–$I \cdot D$ (6), and $D \cdot EC$ (8) involve the addition of two sources of variance in the denominator. Since the error variance, σ_{error}, is a part of both terms of the denominator it is included twice in the denominator and only once in the numerator. Thus, the ratios as presented are too small and may fail to reject the Null Hypothesis when it is true. The denominator can be corrected by subtracting a variance which is at least as large as the σ_{error} variance. If the F' ratio is still not significant, then one can be fairly sure that it would not be if a correct amount of error variance had been removed from the denominator. If it is significant after the correction, then the

Table 12.5. Analysis of variance model

Term	Source of variance	Degrees of freedom	Expectation of the mean square*	F and F' Ratios†
1	T-I	$t-1$	$d\sigma_{C(T-I),S(EC)} + cd\sigma_{T-I,S(EC)} + dem\sigma_{C(T-I)} + cdem\sigma_{T-I}$	$F' = 1/(4 + 11 - 13)$
2	D	$d-1$	$tc\sigma_{D,S(EC)} + em\sigma_{D,C(T-I)} + tcem\sigma_D$	$F' = 2/(12 + 9)$
3	EC	$e-1$	$d\sigma_{C(T-I),S(EC)} + dm\sigma_{EC,C(T-I)} + tcd\sigma_{S(EC)} + tcdm\sigma_{EC}$	$F' = 3/(5 + 10 - 13)$
4	C(T-I)	$t(c-1)$	$d\sigma_{C(T-I),S(EC)} + dem\sigma_{C(T-I)}$	$F = 4/13$
5	S(EC)	$e(m-1)$	$d\sigma_{C(T-I),S(EC)} + tcd\sigma_{S(EC)}$	$F = 5/13$
6	T-I·D	$(t-1)(d-1)$	$c\sigma_{T-I,D,S(EC)} + em\sigma_{D,C(T-I)} + cem\sigma_{T-I,D}$	$F' = 6/(15 + 9)$
7	T-I·EC	$(t-1)(e-1)$	$d\sigma_{C(T-I),S(EC)} + dm\sigma_{EC,C(T-I)} + cd\sigma_{T-I,S(EC)} + cdm\sigma_{T-I,EC}$	$F' = 7/(11 + 10 - 13)$
8	D·EC	$(d-1)(e-1)$	$m\sigma_{D,EC,C(T-I)} + ct\sigma_{D,S(EC)} + tcm\sigma_{D,EC}$	$F' = 8/(12 + 16)$
9	D·C(T-I)	$t(c-1)(d-1)$	$me\sigma_{D,C(T-I)}$	—
10	EC·C(T-I)	$t(c-1)(e-1)$	$d\sigma_{C(T-I),S(EC)} + dm\sigma_{EC,C(T-I)}$	$F = 10/13$
11	T-I·S(EC)	$e(m-1)(t-1)$	$d\sigma_{C(T-I),S(EC)} + cd\sigma_{T-I,S(EC)}$	$F = 11/13$
12	D·S(EC)	$e(m-1)(d-1)$	$ct\sigma_{D,S(EC)}$	—
13	C(T-I)·S(EC)	$et(c-1)(m-1)$	$d\sigma_{C(T-I),S(EC)}$	
14	T-I·D·EC	$(t-1)(d-1)(e-1)$	$cm\sigma_{T-I,D,EC}$	
15	T-I·D·S(EC)	$e(m-1)(t-1)(d-1)$	$c\sigma_{T-I,D,S(EC)}$	
16	C(T-I)·D·EC	$t(c-1)(d-1)(e-1)$	$m\sigma_{D,EC,C(T-I)}$	
17	C(T-I)·D·S(EC)	$et(c-1)(m-1)(d-1)$	$\sigma_{D,C(T-I),S(EC)}$	

* The common source of variance for all these terms, σ_{error}, has been omitted from all these expressions. It should be added to each term.
† These ratios are expressed in terms of the line numbers of the sources of variance involved.

Table 12.6. Analysis of variance table for positive and negative items

Term	Source	d.f.	Positive items		Negative items	
			M.S.	F and F' Ratios	M.S.	F and F' Ratios
1	$T\text{-}I$	3	3,403,695	$F'(3, 15) = 2 \cdot 17$	2,934,762	$F'(3, 16) = 5 \cdot 69^{**}$
2	D	4	2,209,366	$F'(4, 164) = 5 \cdot 70^{*}$	2,246,290	$F'(4, 110) = 2 \cdot 59^{*}$
3	EC	1	3,577,293	$F'(1, \text{—}) < 1 \cdot 0$	3,378,357	$F'(1, \text{—}) < 1 \cdot 0$
4	$C(T\text{-}I)$	16	1,606,987	$F(16, 640) = 7 \cdot 59^{**}$	508,483	$F(16, 640) = 2 \cdot 63^{*}$
5	$S(EC)$	40	6,604,320	$F(40, 640) = 31 \cdot 19^{**}$	5,953,385	$F(40, 640) = 30 \cdot 76^{**}$
6	$T\text{-}I \cdot D$	12	342,912	$F'(12, \text{—}) < 1 \cdot 0$	663,228	$F'(12, \text{—}) < 1 \cdot 0$
7	$T\text{-}I \cdot EC$	3	142,412	$F'(3, 8) = 1 \cdot 24$	209,076	$F'(3, \text{—}) < 1 \cdot 0$
8	$D \cdot EC$	4	83,106	$F'(4, \text{—}) < 1 \cdot 0$	121,172	$F'(4, \text{—}) < 1 \cdot 0$
9	$D \cdot C(T\text{-}I)$	64	216,759		645,433	
10	$C(T\text{-}I) \cdot EC$	16	143,547	$F(16, 640) < 1 \cdot 0$	195,588	$F(16, 640) \simeq 1 \cdot 0$
11	$T\text{-}I \cdot S(EC)$	120	183,464	$F(120, 640) < 1 \cdot 0$	200,714	$F(120, 640) \simeq 1 \cdot 0$
12	$D \cdot S(EC)$	160	171,095		221,202	
13	$C(T\text{-}I) \cdot S(EC)$	640	211,732		193,546	
14	$T\text{-}I \cdot D \cdot EC$	12	310,048		98,398	
15	$T\text{-}I \cdot D \cdot S(EC)$	480	189,504		170,572	
16	$D \cdot EC \cdot C(T\text{-}I)$	64	266,061		147,054	
17	$D \cdot C(T\text{-}I) \cdot S(EC)$	2560	203,939		193,206	

$* \ P < 0 \cdot 05$
$** \ P < 0 \cdot 01$

results are not in doubt. Since each term in Table 12.5 contains σ_{error}, the smallest mean square in the table must be at least as large as σ_{error}. Thus, if the smallest mean square is subtracted from the denominators of the F' ratios with double amounts of σ_{error} and they are checked for significance, we can make a better statement about the results. In no case did such a correction leave the interpretation of the F' ratio in doubt.

Chapter 13

Semantic Equivalence of Verbal and Pictorial Displays

P. H. K. Seymour

Introduction

An important if inadequately understood aspect of word meaning concerns the relationship between sentences and the objects or scenes to which they may refer. For many simple concrete assertions, comprehension may partially be equated with a knowledge of the situation referenced by an utterance. Thus, to understand the sentence, 'The square is inside the circle', a reader must know something about the perceptual properties of square and circular shapes as well as about the locative relation specified by the preposition 'inside'. The appropriate test for the presence of such knowledge is a verification task in which a descriptive sentence and situation are presented, either simultaneously or successively, and the person reports 'Yes' if the picture is included within the class of situations referenced by the sentence, and 'No' if it is not. Alternatively, the person may be asked to construct the situation defined by the sentence, by drawing or by some other means.

It may be noted that accurate performance on these tasks also depends on a more general understanding of the intention of the utterance as an act of communication. In a verification task the subject (S) is invited to treat the sentence as a Yes/No question. In a study of construction, the same sentence may function as a command to produce a drawing. This latter aspect of comprehension is normally manipulated by the experimenter's instructions and explanations about the task. These define the manner in which S must operate on verbal and pictorial events, or the type of transformation which must be applied in the conversion from stimulus to response.

A main goal of the present paper is to formulate an account of the mental operations which occur when a simple locative assertion is matched against a picture, and the outcome of the comparison is indicated by a 'Yes' or 'No' report. From the viewpoint of theory, we may distinguish between statements about the internal representations or memory codes which are utilized in a comparison of this kind, and statements about the sequence of operations or 'processing stages' which occur between presentation of the display and initiation of an appropriate report. Accounts which emphasize distinctions among different types of memory code, or the structure of the representation within a given code, may be termed data base models. Those which emphasize the sequential or iterative character of elementary operations or stages, often with support of assumptions about independence and additivity of the stages, may be termed executive or process models. An adequate statement about performance on the sentence-picture comparison task, or indeed any other semantic memory task, might be expected to include statements about both data base codes and operations or processes, although in practice individual theorists have often emphasized one aspect at the expense of the other.

Figure 13.1 shows a diagrammatic presentation of a data base model which was proposed in the course of a discussion of picture naming and verbal–pictorial comparisons (Seymour, 1973a). This assigns major significance to a system for abstract or modality-free coding (semantic memory), but

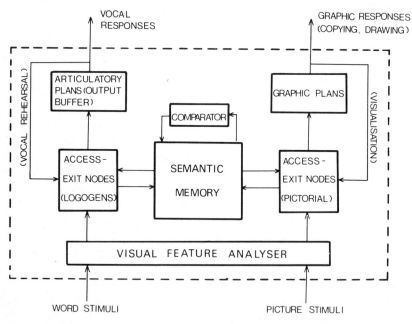

Figure 13.1. Modification of the logogen model incorporating separate verbal and pictorial input channels. (From Seymour, 1973a, *British Journal of Psychology*, **64**, 35–49, with permission.)

also identifies a visual code for literal description of graphemic and pictorial patterns as well as phonological and constructional output codes. Conversion between codes is achieved via systems of access-exit nodes analogous to the logogens of Morton (1969a). A third conversion system is postulated, termed the comparator in Figure 13.1, which mediates transformation of object or relational concepts to a representation of truth or falsity. For the purpose of the present discussion this might be thought of as containing counters which accumulate evidence of sameness and difference (Bindra, Williams and Wise, 1965). The counters within the comparator and within the logogen access–exit system and its pictorial counterpart define the level of evidence required for a conversion from one mode of coding to another. An important property of the model is that these requirements can be manipulated, within the terms of the system, by varying the setting of the threshold (criterion) on a given unit, or by priming the unit.

It will be obvious that various types of procedural description may be mapped on to the data base model. For example, a report of the truth or falsity of a sentence by reference to a picture might depend on the occurrence of the following sequence of operations:

Operation 1.   Visually encode sentence and convert to abstract representation.

Operation 2.   Visually encode picture and convert to abstract representation.

Operation 3.   Transform abstract sentence/picture representation to representation of truth or falsity.

Operation 4.   Transform representation of truth/falsity to vocal 'Yes' or 'No' report.

Research on verbal–pictorial comparisons has generally relied on latency of response (RT) as an index of both (a) the data base codes employed, and (b) the nature of the operations performed upon those codes. Quite often RT has been regarded as a relatively direct measure of congruence/incongruence of memory codes (Tversky, 1969), or structural aspects of the semantic memory system (Collins and Quillian, 1969), or of the occurrence of a sequence of processing stages having additive effects on the overall latency (Clark and Chase, 1972). An alternative position is that the RT differences on which the conclusions of these studies depend are more properly viewed as indices of threshold settings within the 'same'–'different' comparator (Schaeffer and Wallace, 1970), or within the access–exit logogen systems (Warren, 1972). Much recent research into effects of context on word recognition (Morton, 1964), or word reading (Jacobson, 1973), or word/non-word decisions (Meyer and Schvaneveldt, 1971; Meyer, Schvaneveldt and Ruddy, 1972), can be interpreted in terms of priming of logogen units by feedback from the semantic system. This type of facilitation of conversion from a visual to a semantic code may also underlie the small effects for category size and goodness of exemplars which have been obtained in studies of categorization (Collins and Quillian, 1970; Wilkins, 1971). Similarly, Schaeffer and Wallace (1970) have argued that semantic similarity/dissimilarity, as assessed by some rather global comparison process, affects the levels of the thresholds of the 'same' and 'different' counters, and that it is this readjustment which is reflected in the RT

differences. Seymour (1973c, 1974c) has proposed that semantic positivity/negativity may affect the RT in a comparable fashion.

These comments point to a controversy over the nature of the RT differences obtained in semantic information processing tasks. This controversy is of considerable importance, in view of the dependence of semantic memory research on the use of differences in RT as indices of modality and structure of coding, or the identity, independence and additivity of processing stages. An adequate theory about the mechanism by which properties of semantic memory affect the latencies of 'Yes' and 'No' responses is required before RT differences can be used to resolve broad theoretical issues in this area.

Retention and Generation of a Pictorial Code

In the model shown in Figure 13.1 it has been assumed that sentences and pictures may be represented in a single abstract or modality-free code (Clark and Chase, 1972). This position contrasts with the dual code hypothesis of Paivio (1971), and also with Bower's (1972) distinction between propositional memory and memory for appearance. Paivio has argued that stimuli may be represented within a *verbal code* or within an *imaginal code*, or simultaneously in both codes. Similarly, Bower has proposed a separation between that part of semantic memory which represents perceptual properties of objects and scenes (image system), and the part which stores verbal associations and class membership (verbal–semantic system). With respect to Figure 13.1, Paivio's proposal probably deletes the abstract code altogether, but retains the phonological and constructional codes, with the addition of direct connections between the two systems. In a dual code model of this kind, the possibility of judging the truth of a sentence by reference to a picture depends on recoding one input in the modality of the other. Thus, a sentence might initially be represented in the verbal system, but could then be converted to an image representation which is directly comparable to the representation derived from a test picture. Bower's position appears not to delete the abstract system, but to partition it into verbal and spatial components. We might assume, however, that the spatial component is more directly accessible by picture than by verbal inputs, and vice versa for the verbal component. The latter position also retains the phonological and constructional codes, where activity may be generated by output from the semantic system, although, as things are formulated in Figure 13.1, these codes are not directly considered during the comparison.

This section of the paper reports some recent research which was carried out with the aim of testing the dual code hypothesis of Paivio (1971). Support for this position is given in a paper by Tversky (1969) which appeared to demonstrate (a) the utility of the assumption of distinct verbal and pictorial codes, and (b) the possibility of optional verbal–pictorial and pictorial–verbal conversion. In the experiment the stimuli were schematic faces which had been paired, in a previous learning session, with nonsense names. Verbal–verbal, picture–picture, verbal–picture, and picture–verbal trials were run in separate blocks. Modality of the first stimulus was constant within a block, but modality of the second varied on a 79:21 ratio. Thus, in a verbal–pictorial block, the first stimulus was always a name but the second was a picture on a majority of trials, and a name on a minority of trials. *RT*s were delayed in classification of the minority test stimuli irrespective of the modality of the first stimulus. Inter-stimulus interval (ISI) was 3 sec. Tversky concluded that her *S*s were able to retain or generate verbal or pictorial codes to fit the modality of the majority of trials in a block. Alternative explanations, stated in the terms of the model of Figure 13.1, are as follows: the effect would occur (a) if access thresholds were raised for stimuli in the infrequent modality, and lowered for stimuli in the frequent modality (this will affect the time required for the visual–semantic conversion), or (b) if occurrence of an infrequent or unexpected event results in a precautionary rise in the 'same' and 'different' decision thresholds.

A more direct approach to the issue of pictorial recoding is suggested by the work of Posner and his associates on letter matching. Posner's research is not, in itself, relevant to the verbal–pictorial distinction, since he has worked entirely with letters, and these are processed in the left-hand or verbal channel of Figure 13.1. However, the operational definitions of *retention* and *generation* of a visual code given by Posner, Boies, Eichelman and Taylor (1969) may quite readily be applied to verbal–pictorial comparisons. For simultaneously displayed stimuli, picture–picture matching is expected to be faster than description–picture matching because, in the picture–picture (PP) case both stimuli gain direct access to the image system, whereas in the description–picture (DP) case a time-consuming verbal–pictorial (or pictorial–verbal) conversion is required. Retention of a pictorial code may be inferred if PP comparisons are not delayed under conditions of successive presentation. Generation of a pictorial code is inferred if successive DP comparisons produce performance which is equivalent to that observed for successive PP comparisons.

Data obtained in a simple experiment of this type are shown in Figure 13.2 (see Seymour, 1974a). The stimuli were pictures of a square inside a circle, or a circle inside a square, and the printed descriptions 'square inside/outside circle' and 'circle inside/outside square'. The displays were rear-projected onto a screen, and *S* was timed from onset of the PP or DP combination under the simultaneous condition, or from onset of the test picture under the successive PP and DP conditions. The task was to report 'Yes' if the stimuli were equivalent, and 'No' if they were not. Simultaneous and successive trials were run in separate blocks, but DP and PP trials were randomly intermixed. The data are suggestive of retention of a pictorial code, in that PP comparisons were faster under the successive than under the simultaneous condition, and of generation of a pictorial code in that DP and PP comparisons produced equivalent *RT*s under the successive condition.

These results are consistent with some version of the dual coding hypothesis and suggest that verification of a test picture involves a pictorial code which can be set up directly by a picture input (PP trials) but only via a time-consuming

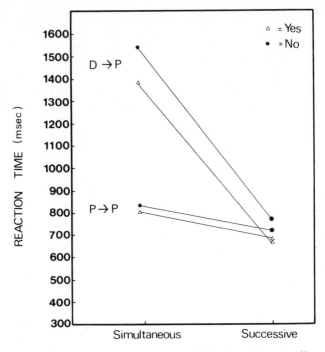

Figure 13.2. Summary of mean *RT*s (msec) to classify simultaneous or successive picture–picture or description–picture combinations. (From Seymour, 1974a, *Quarterly Journal of Experimental Psychology*, **26**, 39–51, with permission.)

conversion for a verbal input (DP trials). However, although successive PP and DP comparisons are equivalent in the general level of the *RT*s, they are distinguished in terms of the magnitude of the 'same'–'different' effect. 'No' *RT*s were delayed relative to 'Yes' *RT*s on DP trials to a much greater extent than on PP trials, and this difference held under both the simultaneous and the successive conditions. This response × displays interaction casts some doubt on the view that a retained and a generated pictorial code provide strictly equivalent bases for verification of a test picture. If we assume that the size of the 'same'–'different' effect depends on the relative settings of the thresholds of the 'same'–'different' counters, then the interaction indicates that input of a verbal description selectively raises the 'different' threshold. It would be difficult to see much utility for such a precautionary adjustment in a dual code system in which retained and generated pictorial codes were equivalent.

Effects of Description Complexity

A second set of criteria against which the dual code hypothesis can be tested concern the effects of verbal complexity on simultaneous and successive DP

comparison *RT*s. Studies of physical identity matching of pairs of simultaneously displayed shapes have provided evidence that 'Yes' *RT* is not much
affected by the number of dimensions which must be considered (Nickerson,
1967a; Hawkins, 1969). This result is also obtained when single test stimuli are
matched against a description which is held constant within a block of trials, e.g.
the description *large red circle* is verified no less rapidly than the description
circle (Nickerson, 1967b; Saraga and Shallice, 1973). Within a dual code
model, therefore, variations in description complexity might be expected to
affect the time required for analysis of the description in the verbal system, but
not time to verify a test picture against a generated pictorial code.

A study by Cohen (1969) provides a test of this prediction. At ISIs of 1 sec,
3 sec, and 5 sec, PP comparisons did not show consistent effects of the
complexity of the pictures; DP comparisons produced *RT*s at the same general
level as PP comparisons, but nonetheless showed effects of description
complexity. Some confirmation of this finding can be obtained from data
reported by Seymour (1974a). The stimuli were pictures of squares or circles

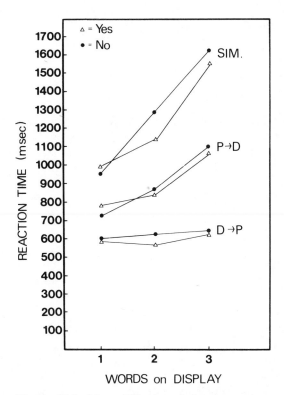

Figure 13.3. Mean *RT*s (msec) for comparisons
between descriptions of varying complexity and
square–circle pictures. (From Seymour, 1974a,
Quarterly Journal of Experimental Psychology, **26**,
39–51, with permission.)

inside squares or circles, and the descriptions either asserted the presence of one shape (e.g. 'circle'), or two shapes (e.g. 'square circle') or two shapes in a specified relation (e.g. 'square outside circle'). Three groups of Ss were tested, under conditions of simultaneous DP presentation, or successive DP presentation, or successive PD presentation. 'Yes' and 'No' RTs were measured from onset of the test stimulus under the successive conditions, and from onset of both stimuli under the simultaneous condition. A summary of the results of the experiment is given in Figure 13.3. It can be seen that the effects of description complexity interacted with presentation conditions, being greatest under the simultaneous condition, and least under the successive DP condition. However, there was a small but highly significant effect of complexity on the DP responses, which depended on a difference of about 40 msec between RTs to verify three-word descriptions and RTs for one- and two-word descriptions. The data obtained under the PD successive condition provide some indication of the increments in time to read descriptions at the three levels of complexity. The effect is not a linear function of number of words to be scanned, since the increment due to addition of a relational term ('inside' or 'outside') is greater than the increment due to addition of an extra noun. For single-word descriptions, RTs were greater under the PD condition than under the DP condition.

Effect of syntactic form of the description

A further prediction of the dual code model is that sentences which differ in syntactic structure but which are nonetheless referentially synonymous will produce equivalent verification RTs, provided sufficient time for pictorial recoding is permitted. The sentences:

(I)   The square is inside the circle
(II) Inside the circle is the square
(III) The circle has the square inside

are all descriptive of a picture of a square contour drawn within a circular contour. On the other hand, the sentence of Type I is intuitively a simpler or more direct statement of the locative relation, and may be regarded as transformationally less complex than sentences of Types II or III (Fillmore, 1968). In a dual code model, these variations in syntactic form might be expected to affect processing time within the verbal–semantic system. However, if the end-product of this analysis is the establishment, in the image system, of a picture-like representation of a square within a circle, and verification of the test picture takes place by reference to this representation, there need be no effect of sentence form on verification RT under conditions of successive presentation of the sentence and picture. Further, successive sentence–picture comparisons should produce RTs at the same general level as successive picture–picture comparisons.

These predictions were tested in experiments reported by Seymour (1974d). Verification *RT*s were obtained for simultaneous and successive comparisons between square–circle pictures (PP condition) or between 'inside' and 'outside' sentences of the three structural types shown above and square–circle pictures (sentence–picture condition). A summary of the data is given in Figure 13.4.

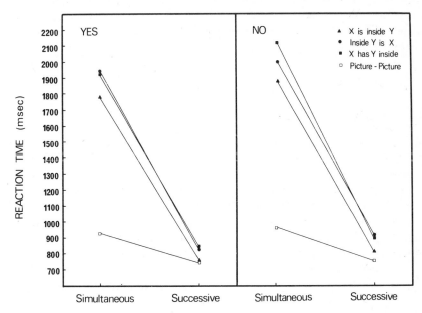

Figure 13.4. Mean *RT*s (msec) for picture–picture and sentence–picture comparisons. (From Seymour, 1974d, *Memory and Cognition*, **2**, 224–232, with permission.)

As in the earlier experiment on three-word descriptions, simultaneous comparisons showed a large difference between the PP and sentence–picture combinations. There was also an effect of sentence type, Type I sentences being verified faster than sentences of Types II or III. Under the successive condition, the general level of *RT*s for sentence–picture comparisons was similar to that obtained for PP comparisons, and there was indeed no significant difference between PP matching and verification of a sentence of Type I. However, the effect of sentence type persisted under the successive condition. Also, the difference between 'Yes' and 'No' *RT*s was greater for sentence–picture than for picture–picture comparisons under both the simultaneous and successive conditions.

These results are not consistent with the assumptions of the dual code model, provided that *RT* can be thought of as an index of match/mismatch of memory codes. Although the data tend to satisfy the criterion of equivalence of successive PP and DP *RT*s, they do not satisfy the criterion of elimination of effects of complexity of syntactic form, or of equalization of the difference between 'Yes' and 'No' responses. We can argue, on the basis of data obtained in visualization and construction tasks by Seymour (1974d), that a period of 2 sec from sentence onset (1 sec display plus 1 sec ISI), is sufficient for derivation of pictorial information from a sentence. Further, a number of studies of sentence–picture comparison have used longer intervals than this and have also shown effects of complexity and logical or syntactic form on verification *RT* (Gough, 1965, 1966; Cohen, 1969; Trabasso, Rollins and Shaughnessy, 1971). Thus, the data fail to provide compelling support for a division of semantic memory into distinct verbal and image systems, and it may be sensible, for the time being, to retain Clark and Chase's (1972) notion of a single modality-free system.

Latency and Order of Construction

In an attempt to clarify the nature of the sentence representation utilized in a verification task Seymour (1974d) obtained some information about constructional responses to square–circle pictures and 'inside'/'outside' sentences of Types I, II and III. A sentence or picture was displayed, and the *S* responded by drawing a square–circle picture. The *RT* was measured from onset of the stimulus to first contact of a ballpoint pen and sheet of conductive paper, and a note was taken of the order in which the shapes were drawn. Various precautions were taken to ensure that the shapes were drawn in a standard size at the inner and outer locations and that the drawing was done straight off. Table 13.1 provides a summary of the reaction time data obtained in this

Table 13.1. Summary of mean latencies (msec) to start construction of a drawing in response to a sentence of Type I, II or III or a picture. (From Seymour, 1974d, *Memory and Cognition*, **2**, 224–232, with permission.)

	Sentence type			
Preposition	I	II	III	Picture
'Inside'	1336	1452	1422	679
'Outside'	1192	1467	1490	
$\bar{X}$	1264	1460	1456	679

immediate construction test. As might be expected, a copying response to a picture was faster than a constructional response to a sentence. Responses to sentences were also affected by sentence type. In a dual code model, in which constructional output is derived from an image representation, these results can be interpreted as indicating (a) faster access to the image code by pictures than by sentences, and (b) an effect of sentence structure on verbal–pictorial conversion time. Rather similar results were obtained in another study in which *S*s pressed a button when they could visualize the shapes in their locations (Seymour, 1974d).

With respect to order of construction, the dual code hypothesis predicts equivalent performance in response to pictures and sentences of the different structural types, since, in each case, output is supposed to derive from a common image-like representation. This prediction was not supported by the data. When the stimulus was a picture, order of construction was highly consistent within an individual S, but differed among Ss. When it was a sentence of Type I, drawing was started, almost without exception, with the subject of the sentence at the location specified by the preposition. For sentences of Types II and III on the other hand, there was much variability, both within and between Ss, in the orders in which the two shapes were drawn.

These findings were confirmed in a subsequent study in which the construction test was delayed until 1500 msec after stimulus offset. At the end of the delay, the S saw either a picture (which required a 'Yes' or 'No' response), or a dot, which required a constructional response. The results of this experiment have been summarized in Figure 13.5. The results for verification are similar to

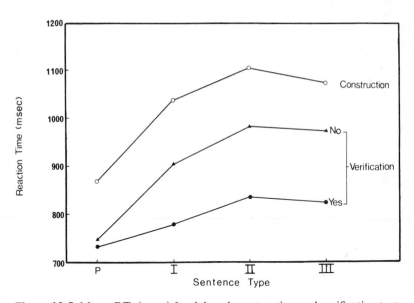

Figure 13.5. Mean RTs (msec) for delayed construction and verification tests on memory for a picture or sentence of varying structural type. (From Seymour, 1974d, *Memory and Cognition*, **2**, 224–232, with permission.)

those obtained at an ISI of 1 sec. 'Yes' responses were equally fast when a picture or a sentence of Type I was in memory. 'No' RTs were delayed relative to 'Yes' RTs for sentence–picture comparisons, but not for picture–picture comparisons. There was a significant effect of sentence type on both 'Yes' and 'No' responses. For construction, the effect of sentence type was not statistically significant. However, the response was faster when a picture was in memory than when a sentence was in memory. Order of construction data were quite similar to those obtained in the immediate test situation, showing idiosyncratic but consistent results for responses to pictures, a significant tendency for the subject of the sentence to be drawn first for sentences of Type I, and variability of output order for sentences of Types II and III (Seymour, 1974d).

These results count as evidence against the view that constructional output derives from a representation in a distinct image system, and thus fail to support the dual code position. The data are also inconsistent with a version of the unitary abstract code model in which sentence and picture inputs are represented in terms of elementary propositions of the form 'X inside Y' or 'X outside Y'. More precisely, the data suggest that Ss have consistent procedures for mapping pictures and sentences of Type I onto one or other of these assertions, but that they lack such procedures for sentences of Types II and III. We might think of the sentence or picture representation as a plan for action, of the form:

First (Draw X at L_1) Then (Draw Y at L_2)

or

First (Test for contour X at L_1) Then (Test for contour Y at L_2)

where X and Y are shape contours, and L_1 and L_2 are locations. The values entered into the plan can be specified by order of scanning for picture inputs, and by the subject and locative preposition for sentences of Type I. Plans derived from pictures and Type I sentences appear about equally efficient in the verification task. This is not so for delayed construction, where responses to pictures are faster than responses to Type I sentences. This could be because a picture has effects on the constructional output code, which facilitates drawing. If verification involves matching of abstract codes rather than constructional codes, there need be no such facilitation in the 'Yes'/'No' task.

Interpretation of the effect on construction and verification RT of sentences of Types II and III can be attempted in terms of a notion of procedurally ambiguous plans. These sentences appear difficult because the surface form separates a mention of a location and a mention of the shape which must occupy that location ('Inside the square is the circle'), or because there is a mismatch between the subject of the sentence and the location specified ('The square has the circle inside'). Given the variability of the order of construction data for these sentences, we may argue that they are encoded as a procedurally ambiguous representation of the form:

First (Draw X at L_1 or Draw Y at L_2)
Then (If X at L_1 Draw Y at L_2) or (If Y at L_2 Draw X at L_1).

The effect on RT of sentence type could then depend on either (a) the time required to resolve the ambiguity or (b) a tendency for a precautionary rise in thresholds of the 'same' and 'different' counters to occur whenever the sentence in memory was classified as potentially procedurally ambiguous.

In general, therefore, we can accommodate the results of the picture–picture and sentence–picture experiments by assuming that the stimuli are represented in an abstract code, and that *RT* differences between 'Yes' and 'No' responses, or between descriptions or sentences of varying degrees of complexity, depend on threshold differences arising at the 'same'–'different' conversion stage. When a picture–picture comparison is made, the 'same' and 'different' thresholds are set at approximately equal levels. There is a selective rise in the 'different' threshold preparatory to a verbal–picture comparison, with the possibility of further increases in caution on both thresholds if the verbal input appears complex, or structurally ambiguous. These threshold adjustments produce *RT* differences which are small relative to the overall latency of the reaction, although they are often treated as a primary indicator of process or coding modality. Major additions to the *RT*, such as the difference between simultaneous picture–picture and sentence–picture comparisons presumably reflect a real change in the complexity and duration of the encoding process, and it will be necessary to devise some criteria for distinguishing between these large effects and small effects of threshold adjustment.

Order of Processing

It is arguable that the data reported in the previous sections are consistent with a version of the dual code hypothesis in which verbal rather than imaginal representations are matched. For example, a verbal description might be generated as a response to a picture, and verbal input could then be matched directly against the resulting phonological representation. Seymour (1970a) argued that this proposition could be investigated by running a word-shape comparison task in which the stimuli were presented simultaneously, but the order in which they were fixated was controlled. In one experiment, Ss matched the prepositions *above* and *below* against location of a dot which appeared above or below a reference square. In the other, they matched the words *square* and *circle* against square and circle shapes. The display components were separated by about 7° of visual angle, and the field of initial fixation was controlled by instruction. On a given trial, the S was uncertain whether a verbal or pictorial display would appear in the field of initial fixation. *RT*s were faster when the word was seen first than when the shape was seen first (Seymour, 1969, 1970a). This result indicates that Ss have a preference for encoding the word before the shape in this kind of simple matching task (see also Seymour, 1970b). Comparable results have been obtained for sentence–picture matching by Chase and Clark (1972) and Clark and Chase (1972). An asymmetry of this kind might be expected to occur in a system in which the first encoding operation was a conversion of the word to a pictorial representation, or, more precisely, a plan for execution of pictorial tests. If the preference was for a verbal test, *RT*s would be expected to be faster for a shape–word scanning order. In an abstract code model, as shown in Figure 13.1, no asymmetry should occur, since both inputs must access their abstract representations before the comparison can be made.

A difference between word–picture and picture–word orders of presentation also occurs in successive versions of the matching task. This can be seen in Figure 13.3, where, at the single-word level of descriptive complexity, 'Yes' and 'No' RTs are faster for description–picture (DP) than for picture–description (PD) comparisons. The same result was reported by Rosenfeld (1967, cited by Paivio, 1971), and was also obtained in a study by Seymour (1972). The latter experiment involved classification of square–circle pictures and three-word 'inside'/'outside' descriptions. PP, DP, PD and DD sequences were randomly intermixed, with the ISI set at 1 sec. RTs were consistently faster when the test was a picture (PP and DP conditions) than when it was a description. These results also suggest the comparison may involve consideration of a code which is more rapidly accessed by a picture than by a word or description, or, at least, that there is a precautionary rise in levels of the 'Yes' and 'No' thresholds when occurrence of a verbal test is detected.

Additional evidence on this point comes from a study of rule identity classification of shape–shape, name–shape and name–name pairs (square, circle, ellipse and rectangular oblong) in which Ss reported 'Yes' if both shape concepts were 'compact' or if both were 'elongated', and 'No' for all other combinations (Seymour, 1973d). Physically identical shape–shape and word–word pairs were also included, and nominally identical word–shape pairs. At the physical identity level, word pairs were classified somewhat faster than shape pairs. However, at the rule identity level, RTs were slower for word–word stimuli than for shape–shape stimuli. Thus, Ss could determine that the shapes square and ellipse were not both compact or both elongated faster when the stimuli were shapes than when they were names. The results for physically identical pairs suggest that the effect cannot be accounted for in terms of a difference in time to establish visual representations of words and pictures. It seems more likely that the data reflect a difference in speed of access to the code used in verification of a pictorially stated classification rule. A conclusion of this sort can be reconciled with the unitary code assumption of Figure 13.1 if we allow that a region of the semantic memory may be specialized for relatively abstract description of pictorial/spatial properties. This region is located, metaphorically speaking, towards the right-hand side of the semantic system. In other words, although a common abstract code may be used to represent procedures and semantic data of various types, we can identify pictorial description as one function of the system. Construction of a pictorial representation proceeds more rapidly when the sensory input is pictorial than when it is verbal.

Pictorial and Semantic Confusability

An implication of the hypothesis that verbal–pictorial comparisons involve the matching of abstract descriptions of pictorial properties is that 'Yes' and 'No' RTs will show effects of pictorial similarity or confusability. It has been shown in many experiments that visual similarity delays a negative response to two simultaneously displayed letters (Posner and Mitchell, 1967) or shapes (Egeth, 1966; Hawkins, 1969). This effect also occurs when single test patterns are matched against a verbally stated criterion which is held constant within a block of trials (Nickerson, 1967; Marcel, 1970). Thus, given a set of shapes which may be defined in terms of values on three dimensions (e.g., colour, size and form), it is generally found that 'No' RTs increase as the number of dimensions on which the patterns have the same value increases. It has been customary to discuss these findings in terms of serial versus parallel models of processing of the component dimensions of the figures (Nickerson, 1967; Egeth, 1966). However, the data are probably better handled in the present context by assuming parallel processing of the component dimensions (Hawkins, 1969; Saraga and Shallice, 1973), and by allowing that similarity (shared values on component dimensions) affects RT by altering the setting of the 'different' decision threshold. This implies a two-stage model of pattern comparison; at a first stage the stimuli are encoded as abstract descriptions of their values on the relevant dimensions, and a global estimate of similarity/difference is made; threshold settings on the 'same' and 'different' counters are revised in a reciprocal manner as the similarity estimate becomes available. (Similarity reduces the 'same' threshold and raises the 'different' threshold, and absence of similarity has the opposite effect.) At the second stage the pattern descriptions are converted to a representation of truth or falsity via the 'same'–'different counters, and the time required for this conversion depends on the revised threshold settings. The adjustment of the thresholds is probably to some degree optional, since the effect of similarity on 'different' RT can be eliminated when Ss attempt to beat an RT deadline (Link and Tindall, 1973).

Seymour (1973b) examined 'Yes' and 'No' vocal RTs for 'same'–'different' judgements of shape–shape and name–shape pairs. The stimuli were the shapes square, circle, ellipse and oblong (rectangle) and their names. In the shape–shape comparison task the contours were drawn one inside the other. In the name–shape task, the word was printed inside the shape. A starting assumption was that the shape concepts might be defined in semantic memory in terms of values on dimensions of contour (rectilinear versus curved) and length (compact versus elongated). Shape–shape 'No' RTs were long when the stimuli shared values on the contour dimension (e.g. circle and ellipse, or square and oblong), but not when they shared values on the length dimension. The effect of similarity was assessed relative to RTs for non-confusable pairs, such as square/ellipse, which share values on neither dimension. Pictorial confusions also occurred in the name–shape comparison task. 'No' RT was long, relative to times for non-confusable pairs, when the stimuli shared the values of curvature, rectilinearity, and elongation. The effect for elongation was not obtained for shape–shape comparisons, but seemed to arise because the name *oblong* is referentially ambiguous as between oval and rectangular elongated shapes. The main point of the study is that it demonstrates the occurrence of *pictorial* confusions in name–shape comparisons. Such confusions would not occur if Ss were matching phonological representations of the shape names, or unitary abstract representations of the shape concepts (such as the nodes in a Collins and Quillian (1969) hierarchy). Matching appears to depend on consideration, at least at stage 1 of the proposed model, of a dimensional representation of pictorial properties.

Much the same conclusion follows from the results of a study of location matching reported by Seymour (1973e). The stimuli consisted of the words *above, below, left* or *right* printed above, below, left or right of a reference dot. In the first experiment, Ss named the location occupied by the word. Vocal *RT* was subject to Stroop interference when the distractor word and the location it occupied specified opposed values on the dimension of verticality or horizontality. There was also an asymmetry in the interference effect, in that the distractor *above* interfered with the report 'below', and the distractor *left* with the report 'right', but not vice versa. These results were interpreted as support for the view that the locative terms are represented in semantic memory by a dimensional feature, (+VERT) or (−VERT), and a specification of polarity on the dimension, (+Polar) or (−Polar), as suggested by Leech (1969) and Clark (1971). The asymmetrical nature of the Stroop effect can be interpreted by reference to Clark's (1969) principle of lexical marking, and will be returned to later. In the second experiment, Ss matched the meaning of the locative against the location it occupied, or the meaning of the word against the location of the dot. There were substantial delays in production of a negative response when the mismatched verbal and locative inputs shared a (+VERT) or (−VERT) feature. Thus, in verifying the location of the word, Ss were slower to classify example (b) below than example (a). This result again indicates that Ss are not matching names or unitary symbols. Also, they are

● above	● left
(a)	(b)

not deriving an image representation from the word which specifies the critical location to be tested. If the whole comparison was based on name matching or location matching of this kind the observed interference effects would not occur. However, it is important to bear in mind that in the proposed two-stage model similarity affects threshold settings on the 'same'–'different' counters. Thus, the model permits an inference from *RT* to the representations considered during the first stage, but makes no statement about the nature of the data which undergo conversion to a representation of truth or falsity.

In situations involving rule identity classifications it is possible to make a clearer distinction between a Stage 1 global test for similarity and a more focussed comparison occurring at Stage 2. For example, Schaeffer and Wallace (1970) instructed Ss to make a positive response if both of two words belonged to one of a small number of specified classes. Given a pair such as oak/tulip, Ss were slow to make a negative response, relative to *RT*s for such pairs as oak/sparrow. This suggested that properties having to do with membership of

ie class of plants were considered at some stage of the comparison of oak and
ilip. However, this kind of global similarity does not provide a sufficient basis
or choice of a 'Yes' or 'No' response, which seems to require focussed
ispection of subsets of semantic features which define the immediate class
iembership of the stimuli. The same point can be made by reference to a study
f rule identity classification of pairs of shape names reported by Seymour
1973b). When the rule was to classify the words by the report 'Yes' if both
amed compact or elongated shapes, 'No' RTs showed delay effects for pairs
iade up of the words circle and ellipse, which share the pictorial property of
urvature. Such an effect would be expected to occur if global consideration of
ontour at Stage 1 resulted in downward adjustment of the 'same' threshold
nd upward adjustment of the 'different' threshold, and this then affected the
uration of focussed inspection of values on the length dimension at Stage 2.

Semantic confusion effects, of the kind obtained by Schaeffer and Wallace
1970), Collins and Quillian (1970), and Rips, Shoben and Smith (1973), can
lso occur in verbal–pictorial comparison tasks. Seymour (1973a) cites a study
y Hutcheon (1970) in which Ss matched simultaneously displayed object
ames and pictures. A category name was defined as a label for a perceptually
iomogeneous class, e.g. flower, table. A specific name differentiated objects
within such a class, e.g. tulip. A superordinate label grouped perceptually
lissimilar object classes which were related by function, e.g. furniture. 'Yes'
esponses for superordinate and specific names were slightly delayed relative to
RTs for category names. 'No' RTs showed an effect of semantic/pictorial
imilarity: RTs were delayed relative to times for non-confusable pairs for
ombinations which shared membership of a functional class (e.g. *glove*/picture
f hat), and to a greater extent for pairs which shared membership of a
ierceptually homogeneous class (e.g., *tulip*/picture of iris). The results for 'Yes'
esponses may reflect a precautionary rise in the 'same' threshold which occurs
when a superordinate or specific name must be verified. The 'No' RTs can be
nterpreted as an effect of global pictorial/semantic similarity on the setting of
he 'different' threshold.

Additive Stages Model of Verbal–Pictorial Comparison

The main conclusions of the discussion to this point may be summarized as
ollows: (1) The data base code utilized in a verbal–pictorial comparison is an
ibstract description of pictorial/semantic properties, rather than a covertly
irticulated name, or a visual image. (2) From the viewpoint of executive
iperations, the comparison involves two gross processing stages prior to
nitiation of a vocal (or manual) report. At Stage 1 the display is encoded as a
eatural description of values on relevant pictorial/semantic dimensions, and
he 'same'–'different' thresholds are revised. Threshold revision may be
irecautionary, as when one or both thresholds are raised to take account of
ierceived difficulty, or anticipatory, as when a global assessment of similarity
eads to the reciprocal raising of one threshold and lowering of the other. Stage

2 involves focussed inspection of a relevant subsection of the semantic data and the conversion of this information to a representation of truth or falsity. The time required for the conversion depends on the settings of the thresholds.

In an *adjustable threshold* model of this kind, RT is seen as an index of the speed with which major coding changes can occur during the translation of the display to a 'Yes' or 'No' report, and not of the occurrence or non-occurrence of additional time consuming operations. The distinction intended here can be clarified by reference to a model of verbal–pictorial comparison proposed by Chase and Clark (1972) and elaborated by Clark and Chase (1972). The model was developed initially to account for the results of a study by Seymour (1969a) in which Ss matched the locatives *above* and *below* against the position of a dot which might appear above or below a reference square. There were significant differences among RTs to classify the four word–picture combinations, principally because 'Yes' responses were faster to *above*/above than to *below*/below. Rather similar effects occur for matching *present* and *absent* against presence or absence of a dot (Chase and Clark, 1971), and for matching *large* or *small* against a large or small square (Seymour, 1971). Chase and Clark (1971) interpreted these results in terms of an *additive stage* model in which increments in RT were thought to index the occurrence of additional operations at the encoding and comparison stages.

The general form of the model is shown as a flow diagram in Figure 13.6. The RT is composed of four successive stages, termed (1) Word encoding, (2) Location encoding, (3) Comparison, and (4) Response execution. Word encoding is a slower operation for *below* than for *above* and location encoding is slower for a dot below the square than for one above it. The comparison operation also takes longer for *false* displays than for *true* displays. Clark has interpreted the above/below differences in terms of the notion of lexical marking (Clark, 1969). The argument here is that certain spatial dimensions such as high–low, tall–short, large–small, are characterized by an unmarked term, which is often also a name for the dimension, and by a marked term which specifies a restricted region at the negative end of the dimension. Chase and Clark (1971) suggested that *above* and *below* refer to the vertical high–low dimensions, and that *below* labels the marked end of the dimension. The semantic representations of the two terms might then take the forms [+VERT(+Polar)] for *above*, and [+VERT(−Polar)] for *below*. The RT difference in classification time for *above* versus *below* can be accommodated by assuming that the (−Polar) feature necessitates an extra step at the encoding stage (Chase and Clark, 1971), which might involve switching a normally positive polarity feature to a negative state. It follows that the *below*/below combination will be classified less rapidly than the *above*/above combination because two additional operations of negating a polarity feature are required. A further assumption is that the outcome of a comparison of word polarity and location polarity is represented by the state of a 'truth index'. This appears to be a semantic representation of truth–falsity which has a normal unmarked state (true), but which can be switched, via some time-consuming operation, to a

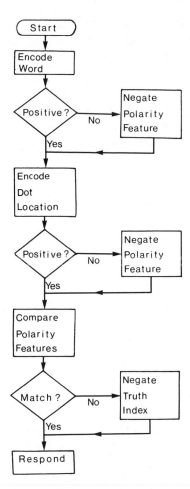

Figure 13.6. Flow diagram representation of the additive stage model for above–below comparisons proposed by Chase and Clark (1971)

negative or marked state (false). Thus, the 'different' combinations *above*/below and *below*/above are processed less rapidly than *above*/above by an amount equivalent to switching time for the truth index and one polarity feature.

As a test of the assumption of additivity of stage durations Chase and Clark (1971) introduced a manipulation designed to interfere selectively with the location encoding stage (*cf*. Sternberg, 1969). This involved masking of the upper location of the word–picture display for one group of Ss, and of the lower location for another group. When the lower location was masked, the S was required to infer presence of the dot below the square from its absence above the square. Similarly, when the upper location was masked, presence of a dot above the square could be inferred from its absence below the square. A summary of the data obtained under these two conditions, and under the normal no mask condition, is given in Figure 13.7. It can be seen that masking

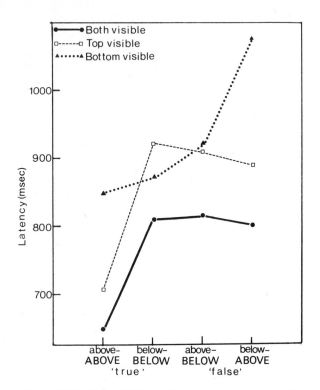

Figure 13.7. Mean *RT*s (msec) for above–below classifications under normal conditions and under conditions of masking of the upper or lower location. (Redrawn from Chase and Clark, 1971, *British Journal of Psychology*, **62**, 311–326, with permission.)

of the lower location made very little difference to the general pattern of the *RT*s, but that masking of the upper location both eliminated the difference between *above*/above and *below*/below, and delayed *below*/above relative to *above*/below. The latter effect can be interpreted as an addition to the time required to encode the above location. Since there is no comparable increment in time to encode the below location when the lower region is masked, it seems reasonable to conclude (a) that attentional scanning of the figure normally proceeds in a top-down direction, and (b) that presence of the dot in the below location is often inferred from its absence in the above location. This means that location encoding, in the model shown in Figure 13.6, is primarily a test for presence of the dot at the upper location. If this test fails, the polarity feature for the picture representation is negated. Under conditions of masking of the upper location, the initial test on the upper location will fail, leading to negation of the polarity feature. A further operation of encoding the lower location is then required. If this also has a negative outcome the polarity feature must be switched back to its positive state, as shown in Figure 13.8. This model provides a good account of the data obtained under the bottom-visible condition of Chase and Clark's study, provided that it can be assumed that initial encoding of the upper location is obligatory.

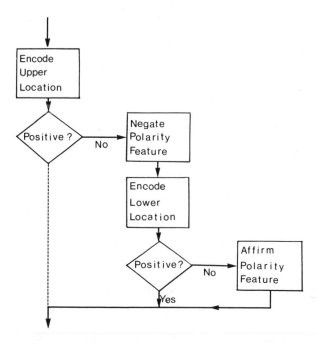

Figure 13.8. Flow diagram representation of picture encoding stage when the upper location is masked, derived from discussion in Chase and Clark (1971)

Thus, the additive stage model differs from the adjustable threshold model in treating *RT* differences as indices of extra operations which add to the durations of the encoding and comparison stages. Extra time is required for negation of the polarity feature and truth index, and also for switching a negated feature back to its positive state.

Semantic Positivity/Negativity

An alternative account of the *above–below* asymmetry can be developed within the framework of the adjustable threshold model. The starting assumption is that the 'same' and 'different' thresholds may also be modifiable by presence of positive or negative components in the featural representation of the display. For example, a (−Polar) feature, or a mismatch outcome of a comparison, may be considered as negative components which effect a reciprocal adjustment in favour of the 'different' threshold, as does semantic dissimilarity in the model of Schaeffer and Wallace (1970). Matching outcomes, or (+Polar) features, effect an adjustment in favour of the 'same' threshold. On a featural analysis of this kind, the representation of an *above*/above display contains only positive components. The representation of *below*/below, on the other hand, contains two (−Polar) features, one for the word representation and one for the location. If inherent positivity/negativity was assessed at Stage 1, downward revision of the 'same' threshold would be rather greater for the *above*/above display than for the *below*/below display. Further, in a system of the type shown in Figure 13.1, the exit logogens for the reports 'Yes' and 'No' may be primed by input of affirmative or negative semantic features. This might provide an additional, or an alternative, mechanism for facilitation of 'Yes' responses to *above*/above displays. Presence of negativity in the *below*/below representation would also prime the 'No' logogen, resulting in some erroneous responses to this display (*cf.* Chase and Clark, 1971). The two 'different' combinations, *above*/below and *below*/above, each have one (−Polar) feature, together with a mismatch outcome on a comparison of word polarity and location polarity. The featural representations of the displays thus contain equal numbers of negative components, producing equivalent settings on the 'different' threshold, and equivalent priming of the 'No' exit logogen. Thus, no difference in RT between these combinations is expected (Seymour, 1969; Chase and Clark, 1971). A similar explanation can be proposed for other pairs which involve a positive/negative (unmarked versus marked) distinction, e.g. *large–small* and *present–absent*.

This discussion indicates that the additive stage and adjustable threshold models make quite similar predictions about classification RTs for above–below displays. In order to obtain opposed predictions, it is necessary to consider cases in which heavily negative displays are classified as 'different' by the report 'No'. In the additive stage model such displays will require extra processing time, because additional operations are required to represent negative properties. In the adjustable threshold model, on the other hand negativity is expected to facilitate selection of a 'No' response. Two sets of experiments reported by Seymour (1974b, 1974c) provide some relevant information on the effects of semantic negativity on classification RT. In the first of these, Ss matched the words *above* and *below* against the location of a dot positioned above or below a schematic face. The face could be upright or inverted, but the above and below locations were defined relative to the top of the face, and not absolute location on the screen. Thus, the word *above* presented with an inverted face and dot in the lower region of the screen counted as an *above*/above display requiring the report 'Yes'. The experiment was undertaken as a test of the additive stages model. If word encoding location encoding and comparison are genuinely independent operations inversion of the reference face will affect the duration of the picture encoding stage only. Also, if 'above' propositions may be represented more rapidly than 'below' propositions, above pictures will be encoded more rapidly than below pictures even when the face is inverted. On these assumptions, the effect of inversion of the face should be to add a constant to the *RT*, but to leave unaltered the basic effects for *above* versus *below* and *true* versus *false*. An alternative account which incorporates the findings of Chase and Clark (1971) might be that the upper location is encoded as dot present or dot absent, with absence resulting in negation of the polarity feature. In order to perform the task, the *S* must then encode the orientation of the face, and change the polarity feature if the face is inverted. This latter version of the location encoding stage is shown as a flow diagram in Figure 13.9. A further possibility is that inversion

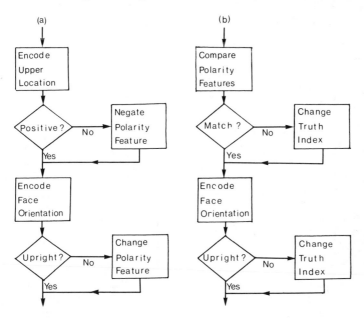

Figure 13.9. Alternative methods of handling inversion of the reference face within an additive stage model, involving (a) additional operations during picture encoding, or (b) additional operations during comparison

of the face may be handled at the comparison stage. *S* might match the polarities of the word and absolute location of the dot, and then use inversion of the face as a cue to change the truth index prior to responding, as has been proposed for processing of linguistic negatives (Chase and Clark, 1972; Clark and Chase, 1972; Trabasso, Rollins and Shaughnessy, 1971). This possibility has also been diagrammed in Figure 13.9.

The model which assumes switching of the polarity feature predicts that *RT*s for *above*/above and *below*/below displays will be about equal, but that 'No'

RTs will be faster for *above*/below than for *below*/above. This is because the *below*/above display requires polarity switching operations at the word encoding and location encoding stages which are not needed for an *above*/below display. Much the same prediction follows from the assumption of switching of the truth index: RTs for *above*/above and *below*/below should be equal, and *above*/below should be faster than *below*/above. The adjustable threshold model makes an opposed prediction with respect to 'No' RTs. In order to demonstrate this, it is necessary to make a number of assumptions about the form of the abstract representation of the word–picture display which is established during the Stage 1 encoding process. Figure 13.10 shows a

	NORMAL				INVERTED			
	above	below	above	below	above	below	above	below
Word	+ VERT + POLAR	+ VERT − POLAR	+ VERT + POLAR	+ VERT − POLAR	+ VERT + POLAR	+ VERT − POLAR	+ VERT + POLAR	+ VERT − POLAR
Dot	+ VERT + POLAR	+ VERT − POLAR	+ VERT − POLAR	+ VERT + POLAR	+ VERT − POLAR	+ VERT + POLAR	+ VERT + POLAR	+ VERT − POLAR
Face	+ VERT + POLAR	+ VERT + POLAR	+ VERT + POLAR	+ VERT + POLAR	+ VERT − POLAR	+ VERT − POLAR	+ VERT − POLAR	+ VERT − POLAR
(Dot / Face-top)	+ MATCH	− MATCH	− MATCH	+ MATCH	+ MATCH	− MATCH	− MATCH	+ MATCH
(Word/Dot Face-top)	+ MATCH	+ MATCH	− MATCH	− MATCH	+ MATCH	+ MATCH	− MATCH	− MATCH
Decision	+ TRUE	+ TRUE	− TRUE	− TRUE	+ TRUE	+ TRUE	− TRUE	− TRUE
Positive	9	6	5	6	7	6	5	4
Negative	0	3	4	3	2	3	4	5

Figure 13.10. Featural representation of above and below displays for normal and inverted orientation of the reference face. (From Seymour, 1974c, *Journal of Experimental Psychology*, **102**, 447–455. Copyright 1974 by the American Psychological Association. Reprinted by permission.)

formulation which was proposed by Seymour (1974c). Word polarity, dot location, and face orientation are encoded in the featural format proposed by Clark, and dot location is matched against face-top location. Presence of positive features at this stage tends to lower the 'same' threshold relative to the 'different' threshold, and presence of negative features has the opposite effect. Stage 2 involves a focussed comparison of word polarity and match/mismatch of dot to face-top. The outcome is a representation of truth or falsity, and time to make the conversion varies as a function of the threshold settings of the 'same'–'different' counters. Further, presence of positive/negative features in the representation of the display may prime the exit logogens for the vocal reports 'Yes' and 'No'. A very gross prediction of RTs within each response category can be made by taking a simple count of positive and negative values for each display. For normal orientation of the face, positivity is greater for *above*/above than for *below*/below, and negativity is greater for *above*/below than for *below*/above. For the inverted face, the prediction is a diminished advantage for *above*/above for 'Yes' responses, and of a reversal in the direction of the difference between *above*/below and *below*/above. This results from the negativity of the *below*/above display, which has negative values for word polarity, dot location, and face orientation, in addition to its classification as false.

The *RT* data obtained in the experiment have been summarized in Figure 13.11. There is clearly an interaction between word–picture combinations and

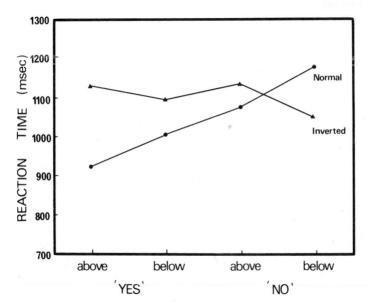

Figure 13.11. Summary of *RT*s (msec) for classification of above and below displays for normal and inverted orientation of the reference face. (From Seymour, 1974c, *Journal of Experimental Psychology*, **102**, 447–455. Copyright 1974 by the American Psychological Association. Reprinted by permission.)

orientation of the reference face: this eliminates the version of the additive stage model in which inversion of the face merely adds a constant to the picture encoding operation. With respect to trials on which the face was normally oriented, the ordering of the mean *RT*s within each response category is adequately predicted both by the adjustable threshold model and by the two versions of the additive stage model outlined in Figure 13.9. For trials on which the face was inverted, the additive stage models correctly predict the elimination of the *above*/above versus *below*/below difference. On the other hand, the additive stage models require that 'No' *RT*s for *below*/above should be longer than *RTs* for *above*/below. The adjustable threshold model makes the converse prediction that 'No' responses to *below*/above inverted face displays should be facilitated, and the data do indeed show a significant advantage for this combination.

In order to investigate this kind of negative response bias slightly more directly, Seymour (1974b) studied a Stroop variant of the *above–below* classification task. The locative *above* or *below* was printed at the centre of a reference square, and an array of Xs or a word appeared above or below the square. The task was to report 'Yes' if either a word or Xs was at the location specified by the preposition, and 'No' if it was not. Three separate experiments were run. The control (Xs) condition was common to all of them, but the words used as Stroop distractors were *yes* and *no* in the first experiment, *right* and *wrong* in the second, and *up* and *down* in the third. The intention was to choose distractors which might selectively interfere with the response stage, the comparison stage, or the encoding stage of the verbal–pictorial comparison. In the first two studies, the distractors *yes* and *no*, or *right* and *wrong*, could be in agreement with the required response, or in conflict with it. In the conflict condition, the negativity of the distractors *no* or *wrong* should interfere with production of a 'Yes' response, whereas the positivity of *yes* and *right* should interfere with a 'No' response. Further, if *S*s define location in terms of presence or absence of a letter configuration at the upper location, interference should occur only for distractors presented above the reference square. These predictions were not supported. Relative to the control condition, the distractors caused a small rise in *RT* which was independent both of agreement/conflict as between the distractor and the required response, and of the usual differences between *above* and *below* or *true* and *false*. This result is important for theories about the nature of Stroop interference, because it demonstrates that these response-related distractors did not gain access to semantic memory. The delay of *RT* observed can be interpreted as a precautionary rise on both the 'same' and 'different' thresholds which occurs when a potential distractor is noted on the display.

In the third experiment the distractors were the locatives *up* and *down*, which are semantically close to the domain of the judgemental task (Klein, 1964; Fox, Shor and Steinman, 1970). If we adopt the assumptions of the additive stage model about the successive and independent nature of the word and location encoding stages, it follows that the distractor will be encountered during location encoding, and might be expected to interfere with that stage. The upper panel of Figure 13.12 shows the data plotted to show the effect of match/mismatch between the distractor and the location it occupied. While it is obvious that the Stroop words had major effects on the pattern of *RTs*, it is also clear that these were not limited to the location mismatch condition, and did not reflect a constant increment to a location encoding stage. Inspection suggested that the data were better characterized in terms of match/mismatch between the meaning of the distractor and the meaning of the locative *above* or *below*. This is shown in the lower panel of Figure 13.12. When there was

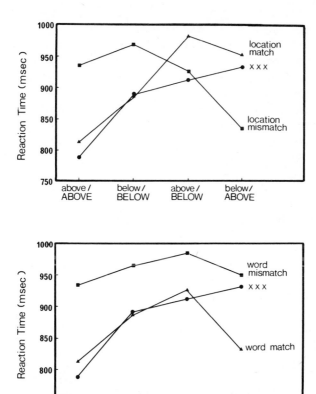

Figure 13.12. Summary of *RT*s(msec) for classification of above and below displays under Stroop conditions. Upper panel shows the data plotted on the assumption that interference will affect picture encoding. Lower panel shows the same data points plotted to show the effect of match/mismatch between the word *above* and *below* and the distractor *up* or *down*. (From Seymour, 1974b, *Memory and Cognition*, **2**, 19–26, with permission.)

mismatch of meaning between the locative and the distractor, *RT*s were delayed and the effects for *above* versus *below* and *true* versus *false* were eliminated. We could interpret the effect on 'Yes' *RT*s within the terms of the additive stage models by arguing that the distractors affect the duration of the word encoding stage, and that the marked term *down* adds more to the time for *above* than does *up* for *below*. However, this account also predicts a difference between 'No' *RT*s in favour of *below*/above, and fails to provide a satisfactory explanation for the disappearance of the *true–false* effect. When the distractors agreed in meaning with the locative, *RT*s for *above*/above and *below*/below were very close to those obtained under the control condition. The important effect was that *below*/above was classified faster than under the control condition, and faster than *above*/below. A consequence of this is that a test for effects of *above* versus *below* and *true* versus *false* produced non-significant results. The facilitation of *RT*s for *below*/above cannot be easily handled by the additive stage model. It is, however, broadly consistent with the notion that accumulated negativity may, under some circumstances, assist production of a 'No' response. Rather as the positivity of the word *above* and the location above can facilitate a 'Yes' reaction, so, it seems, may the negativity of the words *below* and *down* facilitate a 'No' response.

Translation From Decision to Report

In the adjustable threshold model of Figure 13.1, production of a 'Yes' or 'No' report involves conversion of a semantic representation of truth/falsity to a vocal response, following input of semantic features to the exit logogens. In the paper by Morton (1969a) a single logogen system is postulated for access to and exit from semantic memory. However, the Stroop experiments by Seymour (1974b) described in the previous section provide some evidence that exit logogens may be functionally distinct from access logogens. The argument here concerns the 'semantic gradient' in Stroop interference (Klein, 1964), or the tendency for the effect to be greatest for distractors which are related to the domain of the naming task. Morton (1969b) interpreted this in terms of priming of access logogens: when the task and stimuli are defined for the S, logogens of associated words are primed by input of semantic features, and it is for this reason that task-related distractors undergo visual–semantic or visual–phonological recoding and give rise to Stroop interference (Warren, 1972). In a 'same'–'different' variant of the Stroop task the instructions define (a) the domain of the task (here 'verticality') and (b) the judgement and report required (congruence, 'Yes' and 'No' report). We would therefore expect logogens relating both to truth/falsity and to verticality to be primed. However, the results of the Seymour (1974b) experiments indicate that the locative distractors *up* and *down* were semantically recoded (by virtue of the primed state of their logogens?) but that *right*/*wrong* and *yes*/*no* were not. One interpretation of this finding is that access and exit logogen systems are distinct, and that the access units are primed by definition of the domain of the task (colour, location, etc.), whereas the exit units are primed by definition of the response categories and judgemental operation.

Certain effects which are currently being explored in semantic memory research are probably best interpreted in terms of priming of access units. These include context effects on reading *RT* (Jacobson, 1973; Meyer Schvaneveldt and Ruddy, 1974), and on lexical decisions (Schvaneveldt and Meyer, 1973). Meyer has presented arguments, based on experiments involving sequences of three lexical decisions, which suggest that contextual facilitation in the word/non-word task does not depend on adjustments to a 'same' or 'different' threshold of the type considered by Schaeffer and Wallace (1970), or on time to shift between locations in semantic memory. In a logogen model context can affect both lexical decision and reading RT if a 'spread of activation' in the semantic memory primes a subset of access units. It is important to note that the interaction obtained by Meyer, Schvaneveldt and Ruddy (1974) between size of the association effect and stimulus quality is fully consistent with this position. If the association effect depends on the difference between resting states of primed versus unprimed logogens and thresholds for access to the semantic and phonological codes, degradation of the stimulus will be expected to exaggerate this effect. This is because degradation will slow the rate of input of evidence to the access logogens (Sanford, 1972; Coltheart, 1973). A similar analysis may apply for other situations, such as effects of conjoint frequency on categorization RT (Wilkins, 1971).

It is important that techniques should be found for distinguishing between effects occurring at access to semantic memory, and those which occur at the conversion ('same'–'different') or exit stages. One potentially useful method involves a reversal of the usual congruence-report assignment, so that Ss are instructed to report 'No' to 'same' displays and 'Yes' to 'different' displays. In an additive stage model, this manipulation might add the time required for switching a 'truth index' at the end of the latency, but should not alter the magnitudes of effects arising at earlier stages of processing. For example, if the 'same'–'different' effect involves a difference in judgement time, as opposed to a difference in response production time, it should be present when the 'Yes'/'No' assignment is reversed. This appeared to be the case in an experiment reported by Seymour (1970b). Ss matched the labels *square, circle, large, small, black, white* against shapes which varied in shape size and colour. Under a normal congruence-report assignment the size of the 'same'–'different' effect decreased as the number of dimensions considered within a block of trials increased. Ss using the reversed congruence-report assignment were slower by about 235 msec, on average, than those using the normal allocation, but also showed a difference in favour of 'same' displays which decreased with the number of relevant dimensions. This result seems consistent with the view that a distinction can be made between a 'same'–'different' decision process, and a process of response selection and production. The difficulty encountered under the reversed congruence-report condition arises only when a 'same'–'different' judgement is required. If, as in an experiment reported by Seymour (1971), Ss classify word–picture combinations which do not involve a congruence relationship (e.g., the words *black* and *white* paired with large or small squares), no effect of reversal of the report assignment occurs. Thus, the delay of RT observed under the reversed assignment arises when the outcome of a 'same'–'different' judgement is represented as an affirmative or negative state in semantic memory, and there is a mismatch between this state and the meaning of the required report.

If the 'same'–'different' effect is independent of the reversal of the congruence-report assignment, this should also be true of effects arising at the prior stage of access to semantic memory. Some evidence on this point comes from a study by Sanford (1974). Ss classified words as members or non-members of semantic categories using a normal or reversed congruence-report assignment. Under the normal assignment, words of high conjoint frequency with the category name were classified faster than words of low conjoint frequency. Reversal of the assignment raised the general level of the RTs and slightly increased the magnitude of the conjoint frequency effect. This result contrasts with the findings for marked/unmarked pairs reported by Seymour (1971, 1973c). The differences between *above*/above and *below*/below, and between *large*/large and *small*/small, which are observed under the normal congruence-report allocation, were both eliminated under the reversed allocation. An interaction of this kind is difficult to reconcile with the assumptions of an additive stage model in which reversal of the report occurs after the comparison stage. It does fit in, however, with the view that the marked/unmarked difference depends on the possibility of mapping a semantically positive display onto an affirmative report.

In a system of the type shown in Figure 13.1, production of a reversed 'Yes' or 'No' report may depend on a conversion operation in which semantic features for affirmation or denial are replaced by their opposite (Seymour, 1973a). This is because generation of a 'Yes' or 'No' report will occur only when the appropriate semantic features provide input to the exit logogens. If the conversion is mediated by the 'same'–'different' counters, some rewiring is required (a) to redefine the logic of input to the conversion stage (so that matching features are accepted as evidence by the 'different' counter, and vice versa), or (b) to redefine output from the stage (so that a 'same' outcome is semantically represented as denial, and vice versa). This transformation could occur during the focussed comparison of display properties (Stage 2 of the adjustable threshold model), or could involve a second judgemental operation by which the outcome of the first is reversed. On this latter account the delay of response observed under the reversed congruence-report condition reflects the occurrence of an additional judgemental operation, analogous to switching the truth index. If a single conversion is sufficient, RT might increase because maintenance of the revised logic of the conversion takes up limited processing capacity, or because rate of input is much slowed.

Whatever the mechanism involved in congruence-report reversal, the observed elimination of the marked/unmarked effect can quite easily be interpreted in terms of priming of the exit logogens. A strongly positive display, like *above*/above causes a reciprocal rise on the 'different' threshold and has no effect on the 'No' exit logogen. A negative display such as *below*/below, by contrast, reduces the 'different' threshold and also primes the 'No' logogen. If classification of these displays by the report 'No' involves a flow of information through the 'different' counter and the 'No' logogen these adjustments should be sufficient to *reverse* the direction of the marked/unmarked effect. This did not occur in the studies discussed by Seymour (1971, 1973c). One implication of this may be that two judgemental operations are required, one involving recoding of display features in terms of truth/falsity, and the other replacement of truth by falsity, or falsity by truth. The positive display should have some advantage of speed at the first conversion, but not at the second, since positivity will have raised the 'different' threshold somewhat. A negative display will be slow at the first stage, but will gain at the second from reduction of the 'different' threshold, and priming of the 'No' exit logogen. The data suggest that the advantage for the negative display at the second conversion just about compensates for its disadvantages at the first.

Conclusion

The paper has attempted a synthesis of results from a number of studies of verbal–pictorial comparison. Its starting point was an intention to distinguish between dual code and unitary code models of the data base of long term (semantic) memory. No compelling reason to divide the memory system into verbal and pictorial components was found (a) because the data were not consistent with the view that verbal inputs could be recoded in image-like format, and (b) because the data were ambiguous as between coding and threshold adjustment interpretations. It seemed convenient, therefore, to retain Clark and Chase's (1972) notion of a single abstract (propositional) code which incorporates facilities for description of physical properties and locative relations, while allowing that such descriptions may be constructed more rapidly for picture than for verbal input.

With respect to executive processes, the main conclusions of the paper seem to be as follows: (1) RT is at best a rather gross index of component operations occurring during solution of an information processing problem. As the task is altered, alterations occur in the number and complexity of the coding changes involved in translation from input to output, and this is indexed by shifts in the average level of the RT. (2) The average level of the RT for a task of given complexity may be increased or decreased, within some quite limited range, as a consequence of adjustments to the access/exit units and 'same'–'different' decision thresholds. The resulting RT differences do not indicate an increase or decrease in the number of elementary operations occurring, but a slight speeding or retardation for certain essential coding changes. (3) These priming and adjustment effects may occur during the preliminary encoding of a display. It is for this reason that the threshold adjustment model assumes two major stages, one for encoding of the displays and revision of the states of the access, exit and conversion units, and the other for a focussed comparison and translation to a report.

The discussion identified three main types of adjustment, termed *access priming, exit priming,* and *threshold adjustment.* Access priming is exemplified in the dual lexical decision task of Meyer and Schvaneveldt (1971). The mechanism underlying the association effect is one of feedback of semantic features to the access logogens, which reduces the time required for visual–semantic recoding of the second word. The same mechanism is involved in tasks demonstrating context effects on reading RT (Jacobson, 1973) or susceptibility to Stroop interference (Warren, 1972). It may also be important for some effects observed in categorization tasks, such as the conjoint frequency of the exemplar and category name (Wilkins, 1971; Sanford, 1974). A characteristic of the access priming effect is that it may be increased by degradation of the stimulus. It should also be relatively independent of reversal of the congruence-report assignment. Exit priming involves a similar flow of semantic properties to the exit logogens, which may reduce the time for semantic-phonological recoding at output. This kind of exit priming may be partly responsible for the positivity/negativity effects observed in classification tasks involving marked/unmarked terms.

Threshold adjustment effects occur when rather general information about ambiguity, positivity/negativity or similarity of stimuli is derived during the preliminary encoding of a display, and is used as a basis for centrally commanded adjustments of the thresholds of 'same' and 'different' counters. These adjustments affect the time required for semantic–semantic recoding, i.e. replacement of object representations by representations of truth–falsity. There seem to be two main types of adjustment. Precautionary adjustments may involve a tandem rise on both thresholds or an independent rise on one threshold. The data reviewed here suggested that such adjustments might occur when verbal–pictorial, as opposed to picture–picture, matching was involved, and when the description to be verified was structurally complex or ambiguous. An adjustment of this kind could produce the category size effect of Wilkins (1971) and Meyer and Ellis (1970). It may also occur when a stimulus is surprising, as in Tversky's (1969) study, or when a potential distractor is detected, as in the study of *yes/no* and *right/wrong* Stroop interference by Seymour (1974b). The second class of adjustment is probably reciprocal in nature, in that a reduction on one threshold is compensated by a rise on the other. Adjustments of this type underlie the facilitating effect of similarity on 'same' decisions and the retarding effect of similarity on 'different' decisions. This principle can be quite general, applying for similarity effects observed in letter matching (Posner and Mitchell, 1967), shape matching and categorization (Egeth, 1966; Nickerson, 1967), comparison of word meanings (Schaeffer and Wallace, 1970), and verbal–pictorial comparison (Seymour, 1973a, 1973b, 1973e). With respect to semantic comparisons it is important to be clear that the effect of similarity occurs during encoding or at stage 1 of the proposed two-stage model. An effect of similarity therefore says something about the manner in which the stimuli are encoded, but not necessarily about the properties which are considered during the focussed comparison of stage 2. Much the same arguments apply for the effects of positivity/negativity on classification *RT*. Inherent positivity/negativity is a property of the encoded representation of a display which may result in reciprocal revision of the 'same'–'different' thresholds (and some exit priming) at stage 1, although these features may not be explicitly considered during the focussed comparison.

Effects on *RT* which depend on reciprocal threshold adjustments can be identified in the context of rule identity tasks in which stimuli of varying similarity are classified as 'same' under one instruction, and as 'different' under another. The prediction of the adjustable threshold model is that stimuli which show facilitation when classified as 'same' should show retardation when classified as 'different' (*cf.* Schaffer and Wallace, 1969, 1970; Seymour, 1973b, 1973d; Posner and Mitchell, 1967). On the other hand, Meyer has been able to demonstrate that the direction of the association effect in lexical decision is not reversed for stimuli classified by a negative response (Schvaneveldt and Meyer, 1973), implying that this effect does not depend on reciprocal threshold adjustment. Positivity/negativity effects should be identifiable by the same method, or by the technique of reversal of the congruence-report assignment.

Acknowledgements

Much of the research reported here was carried out with the support of a grant, HR 1787, by the Social Science Research Council of the U.K. Thanks are due to Jenny Greenhalgh and Sheila Robinson for their help in collection and analysis of the data, and in preparation of the MS.

References

Bindra, D., Williams, J. A., and Wise, J. S. (1965). Judgements of sameness and difference: experiments on decision time. *Science*, **150**, 1625–1628.

Bower, G. H. (1972). Mental imagery and associative learning. In L. Gregg (Ed.) *Cognition in Learning and Memory*. New York: Wiley.

Chase, W. G. and Clark, H. H. (1971). Semantics in the perception of verticality. *British Journal of Psychology*, **62**, 3, 311–326.

Chase, W. G. and Clark, H. H. (1972). Mental operations in the comparison of sentences and pictures. In L. Gregg, (Ed.) *Cognition in Learning and Memory*, New York: Wiley.

Clark, H. H. (1969). Linguistic processes in deductive reasoning. *Psychological Review*, **76**, 387–404.

Clark, H. H. (1971). Space, time, semantics and the child. Paper presented at the Conference on Developmental Psycholinguistics, State University of New York at Buffalo, August 1971.

Clark, H. H. and Chase, W. G. (1972). On the process of comparing sentences against pictures. *Cognitive Psychology*, **3**, 427–517.

Cohen, G. (1969). Pattern recognition: differences between matching patterns to patterns and matching descriptions to patterns. *Journal of Experimental Psychology*, **82**, 427–434.

Collins, A. M. and Quillian, M. R. (1969). Retrieval time from semantic memory. *Journal of Verbal Learning and Verbal Behavior*, **8**, 240–247.

Collins, A. M. and Quillian, M. R. (1970). Does category size affect categorization time? *Journal of Verbal Learning and Verbal Behavior*, **9**, 432–438.

Coltheart, M. (1973). The organization of word recognition. Paper read at conference of the British Psychological Society, London, 1973.

Egeth, H. E. (1966). Parallel versus serial processes in multi-dimensional stimulus discrimination. *Perception and Psychophysics*, **1**, 245–252.

Fillmore, C. J. (1968). The case for case. In E. Bach, and R. Harms, (Eds) *Universals in Linguistic Theory*. New York: Holt, Rinehart & Winston.

286

Fox, L. A., Shor, R. E. and Steinman, R. J. (1971). Semantic gradients and interference in naming color, spatial direction, and numerosity. *Journal of Experimental Psychology*, **91**, 59–65.

Gough, P. B. (1965) Grammatical transformations and speed of understanding. *Journal of Verbal Learning and Verbal Behavior*, **4**, 107–111.

Gough, P. B. (1966). The verification of sentences: The effects of delay of evidence and sentence length. *Journal of Verbal Learning and Verbal Behavior*, **5**, 492–496.

Hawkins, H. L. (1969). Parallel processing in complex visual discrimination. *Perception and Psychophysics*, **5**, 56–64.

Hutcheon, E. G. (1970). An investigation into stimulus classification under varying instructions. *M.A. Thesis, Dundee University.*

Jacobson, J. Z. (1973). Effects of association upon masking and reading latency. *Canadian Journal of Psychology*, **27**, 58–69.

Klein, G. S. (1964). Semantic power measured through the interference of words with colour-naming. *American Journal of Psychology*, **77**, 576–588.

Leech, G. N. (1969). *Towards a Semantic Description of English.* London: Longmans.

Link, S. W. and Tindall, A. D. (1971). Speed and accuracy in comparative judgements of line length. *Perception & Psychophysics*, **9**, 284–288.

Marcel, A. J. (1970). Sequential and parallel processing and the nature of the decisions in pattern recognition and classification. Unpublished MS. University of Sussex.

Meyer, D. E. and Ellis, G. B. (1970). Parallel processes in word recognition. Paper presented at the annual Psychonomic Society Meeting in San Antonio, Texas, November, 1970.

Meyer, D. E. and Schvaneveldt, R. W. (1971). Facilitation in recognizing pairs of words: Evidence of a dependence between retrieval operations. *Journal of Experimental Psychology*, **90**, 227–234.

Meyer, D. E., Schvaneveldt, R. W. and Ruddy, M. G. (1972). Activation of lexical memory. Paper presented at a meeting of the Psychonomic Society, St. Louis, U.S.A. 1972.

Meyer, D. E., Schvaneveldt, R. W. and Ruddy, M. G. (1974). Loci of contextual effects in visual word-recognition. In P. Rabbitt, (Ed.) *Attention and Performance*, V. New York: Academic Press.

Morton, J. (1964). The effects of context on the visual duration threshold for words. *British Journal of Psychology*, **55**, 165–180.

Morton, J. (1969a). Interaction of information in word recognition. *Psychological Review*, **76**, 165–178.

Morton, J. (1969b). Categories of interference: verbal mediation and conflict in card sorting. *British Journal of Psychology*, **60**, 329–346.

Nickerson, R. S. (1967a) 'Same'–'different' response times with multi-attribute stimulus differences. *Perceptual and Motor Skills*, **24**, 543–554.

Nickerson, R. S. (1967b). Categorization time with categories defined by disjunctions and conjunctions of stimulus attributes. *Journal of Experimental Psychology*, **73**, 211–219.

Paivio, A. (1971). *Imagery and Verbal processes.* New York: Holt, Rinehart and Winston.

Posner, M. I. and Mitchell, R. F. (1967). Chronometric analysis of classification. *Psychological Review*, **74**, 392–409.

Posner, M. I., Boies, S. J., Eichelman, W. H. and Taylor, R. L. (1969). Retention of visual and name codes of single letters. *Journal of Experimental Psychology Monographs*, **79**, 1–16.

Rips, L. J., Shoben, E. J. and Smith, E. E. (1973). Semantic distance and the verification of semantic relations. *Journal of Verbal Learning and Verbal Behavior*, **12**, 1–20.

Rosenfeld, J. B. (1967). Information processing: encoding and decoding. Unpublished doctoral thesis, Indiana University, 1967.

Sanford, A. J. (1972). Loudness and simple reaction time. *Sound*, **6**, 92–96.

Sanford, A. J. (1974). Semantic distance effects in reading, classification and superordinate selection. Paper read at a meeting of the Experimental Psychology Society, London, 1974.

Saraga, E. and Shallice, T. (1973). Parallel processing of attributes of single stimuli. *Perception and Psychophysics*, **13**, 261–270.

Schaeffer, B. and Wallace, R. (1969). Semantic similarity and the comparison of word meanings. *Journal of Experimental Psychology*, **82**, 343–346.

Schaeffer, B. and Wallace, R. (1970). The comparison of word meanings. *Journal of Experimental Psychology*, **86**, 144–152.

Schvaneveldt, R. W. and Meyer, D. E. (1973). Retrieval and comparison processes in semantic memory. In S. Kornblum, (Ed.) *Attention and Performance*, IV. New York: Academic Press.

Seymour, P. H. K. (1969). Response latencies in judgements of spatial location. *British Journal of Psychology*, **60**, 31–39.

Seymour, P. H. K. (1970a). Order of fixation effects in classification of word-shape pairs. *Quarterly Journal of Experimental Psychology*, **22**, 440–449.

Seymour, P. H. K. (1970b). Representational processes in comprehension of printed words. *British Journal of Psychology*, **61**, 207–218.

Seymour, P. H. K. (1970c). Conceptual uncertainty and the latency of judgements of the congruence of word-shape pairs. *Acta Psychologica*, **34**, 451–461.

Seymour, P. H. K. (1971). Perceptual and judgemental bias in classification of word-shape displays. *Acta Psychologica*, **35**, 461–477.

Seymour, P. H. K. (1972). Pictorial coding of locative assertions. Paper read at meeting of the Experimental Psychology Society, Newcastle, 1972.

Seymour, P. H. K. (1973a). A model for reading, naming and comparison. *British Journal of Psychology*, **64**, 35–49.

Seymour, P. H. K. (1973b). Semantic representation of shape names. *Quarterly Journal of Experimental Psychology*, **25**, 265–277.

Seymour, P. H. K. (1973c). Judgements of verticality and response availability. *Bulletin of the Psychonomic Society*, **1**, 196–198.

Seymour, P. H. K. (1973d). Rule identity classification of name and shape stimuli. *Acta Psychologica*, **37**, 131–138.

Seymour, P. H. K. (1973e). Stroop interference in naming and verifying spatial locations. *Perception and Psychophysics*, **14**, 95–100.

Seymour, P. H. K. (1974a). Pictorial coding of verbal descriptions. *Quarterly Journal of Experimental Psychology*, **26**, 39–51.

Seymour, P. H. K. (1974b). Stroop interference with response, comparison and encoding stages in a sentence–picture comparison task. *Memory and Cognition*, **2**, 19–26.

Seymour, P. H. K. (1974c). Asymmetries in judgements of verticality. *Journal of Experimental Psychology*, **102**, 447–455.

Seymour, P. H. K. (1974d). Generation of a pictorial code. *Memory and Cognition*, **2**, 224–232.

Sternberg, S. (1967). Two operations in character recognition. Some evidence from reaction-time measurements. *Perception and Psychophysics*, **2**, 45–53.

Sternberg, S. (1969). The discovery of processing stages: extensions of Donder's method. *Acta Psychologica*, **30**, 276–315.

Trabasso, T., Rollins, H. and Shaughnessy, E. (1971). Storage and verification stages in processing concepts. *Cognitive Psychology*, **2**, 239–289.

Tversky, B. (1969). Pictorial and verbal encoding in a short-term memory task. *Perception and Psychophysics*, **6**, 225–233.

Warren, R. E. (1972). Stimulus encoding and memory. *Journal of Experimental Psychology*, **94**, 90–100.

Wilkins, A. (1971). Conjoint frequency, category size, and categorization time. *Journal of Verbal Learning and Verbal Behavior*, **10**, 382–385.

Chapter 14

Long-term Memory Retrieval During the Comprehension of Affirmative and Negative Sentences

David E. Meyer

Introduction

Among the cognitive functions performed during sentence comprehension, there are a number of fundamental operations. These operations include retrieving individual word meanings and evaluating affirmative or negative information. Thus, some psycholinguistic research has dealt with how people organize and access words stored in long-term memory (e.g., Anderson and Bower, 1973; Collins and Quillian, 1969; Freedman and Loftus, 1971; Kintsch, 1972; Landauer and Freedman, 1968; Meyer, 1970; Rumelhart, Lindsay, and Norman, 1972; Schaeffer and Wallace, 1970; Smith, Shoben, and Rips, 1974; Wilkins, 1971). Other related studies have focused on various situations in which people experience more difficulty understanding negative sentences than understanding affirmative sentences (e.g., Clark and Chase, 1972; Gough, 1965; Greene, 1970; Krueger, 1972; McMahon, 1963; Meyer, 1973; Miller and McKean, 1964; Slobin, 1966; Trabasso, Rollins, and Shaughnessy, 1971; Wales and Grieve, 1969; Wason, 1959, 1961, 1965). One question raised by this work is whether sentence negation influences retrieval from long-term memory (Meyer, 1973). Some data suggest that similar retrieval operations are used in comprehending affirmative and negative sentences, but that word meanings are accessed and compared more slowly when they occur in negatives than when they occur in affirmatives.

The purpose of the current contribution is to consider further the influence of sentence negation on long-term memory retrieval. It concerns the details of both past and present research as follows. First the method and results of a previous reaction-time experiment with two types of sentence will be summarized. To extend that work, a new experiment with two other types of sentence will be reported next. Both experiments demonstrate that certain factors affect the comprehension of negative sentences in the same way as they affect the comprehension of affirmative sentences. However, the effects are greater for negatives than for affirmatives, and negatives take longer to process. A two-stage retrieval model will be outlined to interpret these findings. The results support the view that similar retrieval operations are executed in comprehending affirmative and negative sentences, and that negation reduces the rate at which information is accessed from long-term memory.

Some Previous Research on Negation and Memory Retrieval

The starting point of this work is a reaction-time experiment by Meyer (1973). In that study, people had to judge quickly and correctly the truth values of quantified propositions about familiar semantic categories. Two types of proposition were involved: *particular affirmatives* (PA) of the form SOME S ARE P, e.g. SOME DOCTORS ARE MALES, and *universal negatives* (UN) of the form NO S ARE P, e.g. NO ELMS ARE METALS. Some examples of these propositions are shown in Table 14.1.

Independent variables. Certain aspects of the subject (S) and predicate (P) categories were manipulated in each type of proposition (see Table 14.1). One factor was *category size*. Either the subject category was a 'small' one with relatively few members (e.g., DOCTORS), or it was 'large' (e.g., PERSONS). Similarly, the size of the predicate category varied (*cf.* Landauer and Freedman 1968; Landauer and Meyer, 1972). A second factor was the *set relation* of the subject category to the predicate category, where there were four distinct possibilities. In the first three relations, the subject and predicate categories had common members, so that they *intersected:* either (1) the subject category was a *subset* of the predicate category, e.g. as HOTELS are a subset of BUILDINGS; (2) the subject category was a *superset* of the predicate category, e.g. as FLUIDS are a superset of WINES; or (3) the subject and predicate categories partially *overlapped*, e.g. as DOCTORS and MALES overlap. Alternatively, (4) the subject and predicate categories had no common members and were therefore *disjoint*, e.g. as ELMS and METALS are disjoint.

The truth values of the propositions depended on the set relations of the categories in them. Following conventions of formal logic, the particular affirmatives (SOME S ARE P) were defined to be true whenever the subject category intersected the predicate category, i.e. whenever there was a subset, superset, or overlap relation; the particular affirmatives were false only if the subject and predicate categories were disjoint. In contrast, the universal negatives (NO S ARE P) were false whenever the subject and predicate categories intersected; they were true only if the categories were disjoint. Thus the universal negatives had truth values exactly opposite to the truth values of the particular affirmatives, so that the one type of proposition completely negated the other type.

Dependent variables. Speed and accuracy served as the indices of performance. On each trial of the experiment, a different proposition was presented visually, and people classified it as either 'true' or 'false' by pressing one of two

Table 14.1. Examples of particular affirmatives (PA) and universal negatives (UN) with varying set relations and sizes of the subject (S) and predicate (P) categories. (Adapted from Meyer, D. E., in *Attention and Performance IV*, edited by S. Kornblum. New York: Academic Press, 1973, p. 385, with permission.)

Set relation	S-size	P-size	Particular affirmatives	PA truth value	Universal negatives	UN truth value
Subset	Small Large	Constant	SOME THRONES ARE FURNITURE SOME CHAIRS ARE FURNITURE	True	NO THRONES ARE FURNITURE NO CHAIRS ARE FURNITURE	False
Superset	Small Large	Constant	SOME ROCKS ARE GRANITE SOME SOLIDS ARE GRANITE	True	NO ROCKS ARE GRANITE NO SOLIDS ARE GRANITE	False
Overlap	Small Large	Constant	SOME DOCTORS ARE MALES SOME PERSONS ARE MALES	True	NO DOCTORS ARE MALES NO PERSONS ARE MALES	False
Disjoint	Small Large	Constant	SOME TROUSERS ARE BRIDGES SOME GARMENTS ARE BRIDGES	False	NO TROUSERS ARE BRIDGES NO GARMENTS ARE BRIDGES	True
Subset	Constant	Small Large	SOME HOTELS ARE BUILDINGS SOME HOTELS ARE STRUCTURES	True	NO HOTELS ARE BUILDINGS NO HOTELS ARE STRUCTURES	False
Superset	Constant	Small Large	SOME FLUIDS ARE WINES SOME FLUIDS ARE DRINKS	True	NO FLUIDS ARE WINES NO FLUIDS ARE DRINKS	False
Overlap	Constant	Small Large	SOME PETS ARE DUCKS SOME PETS ARE BIRDS	True	NO PETS ARE DUCKS NO PETS ARE BIRDS	False
Disjoint	Constant	Small Large	SOME ELMS ARE STEELS SOME ELMS ARE METALS	False	NO ELMS ARE STEELS NO ELMS ARE METALS	True

finger keys. Their reaction time was measured from the onset of the stimulus to the response for each type of proposition, set relation, and category size.

Rationale. The experiment was designed to study the retrieval operations used in comprehending affirmative and negative propositions. Although the particular affirmatives and universal negatives had opposite truth values, both types of proposition required people to decide whether or not the subject and predicate categories intersected. Such a decision presumably involves accessing stored semantic information, which depends on the set relations and sizes of the categories. By observing the effects of those factors on reaction time, it was therefore possible to determine whether the same retrieval operations were executed for both the affirmatives and negatives.

Principal findings. Table 14.2 summarizes the mean reaction times of correct responses in the experiment (Meyer, 1973).

Table 14.2. Mean reaction times of correct responses for particular affirmatives (PA) and universal negatives (UN). (From Meyer, D. E. in *Attention and Performance IV*, edited by S. Kornblum. New York: Academic Press, 1973, p. 388, with permission.)

Set relation	S-size	P-size	Mean reaction time (msec)	
			PA	UN
Subset	Small	Constant	1088	1326
	Large		1012	1194
Superset	Small	Constant	973	1173
	Large		1109	1350
Overlap	Small	Constant	1080	1364
	Large		1086	1343
Disjoint	Small	Constant	1160	1302
	Large		1177	1380
Subset	Constant	Small	953	1170
		Large	1084	1332
Superset	Constant	Small	1097	1389
		Large	998	1254
Overlap	Constant	Small	1127	1384
		Large	1094	1367
Disjoint	Constant	Small	1150	1314
		Large	1205	1386

There was a reliable effect of set relation. For example, significantly slower responses to particular affirmatives occurred when the subject and predicate categories partially overlapped than when the subject category was a subset of the predicate category; it took over 60 msec longer on the average to verify a proposition like SOME DOCTORS ARE MALES than to verify a proposition like SOME HOTELS ARE BUILDINGS. Reliable effects of category size also occurred. For example, when the subject category was a subset of the predicate category, increasing the size of the predicate category significantly increased reaction times for particular affirmatives; it took about 130 msec longer to verify a proposition like SOME HOTELS ARE STRUCTURES than to verify a proposition like SOME HOTELS ARE BUILDINGS. The effects of set relation and category size on reaction times for universal negatives were qualitatively similar to their effects on reaction times for particular affirmatives. The results therefore suggest that similar retrieval operations were used in comprehending the two types of proposition.

However, responses to the universal negatives were over 200 msec slower on the average than responses to the particular affirmatives. Furthermore, the set-relation and category-size effects were magnified quantitatively for the universal negatives compared to the particular affirmatives. For example, when the subject category was a superset of the predicate category, increasing the size of the subject category increased reaction time more for universal negatives than for particular affirmatives; a proposition like NO SOLIDS ARE GRANITE took 177 msec longer to judge than a proposition like NO ROCKS ARE GRANITE, whereas the effect of category size was 136 msec for the corresponding particular affirmatives.

These results imply that negation reduces the rate at which retrieval operations are executed in comprehending quantified propositions. One simple way of characterizing the reduction is to assume that the operations are performed serially (Sternberg, 1969), and that the number of operations completed depends on set relation and category size. For example, let us suppose that varying category size increases the number of operations from n to $n + \Delta n$, while negation increases the duration of each operation from r msec to $r + \Delta r$ msec. Then slower responses would occur for universal negatives than for particular affirmatives, and the effect of category size on reaction time would be $(r + \Delta r) \cdot \Delta n$ msec for negatives, compared to only $r \cdot \Delta n$ msec for affirmatives (*cf.* Meyer, 1973).

Further Research on Negation and Memory Retrieval

To elaborate the general argument, a new experiment will be reported here. It employs two additional types of quantified proposition about familiar semantic categories. The first type involves *universal affirmatives* (UA) of the form ALL S ARE P, e.g. ALL HOTELS ARE BUILDINGS, which have also been studied previously by Meyer (1970). The second type involves *particular negatives* (PN) of the form SOME S AREN'T P, e.g. SOME FLUIDS AREN'T WINES. Some examples of such propositions are shown in Table 14.3.

Table 14.3. Examples of universal affirmatives (UA) and particular negatives (PN) with varying set relations and sizes of the subject (S) and predicate (P) categories. (Adapted from Meyer, D. E. in *Attention and Performance IV*, edited by S. Kornblum. New York: Academic Press, 1973, p. 385, with permission.)

Set relation	S-size	P-size	Universal affirmatives	UA truth value	Particular negatives	PN truth value
Subset	Small	Constant	ALL THRONES ARE FURNITURE	True	SOME THRONES AREN'T FURNITURE	False
	Large		ALL CHAIRS ARE FURNITURE		SOME CHAIRS AREN'T FURNITURE	
Superset	Small	Constant	ALL ROCKS ARE GRANITE	False	SOME ROCKS AREN'T GRANITE	True
	Large		ALL SOLIDS ARE GRANITE		SOME SOLIDS AREN'T GRANITE	
Overlap	Small	Constant	ALL DOCTORS ARE MALES	False	SOME DOCTORS AREN'T MALES	True
	Large		ALL PERSONS ARE MALES		SOME PERSONS AREN'T MALES	
Disjoint	Small	Constant	ALL TROUSERS ARE BRIDGES	False	SOME TROUSERS AREN'T BRIDGES	True
	Large		ALL GARMENTS ARE BRIDGES		SOME GARMENTS AREN'T BRIDGES	
Subset	Constant	Small	ALL HOTELS ARE BUILDINGS	True	SOME HOTELS AREN'T BUILDINGS	False
		Large	ALL HOTELS ARE STRUCTURES		SOME HOTELS AREN'T STRUCTURES	
Superset	Constant	Small	ALL FLUIDS ARE WINES	False	SOME FLUIDS AREN'T WINES	True
		Large	ALL FLUIDS ARE DRINKS		SOME FLUIDS AREN'T DRINKS	
Overlap	Constant	Small	ALL PETS ARE DUCKS	False	SOME PETS AREN'T DUCKS	True
		Large	ALL PETS ARE BIRDS		SOME PETS AREN'T BIRDS	
Disjoint	Constant	Small	ALL ELMS ARE STEELS	False	SOME ELMS AREN'T STEELS	True
		Large	ALL ELMS ARE METALS		SOME ELMS AREN'T METALS	

As in the other types of proposition considered before, the subject and predicate categories of universal affirmatives and particular negatives may have various set relations and sizes. But the truth values of the new propositions do not depend simply on whether the categories intersect. By definition, universal affirmatives are true only if the subject category is a subset of the predicate category; they are false whenever there is a superset, overlap, or disjoint relation between the categories. In contrast, particular negatives are true for the superset, overlap, and disjoint relations; a particular negative is false only if the subject category is a subset of the predicate category. Universal affirmatives and particular negatives therefore have truth values exactly opposite to each other, so that the one type of proposition completely negates the other, just as particular affirmatives and universal negatives (Table 14.1) are opposites of each other.

The major question now is whether negation influences retrieval operations beyond those studied already. While universal affirmatives and particular negatives have different truth values, they both require accessing stored information to decide if the subject category is a subset of the predicate category. Thus, it is logically possible to evaluate them through similar operations. However, negation could reduce the rate of processing as observed previously (Meyer, 1973). The present study investigates these possibilities by measuring how long people take to judge the two new types of proposition as a function of set relation and category size.

The Experiment

Method

Subjects. Twelve employees of Bell Laboratories served as subjects. They were divided randomly into two groups of six people each.

Apparatus. The experiment was controlled by a digital computer with a millisecond timer connected to a display oscilloscope and a response panel having finger keys for both hands.

Procedure. Each subject was tested individually for two 1-h sessions. During the first session, subjects in one group judged the truth of universal affirmatives, and subjects in the other group judged the truth of particular negatives. The tasks of the two groups were interchanged for the second session.

Three practice blocks and six test blocks of 24 trials were completed in each session. On every trial, the subject first viewed a visual ready signal. It was formed from a sentence frame for the proposition to be judged, i.e. ALL ____ ARE ____, or SOME ____ AREN'T ____. The display was similar to the one described by Meyer (1970, Experiment I). Next the subject initiated a 1-sec foreperiod by pressing a footswitch. Immediately after the foreperiod, the blanks in the sentence frame were filled with the names of two semantic categories. Then the subject read the proposition and decided whether it was true or false. He pressed a key with the right index finger to respond 'true' or another key with the left index finger to respond 'false'. Reaction time was measured from the presentation of the full proposition to the keypress. The subject was instructed to answer quickly and accurately. After each trial, he received feedback about the speed and accuracy of his response. A 2-sec interval separated one trial from the next. In addition, there was a rest interval of 2 min between trial blocks. During that period, the subject was informed about his mean reaction time and total number of errors for the just-completed block. The propositions occurred in random order on each trial block, and half of them were true.

Stimuli. The category names were selected from a variety of sources (e.g. Battig and Montague, 1969; Cohen, Bousfield, and Whitmarsh, 1957; Riegel 1965; *Roget's International Thesaurus*, 1946; *Webster's Third New International Dictionary*, 1964). They were identical to those employed by Meyer (1973). The names were used to construct a total stimulus set for the test block including 432 test and 24 filler universal-affirmatives, plus 432 test and 24 filler particular-negatives. Some examples of the test propositions are shown in Table 14.3. The filler propositions were included to equate the probabilities of 'true' and 'false' responses. From the total stimulus set, each subject was assigned 120 test universal-affirmatives, 120 test particular-negatives, and all of the filler propositions. A separate set of representative propositions was displayed during the three practice blocks.

The set relations and sizes of the categories varied in the following way (*cf* Meyer, 1970, Experiment I). In half of the propositions presented to a subject including all of the filler propositions, the subject category was a subset of the predicate category; the other three possible set relations (superset, overlap and disjoint) were represented with equal frequencies in the remaining half of the propositions. For each set relation, the propositions belonged to pairs whose members differed with respect to category size. In half of the pairs, the size of the subject category was either 'small' or 'large', while the predicate category was constant; in the other half, the size of the predicate categories was either 'small' or 'large', while the subject category was constant. To produce the variation of category size, 'nested' categories were employed (Landauer and Freedman, 1968; Meyer, 1970). The names of categories used for the different set relations and levels of category size were matched approximately in word frequency (Thorndike and Lorge, 1944) and length.

While there was some overlap in the assignments of stimuli to subjects, each subject did not classify every test proposition. However, a given subject did see the same categories in corresponding universal affirmatives and particular negatives. If he judged a proposition containing the smaller member of a nested category pair, then he also judged the proposition containing the large member.

Results

The principal data are the mean reaction times of correct true-false responses to the universal affirmatives and particular negatives that served as test propositions. These are shown separately in Table 14.4 for each type of proposition, set relation, and category size averaged over individual subjects and stimuli. Data from responses to the filler propositions have been omitted. Approximately 13 per cent of the responses to universal affirmatives and 14 per cent of the responses to particular negatives were incorrect. For each type of proposition, the relative frequencies of incorrect responses correlated positively with mean reaction times over the different set relations and category sizes.

Table 14.4. Mean reaction times of correct responses for universal affirmatives (UA) and particular negatives (PN)

Set relation	S-size	P-size	Mean reaction time (msec) UA	PN	Test of size-effect $F(1, 10)$
Subset	Small	Constant	1309	1845	30·1*
	Large		1200	1715	
Superset	Small	Constant	1338	1838	<1·0
	Large		1386	1732	
Overlap	Small	Constant	1268	1710	<1·0
	Large		1296	1700	
Disjoint	Small	Constant	1206	1601	1·3
	Large		1242	1630	
Subset	Constant	Small	1189	1830	<1·0
		Large	1265	1780	
Superset	Constant	Small	1364	1785	17·1*
		Large	1516	2065	
Overlap	Constant	Small	1319	1711	<1·0
		Large	1330	1778	
Disjoint	Constant	Small	1223	1582	15·8*
		Large	1302	1743	

* $P < 0·01$.

A treatments-by-subjects analysis of variance (Winer, 1971) was performed on the reaction-time data. Because of the way that stimuli were assigned to subjects, both treatment-by-subject and treatment-by-stimulus interactions contributed to the standard deviations of reaction-time differences and to the error variances of statistical tests reported below (*cf*. Clark, 1973). The analysis therefore provides some indication about the reliability of the results over both the subject and stimulus populations.

Effects of negation. Responses took more than 400 msec longer on the average when particular negatives were classified than when universal affirmatives were classified. As Table 14.4 indicates, mean reaction times were greater for particular negatives regardless of the set relation and sizes of the categories in them ($P < 0.001$ by a sign test).

Effects of set relation. Figure 14.1 summarizes mean reaction times for the disjoint, overlap, and super-set relations averaged over category size. The data from universal affirmatives and particular negatives are shown separately. As in earlier work (Meyer, 1970, Experiment I), a large effect of set relation

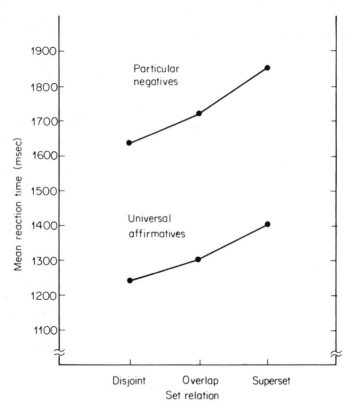

Figure 14.1. Mean reaction times of correct responses as a function of proposition type and set relation

occurred for the universal affirmatives. A qualitatively similar effect was obtained in the present experiment for particular negatives. The main effect of set relation was reliable at the 0.01 level; $F(2,20) = 38.9$. The mean difference plus-or-minus one standard deviation between reaction times for the disjoint and superset relations was 187 ± 26 msec. Set relation and negation did not interact reliably overall. However, the set-relation effect was somewhat larger for the negative propositions, as found previously (Meyer, 1973). For example, the difference in reaction times for the disjoint relation versus the superset relation increased from 158 msec to 216 msec when negatives were classified instead of affirmatives; $t(10) = 1\cdot53$, $0\cdot05 < P < 0\cdot10$ (one tail). Corresponding results for the subset relation will be considered later.

Effects of category size. Tests of the overall category-size effects are summarized by F-ratios in the right column of Table 14.4. Reliable effects were obtained in three cases: when the subject and predicate categories were disjoint, increasing the size of the predicate category increased reaction time by an average of 120 ± 30 msec; when the subject category was a superset of the predicate category, increasing the size of the predicate category increased reaction time by an average of 216 ± 52 msec; and when the subject category was a subset of the predicate category, increasing the size of the subject category decreased reaction time by 120 ± 22 msec. The category-size effects for universal affirmatives were similar in most respects to those obtained previously (Meyer, 1970).

Two of the interactions between category size and negation were at least marginally reliable. When the subject category was a subset of the predicate category, increasing the size of the predicate category increased reaction time for universal affirmatives, but decreased it for particular negatives; the size of the interaction was 126 ± 39 msec, $F(1,10) = 10\cdot5$, $P < 0\cdot01$. Similarly, when the subject category was a superset of the predicate category, increasing the size of the subject category increased reaction time for universal affirmatives, but decreased it for particular negatives; the size of the interaction was 154 ± 78 msec, $F(1,10) = 3\cdot9$, $P < 0\cdot10$.

Two other interactions between category size and negation were relatively large, but not reliable ($P > 0\cdot10$). When the subject category was a superset of the predicate category, the effect of increasing the size of the predicate category was 128 ± 99 msec greater for negatives than for affirmatives; $F(1,10) = 1\cdot68$. Likewise when the subject and predicate categories were disjoint, the effect of increasing the size of the predicate category was 82 ± 71 msec greater for negatives than for affirmatives; $F(1,10) = 1\cdot35$.

Effect of truth value. Table 14.5 compares mean reaction times for the disjoint and subset relations as a function of proposition type. These data

Table 14.5. Mean reaction times of correct responses for the subset and disjoint relations

Set relation	Mean reaction time (msec)	
	UA	PN
Subset	1241	1793
Disjoint	1243	1639

provide a way to measure the main effects of truth value unconfounded with the main effects of set relation and negation. Responses were 78 ± 23 msec faster for true propositions (subset–UA and disjoint–PN) than for false propositions (disjoint–UA and subset–PN); $F(1, 10) = 11.9$, $P < 0.01$. As in previous research, the results suggest that subjects were biased toward making 'true' rather than 'false' responses (Clark and Chase, 1972; Meyer, 1973; Trabasso et al., 1971).

Averaged over true and false propositions, the data in Table 14.5 also supplement the main effects of negation and set relation mentioned above. In particular, the subset relation took 76 ± 28 msec longer than the disjoint relation; $F(1, 10) = 7.3$, $P < 0.05$.

Discussion

Three assumptions may be used to interpret the present results (Meyer, 1973). The first assumption is that set relation and category size influence retrieval operations in comprehending quantified propositions. The second assumption is that the magnitudes of the effects vary inversely with the speed of the operations. Finally, the third assumption is that different retrieval operations lead to different set–relation and category-size effects on reaction time.

With these assumptions, some of the results indicate that universal affirmatives and particular negatives are processed through the same retrieval operations. The effects of set relation (Figure 14.1) were qualitatively similar for the two types of proposition. Similar category-size effects (Table 14.4) also occurred in a number of cases for negatives and affirmatives.

However, some other aspects of the data imply that negation may have influenced the retrieval process. Two comparisons of the category-size effects for universal affirmatives versus particular negatives produced at least marginally significant interactions (i.e., subset relation with P-size varied, and superset relation with S-size varied). Several other comparisons in Table 14.4 produced quantitatively larger category-size effects for the negatives than for the affirmatives. Although not reliably greater, the overall effect of set relation in Figure 14.1 was also about 37 per cent larger for negatives than for affirmatives. These latter findings are reminiscent of previous results obtained for other types of proposition (Meyer, 1973). They could have been caused by negation reducing the rate at which retrieval operations were executed here.

A Two-Stage Retrieval Model

To help interpret the present results further, an explicit retrieval model will be introduced. The model extends a theory formulated earlier to describe the processing of universal affirmatives and particular affirmatives (Meyer, 1970). This is necessary because previous findings indicate that quantified propositions may sometimes require more than one retrieval stage to be evaluated. The model provides a way of separating the effects of negation on various operations.

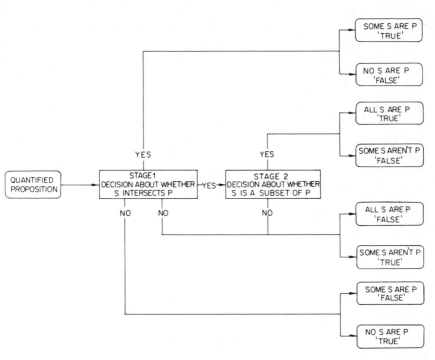

Figure 14.2. A two-stage retrieval model for verifying quantified propositions about familiar semantic categories. (Adapted from Meyer, D. E., *Cognitive Psychology*, 1970, **1**, 242–299, with permission.)

According to the model, quantified propositions about semantic categories are processed in two distinct stages of retrieval, as shown by Figure 14.2. The first stage decides whether or not the subject category of a proposition intersects the predicate category; it has a positive outcome when there is a subset, superset, or overlap relation. The second stage decides whether the subject category is a subset of the predicate category, given that the categories intersect.

Depending on the outcome of the first stage, and on the type of proposition, the process may terminate without the second stage being executed. If Stage 1 has a positive outcome, then particular affirmatives (SOME S ARE P) are classified immediately as 'true', while universal negatives (NO S ARE P) are classified as 'false'. In contrast, if Stage 1 has a negative outcome, then both particular affirmatives and universal affirmatives (ALL S ARE P) are classified as 'false', while universal negatives and particular negatives (SOME S AREN'T P) are classified as 'true'.

However, Stage 2 is executed when Stage 1 has a positive outcome and the proposition is either a universal affirmative or a particular negative. If Stage 2 has a positive outcome, then a universal affirmative is classified as 'true' and a particular negative as 'false'; otherwise, the responses are 'false' and 'true', respectively.

Corresponding to the sequence of stages in Figure 14.2, reaction times are represented as sums of several components (Sternberg, 1969; Meyer, 1970 1973): these components include T_e, the duration of a prerequisite 'encoding stage (not shown in Figure 14.1); T_1, the duration of the first retrieval stage; T_2 the duration of the second retrieval stage; and T_t or T_f, the durations of executing a 'true' or 'false' response, respectively. The expected reaction times for each type of proposition are shown in Table 14.6 as a function of set relation. Presumably T_1 and T_2 may vary with set relation, catefory size, and negation. For the present, however, it is assumed that T_e, T_t, and T_f do not depend on those factors. The validity of this assumption will be considered later.

Table 14.6. Reaction times predicted by the two-stage retrieval model as a function of proposition type and set relation

	Proposition type			
Set relation	Particular affirmative	Universal negative	Universal affirmative	Particular negative
Subset	$T_e + T_1 + T_t$	$T_e + T_1 + T_f$	$T_e + T_1 + T_2 + T_t$	$T_e + T_1 + T_2 + T_f$
Superset	$T_e + T_1 + T_t$	$T_e + T_1 + T_f$	$T_e + T_1 + T_2 + T_f$	$T_e + T_1 + T_2 + T_t$
Overlap	$T_e + T_1 + T_t$	$T_e + T_1 + T_f$	$T_e + T_1 + T_2 + T_f$	$T_e + T_1 + T_2 + T_t$
Disjoint	$T_e + T_1 + T_f$	$T_e + T_1 + T_t$	$T_e + T_1 + T_f$	$T_e + T_1 + T_t$

T_e = duration of prerequisite encoding stage.
T_1 = duration of first retrieval stage.
T_2 = duration of second retrieval stage.
T_t = duration of executing a 'true' response.
T_f = duration of executing a 'false' response.

Mechanism in Stage 1. The model further assumes that the first stage of retrieval involves a *predicate–intersections search process* (Meyer, 1970) During the search, long-term memory is accessed for the names of other categories that intersect the predicate category, including its subsets, supersets and partially overlapping sets; i.e. if the predicate category is one like GEMS then stored names like RUBIES, STONES, and GIFTS are retrieved. As these words become available, they are compared with the name of the subject category. When a match occurs, Stage 1 terminates with a positive decision otherwise, following an exhaustive search without any match, there is a negative decision.

Mechanism in Stage 2. In contrast, the second retrieval stage relies on an *attribute-search process* (Meyer, 1970). Here defining attributes of the predicate category are accessed and compared to the defining attributes of the subject category. If each attribute of the predicate category is found to match some attribute of the subject category, then Stage 2 terminates with a positive decision; otherwise, if some attribute of the predicate category matches no attribute of the subject category, then there is a negative decision.

Applications of the Model

Although some doubts may be raised about certain aspects of the two-stage Model (e.g., Smith *et al.*, 1974), the model accounts for many of the present findings along with previous results. Because universal affirmatives and particular negatives both involve the same retrieval stages, this explains why the effects of set relation and category size for negatives were similar to the effects for affirmatives (Table 14.4). It also explains why the effects of those factors were similar for particular affirmatives compared to universal negatives (Table 14.2; Meyer, 1973).

The model makes a specific prediction about the effects of set relation on reaction times (Meyer, 1970). Responses to universal affirmatives and particular negatives should be slower when the subject and predicate categories intersect than when they are disjoint. This is because intersecting categories require both retrieval stages for those propositions, whereas disjoint categories require only Stage 1 (Figure 14.2). Results from the present experiment support the prediction (Figure 14.1).

The model also makes a number of specific predictions about how increasing category size changes the durations of Stages 1 and 2 for each type of proposition (Meyer, 1970). These predictions are shown in Table 14.7 as a

Table 14.7. Predicted effects of increasing category size on durations in the two-stage model

Set relation	Variable increased	Change in duration[a]	
		Stage 1	Stage 2
Subset	S-size	Decrease	None
	P-size	Increase	Decrease
Superset	S-size	Increase	Decrease
	P-size	Decrease	Increase
Overlap	S-size	?	?
	P-size	?	?
Disjoint	S-size	None	
	P-size	Increase	

[a] Question marks denote cases where the two-stage model does not make any predictions. Blanks denote cases where Stage 2 is never executed.

function of set relation and category-size increase. For example, the model predicts that when the subject and predicate categories are disjoint, increasing the size of the predicate category increases T_1; i.e. Stage 1 takes longer for a proposition like ALL ELMS ARE METALS than for a proposition like ALL ELMS ARE STEELS. The reason is that larger categories intersect more categories, so that increasing the size of the predicate category increases the number of stored names that must be accessed and compared before Stage 1 terminates with a negative decision. On the other hand, when the subject category is a subset of the predicate category, increasing the size of the predicate category decreases T_2; i.e. Stage 2 is shorter for a proposition like ALL HOTELS ARE STRUCTURES than for a proposition like ALL HOTELS ARE BUILDINGS. This is because larger (more abstract) categories have fewer defining attributes, so that increasing the size of the predicate category decreases the number of attributes that must be accessed and compared before Stage 2 terminates with a positive decision. However, in certain cases, category size should have no effect (null entries in Table 14.7), or the expected effects may be indeterminate (question entries in Table 14.7). For a more complete discussion of the reasoning, see Meyer (1970).

Because universal affirmatives and particular negatives involve both retrieval stages, some of these category-size predictions cannot be related directly to the present results. For example, suppose that the subject category is a subset of the predicate category, and the size of the predicate category increases. Then it is not clear whether reaction time should increase or decrease. The reason is that increasing category size here increases the duration of Stage 1 and decreases the duration of Stage 2. Depending on which change is greater, reaction time could go either way.

However, there are certain cases for which the expected category-size effects on the two stages do not conflict (Table 14.7). When the subject and predicate categories are disjoint, increasing the size of the subject category influences neither stage, so that reaction time should remain constant. In contrast, increasing the size of the predicate category increases T_1 without influencing T_2 when the categories are disjoint, so that reaction time should increase. Furthermore, when the subject category is a subset of the predicate category, increasing the size of the subject category decreases T_1 without influencing T_2, so that reaction time should decrease.

In each case, results from the present experiment support these predictions for both universal affirmatives and particular negatives (Table 14.4). The predictions concerning Stage 1 are also consistent with previously observed reaction times for particular affirmatives and universal negatives (Table 14.2; Meyer, 1973), which presumably omitted Stage 2. Another experiment (Meyer, 1970) that used analytic techniques to estimate the duration of Stage 2 substantiates the category-size effects expected for it.

Influence of Negation on Stages 1 and 2

In terms of the two-stage retrieval model, the previous experiment with particular affirmatives (SOME S ARE P) and universal negatives (NO S ARE P) allows conclusions about the influence of negation on Stage 1 (Meyer, 1973). The data suggest that Stage 1 was used to evaluate both types of proposition. But the negatives were comprehended more slowly, while the effects of set relation and category size were magnified for them. As argued earlier (see Introduction), this may have happened because negation reduces the rate of operations performed in Stage 1. For example, when the subject and predicate categories are disjoint, increasing the size of the predicate category increases the number of operations required during the predicate-intersections search process of Stage 1 (Table 14.7). If the extra number of operations is Δn, and if negation increases the duration of each operation by Δr msec, then negation could increase the category-size effect on reaction time by as much as $\Delta r \cdot \Delta n$ msec (Meyer, 1973).

Supplementing the results concerning Stage 1, the present experiment with universal affirmatives and particular negatives permits some inferences about the influence of negation on Stage 2. Such inferences are not possible from reaction times for these two types of proposition alone, because they combine both retrieval stages. However, assuming that the two-stage model is correct, it is possible to estimate the duration of Stage 2 through a *subtraction method* (Sternberg, 1969; Meyer, 1970).

Estimated duration of Stage 2. The subtraction method involves two separate computations, one for affirmative propositions and one for negative propositions. First, reaction times obtained previously for particular affirmatives (Table 14.2; Meyer, 1973) are subtracted from present reaction times for universal affirmatives (Table 4); when the subject and predicate categories intersect, this yields the approximate value of T_2 for universal affirmatives, because the reaction times differ principally in that component (Table 14.6). Second, reaction times obtained previously for universal negatives (Table 14.2; Meyer, 1973) are subtracted from present reaction times for particular negatives (Table 14.4); when the subject and predicate categories intersect, this yields the approximate value of T_2 for particular negatives. The results are shown in Table 14.8 as a function of proposition type, set relation, and category size.

Several points should be noticed about these data. First, the estimates of T_2 are all considerably greater than zero. This is because responses to particular affirmatives and universal negatives (Meyer, 1973) were faster than responses to corresponding universal affirmatives and particular negatives, supporting the conclusion that the latter propositions required two retrieval stages, whereas the former propositions required only one stage (*cf.* Meyer, 1970). For example, when the subject category was a subset of the predicate category, Stage 2 took 207 ± 95 msec on the average for universal affirmatives $[t(20) = 2 \cdot 18, \quad P < 0 \cdot 05]$ and 537 ± 139 msec for particular negatives $[t(20) = 3 \cdot 86, P < 0 \cdot 01]$. Second, the estimates of T_2 are uniformly greater for particular negatives than for universal affirmatives ($P < 0 \cdot 001$ by a sign test). This suggests that negation slows Stage 2 just as it slows Stage 1 (Meyer, 1973).

Table 14.8 also reveals some reliable effects of category size on Stage 2, exactly as predicted by the attribute-search process (Table 14.7). For example, when the subject category was a subset of the predicate category, increasing the size of the predicate category decreased T_2 by 134 ± 44 msec on the average; $t(20) = 3 \cdot 02$, $P < 0 \cdot 01$ (one tail). Wherever category size affected T_2

Table 14.8. Estimated durations of Stage 2 for universal affirmatives (UA) and particular negatives (PN)

Set relation	S-size	P-size	Duration of Stage 2 (msec) UA	PN	Test of size-effect $t(20)$
Subset	Small	Constant	221	519	0·51
	Large		188	521	
Superset	Small	Constant	365	665	3·83*
	Large		277	382	
Overlap	Small	Constant	188	346	0·32
	Large		210	357	
Subset	Constant	Small	236	660	3·02*
		Large	181	448	
Superset	Constant	Small	267	396	5·40*
		Large	518	811	
Overlap	Constant	Small	192	327	0·97
		Large	236	411	

* $P < 0.01$ (one tail).

significantly, the magnitude of the effect was larger for particular negatives than for universal affirmatives. This fact is illustrated more clearly in Table 14.9, which shows the category-size effects on Stage 2 derived from Table 14.8 for each type of proposition. For example, when the subject category was a subset of the predicate category, increasing the size of the predicate category decreased T_2 by 212 msec for particular negatives, but only 55 msec for universal affirmatives; this difference in the category-size effect as a function of negation was significant at the 0·005 level (one tail), $t(20) = 2·92$. An at least marginally significant ($P < 0·10$, one tail) category-size by negation interaction

Table 14.9. Observed effects of increasing category size on the duration of Stage 2

Set relation	Variable increased	Effect on Stage 2 (msec) UA	PN	Negation × size interaction $t(20)$
Subset	S-size	−33	2	0·54
	P-size	−55	−212	2·92***
Superset	S-size	−88	−283	2·14**
	P-size	251	415	1·48*
Overlap	S-size	22	11	0·15
	P-size	44	84	0·51

* $P < 0·10$ (one tail),   ** $P < 0·05$ (one tail),   *** $P < 0·01$ (one tail).

failed to occur only where no main effect of category size on Stage 2 was predicted (Table 14.7) or obtained (Table 14.8, i.e. subset relation with S-size varied, and overlap relation with S-size or P-size varied).

Implications. These last results support the hypothesis that negation reduces the rate of the attribute-search process performed in Stage 2. According to the rate-reduction hypothesis, negation and category size should interact only if there is a reliable main effect of category size. The reason is that an interaction supposedly occurs because negation increases the duration of extra operations required by a change in category size. Since the interaction is 'multiplicative', it cannot occur without the presence of an overall category-size effect. But whenever there are significant size effects, the rate-reduction hypothesis implies that negation should magnify them. This is exactly what happened in the experiment. The present results for Stage 2 are analogous to those obtained previously for Stage 1 (Meyer, 1973).

Possible artifacts. At the same time, one may question whether the subtraction method employed here is valid. Technically, the method relies on a *pure-insertion assumption* (Sternberg, 1969; Meyer, 1970), which presumes that adding Stage 2 to the sequence of operations does not alter the durations of other stages. If the assumption fails to hold, then the method could produce biased estimates of T_2 for universal affirmatives and/or particular negatives.

Some previous experiments support the pure-insertion assumption (Meyer, 1970). One test of it was based on comparing reaction times for universal and particular affirmatives containing disjoint categories. Under such circumstances, the two-stage model predicts that responses should be equally fast for the two types of proposition, since they both supposedly require only Stage 1 when the subject and predicate categories are disjoint (Figure 14.2). The data confirmed this prediction, indicating that Stage 1 was not altered by the possibility of having to execute Stage 2 as well.

The pure-insertion assumption is also consistent with certain aspects of the present data. As before, the difference between reaction times for universal and particular affirmatives (70 ± 96 msec; Table 14.2 and 14.4) did not reach a significant level when the subject and predicate categories were disjoint; $t(20) = 0.73, P > 0.10$. Indeed, with analytic techniques like ones discussed by Clark and Chase (1972), which allow for response-bias effects, it can be argued that the mean duration of Stage 1 was only about 30 msec different for universal and particular affirmatives. Again this suggests that Stage 1 is not altered substantially by the possibility of having to execute Stage 2.

However, some other aspects of the data indicate that the pure-insertion assumption is not strictly satisfied. The problem of response bias (Clark and Chase, 1972; Meyer, 1973; Trabasso *et al.*, 1971) cannot be avoided completely. In the present experiment with universal affirmatives and particular negatives, 'false' responses were approximately 64 msec slower than 'true' responses (Table 14.4); on the other hand, 'false' responses were only about

37 msec slower than 'true' responses in the previous experiment with particular affirmatives and universal negatives (Table 14.2; Meyer, 1973). This suggests that inserting Stage 2 may have altered subjects' bias toward 'true' responses.

A second problem is that slower responses occurred for particular negatives (Table 14.4) containing disjoint categories than for corresponding universal negatives (Table 14.2). The difference was 294 ± 153 msec; $t(20) = 1.92$, $0.05 < P < 0.10$. According to the two-stage model, reaction times should have been equal under those circumstances, because both types of proposition were evaluated through Stage 1 alone (Figure 14.2). The discrepancy may have happened for various reasons. For example, negation could slow Stage 1 more when Stage 2 may also have to be executed. Likewise it could take longer to encode the particular negatives than to encode the universal negatives before retrieval begins (Clark and Chase, 1972). This may happen because particular negatives contain both a quantifier (SOME) and a 'negative particle' (NOT) in their surface structure, whereas universal negatives combine the quantifier and negative particle into one word (NO).

Regardless of their source, these possible violations of the pure-insertion assumption cannot account entirely for the negation effect on Stage 2 (Tables 14.8 and 14.9). If the negation slowed Stage 1 more for particular negatives than for universal negatives, then this would partly explain why larger estimates of T_2 were obtained for negatives than for affirmatives (Table 14.8). But a differential bias favouring 'true' responses would actually deflate the estimates of T_2 for particular negatives in certain cases (i.e., when there is an overlap or superset relation). The reason is that those estimates are obtained by subtracting 'false' reaction times from 'true' reaction times. Moreover, neither response bias nor a stronger influence of negation on Stage 1 would explain why negation magnifies the estimated category-size effects on Stage 2 (Table 14.9). In fact, if negation slowed Stage 1 more for particular negatives than for universal negatives, then it could even attenuate the interaction between category size and negation observed for Stage 2. This is because category size sometimes has opposite effects on the two stages (Table 14.7). Thus, it is still reasonable to entertain the conclusion that negation slows retrieval operations in Stage 2 as well as Stage 1.

Explanation of the Negation Effect on Retrieval

How could sentence negation influence retrieval from long-term memory? One possible answer follows from the theory of negation formulated by Clark and Chase (1972) and by Trabasso et al. (1971). In verifying certain types of sentence, they assume that an abstract 'deep structure' representation of the sentence is formed during encoding (cf. Chomsky, 1957). This representation must be stored temporarily in short-term memory while further information about the referents of the sentence is retrieved from long-term memory (Meyer, 1973). The accessed information, which corresponds to the output of the two-stage retrieval model (Figure 14.2), is then compared with the abstract sentence representation to determine a response. (For a more detailed description of the theory, see Meyer, 1973.)

Now suppose that the underlying representation of a negative sentence is more complex than the representation of an affirmative sentence (cf. Clark and Chase, 1972; Gough, 1965; McMahon, 1963). Then, as mentioned elsewhere (Meyer, 1973), a negative sentence may require more processing capacity to be maintained in short-term memory. Less capacity would therefore be available for searching long-term memory at the same time, and so the rate of retrieval would be reduced for referents of a negative sentence compared to referents of an affirmative sentence. The situation is analogous to time-sharing on a digital computer. When more cycles must be 'stolen' to perform one operation, it takes longer to complete other operations performed concurrently.

Applied to the present findings, these notions explain why negation retards Stage 2 as well as Stage 1 of the two-stage retrieval model. The representation of a proposition has to be maintained in short-term memory until all of the relevant retrieval stages are completed. Thus, whenever Stage 2 is required together with Stage 1, both stages take longer for particular negatives than for universal affirmatives. Since the effects of set relation and category size result from changing the number of component operations executed in each stage, those effects are magnified when the rate of the operations is reduced (Meyer, 1973).

Relations to Other Research

Similar explanations of the present findings could also be developed in terms of other multi-stage retrieval theories related to the two-stage model (e.g., Collins and Quillian, 1969; Smith et al., 1974). In addition, there are some other experiments employing different procedures that complement the interpretation.

One relevant study is an investigation of short-term memory by Howard (1973). In his task, subjects memorized a brief list of digits and then classified a test numeral. Two conditions were included. When a plus sign appeared with the test numeral, subjects had to respond 'yes' if the numeral was a member of the memorized list, and 'no' otherwise (cf. Sternberg, 1969). However, when a minus sign appeared with the test numeral, subjects had to respond 'no' if the numeral was a member of the memorized list and 'yes' otherwise. Thus, the minus sign 'negated' the test numeral. Reaction-time data indicated that minus signs altered the rate at which subjects searched the memorized list for the test digit. The rate of search was approximately 30 per cent less for test numerals preceded by minus signs than for test numerals preceded by plus signs. Howard's data therefore suggest that negation may slow short-term memory retrieval just as it slows long-term memory retrieval.

Another relevant study is an investigation of sentence-picture comparisons by Krueger (1972). Although it did not focus on memory retrieval *per se*, this work has important implications about the interaction of negation, memory

310

load, and processing capacity. The subjects were required to compare an abbreviated test sentence like IS NORTH or ISN'T EAST with the location of a visually presented circle. They responded 'true' when the sentence correctly described the circle's position, and 'false' otherwise. Besides varying the sentence form (affirmative versus negative), truth value, and circle position, Krueger also manipulated a memory load of digits that the subject had to report after classifying each sentence. The data revealed reliable main effects of sentence form, circle position, and memory load. Slower responses occurred when the circle was displayed on the same visual axis as specified by the test sentence (i.e., north–south or east–west). Both sentence negation and larger memory loads magnified this discriminability effect. Thus, Krueger's results are consistent with the hypothesis that negation and memory load both reduce the amount of processing capacity available to deal with demands imposed by other factors.

Conclusion

In summary, various pieces of evidence have been collected about the influence of negation on memory retrieval. The present research compared reaction times for judging the truth values of four types of quantified proposition concerning familiar semantic categories. Reaction times to verify such propositions depended on the set relations and sizes of the categories in them. The set relation and category-size effects were qualitatively similar in many respects for affirmatives and negatives, suggesting that they are evaluated through similar retrieval operations. However, the effects of set relation and category size tended to be larger for negative propositions, and the negatives took longer to classify. An analysis based on a two-stage retrieval model reveals that negation increased the amounts of time needed both for recognizing that two categories intersect (Stage 1) and for recognizing that one category is a subset of another category (Stage 2). The data support the view that sentence negation reduces the rate at which information is accessed from long-term memory.

Acknowledgements

I thank J. R. Gossman, T. K. Landauer, M. G. Ruddy, K. H. Smith, S. Sternberg, and A. M. Wing for their helpful comments on this work.

References

Anderson, J. R. and Bower, G. H. (1973). *Human Associative Memory*. Washington: Winston.
Battig, W. F., and Montague, W. E. (1969). Category norms for verbal terms in 56 categories: A replication and extension of the Connecticut norms. *Journal of Experimental Psychology Monograph*, **80** (3, Part 2).
Chomsky, N. (1957). *Syntactic Structures*. The Hague: Mouton.

Clark, H. H. (1973). The language-as-fixed-effect fallacy: A critique of language statistics in psychological research. *Journal of Verbal Learning and Verbal Behavior*, **12**, 335–359.

Clark, H. H. and Chase, W. G. (1972). On the process of comparing sentences against pictures. *Cognitive Psychology*, **3**, 472–517.

Cohen, B. H., Bousfield, W. A. and Whitmarsh, G. A. (1957). Cultural norms for verbal items in 43 categories. *Technical Report No. 22*, Department of Psychology, The University of Connecticut.

Collins, A. M. and Quillian, M. R. (1969). Retrieval time from semantic memory. *Journal of Verbal Learning and Verbal Behavior*, **8**, 240–247.

Freedman, J. L. and Loftus, E. F. (1971). Retrieval of words from long-term memory, *Journal of Verbal Learning and Verbal Behavior*, **10**, 107–115.

Gough, P. B. (1965). Grammatical transformations and speed of understanding. *Journal of Verbal Learning and Verbal Behavior*, **4**, 107–111.

Greene, J. M. (1970). The semantic function of negatives and passives. *British Journal of Psychology*, **61**, 17–22.

Howard, J. H. (1973). Information processing demands in a short-term memory task. Unpublished doctoral dissertation, Brown University.

Kintsch, W. (1972). Notes on the structure of semantic memory. In E. Tulving and W. Donaldson (Eds), *Organization of Memory*. New York: Academic Press.

Krueger, L. E. (1972). Sentence-picture comparison: A test of additivity of processing time for feature matching and negation coding. *Journal of Experimental Psychology*, **95**, 275–284.

Landauer, T. K. and Freedman, J. L. (1968). Information retrieval from long-term memory: Category size and recognition time. *Journal of Verbal Learning and Verbal Behavior*, **7**, 291–295.

Landauer, T. K. and Meyer, D. E. (1972). Category size and semantic memory retrieval. *Journal of Verbal Learning and Verbal Behavior*, **11**, 539–549.

McMahon, L. E. (1963). Grammatical analysis as part of understanding a sentence. Unpublished doctoral dissertation, Harvard University.

Meyer, D. E. (1970). On the representation and retrieval of stored semantic information. *Cognitive Psychology*, **1**, 242–299.

Meyer, D. E. (1973). Verifying affirmative and negative propositions: Effects of negation on memory retrieval. In S. Kornblum (Ed.), *Attention and Performance IV*. New York: Academic Press.

Miller, G. A. and McKean, K. (1964). A chronometric study of some relations between sentences. *Quarterly Journal of Experimental Psychology*, **16**, 297–308.

Riegel, K. F. (1965). The Michigan Restricted Association Norms. *Report No. 3*, Department of Psychology, University of Michigan.

Roget's International Thesaurus (1946). New York: Crowell.

Rumelhart, D. E., Lindsay, P. H. and Norman, D. A. (1972). A process model for long-term memory. In E. Tulving and W. Donaldson (Eds.), *Organization of Memory*. New York: Academic Press.

Schaeffer, B. and Wallace, R. (1970). The comparison of word meanings. *Journal of Experimental Psychology*, **86**, 144–152.

Slobin, D. I. (1966). Grammatical transformations and sentence comprehension in childhood and adulthood. *Journal of Verbal Learning and Verbal Behavior*, **5**, 219–227.

Smith, E. E., Shoben, E. J. and Rips, L. J. (1974). Structure and process in semantic memory: A featural model for semantic decisions. *Psychological Review*, **81**, 214–241.

Sternberg, S. (1969). Memory-Scanning: Mental processes revealed by reaction-time experiments. *American Scientist*, **57**, 421–457.

Thorndike, E. L. and Lorge, I. (1944). *The Teacher's Wordbook of 30,000 Words*. New York: Columbia University Press.

Trabasso, T., Rollins, H. and Shaughnessy, E. (1971). Storage and verification stages in processing concepts. *Cognitive Psychology*, **2**, 239–289.

Wales, R. G. and Grieve, R. (1969). What is so difficult about negation? *Perception and Psychophysics*, **6**, 327–332.

Wason, P. C. (1959). The processing of positive and negative information. *Quarterly Journal of Experimental Psychology*, **11**, 92–107.

Wason, P. C. (1961). Response to affirmative and negative binary statements. *British Journal of Psychology*, **52**, 133–142.

Wason, P. C. (1965). The contexts of plausible denial. *Journal of Verbal Learning and Verbal Behavior*, **4**, 7–11.

Webster's Third New International Dictionary (1964). Springfield, Massachusetts: Merriam.

Wilkins, A. (1971). Conjoint frequency, category size, and categorization time. *Journal of Verbal Learning and Verbal Behavior*, **10**, 382–385.

Winer, B. J. (1971). *Statistical Principles in Experimental Design*. New York: McGraw-Hill.

Part V

Pathology

Chapter 15

Lexical Memory: A Linguistic Approach

John C. Marshall, Freda Newcombe and Jane M. Holmes

Introduction

We are concerned in this paper with one aspect of 'Memory Without Record'. The expression is due to Bruner (1969) who uses it to describe experiences which ' . . . are converted into some process that changes the nature of an organism, changes his skills, or changes the rules by which he operates but which are virtually inaccessible in memory as specific encounters'. Encounters with language change the organism in particularly dramatic ways, converting the young *homo alalus* into a mature member of a speech community capable of producing and understanding ' . . . more different statements about grass than there are blades of grass in the world' (Thorndike, 1943). The capacity to comprehend an indefinitely extended number of utterances can, in part, be explicated by referring to the recursive nature of certain grammatical rules and to the large, albeit finite, number of words which are represented in the internal lexicon of all normal adults. Our primary concern here is with the structure of this latter 'component' of a language-user. We seek to understand some basic properties of lexical storage—'memory without record' for a large vocabulary. This task can be regarded as the elucidation of the filing system used by the cerebral librarian. Preserving the metaphor, it is crucial to note that the most important constraint upon the librarian is that his system of lexical storage be maximally useful to the cerebral grammarian. Informative utterances are, typically, longer than one word.

Syntax, Frequency and Word-Retrieval

If the preceding constraint is to be met, one critical faculty the librarian must possess is the ability to distinguish between different parts of speech (i.e., grammatical categories); according to what storage and retrieval strategies does he organize them?

It has often been reported (Elder, 1900; Siegel, 1959; Halpern, 1965; Marshall and Newcombe, 1966) that (many) subjects with acquired dyslexia find it easier to read (individual) concrete nouns than either, for example, adjectives or verbs. This effect is demonstrable when, as in our own and Halpern's studies, letter-length and orthographic frequency are controlled. The data in Table 15.1 are representative of our findings; the figures are the mean number of erroneous (vocal) responses for a group of 10 subjects, nine men and one woman (with a variety of left-hemisphere injuries), attempting to read aloud (with no time pressure) individual high and low frequency (Hf, Lf) concrete nouns, adjectives and verbs (between four and seven letters in length). The maximum possible number of errors in any one cell is ten.

Table 15.1. Mean number of erroneous responses to high and low frequency concrete nouns, adjectives and verbs

N		A		V	
Hf	Lf	Hf	Lf	Hf	Lf
1·6	3·6	3·2	5·2	3·8	5·3

Analysis of variance shows significant main effects of syntactic class ($P < 0.05$) and of word-frequency ($P < 0.01$). There is no significant interaction between these two variables. The Wilcoxon matched-pairs signed ranks test shows that the difference between nouns and adjectives is significant at the $P < 0.025$ level, and between nouns and verbs significant at the $P = 0.01$ level. The difference between adjectives and verbs is not significant. 'Noun facilitation' is thus responsible for the main effect of syntactic class in the analysis of variance.

We have also tested, on the same material and task, a group of 32 normal children, 16 boys and 16 girls, from a school in Southern England. The age range of the children is 10·0 to 11·1 years. The total number of errors per syntactic and frequency class for the children (boys and girls separately) is shown in Table 15.2.

Table 15.2. Total number of errors per syntactic and frequency class for children

	N		A		V	
	Hf	Lf	Hf	Lf	Hf	Lf
Boys:	2	13	3	15	9	40
Girls:	0	10	3	10	3	23
Total:	2	23	6	25	12	63

Analysis of variance shows that the effect of syntax, frequency, and syntax × frequency are all significant ($P < 0.001$). The main effect of sex is not significant, although the interaction of syntax × sex is significant ($P < 0.05$). We interpret these data, as indicating that word-frequency has a more pronounced effect upon the reading of verbs than upon nouns and adjectives. Verbs are the most difficult items for both the boys and the girls, and it is only when reading verbs that the performance of the boys appears to be significantly poorer than that of the girls. (In contradistinction to the data on acquired dyslexia, adjectives seem to resemble nouns, rather than verbs, in terms of their 'difficulty-level').

We have previously shown (Holmes, Marshall and Newcombe, 1971), on the same stimulus material, that similar effects can be obtained from normal adult subjects, using tachistoscopic presentation (ascending method of limits with central presentation). Table 15.3 shows the results, under a new analysis, for tachistoscopic presentation (mean threshold in milliseconds) to a group of 18 Edinburgh University students, nine men and nine women.

Table 15.3. Reading threshold as a function of syntactic class and frequency

	N		A		V	
	Hf	Lf	Hf	Lf	Hf	Lf
Men:	30·4	35·6	28·8	37·5	29·7	49·5
Women:	30·7	34·8	33·9	41·8	32·8	48·2
Mean:	30·6	35·2	31·4	39·7	31·3	48·9

A preliminary analysis with sex as a factor gave no significant main effect of sex and no significant interactions with sex. Accordingly we then treated the 18 subjects as one group. Analysis of variance showed significant main effects of syntax ($P < 0·01$) and of frequency ($P < 0·001$), and a significant syntax × frequency interaction ($P < 0·05$).

Although there are a number of interesting differences between these three studies (which we do not propose to discuss in this paper), the claim that, when differences emerge as a function of syntactic class, then the order of difficulty is Verb > Adjective > Noun, would appear to be substantiated. The observation that a substantial proportion of subjects with acquired dyslexia show significantly better reading of nouns than adjectives or verbs (with the latter two classes being of roughly equivalent difficulty) may be recorded as a reliable datum. Prior to our own results, Siegel (1959) and Halpern (1965) had reported similar effects with n's of 31 and 32 respectively. It is, however, our experience and that of Hécaen and his colleagues (H. Hécaen, personal communication) that the syntax effect does not obtain in *all* subjects with acquired dyslexia; in particular, subjects with 'pure' dyslexia (and injuries which do not encroach beyond occipital cortex) may be exceptions to the pattern. In general, however, studies of word-recognition and retrieval in normal subjects (e.g. Riegel and Riegel, 1961; Roydes and Osgood, 1972) are consistent with the 'noun facilitation' effect which is such a striking aspect of our own data.

We have furthermore confirmed this effect on a new set of words, three-letter concrete nouns and verbs, matched for word-frequency (Holmes and Marshall, unpublished data, 1971). Fourteen normal adult subjects were tested in an ascending method of limits design (with central presentation); the results (mean threshold values) indicated that the nouns were recognized at a significantly lower threshold than the verbs ($P < 0.05$). neither the frequency effect, nor the interaction of syntax × frequency was significant. The absence of an (overall) frequency bias is consistent with earlier observations, using central presentation, that the magnitude of the frequency affect varies directly with word-length; longer words show a more pronounced frequency effect than do shorter words (McGinnies, Comer and Lacey, 1952).

Our three-letter stimuli were then used in a study of recognition in the visual half-fields (left and right visual fields), using a percentage correct measure at a fixed exposure duration (Marshall and Holmes, 1974). The results of this experiment can be interpreted in the following fashion: the left hemisphere (= presentation in the right visual field) is organized to give preferential access to nouns, irrespective to a considerable extent, of frequency considerations; the right hemisphere (= presentation in the left visual field) gives preferential access to high frequency items, irrespective to a considerable extent of part-of-speech classification (Marshall, 1973). *Prima facie*, this result would appear to be incompatable with certain findings that have been reported on split-brain patients (Gazzaniga, 1970). There are, however, methodological problems in the commissurotomy studies; the stimuli appear to be uncontrolled for some parameters known to be relevant to word-recognition thresholds. Furthermore, recent discussion suggests the possibility that 'the mode of operation of the components of the "split brain" may be radically different from that characteristic of the normal "integrated" brain' (Caplan, Holmes and Marshall, 1974).

We have seen, then, that in single word perceptual tasks one cerebral hemisphere appears to give priority to concrete nouns over verbs. Why should this be the case? It could be argued that the concrete–abstract dimension, or the related but not identical parameter of imagery value (Richardson, 1974), is implicated in the effect. That nouns are easier than verbs would thus be interpreted as an artifact of differences in 'concreteness' associated with the two syntactic classes; or alternatively, the 'imagery' associated with concrete nouns is perhaps 'stronger' or more 'vivid' than that characteristic of other parts-of-speech. An explanation along such lines cannot be conclusively ruled out, yet we find the speculation implausible when advanced as the *sole* reason for the noun-facilitation effect.

Words, Images and Things

The usefulness of imagery in traditional recognition and recall tasks (memory *with* record) has been amply documented (see Paivio, this volume). Paivio has furthermore shown that recall is facilitated by dual-coding; there appears to be additivity in recall of imaginal and verbal memory codes. In part, this is no doubt due to the fact that concepts whose visual referents *look* alike do not have vocal representations which *sound* alike. The dimensions of visual and verbal confusibility are orthogonal; dual-coding should therefore serve to keep items apart in memory. It is difficult to see, however, how arguments of this nature could be extended to the type of task with which we have been concerned; indeed Paivio's (1971) two-process model implies that imagery variables should not affect immediate perceptual recognition.

In reading (either normally or under conditions of tachistoscopic presentation) the subject's problem is to recognize an initially unknown stimulus and identify that configuration as a particular (long-term) vocabulary item. Attaching the 'correct' image to CAT presupposes that CAT has been identified and assigned its full semantic specification. It is consistent with this line of argument that tachistoscopic experiments with *normal* subjects have not shown any strong influence of imageability (or concreteness) on recognition thresholds (Riegel and Riegel, 1961; Winnick and Kressel, 1965).

Although we have not controlled for 'imagery' or 'concreteness' variables in our own studies, the words used in Halpern's (1965) investigations of dyslexic reading errors are counterbalanced for (rated) abstraction level and part-of-speech (in addition to the usual matching for word length and frequency of occurrence). Halpern does find a significant main effect of abstraction level, but despite the matching of words on this parameter, his subjects still made a significantly greater number of errors on adjectives and verbs than they did on nouns. Similarly, Siegel's (1959) study of dyslexic reading found a noun facilitation effect in spite of the words (nouns, adjectives and verbs) having been counterbalanced for level of abstraction. (It is true that rated abstractness is not the same as imagery value, but the correlation between the two attributes is very high, +0·83 according to Paivio, Yuille and Madigan, 1968.)

This leads one to wonder if, in addition to the basic noun-facilitation effect, there might be a 'response-bias' (Morton, 1969) towards guessing highly 'concrete' items; such a 'concreteness effect' would appear, however, to be much more pronounced in dysphasic than in normal subjects. If it is legitimate to extrapolate from Brook's (1967) results on 'the suppression of visualization by reading' to simple word-recognition tasks, then perhaps the visual mode of presentation actively militates against any 'on-line' use of imagery by normal subjects.

There are yet alternative ways of looking at the 'imaginal-concreteness' hypothesis. For example, attempts have been made to assimilate it to an extended notion of frequency of occurrence. When Riegel and Riegel (1961) found, with normal German-speaking subjects, that concrete nouns had lower tachistoscopic recognition thresholds than other parts of speech, they proposed the following explanation: word-frequency summates with the 'experiential' frequency of the object that the word refers to. That is, to the frequency of CATS, one adds the frequency of cats in order to predict the recognition threshold of CATS. Whilst such a procedure is conceivable for concrete nouns, it is, of course, considerably less plausible for many instances of other parts of speech. Adding the frequency of ANGRY, or GO, to the frequency of anger or goings respectively does not have the ring of conceptual coherence.

A related line of argument has recently been advanced by Gardner (1973). Following Piaget, Gardner distinguishes between operative and figurative categories; the operative elements are ' . . . objects, parts of objects, and other entities which can be readily grasped, manipulated and operated upon'. In confrontation naming tasks, Gardner found that aphasic subjects were more successful at naming 'objects' which 'could be easily handled and which were relatively discrete and separate entities (like nose or finger) than in naming instances of equal frequency and articulability which could not be easily grasped and which were continuous with the surrounding context (like hip or chin)'. Both Gardner's and the Riegels' studies suggest that some multi- (or supra-) modal concept of stimulus frequency may be required. This in turn may be related to the parameter of 'age-of-acquisition' of words which Carroll and White (1973) have shown to be an important factor in predicting object-naming latencies.

Finally, with respect to our own data, we have previously noted that the superior ease of recognition of concrete nouns (as opposed to verbs) is primarily associated with presentation to the right visual field (in normal subjects). On the standard interpretation, then, the noun superiority effect arises in the left (language) hemisphere, not in the right (visuo-spatial) hemisphere. Seamon and Gazzaniga (1973) have suggested that the use of imagery (in tasks where mnemonic instructions are manipulated) is a right-hemisphere function. Yet our data seem to implicate left-hemisphere functions when visual word-recognition is biased in favour of nouns. We are thus led to seek a linguistic explanation for (at least a part of) the effect.

Following Reichenbach (1947), we make the following proposal: lexical items can be regarded as functions which differ according to the number of variables they take. Thus MAN, TALL, and SLEEPS are one-place functions, $f(X)$; they occur in sentences such as X IS A MAN; X IS TALL; X SLEEPS. Words like FRIEND, TALLER, SEES are two-place functions, $f(X, Y)$; they occur in sentences such as X IS A FRIEND OF Y; X IS TALLER THAN Y; X SEES Y. Words like GIFT, TALLEST, SEND are three-place functions $f(X, Y, Z)$, they occur in sentences such as X IS A GIFT FROM Y TO Z; X IS THE TALLEST OF X, Y, Z; X SENT Y TO Z.

We have illustrated in the above examples that there are functions of one, two, and three variables in each grammatical category, noun, adjective and verb. Yet, as Reichenbach notes, the functions are 'unequally distributed' among the categories; nouns and adjectives predominate among the one-place functions; verbs predominate among the two- and three-place functions.

The possibility thus arises that the notion of 'lexical complexity' is to be explicated in terms of the number of variables which are associated with particular vocabulary items. Ideas of this nature have recently been developed, in logic, by Montague (1970), and, in syntax, by Fillmore (1969). In the psycholinguistic literature, it is clear that the Fodor, Garrett and Bever (1968) 'verb complexity hypothesis' is a closely related proposal. These latter scholars have attempted to show, in a variety of psychological tasks, that sentential complexity is determined (in part) by the number of deep structure trees in which the main verb of the sentence *may* appear. Fodor (1971) reviews the evidence which suggests that lexical items are cross-classified for the type of base structures in which they may appear, rather than, e.g. types of clauses being cross-classified by the lexical items which may select them. Our proposal, then, simply extends this line of argument to cover lexical categories other than verbs. In earlier work (Marshall and Newcombe, 1966), we argued that 'the process of reading an individual word involves the retrieval of the full lexical entry associated with the particular visual stimulus'. Current linguistic accounts suggest that the information represented in the lexicon must include features that specify the number and type of syntactic and semantic relationships into which particular lexical items may enter. On average, it will be the case that these relationships are more extensive for verbs than for nouns.

It seems that a particular type of lexical organization—cross-classification of items for the structures they take—is necessary in order to provide the integration of stimulus and contextual information required in efficient 'predictive' sentence recognition. Noun-facilitation in single-word tasks may result, then, from a form of organization which derives from the requirements of sentence processing.

References

Brooks, L. R. (1967). The suppression of visualization by reading. *Quarterly Journal of Experimental Psychology*, **19**, 289–299.

Bruner, J. S. (1969). Modalities of memory. In G. A. Talland and N. C. Waugh (Eds) *The Pathology of Memory*. London: Academic Press.

Caplan, D., Holmes, J. M. and Marshall, J. C. (1974). Word classes and hemispheric specialization. *Neuropsychologia*, in press.

Carroll, J. B. and White, M. N. (1973). Word frequency and age of acquisition as determiners of picture-naming latency. *Quarterly Journal of Experimental Psychology*, **25**, 85–95.

Elder, W. (1900). The clinical varieties of visual aphasia. *Edinburgh Medical Journal*, **49**, 433–454.

Fillmore, C. J. (1969). Types of lexical information. In F. Kiefer (Ed.) *Studies in Syntax and Semantics*. Dordrecht: Reidel.

Fodor, J. A. (1971). Current approaches to syntax recognition. In D. L. Horton and J. J. Jenkins (Eds) *The Perception of Language*. Columbus: Merrill.

Fodor, J. A., Garrett, M. and Bever, T. (1968). Some syntactic determinants of sentential complexity, II: verb structure. *Perception and Psychophysics*, **3**, 453–461.

Gardner, H. (1973). The contribution of operativity to naming capacity in aphasic patients. *Neuropsychologia*, **11**, 213–220.

Gazzaniga, M. S. (1970). *The Bisected Brain*. New York: Appleton, Century, Crofts.

Halpern, H. (1965). Effects of stimulus variables on dysphasic verbal errors, *Perceptual and Motor Skills*, **21**, 292–298.

Holmes, J. M., Marshall, J. C. and Newcombe, F. (1971). Syntactic class as a determinant of word-retrieval in normal and dyslexic subjects. *Nature*, **234**, 416.

Marshall, J. C. (1973). Language, learning and laterality. In R. A. and J. S. Hinde (Eds) Constraints on Learning: Limitations and Predispositions. London: Academic Press.

Marshall, J. C. and Holmes, J. M. (1974). Sex, handedness and differential hemispheric specialization for components of word perception. Journal of International Research Communications: Medical Science, 2, 1344.

Marshall, J. C. and Newcombe, F. (1966). Syntactic and semantic errors in paralexia Neuropsychologia, 4, 169–176.

McGinnies, E., Comer, P. B. and Lacey, D. L. (1952). Visual recognition thresholds as a function of word length and word frequency. Journal of Experimental Psychology, 44, 65–69.

Montague, R. (1970). English as a formal language. In Linguaggi nella Società e nella Tecnica. Milan: Edizioni di Comunita.

Morton, J. (1969). Interaction of information in word recognition. Psychologica Review, 76, 165–178.

Paivio, A. (1971). Imagery and Verbal Processes. New York: Holt, Rinehart, and Winston.

Paivio, A., Yuille, J. C. and Madigan, S. (1968). Concreteness, imagery, and meaningfulness values for 925 nouns. Journal of Experimental Psychology, 76 (1, Pt. 2).

Reichenbach, H. Elements of Symbolic Logic. Illinois: The Free Press.

Richardson, J. (1974). Word reading and word recognition. Quarterly Journal of Experimental Psychology, in press.

Riegel, K. F. and Riegel, R. M. (1961). Prediction of word-recognition thresholds on the basis of stimulus parameters. Language and Speech, 4, 157–170.

Roydes, R. L. and Osgood, C. E. (1972). Effects of grammatical form-class set upon perception of grammatically ambiguous English words. Journal of Psycholinguistic Research, 1, 165–174.

Seamon, J. G. and Gazzaniga, M. S. (1973). Coding strategies and cerebral laterality effects. Cognitive Psychology, 5, 249–256.

Siegel, G. M. (1959). Dysphasic speech responses to visual word stimuli. Journal of Speech and Hearing Research, 2, 152–160.

Thorndike, E. L. (1943). Man and His Works. Cambridge: Harvard University Press.

Winnick, W. A. and Kressel, K. (1965). Tachistoscopic recognition thresholds, paired-associate learning, and immediate recall as a function of abstractness-concreteness and word frequency. Journal of Experimental Psychology, 70, 163–168.

Chapter 16

Retrograde Amnesia

Moyra Williams

The deterioration of a skill—particularly a verbal skill—is rather different from what the clinician usually thinks of as a disorder of Memory. To him, memories are the recollection of personal experiences—what Tulving (1972) has termed Episodic Memory as opposed to Semantic Memory.

Two important characteristics of these memories are (a) that they are remembered in a unique *context*, and (b) that they are accompanied by a sense of *familiarity*—what Claparède (see MacCurdy, 1926) has referred to as Me-ness. The fact that these two characteristics are related to one another does not appear to be fortuitous. A sense of familiarity is almost always dependent on a person being able to recall the full context of a past experience and relate it to the total stream of his awareness. Where he is unable to do this, he has a sense of 'unreality' or of uncertainty.

Retrograde Amnesia (RA) is the inability to recall events experienced before the onset of cerebral injury or disease—events which were perceived and encoded by the 'normal' healthy brain and which, had it not been for the cerebral insult, would undoubtedly have been available to recall. It can be due to a variety of causes.

Causes and Concomitants of Retrograde Amnesia

Three principal causes may be identified:

(a) Sudden loss of consciousness due to concussional head injury or seizure. It is to be noted that head injuries which do not cause loss of conscious (e.g., penetrating wounds) are very seldom followed by RA (Russell and Nathan, 1946). In the case of seizures, it has been suggested recently that electrically-induced convulsions (ECT) cause varying degrees and extents of RA depending on the position of the electrodes (d'Elia, 1970); that if both are applied to the Non-dominant hemisphere (Unilateral Non-dominant ECT) the retrograde amnesia is less extensive than if applied to the temporal areas of the two hemispheres.

(b) Illnesses involving areas of the limbic system either chronically (as in some post-Alcoholic Korsakov conditions) or temporarily (as in Tuberculous

Meningitis—TBM) are associated with RA. In both (a) and (b) above, some degree of RA is usually found to persist after full restitution of normal intellectual and mnemonic activity, and in this way such conditions differ from cerebral atrophy.

(c) In the first stages of cerebral atrophy (e.g., Senility) the amnesia affects recent experiences only, long past events (or remote memories) being comparatively well preserved. As the lesions progress, more and more distant memories also become affected, a process noted in 1885 by Ribot and leading to his Law of Regression. The degree to which acquired skills are also lost varies greatly in different individuals. Although there are suggestions that the losses depend on the site of the lesions, no one-to-one relationship has ever been established between extent of amnesia and lesion site.

Characteristics of RA

There is usually a residual short 'gap' for events immediately preceding impact (in concussional head injuries), seizure (in the case of electrically-induced convulsions), or onset of illness (in TBM). Frequently a 'haziness of recollection' for scattered events precedes this gap, roughly (but not exactly) proportional to the length of time dividing them. The more recent the experience, the hazier and less well defined it is but incidents are well documented of amnesia (especially after TBM) covering events which occurred two or more years before the onset of illness.

In the course of time *following* the cerebral impact there is a recovery or restitution of availability to recall ('shrinkage' of the amnesia), as a result of which the past is often reconstructed. Restitution does not necessarily depend on 'prompting'. Rats which have apparently forgotten the experience of foot-shock 24 hours after ECS, may apparently 'remember' it after 7 days (Zinkin, 1967). However, in the case of humans, much of the reconstruction stems from 'prompts' or 'cues'. The availability of an experience to recall depends on the manner in which it was assimilated and the different cerebral areas dislocated by the accident, illness or treatment.

Factors Affecting Recall in RA

From the above very brief review, it is apparent that not all past events are equally affected by RA.

The effect of time

In general, the greater the time-lapse between the occurrence of an event and the cerebral injury, the more easily it is recalled, following Ribot's Law of Regression (Ribot, 1885). Thus remote events are recalled before recent ones and shrinkage is from past to present (Russell and Nathan, 1946; Williams and Zangwill, 1952; Talland, 1965). There are exceptions to this rule, however and much reconstruction occurs as a result of prompting by friends and relatives.

The nature of the event

Events of particular personal importance are recalled before others. In the experimental situations afforded by ECT, it has been found that the ability to recall stimuli presented before the treatment is related to Familiarity and ease of Assimilation. Thus easy word-pairs are remembered better than difficult ones.

In some cases the affect aroused by a stimulus may, however, be recalled without recollection of the stimulus itself, or it may be 'projected' on to another stimulus and become associated in recollection with it (Williams, 1952).

The manner of assimilation

This has already been referred to briefly. It has been found in experiments associated with ECT that events to which particular attention was paid at the time are remembered better than others.

Area and extent of cerebral lesion

As already mentioned, short circumscribed RA is seldom seen in association with head injuries unless these cause a period of unconsciousness. The cerebral areas involved are those involving the reticular and limbic systems rather than the cerebral cortex; but in the case of ECT, as already mentioned, it is claimed that recall of past personal events is more seriously affected if an electrode is placed over the Dominant temporal lobe (Bilateral ECT) than in either Bilateral Frontal ECT or Unilateral Non-dominant ECT (Abrams and Taylor, 1973).

Retrograde Amnesia and Normal Forgetting

Since RA is—almost by definition—inability to recall events which were registered (or encoded) normally, it must consist essentially of either a storage or a retrieval failure. The characteristic of 'shrinkage' already referred to places the likelihood of the defect in the retrieval rather than the storage phase; hence the study of RA should throw light on some mechanisms involved in this process.

Comparing RA with normal forgetting, shows many similarities between them. The changes which occur in normal Episodic memory with the passage of time (based on the recall of stories and pictures) have been familiar to psychologists since the classical work of Bartlett; and although there have been few systematic studies of the recall of past personal events, one such study undertaken by the present author (see Williams, 1969), shows that these memories seem to undergo the same sort of changes as those found by Bartlett in the recall of laboratory stimuli. Thus, recent events (like other items in Short-term memory stores) are reproduced in sequences, in detail, and without reference to importance, whereas remote ones (like those in Long-term store) are schematized and organized in some form of importance-hierarchy.

Between these two extremes, however, is an area of half-forgotten items which could be retained for future reference if needed and rehearsed, but which would otherwise be dropped out: 'Now I think about it, I remember that was the day I went . . .'

These items appear to undergo some process by means of which their threshold to retrieval is progressively raised, until perhaps the time comes when even total reconstruction of them fails to arouse a sense of familiarity.

The similarity between memories in this stage and memories affected by RA is so close that it is tempting to presume that both time and cerebral pathology have the same effect. Both cause 'Forgetting' due to the raising of threshold to retrieval; but whether this is due to alterations in the neural traces or to alterations of the retrieval strategies is not yet clear. Future work, which appears to be turning more towards the study of strategy than has been evident in recent past publications, may well throw more light on this question.

References

Abrams, R. and Taylor, M. A. (1973). Anterior bifrontal ECT. A clinical trial. *British Journal of Psychiatry*, **122**, 587–590.

d'Elia, G. (1970). Unilateral ECT. *Acta Psychiatrica Scandinavica Suppl.*, 215.

McCurdy, J. T. (1926). *Common Principles in Psychology and Physiology*. Cambridge: Cambridge University Press.

Ribot, T. (1885). *Diseases of the Memory*. London: Kegan Paul.

Russell, W. R. and Nathan, P. W. (1946). Traumatic amnesia. *Brain*, **69**, 280–301.

Talland, G. A. (1965). *Deranged Memory*. New York: Academic Press.

Tulving, E. (1972). Episodic and semantic memory. In E. Tulving and W. Donaldson (Eds) *Organization of Memory*. New York: Academic Press.

Williams, M. (1952). A case of displaced affect following ECT. *British Journal of Medical Psychology*, **25**, 156–157.

Williams, M. (1966). Memory disorders associated with ECT. In C. W. M. Whitty and O. L. Zangwill (Eds) *Amnesia*. London: Butterworths.

Williams, M. (1969). Traumatic amnesia. In G. A. Talland and N. C. Waugh (Eds) *The Pathology of Memory*. New York: Academic Press.

Williams, M. and Zangwill, O. L. (1952). Memory defects after head injury. *Journal of Neurology, Neurosurgery and Psychiatry*, **15**, 54–58.

Zinkin, S. (1967). ECS and RA. *Proceedings of the Experimental Psychology Society*. Oxford, 1967.

Chapter 17

Theories of Amnesia

A. D. Baddeley

Introduction

As in Chapter 16, the subject under discussion will be amnesia. However, this paper will differ from that of Dr Williams in a number of respects. Firstly, whereas she was concerned with retrograde amnesia, the inability to recall events preceding the cause of the amnesia, this chapter is concerned primarily with anterograde amnesia, reflected in the defective ability to learn new material. A second major difference between the two chapters stems from the fact that whereas Dr Williams is a neuropsychologist with wide experience of both clinical work and experimentation, the present author is an experimental psychologist who has been fortunate enough to do a limited amount of experimental work in conjunction with neuropsychologists on amnesic patients. The author's interest is in normal human memory, and the interest in amnesia stems from the belief that an understanding of the way in which human memory breaks down in amnesic patients can have considerable implications for our understanding of normal intact memory. This chapter, therefore, differs from Dr Williams' in being primarily concerned with theoretical interpretations of amnesia. The review will necessarily be rather superficial since it ranges across a wide number of sources of evidence, many of them based on clinical observations and physiological experiments on animals, areas in which the author is not competent to provide anything other than a superficial survey. The intention is however, to persuade the reader that the question of why amnesics are amnesic is both intrinsically interesting and tractable, and that the suggested answers have considerable potential implications for the understanding of normal memory. If it succeeds, it is hoped that the reader will go beyond this limited survey, and read the original papers on which it is based.

The Amnesic Syndrome

Amnesic patients come from three main sources. Probably the best known of these is typified by the patient H.M. described by Milner (1966) and her co-workers. This patient showed gross memory defects following the bilateral

328

removal of his temporal lobes and hippocampus, an operation performed in order to try to reduce the frequency of epileptic seizures. A second group of amnesic patients are those suffering from the Korsakov Syndrome. This is an alcoholic condition which probably results from a vitamin deficiency associated with excessive alcohol consumption over a long period of time. It is frequently associated with general intellectual deterioration, but it is possible by careful selection to obtain patients with a pure memory defect, unassociated with dementia. The third class of patient comes from those who have suffered from encephalitis. As in the Korsakov Syndrome this seems to lead to damage in the region of the hippocampus. While these three types of amnesics may differ, there is as yet no conclusive evidence to suggest that they do so, provided relatively pure cases are used.

The general clinical picture has been described elsewhere (Zangwill, 1966) and therefore a very brief description of the main characteristics of an amnesic patient will be given here. The most striking feature of such patients is that they appear to forget incidents in their daily life just as fast as they occur. Typically they are unable to tell you where they are, what year it is, who is the Prime Minister, what they had for breakfast or to supply any of the vast number of details of daily existence that a normal person takes for granted. One can spend all morning testing an amnesic and on resuming experimentation in the afternoon discover that he has no apparent recollection of ever having met you

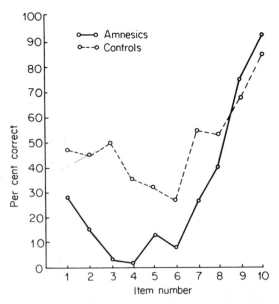

Figure 17.1. Serial position curve for immediate free recall. (Reprinted with permission from Baddeley and Warrington, *Journal of Verbal Learning and Verbal Behavior*, 1970, **9**, 176–189.)

before. On the other hand, his ability to converse is quite unimpaired and he is quite capable of providing information about his early life, his job, etc. In psychological terms he appears to have grossly defective long-term memory, but an intact short-term memory. This is illustrated in Figure 17.1 which shows the free recall performance of amnesics and of comparable control patients (Baddeley and Warrington, 1970). Subjects were presented with a sequence of 10 unrelated words and asked to repeat them back in any order they liked. As Figure 17.1 shows, the amnesic patients had grossly impaired performance on early items which are usually regarded as residing in long-term or secondary memory, whereas their ability to retain the most recent items presented was quite unimpaired, suggesting normal short-term or primary memory. The implications of this and other data for the proposed distinction between long and short-term memory are discussed by Warrington and Weiskrantz (1973) and will not be considered here. The present chapter will be concerned with suggested explanations of the defective long-term memory performance of amnesic patients. To start with, five current hypotheses will be described briefly, and each will be illustrated with one characteristic piece of empirical evidence. Then a range of potentially critical empirical findings will be described, and the relevance of each for the five theories will be discussed.

Theories of Amnesia

Consolidation

This is probably the oldest interpretation of amnesia. It is based on the assumption that in order to become durable a memory trace must undergo a process of consolidation, rather like a concrete mould which when it has just been made is soft and easily broken whereas after being allowed to set it is hard and very durable. The implication of this interpretation is that amnesics somehow lack the ability to consolidate their memory traces, hence they are present for a short time (i.e., in short-term memory), but leave no durable record. The chief proponent of a consolidation hypothesis of amnesia is probably Milner (1968), although she does also talk in rather general terms about the transfer of information from STM to LTM. The sort of evidence that is typically cited in support of the consolidation hypothesis comes from the clinical observation that patients appear to be able to recall their early life, where they were born, what their job was, how many children they had, etc., while being unable to recall more recent events. This marked contrast between an amnesic's recall of old information and his inability to remember recent events suggests that in some sense the recent events are not being learned. Since his ability to repeat back for example, a telephone number, is unimpaired it seems plausible to suggest that the recent material does get into the memory system but is not preserved, and if one regards consolidation as an important feature of long-term learning then failure of the memory trace to consolidate clearly offers a possible explanation.

Pro-active Interference

In a number of experimental papers and in a persuasive recent review, Warrington and Weiskrantz (1973), have argued that amnesics have difficulty in remembering, not because they are unable to learn new material but because they are unable to retrieve it. The retrieval difficulty occurs because they are unable to inhibit competing irrelevant material, paradoxically then their problem is not that they forget too much but that they do not forget enough. Perhaps the most striking piece of evidence in favour of this view comes from the observation made by Warrington and Weiskrantz that amnesic patients show much better recall if they are tested using a procedure which minimizes the possibility of interference from competing responses. One way of achieving this is to cue the subject with a part of the item to be remembered. For example, if the subject is attempting to recall the word STAMP then he might be cued using the letters ST. While this would not provide enough information for a subject to guess the word, since there are many words beginning with ST, it does allow him to eliminate all possible competing responses which do not begin with those two letters. Regardless of how the original material is learnt, when it is tested in this way the difference between amnesic patients and normals is very considerably reduced (Warrington and Weiskrantz, 1973).

Semantic Coding Defect

This is a tentative explanation of my own based on the general association observed between semantic coding and long-term memory (Baddeley, 1972). It is clearly not the case that amnesics are unable to encode material semantically, since they can talk quite effectively and discuss their early life with no apparent impairment. However if one accepts the division of semantic memory proposed by both Paivio (1971) and Bower (1972) into a linguistic and an imagery component, there is evidence that amnesics may be defective in their ability to utilize the imagery component of semantic memory. The evidence for this comes from a study (Baddeley and Warrington, 1973) which showed that while amnesics are quite able to take advantage of word clustering based on taxonomic category membership, they gain no apparent advantage from clustering based on visual imagery, a technique which is very helpful to normal subjects.

The Cognitive Map Hypothesis

This hypothesis has been proposed by O'Keefe and Nadel (1974) on the basis of the enormous body of experiments on animals with lesions of the hippocampus. On the basis of both this and the human data they suggest that the role of the hippocampus is to form a cognitive map of the environment. When the hippocampus is removed the animal is still capable of learning to associate stimuli and responses but is unable to build up this spatial picture of its world. This is a very inadequate summary of a very lengthy draft mono-graph. The author's interpretation is probably further distorted by the apparent similarity of this view to his own interpretation of amnesia as due to the disruption of the imagery component of semantic memory. Evidence in favour of the cognitive map hypothesis comes from experiments in which rats are shown to have unimpaired ability to learn a position habit, but have great difficulty in learning that food is to be found at a particular location, when the starting point is varied from trial to trial. When they do exhibit this type of learning it appears to be the case that they are associating specific cues with food rather than acquiring a general knowledge of the geography of the test room. When these cues are reduced by surrounding the area with black curtains normal rats have little difficulty whereas the performance of hippocampal rats is grossly impaired (O'Keefe and Nadel, 1974).

The Familiarity Hypothesis

This hypothesis which has recently been proposed by Gaffan (1972) was also based principally on animal experiments but can with little difficulty be extended to cover human amnesia. Gaffan suggests that the basic cause of amnesia is the loss of the ability to judge the familiarity of an item, whether this is a stimulus item which the subject is required to recognise, or a potential response which he is checking before outputting. Gaffan supports his view with a series of experiments based on both rats and monkeys in which the output of the hippocampus has been cut by a lesion in the fornix. One such experiment compared associative and recognition memory in fornical and control monkeys. The monkeys were seated in front of a discrimination apparatus containing two small wells. One of these was covered always by a brass plate while the other was covered by a series of junk objects (a junk object is an item found lying around the laboratory, e.g. a torch battery, an ink bottle, a tobacco tin). The monkeys were tested in blocks of ten trials, on each of which a small reward (a sugar puff) was placed under either the junk object or the brass plate. Recognition memory was tested by ensuring that each block of ten trials comprised five presentations of the same junk objects and five presentations of completely new objects. When an 'old' object was presented the reward was always underneath it, whereas when a new object was shown the reward was always under the brass plate. Hence in order to perform this task perfectly, all the monkey needed to do was to decide whether the junk object was new and unfamiliar or old and familiar and respond accordingly. As Figure 17.2 shows the fornical monkeys were extremely bad at performing this recognition task; in this respect they are very similar to amnesic human patients who find recognition memory extremely difficult (Warrington and Weiskrantz, 1973). The procedure for testing associative learning was very similar except that only the initial set of ten junk objects were used. Once again, for five of them a reward was placed under the object while in the case of the other five the reward was placed under the brass plate. The procedure differs from the recognition memory task however in that the same ten objects were used repeatedly, with the positively rewarded objects continuing to be positively

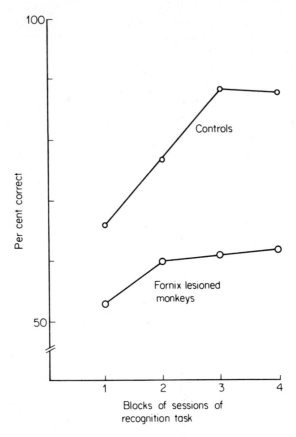

Figure 17.2. Performance of amnesic and control monkeys on a discrimination task based on familiarity. (From Gaffan, *Journal of Comparative and Physiological Psychology*, 1974, **86**(6), 1100–1109. Copright 1974 by the American Psychological Association. Reprinted by permission.)

rewarded and the remainder continuing to be unrewarded. Hence the monkey needs to learn what object is associated with food, and cannot solve the task simply by deciding whether a given object is familiar or not, since all óbjects are presumably equally familiar. The performance of the two groups of monkeys on this task is shown in Figure 17.3, from which it is clear that the gross difference between the amnesic and control monkeys has virtually disappeared. Apart from a pilot study on a single patient (Gaffan, 1972) this procedure has yet to be tried on human subjects; if it be shown to generalize however it clearly presents a striking and counter-intuitive piece of evidence in favour of the familiarity hypothesis.

Following this brief description of five current hypotheses about the nature of amnesia, a number of potentially critical experimental results will be presented and the ability of the various hypotheses to account for the data in question will be discussed.

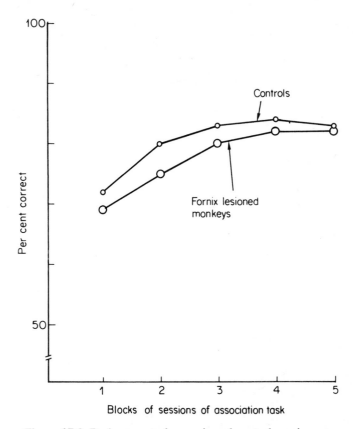

Figure 17.3. Performance of amnesic and control monkeys on a discrimination involving associative learning. (From Gaffan, 1973, *Journal of Comparative and Physiological Psychology*, 1974, **86**(6), 1100–1109. Copyright 1974 by the American Psychological Association. Reprinted by permission.)

The Evidence

Retrograde Amnesia (R.A.)

At a clinical level it is clearly the case that amnesic patients do not show gross retrograde amnesia since they can quite happily talk about their early life, and indeed the very fact that they can talk suggests that all early learning has clearly not been lost. It does not however follow that their retention of events occurring before the onset of their amnesia is unimpaired. This question has been investigated by Sanders and Warrington (cited in Warrington and Weiskrantz, 1973) who tested both amnesic patients and normals on a questionnaire relating to public events which had occurred over the past 40 years. The amnesics showed grossly impaired retention of such events whether tested by recall or by forced choice recognition. These results are shown in Figure 17.4 from which it should be clear that the impairment is not limited to recent events but applies almost equally to events of the remote past which in

334

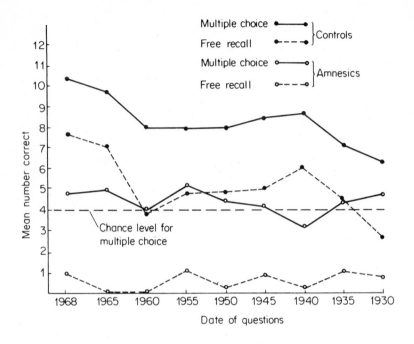

Figure 17.4. Performance of amnesic and control patients on a long-term memory questionnaire. (Reprinted with permission from Sanders and Warrington, *Brain*, 1971, **94**, Part IV, 661–668.)

all cases happened before the onset of the amnesia. Taken at face value then this finding suggests that far from being free from retrograde amnesia, amnesic patients show gross R.A., though this is probably mixed with 'islands' of accurate memory, possibly associated with particularly over-learnt information, such as the person's own name and family background. If this is so, then all interpretations which suggest that amnesia results from encoding or consolidation run into considerable difficulty since we appear to have evidence of amnesia which operates on material which had already presumably been both encoded and consolidated by the time the patient became amnesic. Unfortunately, however, interpretation of this result is not straightforward. We continue to read about, hear about and see significant events from the past long after they are over, in newspapers, in films, and on television. Consequently the questionnaire used by Sanders and Warrington was probably testing the combination of retention of the original event together with the effect of an unknown number of 'reminders' that had occurred during the intervening delay. Once an amnesic developed a memory defect these reminders would be likely to become ineffective, and consequently his poorer performance may simply reflect his inability to take advantage of this subsequent information. At present then retrograde amnesia presents an important question rather than a piece of critical empirical evidence.

Recognition

There is considerable evidence both from the questionnaire task illustrated in Figure 17.4 and from verbal learning tasks (Warrington and Weiskrantz, 1973) that amnesic patients are no better at recognition memory than they are at recall. This observation presents no problem for either the consolidation hypothesis or the semantic coding and cognitive map hypotheses, and fits in very well with the familiarity hypothesis. Although Warrington and Weiskrantz would no doubt disagree, the author considers that it does present something of a problem for the pro-active interference hypothesis. From what we know about interference in normal verbal learning it is clearly the case that recognition memory does lead to less interference, particularly if the specific competing item is not included in the recognition set (Postman, Stark and Fraser, 1968). While Warrington and Weiskrantz do not necessarily need to identify the interference effects in amnesics with the interference phenomena shown in verbal learning experiments, assumption of a distinction between the interference effects they postulate, and the classical phenomena of the verbal learning laboratory inevitably reduces the generality of their conclusions. One clearly needs to know more about the interference process proposed before accepting it as an adequate explanation of amnesia.

Motor Skills

There have been a number of observations that amnesics are apparently still able to acquire motor skills. Figure 17.5 shows the acquisition of a pursuit rotor

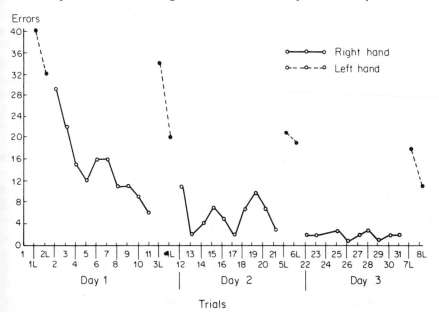

Figure 17.5. Performance of an amnesic patient on the mirror drawing task. (Reprinted with permission from Milner, 1962. *Physiologie de l'hippocampe*. Series Colloques International, Paris. Centre Nationale de la Recherche Scientifique.)

tracking by H.M. the patient with bilateral hippocampal damage studied extensively by Milner and her associates (Milner, 1968). Although he shows clear evidence of learning, the rate of learning does not appear to be normal, and further work on a wider range of patients is clearly needed before one can draw any conclusions other than that amnesic patients are capable of motor learning. This conclusion does not present problems for any of the hypotheses with a possible exception of the consolidation theory. It is not clear why certain types of learning should consolidate and certain others should not but so little appears to be known about consolidation that one could presumably exclude motor learning from the generalization without doing too much violence to the original hypothesis.

Intrusions

As Warrington and Weiskrantz (1973) observed, amnesics are particularly prone in verbal memory tasks to give as responses items from previous lists. Such intrusions would not be expected on a simple consolidation hypothesis since they do appear to reflect new material which has apparently been consolidated. Their existence presents no problem for any of the alternative hypotheses, and indeed fits in very neatly with both the pro-active interference and the familiarity hypotheses.

Partial Cueing

Using a technique based on some earlier studies by Moira Williams (1953), Weiskrantz and Warrington showed that even densely amnesic patients are able to show substantial learning when tested by a partial prompting proce- dure. In the first of these Warrington and Weiskrantz (1968) required their subjects to learn to recognize a series of fragmented pictures or words, examples of which are shown in Figure 17.6. The subject's task was to learn to recognize the most fragmentary version of each item. He was prompted by being shown progressively less and less fragmentary versions of the stimulus until eventually, if necessary the complete stimulus was presented. Over a series of trials both amnesic and normal subjects learned to recognize the fragmented item without further prompting, and were able to retain this for a period of several days with relatively little forgetting. Subsequent research (Weiskrantz and Warrington, 1970) showed that this was not a simple case of perceptual learning, since the same phenomenon was shown using words and prompting with the first few letters. Furthermore the crucial factor appears to be method of testing since regardless of how the material is learned, the amnesic is always assisted by partial prompting. Warrington and Weiskrantz interpret their result in terms of the pro-active interference hypothesis suggesting that the partial information allows the subject to eliminate compet- ing responses. This result is also consistent with the familiarity hypothesis since when the subject is simply required to perform the task of identifying the incomplete item he presumably produces the first available item that will

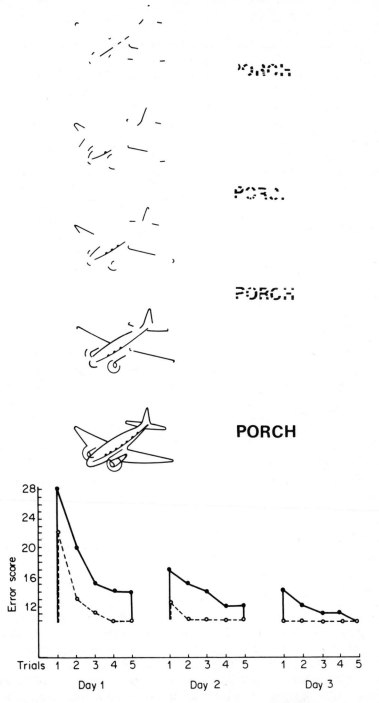

Figure 17.6. A sample of material and learning curve for amnesic and control patients on a prompted learning task. (Reproduced with permission from Warrington and Weiskrantz, *Nature*, 1968, **217**, 972–974.)

complete the fragment, not worrying about whether the response seems familiar or not as he would in a recognition task.

Interpretation in terms of the semantic coding hypothesis is somewhat more complex. Let us suppose that subjects typically do such long-term learning in terms of their semantic memory system (Baddeley, 1966). Because of their defective semantic memory, amnesic patients typically learn this material in acoustic or visual terms. The partial cueing technique works by giving the subject either visual or acoustic information and this will presumably be particularly helpful to a subject who has been encoding the material in this way, that is to the amnesic. On the other hand the control patient will be helped relatively much less since there is a mismatch between the optimal code for learning and the retrieval cue provided by the experimenter. It is suspected a similar interpretation could be phrased in terms of the cognitive map hypothesis but the author is not sufficiently familiar with the hypothesis to do so in any detail. Once again then the only hypothesis which appears to have real difficulty with the evidence is a simple consolidation theory which would appear to have nothing to say on the role of prompting in recall.

Category Cueing

When a list for free recall is divided into groups of words on the basis of either acoustic similarity or taxonomic category membership, amnesics are able to take advantage of the grouping to improve their recall (Baddeley and Warrington, 1973) and are also assisted by being cued with the appropriate category name (Warrington and Weiskrantz, 1971), or by being given the first word of the relevant category group (Baddeley and Warrington, 1973). Once again this fits in reasonably well with the pro-active interference and familiarity hypotheses since cueing presumably reduces the need to discriminate between potential competing responses. It is consistent with the semantic coding, and probably the cognitive map hypotheses, as long as one assumes that the semantic coding defect does not apply to material that is categorized linguistically rather than in terms of the imagery system (Paivio, 1971). Once again it is not clear how the consolidation hypothesis would account for this phenomenon.

Imagery

Baddeley and Warrington (1973) have shown that amnesic patients appear to gain virtually no assistance from the instruction to use a mnemonic involving visual imagery. Subjects were given lists of 16 concrete words grouped into four sets of four. On half the trials they were instructed to attempt to form a visual image linking the four words into a single composite picture and the experimenter provided linking words to help them to do this. For example if the four words were Irishman, Penny, Monkey and Violin they would be told 'The *Irishman* gave a *penny* to the *monkey* playing the *violin*' and instructed to form a clear visual image of this. Performance in this condition was contrasted with one in which the four words were repeated rapidly, a condition which is known to make the formation of composite visual images extremely difficult. Under these conditions the normal control patients showed considerable enhancement in the visual imagery condition whereas the amnesics were not at all helped by the imagery instruction.

This result fits in well with the semantic coding hypothesis, which is hardly surprising since the current version of the hypothesis was largely based on this result. Similarly it fits in well with the cognitive map hypothesis and can be fitted into the familiarity hypothesis, on the assumption that subjects can create the necessary images but are unable to recognize the image and therefore use it for aiding subsequent recall. It is not clear how this phenomenon is handled by pro-active interference interpretation nor is it easy to see how a general consolidation hypothesis would predict this result.

McGill Anomalies Test

Warrington and Weiskrantz (1973) present evidence that amnesics are able to show learning on the McGill Anomalies Test, a task in which a subject is shown a picture which has one anomalous feature. His task is to point out the anomalous feature as quickly as possible. At the time of reporting, only two amnesic patients had been tested on this but both showed a consistent increase in the number of anomalous features detected when the test was presented on repeated trials and the anomaly pointed out when the subject failed to detect it. This fits in well with the familiarity hypothesis since again the subject is required to learn an association but not to discriminate something as familiar or unfamiliar. It also fits in reasonably well with the pro-active interference hypothesis since one would not expect this task to be particularly susceptible to P.I. It is less clear how either the semantic coding or cognitive map hypotheses could handle this result. It could be argued that the subjects were learning a visual scanning strategy, and that this is essentially an example of motor learning. This possibility could probably be checked by having the same anomaly located at different points in the picture on different trials; on the scanning hypothesis this should make the task extremely difficult for amnesics, while giving no substantial problem to normal subjects.

Jigsaw Learning

Another potentially important but still tentative observation has been made recently by Brooks of the Southern General Hospital, Glasgow and the author in testing two 14-year old boys who became amnesic following an attack of encephalitis. The task simply involved assembling a child's 12-piece jigsaw puzzle as rapidly as possible. Subjects were given six successive trials and timed on each. Results are shown in Figure 17.7, together with their performance when tested 1 week later on the same puzzle and on a puzzle of equivalent difficulty. It is clear that learning as measured by time to complete the puzzle, did occur and that it was retained over a week's delay. Furthermore since

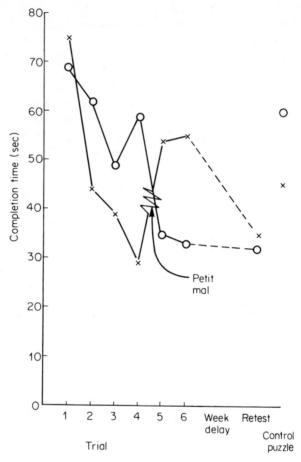

Figure 17.7. Learning and retention of a simple jigsaw by two amnesic patients. (Brooks and Baddeley, unpublished.)

performance on an equivalent puzzle was considerably slower it is clear that the subject was not simply learning something rather general about doing jigsaw puzzles quickly. This result fits in rather well with the familiarity hypothesis since it presumably reflects associative learning but does not require the subject to recognize the puzzle as familiar. It is also consistent with a P.I. interpretation since there is no reason to anticipate P.I. in such a task. It does however present problems for both the coding and the cognitive map interpretations since such learning might be expected to involve the imagery or locational system. Again of course it could be argued that the subjects were acquiring a particular motor or perceptual pattern, but casual observation suggested that this was probably not the case since subjects appeared to assemble the puzzle in somewhat different ways on different trials. This latter point should obviously be checked more carefully and the task clearly needs to be replicated on a larger sample of patients before drawing any very firm conclusions. Once again, a simple consolidation hypothesis appears to have difficulty, unless the motor learning interpretation can be sustained.

How Well do the Hypotheses Fit the Evidence?

The ability of the five hypotheses to account for the evidence just described is summarized in Table 17.1 using a double plus to represent a piece of evidence

Table 17.1. Five hypotheses as assessed against clinical evidence

Hypothesis	Familiarity	Cognitive map	Semantic coding	Proactive interference	Consolidation
Phenomena:					
Retrograde amnesia	?	?	?	?	?
Recognition memory	++	+	+	?–	+
Motor skills	+	+	+	+	?
Prior-List intrusions	++	+	+	++	–
Partial cueing	+	?+	+	++	–
Category cueing	+	+	+	+	–
Imagery	+	++	++	–	–
Anomalies test	+	?–	?–	?+	–
Jigsaw learning	+	–	–	?+	–

which fits in particularly well with the hypothesis, a single plus to indicate evidence that is consistent, a minus to indicate inconsistent evidence, and a question mark to indicate doubt either as to the phenomenon in question (as in the case of retrograde amnesia) or when there is serious doubt about the prediction to be made. In interpreting the Table it should be borne in mind that the plusses and minuses represent a very crude categorization of my own subjective judgment, which in a number of cases would almost certainly conflict with that of others, at least as competent as I to assess the evidence in this field. Furthermore some of the phenomena are more robust than others and in the case of the McGill Anomalies Test and Jigsaw Learning further evidence is clearly needed before any firm conclusions are drawn. It should also be borne in mind that the various hypotheses do not all refer to the same conceptual level and are therefore not mutually exclusive. To take an extreme example, it is logically conceivable that amnesics suffer from excessive P.I., which occurs because the patient is defective in making familiarity judgments, which in turn is the result of defective consolidation of material encoded via the imagery sub-system of semantic memory? Needless to say parsimony suggests that such multiple hypotheses could only be accepted with great reluctance when all simpler hypotheses fail.

On the evidence available however one can draw the following tentative conclusions. First, a general consolidation hypothesis seems unlikely. One could of course talk about the defective consolidation of certain types of material but it is not easy to see how such a hypothesis would be distinguishable from, for example, a coding hypothesis. Similarly, general statements of the kind 'amnesia reflects the inadequate transfer of information from short-term to long-term memory' do not appear to do justice to the complexity of the data. Furthermore since the concept of entry to long-term memory necessarily being via short-term memory, is a somewhat controversial one (Shallice and Warrington, 1970), this interpretation probably presents far more problems than it solves. On the evidence available none of the remaining four alternatives can be confidently rejected. There are however a number of potentially critical results which seem to present problems for at least some of these hypotheses and it is surely not too optimistic to expect that within the next two or three years we shall have narrowed down the number of contenders considerably.

One final point of interest is that all the remaining four hypotheses if supported would have interesting implications for normal memory. The P.I. hypothesis has obvious implications for the role of interference in normal learning and more importantly for the mechanisms that normal subjects have for overcoming interference from prior learning. The encoding and cognitive map hypotheses suggest that amnesic patients may provide interesting techniques for further investigation of the semantic memory system, particularly if they allow an easier separation of the imagery and linguistic systems than is possible with normal subjects. On the very limited evidence so far available however Gaffan's familiarity hypothesis appears to be particularly interesting, both as an explanation of amnesia, and also for its implications for normal long-term memory. In suggesting that the process of recognition is both separable from that of recall and also of absolutely fundamental importance in human learning, the familiarity hypothesis has implications not only for recent controversies as to the role of retrieval in recognition memory (Kintsch, 1970; Mandler, 1972), but also in suggesting that recognition processes are vital in recall. It has of course, often been suggested that recognition may be used as a post-retrieval check on recalled items (Underwood, 1964; Baddeley, 1972). However if the inability to perform such a recognition check is responsible for the dramatic memory decrement found in amnesic patients, as Gaffan's hypothesis might suggest, then the role of recognition in recall must be considerably greater than is commonly assumed. However, critical evidence on all the more recent explanations of amnesia is still extremely sparse, and firm conclusions would clearly be premature.

References

Baddeley, A. D. (1966). The influence of acoustic and semantic similarity on long-term memory for word sequences. *Quarterly Journal of Experimental Psychology*, **18**, 302–309.

Baddeley, A. D. (1972). Retrieval rules and semantic coding in short-term memory. *Psychological Bulletin*, **78**, 379–385.

Baddeley, A. D. and Warrington, E. K. (1970). Amnesia and the distinction between long- and short-term memory. *Journal of Verbal Learning and Verbal Behavior*, **9**, 176–189.

Bower, G. H. (1972). Mental imagery and associative learning. In L. Gregg (Ed.) *Cognition in Learning and Memory*. New York: Wiley.

Gaffan, D. (1972). Loss of recognition memory in rats with lesions of the fornix. *Neuropsychologia*, **10**, 327–341.

Gaffan, D. (1973). Recognition impaired and association intact in the memory of monkeys after transection of the fornix. (Unpublished manuscript.)

Kintsch, W. (1970). Models for free recall and recognition. In D. A. Norman (Ed.) *Models of Human Memory*. New York: Academic Press.

Mandler, G. (1972). Organization and recognition. In E. Tulving and W. Donaldson (Eds) *Organization of Memory*. New York: Academic Press.

Milner, B. (1966). Amnesia following operation on the temporal lobes. In C. W. M. Whitty and O. L. Zangwill (Eds) *Amnesia*. London and Washington, D.C.: Butterworths.

Milner, B. (1968). Preface; material specific and generalized memory loss. *Neuropsychologia*, **6**, 175–179.

Milner, B. (1970). Memory and the medial temporal regions of the brain. In K. H. Pribram and D. E. Broadbent (Eds) *Biology of Memory*. New York: Academic Press.

O'Keefe, J. and Nadel, L. The hippocampus as a cognitive map. (In preparation.)

Paivio, A. (1971). Imagery and language. In S. J. Segal (Ed.) *Imagery: Current Cognitive Approaches*. New York: Academic Press.

Postman, L., Stark, K. and Fraser, J. (1968). Temporal changes in interference. *Journal of Verbal Learning and Verbal Behavior*, **7**, 672–694.

Shallice, T. and Warrington, E. K. (1970). Independent functioning of verbal memory stores; a neuropsychological study. *Quarterly Journal of Experimental Psychology*, **22**, 261–273.

Underwood, P. J. (1964). The representativeness of rote learning. In A. W. Melton, (Ed.) *Categories of Human Learning*. New York: Academic Press.

Warrington, E. K. and Weiskrantz, L. (1968). A study of learning and retention in amnesic patients. *Neuropsychologia*, **6**, 283–291.

Warrington, E. K. and Weiskrantz, L. (1971). Organizational aspects of memory in amnesic patients. *Neuropsychologia*, **9**, 67–73.

Warrington, E. K. and Weiskrantz, L. (1973). An analysis of short-term and long-term memory defects in man. In J. A. Deutsch (Ed.) *The Physiological Basis of Memory*. New York: Academic Press.

Williams, M. (1953). Investigation of amnesic defects by progressive prompting. *Journal of Neurology, Neurosurgery, and Psychiatry*, **16**, 14–18.

Zangwill, O. L. (1966). The amnesic syndrome. In C. W. M. Whitty and O. L. Zangwill (Eds) *Amnesia*. London and Washington D.C.: Butterworths.

Name Index

346

Chase, W. G., 82, 84, 136, 141, 255, 256, 262, 265, 270, 271, 273, 274, 275, 283, 285, 289, 300, 307, 308, 311
Chomsky, N., 126, 141, 308, 310
Christal, R. E., 155, 160
Claparède, 323
Clark, E. V., 176, 179
Clark, H. H., 136, 141, 155, 160, 236, 237, 247, 255, 256, 262, 265,·268, 270, 271, 272, 273, 274, 275, 283, 285, 289, 297, 300, 307, 308, 311
Claxton, G., 90, 183, 198
Cofer, C. N., 82
Cohen, B. H., 9, 18, 222, 226, 247, 259, 262, 288, 296, 311
Collins, A. M., 45, 54, 58, 82, 90, 97, 101, 123, 124, 125, 128, 141, 219, 220, 221, 224, 245, 255, 268, 269, 285, 289, 309, 311
Colman, F., 64, 82
Colotla, V. A., 71, 85
Coltheart, M., 6, 18, 281, 285
Comer, P. B., 312, 322
Conrad, C., 125, 141, 220, 246, 247
Cook, J., 171
Coope, E., 126
Cooper, G. S., 134, 141
Cooper, L. A., 58, 67, 68, 82
Corbett, A., 16, 219, 247
Craik, F. I. M., 44, 45, 53, 54, 69, 82
Crowder, R. G., 7, 18
Crown, I., 185, 187, 198
Csapo, K., 51, 53, 55, 63, 66, 72, 73, 83
Cunitz, A. R., 70, 83
Cushman, W., 198

Dansereau, D., 31, 41
Davidson, D., 131, 132
Davies, D. J. M., 129, 137, 142
Dean, P. J., 75, 83
Deese, J., 45, 46, 54, 104, 121
d'Elia, G., 323, 326
Dirlam, D. K., 6, 18
Dowell, P. C., 18
Donaldson, W., 55, 82, 84, 101, 141, 160, 311, 326, 343

Eagle, M., 53, 54
Easton, R. D., 51, 54
Egan, J. P., 183, 198
Egeth, H. E., 267, 284, 285
Eggleston, V. H., 165, 168, 180
Eichelman, W. H., 257, 286
Elder, W., 315, 321

Elias, C. S., 46, 53, 54
Elkind, D., 179
Ellis, G. B., 248, 284
Elshout, J. J., 143, 153, 155, 160
Endler, N. S., 180
Engelkamp, J., 203, 204, 215
Epstein, W., 51, 54, 66, 82
Ernest, C. H., 61, 62, 64, 82, 83
Ervin, S. M., 177, 179
Ervin-Tripp, S. M., 214, 215

Farvis, K., 104, 120, 121
Feigenbaum, E. A., 158
Feng, C., 67, 84
Fillenbaum, S., 51, 54, 181, 184, 201, 215, 298
Fillmore, C. J., 260, 285, 320, 322
Flavell, J. H., 174, 179
Flores d'Arcais, G. B., 201, 215
Fodor, J. A., 19, 41, 321
Foth, D., 64, 65, 66, 76, 84
Fox, L. A., 278, 280
Francis, W. N., 222, 234, 235, 247
Frankish, C., 6, 7
Franks, J. J., 201, 215
Fraser, J., 335, 343
Freedle, R. O., 142
Freedman, J. L., 48, 54, 124, 141, 219, 221, 244, 247, 289, 290, 296, 311
Frijda, N. H., 18, 45, 49, 54, 143, 150, 160, 213, 215
Frincke, G., 78, 83

Gaffan, D., 331, 332, 333, 342, 343
Galanter, E., 45, 55, 82
Gardner, H., 320, 321
Garrett, M., 321
Gazzaniga, M. S., 62, 83, 84, 318, 320, 321, 322
Gibbs, G., 126
Glanzer, M., 70, 83
Goldman-Eisler, F., 20, 41
Good, S. J., 52, 54
Goodnow, J. H., 165, 179
Gough, P. B., 262, 286, 289, 309, 311
Grant, S., 63, 82
Green, D. W., 129, 141
Greenberg, S. N., 17, 18
Greene, J. M., 289, 311
Gregg, L. W., 19, 41
Grieve, R., 289, 312
Groninger, L. D., 73, 83
Gross, A. E., 69, 84

350

Subject Index